Redesigning Research on Post-Traumatic Growth

Redesigning Research on Post-Traumatic Growth

Challenges, Pitfalls, and New Directions

EDITED BY FRANK J. INFURNA

AND

ERANDA JAYAWICKREME

OXFORD
UNIVERSITY PRESS

OXFORD
UNIVERSITY PRESS

Oxford University Press is a department of the University of Oxford. It furthers the University's objective of excellence in research, scholarship, and education by publishing worldwide. Oxford is a registered trade mark of Oxford University Press in the UK and certain other countries.

Published in the United States of America by Oxford University Press
198 Madison Avenue, New York, NY 10016, United States of America.

Library of Congress Cataloging-in-Publication Data
Names: Infurna, Frank J., editor. | Jayawickreme, Eranda, editor.
Title: Redesigning research on post-traumatic growth : challenges,
pitfalls, and new directions / edited by Frank J. Infurna and Eranda Jayawickreme.
Description: New York, NY : Oxford University Press, [2021] |
Includes bibliographical references and index.
Identifiers: LCCN 2021016421 (print) | LCCN 2021016422 (ebook) |
ISBN 9780197507407 (hardback) | ISBN 9780197507421 (epub) |
ISBN 9780197507438
Subjects: LCSH: Psychic trauma. | Life change events. | Personality assessment. | Well-being.
Classification: LCC BF175.5.P75 R43 2021 (print) |
LCC BF175.5.P75 (ebook) | DDC 155.9/3—dc23
LC record available at https://lccn.loc.gov/2021016421
LC ebook record available at https://lccn.loc.gov/2021016422

DOI: 10.1093/med-psych/9780197507407.001.0001

9 8 7 6 5 4 3 2 1

Printed by Integrated Books International, United States of America

CONTENTS

CONTRIBUTORS

Kinan Alajak, BSc
Utrecht University

Eva Alisic, PhD
University of Melbourne

Michael H. Antoni, PhD
University of Miami

Lara M. Baez, MS
University of Miami

Elana Bayer-Pacht, MA
William James College

Thröstur Björgvinsson, PhD
McLean Hospital/Harvard Medical School

Laura E. R. Blackie, PhD
University of Nottingham

Adriel Boals, PhD
University of North Texas

Gustavo Carlo, PhD
University of California, Irvine

Elaine O. Cheung, PhD
Northwestern University Feinberg School of Medicine

William J. Chopik, PhD
Michigan State University

Sy-Miin Chow, PhD
The Pennsylvania State University

Joanne M. Chung, PhD
University of Toronto

J. Doug Coatsworth, PhD
University of Tennessee

Alexandria Curlee, PhD
Arizona State University

Anna Dorfman, PhD
University of Waterloo

Ina Fassbender, PhD
Ruhr University Bochum

Sarah C. Flury, MD
Vanderbilt University School of Medicine

Marie Forgeard, PhD
William James College
McLean Hospital/Harvard Medical School

Molly J. Gardner, BSc
Arizona State University

Nancy A. Gonzales, PhD
Arizona State University

Kevin J. Grimm, PhD
Arizona State University

Igor Grossmann, PhD
University of Waterloo

Aaron S. Heller, PhD
University of Miami

Frank J. Infurna, PhD
Arizona State University

Eranda Jayawickreme, PhD
Wake Forest University

Sheetal M. Kircher, MD
Northwestern University Feinberg School of Medicine

George P. Knight, PhD
Arizona State University

Shilajit D. Kundu, MD
Northwestern University Feinberg School of Medicine

Odilia M. Laceulle, PhD
Utrecht University

Maike Luhmann, PhD
Ruhr University Bochum

Gloria Luong, PhD
Colorado State University

Suniya S. Luthar, PhD
Arizona State University
Authentic Connections

Kate C. McLean, PhD
Western Washington University

Sara Etz Mendonça, PhD
Wake Forest University

Patricia I. Moreno, PhD
University of Miami Miller School of Medicine

David A. Moscovitch, PhD
University of Waterloo

Judith T. Moskowitz, PhD, MPH
Northwestern University Feinberg School of Medicine

Crystal L. Park, PhD
University of Connecticut

Frank J. Penedo, PhD
University of Miami
University of Miami Miller School of Medicine

Haza F. Rahim, MSc
Utrecht University

Ann Marie Roepke, PhD
Evoke Training and Consulting, PLLC

Zeina Al Sawaf, BA
Utrecht University

Paul J. Silvia, PhD
University of North Carolina Greensboro

Omar E. Staben, MA
Arizona State University

Valerie Tiberius, PhD
University of Minnesota

Rebecca M. B. White, PhD, MPH
Arizona State University

Betina Yanez, PhD
Northwestern University Feinberg School of Medicine

Jenn Yun-Tein, PhD
Arizona State University

Areti Zikopoulos, MA
William James College
McLean Hospital/Harvard Medical School

Renée Zonneveld, MSc
Tilburg University

1

Growth and the Multiple Dimensions of Well-Being

A Philosopher's Take on the Idea of Post-Traumatic Growth

VALERIE TIBERIUS

In the novel *Bel Canto*, the vice-president of a small Latin American country and about 50 others are being held hostage by terrorists. They have been held in the vice-president's mansion for months and they fear they will not survive.

> Vice President Ruben Iglesias, who thought he would not live to feel once again the sensation of grass beneath his feet, stepped off the shale stone walkway and sank into the luxury of his own yard. He had stared at it every day from the living-room window but now that he was actually there it seemed like a new world. Had he ever walked around his own lawn in the evening? Had he made a mental note of the trees, the miraculous flowering bushes that grew up around the wall? What were they called? He dropped his face into the nest of deep purple blossoms and inhaled. Dear God, if he were to get out of this alive he would be attentive to his plants. (Patchett, 2001, p. 281)

I've thought of this example many times, and I've used it before to illustrate a kind of wisdom that one might gain from a traumatic experience: the wisdom needed to put things in perspective and focus on what matters most to us (Tiberius, 2002). Literature is full of characters who grow after adversity. Popular literary themes—rags to riches, stories of redemption, journeys of self-discovery—are built on the idea that good can come of suffering. People like literature and films with these characters and themes. Characters who do not grow are not very interesting, and uplifting themes are—well—uplifting! But how realistic is this portrayal of life? Does life imitate art in this respect? I'm skeptical.

I'm skeptical in part because my own experience of life is that some things get better, some things get worse, I improve in some respects and fall back in others. There is no grand, elevating narrative. Moreover, as I've watched friends and loved ones who have experienced truly traumatic experiences, I've noticed that sometimes things are learned, but mostly they are just really bad for the person who suffers them. This anecdotal evidence is confirmed by the research I have seen coming out of this project. Putting the various studies together, to my untrained eye, the answer to the question of whether there is post-traumatic growth (PTG) seems to be sometimes, for some people, there is some kind of growth; for other people, at other times, or in other ways, there isn't. My skepticism is joined by a sense that growth narratives can be hurtful to people who aren't "growing" from their trauma. This can be because the possibility of growth makes people who are suffering feel inadequate if they aren't growing from it or (more perniciously) because the narrative of PTG can be taken to support blaming people who do not get over their troubles and become better people.

Given this background, my gut feeling is that the response to the question "do trauma, adversity and suffering create growth?" has to be a big "it depends." It depends not just on the person or personality enduring the suffering, but also on what kind of suffering it is and what kind of growth is at issue. This matters for PTG research and how it will invariably be interpreted by the public. In this chapter, I'll lay out the various ways in which whether growth occurs depends on what you mean by "growth." I'll also consider three ways in which one might try to amalgamate the various dimensions of growth to enable general conclusions, and I'll argue that they are all problematic. Though I'm skeptical about *general* growth from trauma, I am not skeptical about PTG research. Rather, I think that researchers just need to take care in defining the type of growth that they find in their studies. I am not a scientist and I do not have the expertise to make specific recommendations about how to do this, but I hope this chapter will provide some guidance by describing the large domain of possible assessments of growth and the challenges involved in trying to put them together.

GROWTH, CHANGE, AND THICK CONCEPTS

Before we turn to well-being and virtue, it will be helpful to think about the concepts employed in this area. The conference I attended was billed as a conference on post-traumatic *growth*, and it is PTG that has achieved acronym status (PTG was everywhere in the slides presented). Yet many at the conference appeared to be talking about personality *change*. The question "Do we grow from trauma?" is, obviously, quite different from the question "Is there personality change after trauma?" In his comments at the Pathways to Character conference at Wake Forest University in 2019, William Fleeson urged us to reflect on and clarify the concepts "growth, change, reaction, resilience, and recovery."

One thing that strikes me, as an outsider to psychological research, is that some of these concepts are typically used to convey an evaluation while others are not. Philosophers have a term for concepts that are used both to report the facts *and* convey an evaluation of those facts: we call them "thick concepts." Concepts that merely describe the facts (e.g., "square") or concepts that mere convey evaluations (e.g., "good") are "thin concepts." The word "growth" strikes me as a thick concept. It is defined in terms of "increasing, developing, or maturing," which is naturally interpreted teleologically: something that is growing is making progress toward its natural telos. In common usage, it seems to me that, when people talk about growth, unless they're talking about a tumor, they tend to mean something positive. The word has a positive evaluative spin. "Change" is not like this. Something may change for the better or the worse, and no particular direction is implied when the word is used. If I say that I *grew* from my time in Italy, I would bet that you'll think about what interesting things I learned, how my mind opened, and so on. Whereas, if I say that I *changed*, you could just as easily think that I became more of a snob about wine.

If I'm right that "growth" (but not "change") is a thick concept, this means that it will be difficult for people to read discussions of PTG without thinking that the change in question is change for the good. Moreover, "growth" may even suggest overall positive change, at least unless it is explicitly qualified. My point is not that psychologists should stop using the word "growth," but it does seem to me worth being aware that the word carries this evaluative meaning for most of us. Those who really want to eschew evaluations might be better off using the word "change." I have no such scruples as a philosopher, so in the remainder of this chapter, I will use the word "growth" with its positive evaluative spin.

People can change for the good, or grow, in various ways. Someone might grow aesthetically from exposure to new art forms, grow intellectually by taking college courses, or grow as an athlete with training. I'm going to focus on a kind of personal growth that I think is of primary interest in the literature on PTG: growth with respect to well-being or well-being–related virtues. In other words, my focus will be on growth that is good *for the person* him- or herself. It may be that such growth also produces moral improvement; happier people might do more for others, for example, and well-being may be intertwined with other people in ways that make improvements in well-being overlap with being better to others (empathy may make one's own life better at the same time as it makes one nicer to others). But my focus will be on growth in well-being and the virtues that are required for it.

POST-TRAUMATIC GROWTH, WELL-BEING, AND VIRTUE

To consider whether trauma increases well-being, we need to know what well-being is. Philosophical theories of well-being have standardly been divided into three types: hedonism, objective list theories, and desire satisfaction theories (Crisp, 2017). Hedonism takes well-being to consist in pleasure (positive affective experience) and the absence of pain. Objective list theories take well-being to consist in certain objective goods such as pleasure, knowledge, achievement, and friendship. The more popular version of objective theory these days is a theory called "perfectionism" or "developmentalism," which takes well-being to consist in the excellent activity of essential human capacities. Goal fulfillment theories (like desire satisfactionism or value fulfillment theory) take well-being to consist in achieving what you want or value. These three types of theory offer different explanations of what makes something good for a person. According to hedonism, pleasure is intrinsically good for you and anything other than pleasure is instrumentally good for you if (and only if) it causes pleasure or prevents pain. According to objective list theories, particular pleasures, pieces of knowledge, and other things are intrinsically good for you because they are just good, period, and so your having them is good for you. According to perfectionism, learning, relating to others, and achieving goals are good for you because they use our essentially human capacity for practical reasoning. According to desire satisfaction or value fulfillment theories, pleasures, knowledge, friendships, and so on are good for you if and only if you desire or value them.

Psychological measures of well-being target various aspects of these three theories (Tiberius, 2006). Positive affect measures and life satisfaction measures target the positive mental states that are the heart of hedonism. Life satisfaction and domain satisfaction scales also likely target goal fulfillment, insofar as felt satisfaction is correlated with actual achievement of goals. Some dimensions of eudaimonist measures target the objective goods at the heart of objective theories in philosophy. For example, Ryff and colleagues list six goods as constitutive of psychological well-being: autonomy, environmental mastery, personal growth, purpose in life, self-acceptance, and positive relationships (Ryff, 1989). Although Ryff and colleagues use self-report, their scales target not just how we feel about our relationships and so on, but also how we are actually doing. The important thing that all of these theories have in common is that they all countenance a long list of things that are good for people either instrumentally or intrinsically. Objective list theories have lists of multiple items, and each of those items is typically achieved through a variety of experiences and activities. There are many eudaimonist theories in psychology that include various lists of goods. Ryff's list (just mentioned) has six; Ryan and Deci (2001) list three main components (autonomy, competence, and relatedness), and Seligman's (2011) PERMA model has five (positive emotion, engagement, positive relationships, meaning, and accomplishment). Goal fulfillment theories countenance as many good things as there are desires or values. Even hedonism, which seems to have a very short list of intrinsic goods, will say that there are various instrumental goods that are no less important for being instrumental. Hedonism can also accept that there are different types of pleasures that arise from different activities. Moreover, for any of these three theories, there are facilitating conditions and requirements for getting the recommended goods. Poor physical health produces pain, frustrates desire satisfaction, and can make it difficult to pursue knowledge. Lack of basic civil liberties can also impede desire satisfaction, produce mental anguish, and prevent achievement.

If this is the state of things, a problem emerges: How do we commensurate all the various goods in order to make overall judgments about whether someone has improved or deteriorated? How could we possibly tell if a person has grown or changed for the better (after trauma or just in general) when there are so many dimensions of well-being? Hedonism makes things somewhat easier for us because it has only one intrinsic value, which means that there is a single metric for putting everything together. But even hedonism doesn't make things simple because there are so many different pleasures, and it can be extremely difficult to compare them in a meaningful way. How would you compare the pleasure of the sun on your face on a warm summer day to the pleasure of listening to a good piece of music? Or the pleasure of an orgasm to the pleasure of learning that a terrible political leader had been defeated? We'll come back to comparing pleasures and other aspects of well-being momentarily, but first, let's make the picture even more complicated.

Along with the long list of things that are good for us and prerequisites for procuring these things goes a long list of virtues and vices that help or hinder our achieving well-being. Philosophers tend to think of virtues as intimately related to well-being. This is either because they take the virtues to be instrumental to other things that are intrinsically good or because they take acting virtuously to be just part of what it is to live a good human life. Any theory can acknowledge the instrumental value of virtues; for example, we seem to need a certain degree of perseverance and courage to pursue important goals in life, for example, and empathy and kindness help us achieve good personal relationships. Some theories will say that virtues also have intrinsic value. Aristotle in particular is known for the view that virtuous action is part of the very definition of flourishing.

Whatever the theoretical background, the foreground is almost always messy. There are numerous virtues. Aristotle emphasizes the cardinal virtues but discusses many others. David Hume lists dozens of virtues in his various works, including good sense, justice, honesty, capacity to keep a secret, knowledge, wit, eloquence, humanity, fidelity, courage (preferably off the battlefield), temperance, constancy, dignity of mind, sociability, good nature, mercy, gratitude, kindness, tenderness, friendliness, generosity, beneficence, integrity, moderate chastity combined with sexual enterprise, discretion, caution, industry, assiduity, frugality, economy, prudence, forethought, considerateness, presence of mind, quickness of conception, ingenuity, facility of expression, and veracity. According to Hume's account of the virtues, virtues are traits of character ("qualities of the mind," as he puts it) that are useful or agreeable to the self or others, and we can see how the qualities he lists—and others we might think of—count as virtues. Psychologists also have lists of virtues and various methods for measuring them. For example, the Virtues in Action (VIA) survey includes 24 character strengths organized into six types: wisdom, courage, humanity, justice, temperance, and transcendence. There is, naturally, a great deal of overlap among the various lists, even among those who have different ideas about the nature of virtue.

The important lesson for our purposes is that even if we could settle on a single theoretical approach to the nature of virtue, we are likely to end up with numerous virtues. Once again, we can ask: If this is the state of things, how do we commensurate all the various virtues in order to make overall judgments about whether someone's personality has grown or improved after trauma, or at all? Once again, there is one theoretical approach that makes things easier. For those who think that the virtues are "unified," improvement is easier to conceptualize. According to the doctrine of "the unity of the virtues," no virtue can be fully possessed without the possession of practical wisdom, and no one can truly have practical wisdom unless they possess all the other virtues. The idea here, which has its roots in Aristotle's ethics, is that practical wisdom includes knowledge of the general nature of a good human life and of the particulars of what to do in any given situation. Wisdom is, therefore, the virtue that adjudicates between the other virtues. For example, consider the case of Jo who, out of desperation and without other options, steals life-saving medication for her son. The virtue of justice might incline someone to report Jo, or at least judge her harshly; the virtue of compassion counsels a quite different response. The person with practical wisdom will know which of these virtues is the relevant one in the case, and she will act appropriately. Unfortunately, the unity of the virtues has invited a lot of skepticism, particularly from those who try to ground their accounts of virtue in personality psychology. Moreover, even if one were to succeed in arguing that virtues are unified *in theory*, they are not unified in practice. People vary in the degree to which they are just, merciful, compassionate, and so on, and it does seem that some people can be fairly high in compassion while being rather low on, say, courage. For someone who holds fast to the unity doctrine, this means that no one has complete virtue. That's fine to say, but it doesn't help solve the practical problem of assessing how people's lives are going; to do that, we need to be able to distinguish degrees of virtue and say something sensible about how much a certain degree of change contributes to overall improvement.

PUTTING THINGS TOGETHER

Let's take stock of where we are. No matter what theory you hold, there are numerous components or ingredients of well-being. Plausible candidates include psychological happiness, health, friendship and family relationships, meaningful work, personal liberty, pleasure, and virtues of various kinds. Different theories are likely to emphasize different ingredients and how they are prioritized, but pluralism in practice (if not in theory) is highly likely. Some theories promise to simplify this mess—hedonism by limiting the number of intrinsic goods and the unity doctrine by amalgamating the virtues into one, but neither of these theoretical approaches succeeds in eliminating questions about how (in practice) to commensurate all the various components of a good human life.

How do we solve this daunting problem? Fortunately, it's a problem that has been noticed before, so there are solutions out there. John Stuart Mill thought we could appeal to "qualified judges." Economists appeal to money and willingness-to-pay measures as a commensurating standard. Some philosophers appeal to ideals or paradigms in order to adjudicate, and psychologists might argue that relying on life satisfaction reports allows individuals to determine how to put the variety of goods together for themselves. Unfortunately, each of these solutions has its problems.

Let's consider the more "objective" solutions first. John Stuart Mill's (1985) famous qualified judge argument aimed to show that higher quality pleasures (by which he meant pleasures that arise from using our higher, human capacities of understanding and moral imagination) are worth more than lower quality pleasures (by which he meant the pleasures that arise from the capacities we share with animals, such as the pleasures of eating and drinking). Mill's thought was that if you want to know which of two things is *better*, you should ask someone who knows both. Therefore, if we want to know whether higher or lower pleasures are better, we should ask someone who has experienced both, a "qualified judge." According to Mill, qualified judges prefer the higher pleasures: "It is better to be a human being dissatisfied than a pig satisfied; better to be Socrates dissatisfied than a fool satisfied. And if the fool, or the pig, are a different opinion, it is because they only know their own side of the question." While this argument does establish that higher pleasures are very important to the people who are able to experience them, it doesn't seem to warrant the conclusion that higher pleasures are better, full stop. A further and perhaps more serious problem for our purposes is that it's hard to see how we could use Mill's strategy to help us understand growth: we would have to appeal to competent judges about packages of goods, or whole lives, but there are no competent judges here. We won't find anyone who has experienced both a life with no trauma and a life with trauma who can decide which is preferable.

Jason Raibley, who defends a value fulfillment theory of well-being, makes use of the notion of a paradigm of a robustly functioning agent. The degree to which "an agent who is realizing his or her values is a central aspect of robustly functioning agency. So is the degree to which the agent is stably disposed to realize these values—i.e., the degree to which the agent is in good emotional and physical health and has the habits of thought and action mentioned above" (Raibley, 2013, p. 207). On this view, attributions of overall growth could be made by comparing the person to this paradigm or exemplar of flourishing agency. This solution to our problem doesn't have the same difficulties as the qualified judge solution. It does not depend on the assumption that someone could be fully informed about what it is like to live several entirely different lives. However, Raibley's view as a solution to our problem does have other problems. Most significantly, it does rely on an ideal of agential flourishing, which would have to be detailed enough to support comparisons to many different lives. Moreover, to use this paradigm of flourishing as a means for attributing overall growth to someone, we must assume that we can (1) compare the post-traumatic life to the ideal, (2) compare the counterfactual life that the person would have had without the trauma to the ideal, and (3) compare the results of 1 and 2 to each other to determine which is better or closer to the ideal. These assumptions might be fine for a philosophical theory of flourishing, but they are unlikely to be met in practice.

Not all goal fulfillment theories appeal to a paradigm in this way. According to my own version of value fulfillment theory, well-being consists in the fulfillment of psychologically integrated, mutually achievable values over time (Tiberius, 2018). Unfortunately, it does not offer a neat way to aggregate the fulfillment of values. I think of this as a virtue of the theory—neat algorithms seem inadequate to the complexities of life—but it does mean that there's no magic solution here for someone who wants to investigate general well-being empirically. Overall well-being would have to be evaluated by assessing how well people are doing in terms of all of their values (such as friendship, career, fitness, music) and how well disposed they are (in terms of their character and the environment) to continue to fulfill their values in the future.

The approaches we have just considered provide ways of putting together the multifarious components of well-being in order to make a reasonable overall assessment of progress that does not rely on the self-report of the person in question. An alternative approach is to leave it to the individual to determine what counts as overall improvement or not. Such approaches have the advantage that they are more empirically tractable because they do not invoke ideals of full information or flourishing agency. Let's consider two examples of this approach.

First, one could prompt individuals to "put together" different components of well-being into an overarching assessment by asking them to convert the components into a commensurating value like money. This is what "willingness-to-pay" measures do. Put simply, willingness-to-pay is just the maximum amount that a person is willing to pay for a product or service. The promise of this as a measurement tool is that it can be used to assess the strength of people's preferences for things that are difficult to quantify and compare. For example, you can ask someone how much they would pay to avoid dialysis, or to live near public parks, or to prevent a highway from being built through their neighborhood. Ostensibly, the results of these questions will tell you how important these things are in comparison to other goods that the person could secure with that money.

Unfortunately, willingness-to-pay measures also have problems. For one thing, what people are willing to pay is sensitive to various features of context, such as how much money they have or are used to having. For another, forcing people to put a price on everything may distort how people actually feel about the things they care about in life. As Haybron and Alexandrova put the problem:

> Suppose there is some amount of money for which farmers in a region have been observed to be willing to sell off their land. It may seem we can infer that they value their property to that extent, but the appearance may be misleading. Perhaps—indeed, this may be the standard case—they accept the trade purely to protect other cherished values; for example, you sell your land during hard times to save your family from ruin. They may not generally be willing to make such tradeoffs at all . . . because mere commodities (mere wants) aren't comparable at all to [their] core values, which serve to

> constrain the pursuit of commodities. (Haybron and Alexandrova, 2013, p. 166)

Asking people to compare different goods by ranking them in terms of a common metric like money invites distortion, and the problem seems to be even worse if we're interested in comparisons of life before and after a traumatic experience. Asking someone post-trauma how much they would be willing to pay to have avoided the trauma in the first place seems likely to trigger major post-hoc rationalization as well as other biases.

Another possibility is to use life satisfaction measures to elicit people's own ideas about how their lives are going overall, putting all the many facets of well-being together. Some psychologists argue that life satisfaction is fairly stable, which may mean that it is less subject to the kinds of biases that plague willingness-to-pay measures (Schimmack, Diener, and Oishi, 2002). Life satisfaction may have other problems, however, as a commensurating evaluation. As Dan Haybron (2007) has argued, we can be satisfied with a life that isn't actually very good for us, because of our perspective or ethical commitments. A person may be grateful to be alive and therefore inclined to be satisfied with her life. Or, she may take the perspective of downward comparison and be satisfied with her life because things could be worse. A person who endures certain kinds of trauma—cancer, natural disaster, car accident—might compare herself to those who fared worse and feel lucky to be doing as well as she is.

Importantly, this isn't a problem with the life satisfaction measure per se; if a person feels better about her life after a traumatic experience because she has shifted perspectives in this way, then she does have more positive feelings, and, perhaps, she has grown in a kind of wisdom that has redounded to her benefit. It is, rather, a problem with thinking that measuring life satisfaction will give you evidence for *overall* improvement. The point is that we cannot conclude from an increase in life satisfaction that the person is better off, all things considered. For example, we can't conclude that her life is better than it would have been had she not had the trauma but gained wisdom and perspective by some other means (mindfulness training, say). If we could ascertain that she has gained the virtue of perspective, we can't conclude anything about how she is doing with respect to other virtues like generosity or friendliness. We also don't know if she is better off in terms of eudaimonist goods like autonomy and relationships. What if one of the reasons that the traumatic experience causes a person to evaluate her life as more satisfying is that it causes her to downplay the importance of some of the things she is no longer able to do (say, if she has lost mobility due to an illness or accident)? Could we conclude that those things aren't good for her? That it wouldn't be good for her to regain them if she could? It doesn't seem to me we can draw any of these conclusions. We can say only that she is somewhat more satisfied with her life perhaps because her perspective on what matters and her level of gratitude have changed.

We started with the problem of how to put the various ingredients of well-being together in order to make overall assessments of how well a person's life is going.

Such assessments are needed for talking about "growth," full stop. We have seen that no method is perfect, and, indeed, they all have serious problems. One response to this situation would be to try to consult multiple methods and make explicit the process by which we are making overall judgments about growth. As a philosopher, I don't have any particular expertise about how this would go, but one thought would be to bring together methods that derive from different dimensions of well-being and virtue. My thought here is that if you could show that trauma increases life-satisfaction *and* joyful emotions *and* objective components of flourishing like relationships, you will have a much better case for making claims about all things considered growth.

Another way forward would be just not to talk about "growth" but always to talk about improvement *in some respect*. One advantage of this approach is that it might encourage thinking about the ways in which trauma makes us worse off in some respects. This is an advantage because people who are suffering due to trauma are sometimes offended by claims about PTG, and an acknowledgment that trauma has measurable negative consequences would alleviate this. These two paths forward are not mutually exclusive, of course. PTG researchers might look for evidence for broader conclusions while at the same time qualifying the conclusions that are warranted from the methods they use.

CONCLUSION

I would hazard a guess that what motivates the interest in PTG is the fact that we all know we're going to face some kind of trauma or other, and we want to believe it won't ruin our lives. Stories about centered cancer survivors and grateful victims of hurricanes give us hope that we'll emerge from whatever bad things happen to us even better than we were before. This is comforting. The message that you may not lose *everything* because of trauma, or that your life may be better in one respect, even if it's worse in others, isn't as comforting. It might be more accurate, though, and more respectful to the people who notice and grieve the ways in which their lives have been made worse by trauma.

REFERENCES

Crisp, R. (Fall 2017). Well-being. In Edward N. Zalta (Ed.), *The Stanford Encyclopedia of Philosophy*. https://plato.stanford.edu/archives/fall2017/entries/well-being/

Haybron, D. (2007). Life satisfaction, ethical reflection, and the science of happiness. *Journal of Happiness Studies, 8*(1), 99–138.

Haybron, D. M., & Alexandrova, A. (2013). Paternalism in economics. In C. Coons & M. Weber (Eds.), *Paternalism: Theory and Practice* (pp. 157–177). Cambridge: Cambridge University Press.

Mill, J. S. (1895). *Utilitarianism*. London: Longmans, Green and Company.

Patchett, A. (2001). *Bel Canto*. New York: HarperCollins Perennial.

Raibley, J. R. (2013). Values, agency, and welfare. *Philosophical Topics, 41*(1), 187–214.

Ryan, R. M., & Deci, E. L. (2001). On happiness and human potentials: A review of research on hedonic and eudaimonic well-being. *Annual Review of Psychology, 52*(1), 141–166.

Ryff, C. D. (1989). Happiness is everything, or is it? Explorations on the meaning of psychological well-being. *Journal of Personality and Social Psychology, 57*(6), 1069.

Schimmack, U., Diener, E., & Oishi, S. (2002). Life-satisfaction is a momentary judgment and a stable personality characteristic: the use of chronically accessible and stable sources. *Journal of Personality, 70*(3), 345–384.

Seligman, M. E. P. (2011). *Flourish: A visionary new understanding of happiness and well-being.* Free Press.

Seligman, M. E. P. (2018). PERMA and the building blocks of well-being. *The Journal of Positive Psychology, 13*(4), 333–335.

Tiberius, V. (2002). Perspective: A prudential virtue. *American Philosophical Quarterly, 39*(4), 305–324.

Tiberius, V. (2006). Well-being: Psychological research for philosophers. *Philosophy Compass, 1*(5), 493–505.

Tiberius, V. (2018). *Well-Being as Value Fulfillment: How We Can Help Each Other to Live Well.* New York: Oxford University Press.

2

Current Assessment and Interpretation of Perceived Post-Traumatic Growth

CRYSTAL L. PARK AND ADRIEL BOALS

Friedrich Nietzsche's (1998) famous quote "What doesn't kill me makes me stronger" is among the most optimistic and hopeful notions held by human beings. Drawing on this idea in the aftermath of traumatic experiences has long been one of our primary ways of moving forward, beyond pain and suffering, and attempting to re-establish happier, healthier lives. In dealing with smaller stresses as well, positive reappraisal is a key method for managing distressing emotions and reframing the situation into a challenge that is more easily handled or resolved (Aldwin, 2007; Garland et al., 2017). One of the main ways that people positively reframe their stressful experiences is by perceiving that they have grown or benefitted from them (Tennen & Affleck, 2002).

Research interest in this specific type of positive reappraisal has proliferated, starting in earnest in the late 1980s and early 1990s (e.g., Collins, Taylor, & Skokan, 1990; Ebersole & Flores, 1989; Lehman et al., 1993; Park & Cohen, 1993; Schaefer & Moos, 1992) and then expanding exponentially later that decade (e.g., Affleck & Tennen, 1996; Park, Cohen, & Murch, 1996; Tedeschi & Calhoun, 1996). Yet as psychologists began to study this phenomenon empirically, this field of study took an unfortunate turn. Rather than explicitly focusing on these beliefs and the cognitive processes underlying them, many researchers began to conflate perceptions of positive change with veridical growth. Although lacking evidence, they claimed that the measures of personal growth or positive change that they developed assessed not experiences of self-enhancement through reappraisal but rather actual positive change. The development of these assessment tools quickly led to an explosion of studies employing retrospective measures of positive change as a result of a wide variety of stressful experiences. From earthquakes to mass shootings to serious illness—wherever investigators looked, they found fairly large degrees of so-called *post-traumatic growth* (PTG). This wonderful news, that science apparently verified our deeply entrenched and heartfelt belief in the possibility of growth—and indeed its widespread occurrence—in the face of hardship, spread quickly in the lay public (e.g., Rendon, 2016) as well as through cultural institutions such as the US military (e.g., Falke & Goldberg, 2019).

This trajectory of scientific inquiry into self-reported positive change omitted a key step in standard psychological science: *validation of the self-report instruments* used to assess the construct. To date, few studies have attempted to properly validate measures of PTG, and these few studies generally demonstrated that these measures do *not* correspond well with observed changes (e.g., Frazier et al., 2009). In this chapter, we describe the most widely used self-report measures, their limitations, and researchers' efforts to modify them to reduce some of their inherent biases. We then consider the meaning of these measures, which appear to tap into an important aspect of individuals' adjustment following stressful experiences, albeit not actual positive personal change, the construct it is widely purported to assess. We conclude with suggestions for future research.

MEASURES OF PERCEIVED (AND ACTUAL) POST-TRAUMATIC GROWTH

Numerous measures of PTG have been developed; in this section, we describe three of the most commonly used. We start with the Posttraumatic Growth Inventory (PTGI; Tedeschi & Calhoun, 1996) because it is the most widely used measure of PTG (Boals, Jayawickreme, & Park, 2021). This 21-item scale comprises five subscales: Relating to Others (e.g., "I have a greater sense of closeness with others"), New Possibilities (e.g., "I developed new interests"), Personal Strength (e.g., "I have a greater feeling of self-reliance"), Spiritual Change (e.g., "I have a better understanding of spiritual matters"), and Appreciation of Life (e.g., "I can better appreciate each day"). Correlations between these five factors usually range from $r = .62$ to .83, suggesting separate factors with a fair amount of overlap. All 21 items are scaled from 0 ("I did not experience this change as a result of my crisis") to 5 ("I experienced this change to a very great degree as a result of my crisis"). The reported internal consistency for both the overall total score ($\alpha = .90$) along with the internal consistencies for the five subscales (α ranged from .67 to .85) are good. The test-retest reliability over a period of 2 months was reported to be $r = .71$. There are several variations of this scale, including the PTGI-42, which includes a separate set of items to assess post-traumatic depreciation (Baker, Kelly, Calhoun, Cann, & Tedeschi, 2008), and the PTGI-X, which included an expanded spirituality/existential subscale (Tedeschi, Cann, Taku, Senol-Durak, & Calhoun, 2017).

The Stress-Related Growth Scale (SRGS; Park et al., 1996) was published in the same year as the PTGI. The SRGS comprises 50 items that load onto a single factor; hence, this measure has no subscales. Example items include, "I became more accepting of others," "I learned to be nicer to others," and "I feel freer to make my own decision." The stem for all items is "Because of this event. . . ." All items are rated on scale from 0 (not at all) to 2 (a great deal). The reported internal consistency is acceptable (α = .94). The test-retest reliability over a period of 2 weeks was reported to be *r* = .81. A 15-item short form of the SRGS is available (Cohen, Hettler, & Pane, 1998). At least two studies have revised the wording of the items from positive to neutral and used a response scale that included positive and negative change (Armeli, Gunthert, & Cohen, 2001; Boals & Schuler, 2018).

The Benefit Finding Scale (BFS; Antoni et al., 2001; Tomich & Helgeson, 2004) was designed to assess positive growth in women with breast cancer, although it has also been used in relation to other types of cancer. The number of items varies from 14 to 30, depending on the specifics of the sample and study design. The stem for all items is "Having had cancer: . . . " Example items include, "has showed me that all people need to be loved" and "has taught me that everyone has a purpose in life." Factor analysis of the 20 most commonly used items revealed a single factor (Tomich & Helgeson, 2004). Items are scored on a 5-point scale from "a little" to "extremely." The reported internal consistency is acceptable (α = .95). We could find no published test-retest reliability for the standard version of the BFS, but a Chinese version demonstrated good test-retest reliability over a period of 4 weeks (*r* = .85) (Wang et al., 2015), and a version for multiple sclerosis patients similarly demonstrated good test-retest reliability over a period of 12 months (*r* = .74) (Pakenham & Cox, 2009).

Given the multiple measures of PTG available, we examined the usage rates of these measures. We conducted a systematic search of the databases Medline, PsychInfo, and Scopus from January 1, 2018, to December 16, 2019 using the search terms "stress-related growth" or "stress related growth" or "benefit-finding" or "benefit finding" or "posttraumatic growth" or "post-traumatic growth" or "adversarial growth." Our initial search turned up 846 results; after removing duplicates, conceptual works, and abstract-only publications, 363 abstracts with full-text articles available remained. We decided to focus on those articles published in the highest impact journals as a proxy for high influence and study quality. Thus, we included all articles in journals published with IF ≥1.5 based on the Scientific Journal Ranking (SJR; Scimago, 2018), resulting in 51 articles. We (AB and CP) independently coded each full-text article for the measure of PTG used. Discrepancies in ratings were resolved by discussion. Twelve of the papers were review papers, which do not assess PTG, and hence were omitted. Of the remaining 39 empirical studies, six articles discussed PTG (which is why they showed up in our search), but PTG was not a measured variable in their study. Of the remaining 33 empirical studies, six papers used qualitative measurement. Of the remaining 27 empirical studies that used a quantitative measure of PTG, 23 used the PTGI. Three of the empirical studies used the BFS. One empirical paper used three items created by the author to assess "benefit finding." The takeaway from our search is that the PTGI is currently far and away the most used commonly used measure of PTG.

LIMITATIONS OF SELF-REPORT MEASURES

Self-report questionnaires are the most commonly used method for assessing PTG. However, these self-reports of personal growth contain a number of inherent limitations. These measures require respondents to make very cognitively complex judgments. Completing items on most psychological questionnaires only requires one step: judging one's current standing on a particular dimension (e.g., "Please rate how sad you feel"). As outlined by Coyne and Tennen (2010), assessing growth as a result of a distressing event involves *five* distinct steps. The first is to evaluate one's current standing on a particular dimension (e.g., appreciation of life). The second is to recall one's standing on this same dimension prior to the distressing event. The third is to compare one's current and previous standing. The fourth is to assess how much change has occurred. The fifth and final step is to determine how much of this change can be attributed to the distressing event. Not only are these steps numerous, but potential biases at each step can distort and diminish the accuracy of the judgment.

Step one is fairly straightforward and not much different than the single step required to complete most psychological assessments. Steps two and three require the respondent to recall their previous standing (Step 2) and compare it to their current standing (Step 3). These two steps are likely to be influenced by *egocentric bias* (sometimes also called *self-enhancing bias*). Egocentric bias is the tendency to view oneself in an overly positive manner and have an inflated opinion of one's personal attributes, in lieu of reality (Ross & Sicoly, 1979). People have a tendency to denigrate their perceptions of their past self as a way to perceive improvement over time (Conway & Ross, 1984; Breckler, 1994; Keuler & Safer, 1998). Furthermore, this bias can be exacerbated when participants expect to improve (Conway & Ross, 1984) and/or focus on a distressing event (McFarland & Alvaro, 2000). Given that these latter two factors are exceptionally salient when completing items about PTG, self-reports of PTG are particularly vulnerable to egocentric bias.

Step 4 requires the respondent to assess how much change has occurred. This is a difficult judgment for respondents to make and is also prone to biases. Individuals' desire for improvement can cause them to perceive improvement even in the absence of genuine change (Sprecher, 1999). Most people who experience distressing events are motivated to believe they have changed for the better, which influences their perceptions of how much they have grown over time.

Step 5 involves judging how much of any perceived improvement is attributable to the distressing event. This judgment is perhaps the most vulnerable to biases. When judging the impact of an event on emotional well-being, most people focus on the one event while ignoring the multitude of other events and factors that might also have an impact. This phenomenon is referred to as *focalism* (Gilbert, Pinel, Wilson, Blumberg, & Wheatley, 1998). For instance, a respondent indicates that the death of a loved one that occurred 2 years earlier is their most life-altering event. When completing a self-report of PTG, the respondent perceives that he or she has grown immensely in the 2 years since the event. However the respondent focuses solely on the single event of death of a loved one while ignoring other events and experiences in the previous 2 years that have also impacted his or her growth. The result is a gross overestimation of the impact of the single event on total growth over time, including the strong possibility that much of said growth may be due to normal development over time, in which case the growth is not attributable to any event(s).

A second problem with self-reports of PTG is the wording of the items and corresponding response scales. Items are typically worded in a positive manner (e.g., "I established a new path for my life") and use a response scale that only includes options for positive growth. When it comes to views of the self and corresponding personal attributes, most people believe they are above average and improving over time (Ross & Wilson, 2003). From a respondent's perspective, reporting little to no growth can be potentially threatening to one's self-concept and is wholly inconsistent with beliefs of being "above average and improving." Respondents may report PTG simply to maintain consistency between their self views and their corresponding beliefs about their growth. Furthermore, the fact that these questionnaires solely use positive items and positive response scales implicitly suggests that most people experience positive changes after a distressing event; it is just a matter of *how much* positive change they have experienced. This implicit message could encourage respondents to report PTG even when none exists (Boals & Schuler, 2018). Consistent with this idea, one study that asked respondents to complete the PTGI in reference to a distressing but clearly non–life-altering event: a cracked cell phone screen (Boals & Schuler, 2019). This study found that 81% of participants reported at least some PTG and a small percentage (12%) reported extreme levels of PTG (above the midpoint of the scale) in a scenario where the possibility of genuine PTG seems highly unlikely.

EFFORTS TO VALIDATE SELF-REPORTS OF POST-TRAUMATIC GROWTH

In light of the many inherent potential response biases, researchers have made numerous attempts to validate self-reports of PTG. The findings have produced mixed results, at best. Given that respondents may be motivated to report elevated levels of PTG to project a positive image, the initial papers on the PTGI and SRGS examined possible correlations with social desirability (Tedeschi & Calhoun, 1996; Park et al., 1996). Both papers reported no relationship with social desirability. This lack of a significant relationship is important but does not rule out the possibility of all motivations to project a positive image. Social desirability is a response bias motivated by a desire to look favorable to *others*. Theories of illusory PTG purport that respondents will convince *themselves* they have grown as a means to cope with the distress of the event (Zoellner & Maercker, 2006). If respondents hold fictitious positive beliefs about themselves, they can report PTG when no genuine growth has taken place, and, because they believe their reports are veridical, these reports will be unrelated to social desirability.

Another way to test validity is to examine concordance rates with reports from those who know the respondent well. Park et al. (1996) asked a friend or relative of the respondent to rate the changes they had seen in the respondent using the SRGS. The mean scores of the respondent and the informant did not significantly differ, and the correlation between the two measures was $r = .21$. This correlation increased to $r = .31$ when informants said they were extremely close to respondents. Although this finding is encouraging, the size of these correlations is underwhelming, suggesting only mild agreement between respondents and informants. Furthermore, if respondents have convinced themselves that they grown (i.e., illusory growth), they may act and speak in ways that similarly convince close others of this growth. In other words, informants' perceptions of respondents' PTG likely relies heavily on respondents' own beliefs. In addition, not only do individuals believe they are above average and improving over time, but they also tend to hold similar beliefs about others close to them (Wilson & Ross, 2001). Thus, these modest correlations between respondents' and informants' reports of PTG may simply result from shared biases.

In perhaps the most direct examination of the validity of self-reports of PTG, Frazier and colleagues (2009) directly compared PTGI scores with actual change in the domains that comprise PTG. In a prospective study, college students completed measures of the domains comprising PTG pre-event (Time 1) and again approximately 2 months later (Time 2). Participants who experienced a traumatic event between Time 1 and Time 2 completed the PTGI at Time 2 regarding PTG from the interim event. PTGI scores were unrelated to changes in actual growth. Furthermore, increased reports of PTG were significantly related to increases in distress from Time 1 to Time 2 and to higher levels of positive reinterpretation coping at Time 2. In contrast, increases in actual growth related to decreases in distress. These results suggest that self-reports of PTG such as the PTGI do not assess genuine growth but rather perceived PTG that is in part a defensive coping attempt (Boerner et al., 2017). At least two similar prospective studies subsequently replicated and extended these findings (Boals, Bedford, & Callahan, 2019; Owens & Fowers, 2019; Yanez et al., 2011).

In addition to the Frazier et al. (2009) study and subsequent replications, six other studies have similarly examined associations between self-reported PTG and measures of actual growth. Results of these studies are mixed. Several studies have found relations between perceived changes in spirituality and actual changes in spirituality (e.g., Frazier et al., 2009; Blackie et al., 2017). For example, Trevino, Naik, and Moye (2016) assessed religiosity and spirituality in a sample of military veteran cancer survivors at initial diagnosis and 6 and 12 months post-diagnosis. Self-reports of PTG were related to actual changes in religiosity and spirituality. However, actual increases in religiosity and spirituality and increases in self-reported PTG were related to increases in anxiety, suggesting both may have been attempts at coping. One study found a relationship, albeit a weak one. Kunz, Joseph, Geyh, and Peter (2019) examined changes in self-efficacy and purpose in life in patients with a spinal cord injury undergoing rehabilitation. Reported levels of PTG at discharge were weakly related to actual changes in self-efficacy and purpose in life, although the changes were only observed during rehabilitation whereas the PTG referred to changes from the injury. Another study obtained mixed results. Ransom, Sheldon, and Jacobsen (2008) assessed life goals and personal attributes of cancer patients before and after radiotherapy. They found that self-reports of PTG were related to actual changes in life goals, but unrelated to actual change in personal attributes; again, the PTG referred to cancer rather than treatment while the changes were only assessed at time points following diagnosis. Another study examined a behavioral outcome of PTG and found no relationship with self-reported PTG. Cohen and Numa (2011) compared reports of PTG between a sample of breast cancer survivors who had volunteered to help with other survivors to a sample of nonvolunteer breast cancer survivors. No differences in self-reported levels of PTG were observed between the groups. Finally, two studies used prospective designs. Johnson and Boals (2015) found that self-reports of PTG in a college student sample were only weakly related to actual change (*r* ranged from .09 to .23). Iimura and Taku (2018) examined self-reports of PTG in a sample of Japanese adolescents transitioning to high school. They found no significant relationship between self-reports of PTG and measures of actual change. However, both of these studies obtained a different pattern of results when they examined only participants who rated their distressing event as high in event centrality.

In sum, the bulk of the empirical evidence suggests that self-reports of PTG do not assess genuine growth. Rather, these measures assess *perceived* PTG, a distinct and separate construct from genuine growth (Jayawickreme & Blackie, 2014). The studies that directly examined relations between self-reports of PTG and actual positive change are methodologically rigorous, included a variety of samples and trauma types, and employed either a prospective or longitudinal design. These studies generally fail to find a relationship between perceived PTG and actual changes. It is entirely possible that many perceptions of PTG stem from misattribution errors. A recent meta-analysis found that although there is evidence of growth after traumatic events, the amount of growth is no different from the amount of growth observed in those who did not experience a traumatic event over similar time periods (Mangelsdorf, Eid, & Luhmann, 2019). Hence, people grow over time as part of normal development, and the experiencing of a traumatic event has little to no effect on this growth. Most perceptions of growth from trauma are likely the result of misattributions and other types of cognitive biases.

Efforts to Modify Measures to Reduce Bias

Ideally, there would be two types of self-report measures available to assess PTG: what we have available now (i.e., measures that assess perceived PTG) and measures that assess the much more elusive genuine PTG. Unfortunately, no such self-report measures of genuine PTG are currently available because it is difficult for any self-report measure to overcome the aforementioned response biases and motivated illusions. However, researchers have made some efforts to at least reduce biased reporting. The two primary methods researchers have investigated thus far are altering the rating scale and examining responses only for events that have become central to the respondent's identity. We next detail these two methods and the subsequent findings.

One of the critiques of self-reports of PTG is that the rating scales only include options for reporting positive change. A number of researchers have altered the rating scale to include options for both positive and negative changes (Arpawong, Richeimer, Weinstein, Elghamrawy, & Milam, 2013; Armeli et al., 2001; Boals & Schuler, 2018; Marshall, Frazier, Frankfurt, & Kuijer, 2015; Milam, 2004; Milam, 2006). As a side note, this methodological change is similar to, but still different from the PTGI-42 (Baker et al., 2008). The PTGI-42 asks separate questions about positive and negative impact: the original 21 items on the PTGI (all positively worded; e.g., "I appreciate each day more") followed by the same 21 items negatively worded (e.g., "I appreciate each day less").

Boals and Schuler directly investigated the effect of using an altered response scale that includes both positive and negative options. They randomly assigned participants to complete either the SRGS, the PTGI, or a revised version of the SRGS that contained neutral wording of items and a response scale that ranged from +3 (very positive change) to −3 (very negative change). The results suggest the revisions made to the SGRS greatly reduced the response bias. The revised SRGS evidenced significantly stronger relationships with measures of convergent validity. The correlations between the original versions of the PTGI and SRGS and mental health outcomes replicated previous findings from a meta-analysis (Helgeson, Reynolds, & Tomich, 2006)—null relationships with depression, anxiety, global distress, and quality of life, and a *positive* relationship with post-traumatic stress disorder (PTSD) symptoms. In contrast, the correlations with the revised SRGS were significant and in the expected directions—less depression, anxiety, global distress, and greater quality of life. Importantly, the revised SRGS was also *negatively* related with PTSD symptoms. Furthermore, PTGI scores were related to avoidance coping (particularly denial coping), whereas the revised SRGS was related to less avoidance coping. Thus, self-reports of PTG that use the altered response scale appear to produce stronger convergent and predictive validity.

The second method researchers have attempted is to limit the analyses to individuals who rated their distressing event as high in event centrality. "Event centrality" refers to the extent to which individuals perceive an event as a central aspect of their identity and life story (Berntsen & Rubin, 2006). Johnson and Boals (2015) argued that genuine PTG is only likely to occur when respondents perceive the event as a turning point in their life story. They employed a prospective research design similar to that of Frazier et al. (2009) in which participants complete measures of current standing on PTG domains before and after a distressing event, and actual change is calculated. The results replicated the aforementioned lack of relations with actual growth obtained by Frazier et al. (2009), but when they examined only participants who rated the distressing event as high in event centrality, self-reports of PTG were related to actual change in the domains that comprise PTG. Furthermore, self-reports of PTG in this subsample were associated with decreases in distress. Iimura and Taku (2018) employed a similar design in their study of Japanese adolescents transitioning to high school. Self-reported PTG was significantly related to change in actual growth but only for students who reported that their transition to high school was high in event centrality. The results from these two studies suggest that self-reports of PTG are more likely to reflect genuine growth when the event is central to the respondent's view of the self.

Although these two methodological "tweaks" of altering the response scale and only examining events high in event centrality appear to reduce some of the inherent response biases, they likely do not reduce the numerous motivations to perceive illusory growth. Hence, these tweaks may make the measures less prone to biased responding, but do not produce a pure measurement of genuine PTG. Creating valid measures of genuine PTG is one of the most important challenges facing the science of PTG.

MEANING OF PERCEIVED POST-TRAUMATIC GROWTH

Given that measures of self-reported growth continue to be widely used—a trend that does not appear to be waning (Jayawickreme, Rivers, & Rauthmann, 2018)—and given the voluminous information we already have on perceived PTG, we believe that now is an opportune time to thoughtfully consider what these perceptions of growth *actually mean*. A number of researchers have argued that reports of growth may sometimes reflect veridical change but often reflect, instead, efforts at coping with the aftermath of the traumatic event or stressful situation (e.g., Zoellner & Maercker, 2006). Indeed, given their subjective nature, the stressful context to which they refer, and their widespread reporting, these appraisals of growth may best be viewed as important aspects of individuals' efforts to make meaning of stressful and traumatic events (Park, 2010). Thus, although these perceptions largely do *not* reflect the degree of actual growth experienced by individuals following trauma, the perceived growth becomes an important part of individuals' narratives, incorporated into the ways that they view the events and their consequences (Bauer et al., 2019).

Perceiving PTG in the aftermath of trauma serves at least two key meaning-related functions for those reporting it: (1) it provides a positive reinterpretation of the event to make it seem less aversive, minimizing the damage and loss sustained; and (2) it enhances one's views of oneself, which enables traumatized individuals to maintain and bolster their sense of self-worth. Both of these functions have been well-described by coping researchers and both may help individuals cope with the sequelae of trauma, reducing event-related distress and promoting better adjustment following major life traumas. Understanding more about these processes of reappraising the difficulties one has encountered is a worthy goal and may lead to more sensitive clinical care as well as effective interventions for those exposed to trauma.

Positive reinterpretation is a type of active coping that involves focusing on the positive aspects of a stressful situation. In positive reinterpretation, individuals reappraise difficult or challenging circumstances to reduce their aversive meaning and heighten the salience of potentially positive aspects of those circumstances (Park, 2010). These more favorable reappraisals of stressful situations do not in themselves involve any actual change in the circumstances (e.g., real change or growth) but rather a more positive perspective on the event. These positive perspectives are very effective at alleviating distress (Aldwin, 2007), and sometimes may actually help individuals to remain engaged in their ongoing coping efforts.

These reappraisal efforts may sometimes lead to positive change, perhaps seen most clearly in the aftermath of health-related crises, where life-threatening health issues such as a cardiac event or cancer can be reframed as an opportunity to make healthy lifestyle changes (e.g., Demark-Wahnefried, Aziz, Rowland, & Pinto, 2005). For instance, a person recovering from a cardiac event may reappraise the event as a second chance at life and an opportunity to develop a healthier lifestyle, which they may then actually adopt (e.g., Tofler et al., 2015). Positive reappraisals may also lead to other behaviors that likely would not have been manifested if the traumatic experience had not occurred, as with individuals who devote their lives to charitable causes following their own crisis or traumatic exposure (e.g., Michael J. Fox Foundation for Parkinson's Research; Christopher & Dana Reeve Foundation). These anecdotal reports suggest that behavioral manifestations of perceiving growth may actually lead to some observable behavior changes, but minimal empirical research documenting such changes exists, and they may be rare occurrences. Moreover, these changes likely do not correspond closely to individuals' perceptions of change. Future research is needed to see how common are lifestyle changes following health crises and the extent to which perceived growth associates with such behavior change.

Perceiving that one has grown as a result of traumatic experiences can also function as *self-enhancement*, the maintenance of positive views of oneself that help individuals to maintain self-esteem, especially in the context of threat or loss (Belsher, Ruzek, Bongar, & Cordova, 2012). Although self-enhancement is typically studied as a tendency or trait, self-enhancement motives can come to the fore in stressful situations, manifesting as self-affirming reflections (Hepper, Gramzow, & Sedikides, 2010). Self-enhancement is generally associated with well-being (e.g., life satisfaction, positive affect, negative affect, depression) (e.g., Dufner, Gebauer, Sedikides, & Denissen, 2019) and resilience following trauma exposure (Bonanno, Rennicke, & Dekel, 2005; Gupta & Bonanno, 2010).

Perceiving growth following stressful and traumatic experiences may be expected to promote well-being, then, given its promotion of both positive reappraisal and self-enhancement because both of these phenomena are associated with positive adaptation. Curiously, however, the associations of self-reported growth and post-trauma adaptation are inconsistent, with some studies finding positive associations but many noting negative associations and others no relationships at all (Park & Sinnott, 2018). This lack of consistent findings may be due to the fact that perceiving growth from stressful events is also strongly associated with continued struggle to cope with and make meaning from them (Park, 2009).

SUGGESTIONS FOR FUTURE RESEARCH

The lack of clear conceptual understanding of what perceptions of PTG mean along with the myriad mixed findings regarding how these perceptions of growth relate to post-trauma recovery highlight the need for more research. To advance our knowledge of perceived PTG, however, future work must take a thoughtful approach to unpacking the potential multiple phenomena encompassed by these perceptions. Given that, at best, these perceptions of growth have a tenuous connection with actual positive change yet seem to be widely experienced and meaningfully related to well-being and adjustment in some studies, we need to understand their value and meaning for individuals in their efforts to recovering from traumatic and stressful experiences.

As we described earlier, when assessing perceived growth, different results may be obtained if participants are simply asked to describe post-traumatic changes in themselves that they have observed versus if participants are asked to rate multiple items presented to them in a long list. If the latter (questionnaire-based) approach is taken, it may also matter whether the items that participants rate are all biased toward positive reports (e.g., having no opportunity to report negative change, such as with the PTGI) versus presenting options to rate each item with a valence from negative change to no change to positive change (Park & Sinnott, 2018). Researchers should consider their choice of assessment carefully and justify their choice in their research reports. They should also note limitations of the method used.

Researchers should also rely on theoretical and previous empirical literature when investigating the meaning of perceiving growth from or through traumatic experiences. In this chapter, we drew on coping theory and specifically positive reappraisal and self-enhancement as obvious mechanisms underlying these perceptions, and both of these notions warrant continued exploration. In addition, researchers may identify other helpful theoretical perspectives (e.g., narrative self-identify: Bauer et al., 2019) from which to conceptualize and study perceived growth. The body of existing work on perceived growth is already quite large and should be fully interpreted and integrated within this framework.

Embracing the notion that the phenomenon of perceived growth is distinct from actual growth and potentially important in its own right will open the door for much important research that will deepen our understanding of these perceptions and, ideally, identify for whom and under what circumstances perceiving growth is helpful. Taking these steps will propel this research area forward onto a more solid scientific footing.

REFERENCES

Affleck, G., & Tennen, H. (1996). Construing benefits from adversity: Adaptational significance and dispositional underpinnings. *Journal of Personality, 64*, 899–922.

Aldwin, C. M. (2007). *Stress, Coping, and Development*. New York: Guilford.

Antoni, M. H., Lehman, J. M., Kilbourn, K. M., Boyers, A. E., Culver, J. L., Alferi, S. M., Yount, S. E., McGregor, B. A., Arena, P. L., Harris, S. D., Price, A. A., & Carver, C. S. (2001). Cognitive-behavioral stress management intervention decreases the prevalence of depression and enhances benefit finding among women under treatment for early-stage breast cancer. *Health Psychology, 20*(1), 20–32. https://doi.org/10.1037/0278-6133.20.1.20

Armeli, S., Gunthert, K. C., & Cohen, L. H. (2001). Stressor appraisals, coping, and post-event outcomes: The dimensionality and antecedents of stress-related growth. *Journal of Social and Clinical Psychology, 20*, 366–395. https://doi.org/10.1521/jscp.20.3.366.22304

Arpawong, T. E., Richeimer, S. H., Weinstein, F., Elghamrawy, A., & Milam, J. E. (2013). Posttraumatic growth, quality of life, and treatment symptoms among cancer chemotherapy outpatients. *Health Psychology, 32*(4), 397–408. https://doi.org/10.1037/a0028223

Baker, J. M., Kelly, C., Calhoun, L. G., Cann, A., & Tedeschi, R. G. (2008). An examination of posttraumatic growth and posttraumatic depreciation: Two exploratory studies. *Journal of Loss and Trauma, 13*, 450–465. doi:10.1080/15325020802171367

Bauer, J. J., Graham, L. E., Lauber, E. A., & Lynch, B. P. (2019). What growth sounds like: Redemption, self-improvement, and eudaimonic growth across different life narratives in relation to well-being. *Journal of Personality, 87*, 546–565.

Belsher, B. E., Ruzek, J. I., Bongar, B., & Cordova, M. J. (2012). Social constraints, posttraumatic cognitions, and posttraumatic stress disorder in treatment-seeking trauma survivors: Evidence for a social-cognitive processing model. *Psychological Trauma: Theory, Research, Practice, and Policy, 4*, 386–391.

Berntsen, D., & Rubin, D. C. (2006). The centrality of event scale: A measure of integrating a trauma into one's identity and its relation to post-traumatic stress disorder symptoms. *Behaviour Research and Therapy, 44*(2), 219–231.

Blackie, L. E., Jayawickreme, E., Tsukayama, E., Forgeard, M. J., Roepke, A. M., & Fleeson, W. (2017). Post-traumatic growth as positive personality change: Developing a measure to assess within-person variability. *Journal of Research in Personality, 69*, 22–32.

Boals, A., Bedford, L. A., & Callahan, J. L. (2019). Perceptions of change after a trauma and perceived posttraumatic growth: A prospective examination. *Behavioral Sciences, 9*(1), 10.

Boals, A., Jayawickreme, E., & Park, C. L. (2021). Advantages of distinguishing perceived and veridical posttraumatic growth: Recommendations for future research on both constructs. *Manuscript under review*.

Boals, A., & Schuler, K. (2018). Reducing reports of illusory posttraumatic growth: A revised version of the Stress-Related Growth Scale (SRGS-R). *Psychological Trauma: Theory, Research, Practice, and Policy, 10*, 190–198.

Boals, A., & Schuler, K. (2019). Shattered cell phones, but not shattered lives: A comparison of reports of illusory posttraumatic growth on the Posttraumatic Growth

Inventory and the Stress-Related Growth Scale—Revised. *Psychological Trauma: Theory, Research, Practice, and Policy, 11*(2), 239–246.

Boerner, M., Joseph, S., & Murphy, D. (2017). Reports of post-traumatic growth and well-being: Moderating effect of defense style. *Journal of Social and Clinical Psychology, 36*(9), 723–737.

Bonanno, G. A., Rennicke, C., & Dekel, S. (2005). Self-enhancement among high-exposure survivors of the September 11th terrorist attack: Resilience or social maladjustment? *Journal of Personality and Social Psychology, 88*, 984–998.

Breckler, S. (1994). Memory for the experience of donating blood: Just how bad was it? *Basic and Applied Social Psychology, 15*(4), 467–488. doi:/10.1207/s15324834basp1504_5

Cohen, L. H., Hettler, T. R., & Pane, N. (1998). Assessment of posttraumatic growth. In R. G. Tedeschi, C. L. Park, & L. G. Calhoun (Eds.), *The LEA series in personality and clinical psychology. Posttraumatic growth: Positive changes in the aftermath of crisis* (pp. 23–42). Lawrence Erlbaum Associates Publishers.

Cohen, M., & Numa, M. (2011). Posttraumatic growth in breast cancer survivors: A comparison of volunteers and non-volunteers. *Psycho-Oncology, 20*(1), 69–76. https://doi.org/10.1002/pon.1709

Collins, R., Taylor, S., & Skokan, L. (1990). A better world or a shattered vision? Changes in life perspectives following victimization. *Social Cognition, 8*, 263–285.

Conway, M., & Ross, M. (1984). Getting what you want by revising what you had. *Journal of Personality and Social Psychology, 47*(4), 738–748. doi:10.1037/0022-3514.47.4.738

Coyne, J. C., & Tennen, H. (2010). Positive psychology in cancer care: Bad science, exaggerated claims, and unproven medicine. *Annals of Behavioral Medicine, 39*(1), 16–26. https://doi.org/10.1007/s12160-009-9154-z

Demark-Wahnefried, W., Aziz, N. M., Rowland, J. H., & Pinto, B. M. (2005). Riding the crest of the teachable moment: promoting long-term health after the diagnosis of cancer. *Journal of Clinical Oncology, 23*(24), 5814–5830.

Dufner, M., Gebauer, J. E., Sedikides, C., & Denissen, J. J. (2019). Self-enhancement and psychological adjustment: A meta-analytic review. *Personality and Social Psychology Review, 23*, 48–72.

Ebersole, P., & Flores, J. (1989). Positive impact of life crises. *Journal of Social Behavior and Personality, 4*, 463–469.

Falke, K., & Goldberg, J. (2019). Posttraumatic growth proves you can be stronger after trauma. https://www.military.com/daily news/2019/06/03/posttraumatic-growth-proves-you-can-be-stronger-after-trauma.html

Frazier, P., Tennen, H., Gavian, M., Park, C., Tomich, P., & Tashiro, T. (2009). Does self-reported posttraumatic growth reflect genuine positive change? *Psychological Science, 20*, 912–919. doi:10.1111/j.1467-9280.2009.02381.x

Garland, E. L., Kiken, L. G., Faurot, K., Palsson, O., & Gaylord, S. A. (2017). Upward spirals of mindfulness and reappraisal: Testing the mindfulness-to-meaning theory with autoregressive latent trajectory modeling. *Cognitive Therapy and Research, 41*, 381–392.

Gilbert, D. T., Pinel, E. C., Wilson, T. D., Blumberg, S. J., & Wheatley, T. P. (1998). Immune neglect: A source of durability bias in affective forecasting. *Journal of Personality and Social Psychology, 75*(3), 617–638. https://doi.org/10.1037/0022-3514.75.3.617

Gupta, S., & Bonanno, G. A. (2010). Trait self-enhancement as a buffer against potentially traumatic events: A prospective study. *Psychological Trauma: Theory, Research, Practice, and Policy, 2*, 83–92.

Helgeson, V. S., Reynolds, K. A., & Tomich, P. L. (2006). A meta-analytic review of benefit finding and growth. *Journal of Consulting and Clinical Psychology, 74*(5), 797–816. https://doi.org/10.1037/0022-006X.74.5.797

Hepper, E. G., Gramzow, R. H., & Sedikides, C. (2010). Individual differences in self-enhancement and self-protection strategies: An integrative analysis. *Journal of Personality, 78*, 781–814.

Iimura, S., & Taku, K. (2018). Positive developmental changes after transition to high school: Is retrospective growth correlated with measured changes in current status of personal growth?. *Journal of Youth and Adolescence, 47*(6), 1192–1207.

Jayawickreme, E., & Blackie, L. E. R. (2014). Post-traumatic growth as positive personality change: Evidence, controversies and future directions. *European Journal of Personality, 28*(4), 312–331.

Jayawickreme, E., Rivers, J., & Rauthmann, J. R. (2018). Do we know how adversity impacts human development? *Research in Human Development, 15*, 294–316.

Johnson, S. F., & Boals, A. (2015). Refining our ability to measure posttraumatic growth. *Psychological Trauma: Theory, Research, Practice, and Policy, 7*(5), 422–429. https://doi.org/10.1037/tra0000013

Keuler, D. J., & Safer, M. A. (1998). Memory bias in the assessment and recall of pre-exam anxiety: How anxious was I? *Applied Cognitive Psychology, 12*(Special Issue), S127–S137. doi:2147/10.1002

Kunz, S., Joseph, S., Geyh, S., & Peter, C. (2019). Perceived posttraumatic growth and depreciation after spinal cord injury: Actual or illusory? *Health Psychology, 38*, 53–62. doi:10.1037/hea0000676.supp

Lehman, D., Davis, C, DeLongis, A., Wortman, C., Bluck, S., Mandel, D., & Ellard, J. (1993). Positive and negative life changes following bereavement and their relations to adjustment. *Journal of Social and Clinical Psychology, 12*, 90–112.

Mangelsdorf, J., Eid, M., & Luhmann, M. (2019). Does growth require suffering? A systematic review and meta-analysis on genuine posttraumatic and postecstatic growth. *Psychological Bulletin, 145*(3), 302–338. https://doi.org/10.1037/bul0000173

Marshall, E. M., Frazier, P., Frankfurt, S., & Kuijer, R. G. (2015). Trajectories of posttraumatic growth and depreciation after two major earthquakes. *Psychological Trauma: Theory, Research, Practice, and Policy, 7*(2), 112–121. https://doi.org/10.1037/tra0000005

McFarland, C., & Alvaro, C. (2000). The impact of motivation on temporal comparisons: Coping with traumatic events by perceiving personal growth. *Journal of Personality and Social Psychology, 79*(3), 327–343. https://doi.org/10.1037/0022-3514.79.3.327

Milam, J. E. (2004). Posttraumatic growth among HIV/AIDS patients. *Journal of Applied Social Psychology, 34*(11), 2353–2376.

Milam, J. E. (2006). Posttraumatic growth and HIV disease progression. *Journal of Consulting and Clinical Psychology, 74*(5), 817–827. https://doi.org/10.1037/0022-006X.74.5.817

Nietzsche, F. (1998). *Twilight of the idols*. Oxford: Oxford University Press.

Owens, M., & Fowers, B. J. (2019). Perceived post-traumatic growth may not reflect actual positive change: A short-term prospective study of relationship dissolution. *Journal of Social and Personal Relationships, 36*, 3098–3116.

Pakenham, K. I., & Cox, S. (2009). The dimensional structure of benefit finding in multiple sclerosis and relations with positive and negative adjustment: A longitudinal study. *Psychology & Health, 24*(4), 373–393. doi:10.1080/08870440701832592

Park, C. L. (2009). Overview of theoretical perspectives. In C. L. Park, S. Lechner, M. H. Antoni, & A. Stanton (Eds.), *Positive Life Change in the Context of Medical Illness: Can the Experience of Serious Illness Lead to Transformation?* (pp. 11–30). Washington, DC: American Psychological Association.

Park, C. L. (2010). Making sense of the meaning literature: An integrative review of meaning making and its effects on adjustment to stressful life events. *Psychological Bulletin, 136*(2), 257–301. https://doi.org/10.1037/a0018301

Park, C. L., & Cohen, L. H. (1993). Religious and nonreligious coping with the death of a friend. *Cognitive Therapy and Research, 17*, 561–577.

Park, C. L., Cohen, L. H., & Murch, R. L. (1996). Assessment and prediction of stress-related growth. *Journal of Personality, 64*, 71–105.

Park, C., & Sinnott, S. (2018). Testing the validity of self-reported posttraumatic growth in young adult cancer survivors. *Behavioral Sciences, 8*(12), 116.

Ransom, S., Sheldon, K. M., & Jacobsen, P. B. (2008). Actual change and inaccurate recall contribute to posttraumatic growth following radiotherapy. *Journal of Consulting and Clinical Psychology, 76*(5), 811–819. https://doi.org/10.1037/a0013270

Rendon, J. (2016). *Upside: The New Science of Post-Traumatic Growth*. New York: Simon & Schuster.

Ross, M. (1989). Relation of implicit theories to the construction of personal histories. *Psychological Review, 96*(2), 341–357. doi:10.1037/0033-295X.96.2.341

Ross, M., & Sicoly, F. (1979). Egocentric biases in availability and attribution. *Journal of Personality and Social Psychology, 37*, 322–336. doi:10.1037/0022-3514.37.3.322.

Ross, M., & Wilson, A. E. (2003). Autobiographical memory and conceptions of self: Getting better all the time. *Current Directions in Psychological Science, 12*(2), 66–69.

Schaefer, J. A., & Moos, R. H. (1992). Life crises and personal growth. In B. N. Carpenter (Ed.), *Personal coping: Theory, research, and application* (pp. 149–170). Praeger Publishers/Greenwood Publishing Group.

Sprecher, S. (1999). "I love you more today than yesterday": Romantic partners' perceptions of changes in love and related affect over time. *Journal of Personality and Social Psychology, 76*(1), 46–53. https://doi.org/10.1037/0022-3514.76.1.46

Tedeschi, R. G., & Calhoun, L. G. (1996). The posttraumatic growth inventory: Measuring the positive legacy of trauma. *Journal of Traumatic Stress, 9*, 455–471. doi:10.1007/BF02103658

Tedeschi, R. G., & Calhoun, L. G. (2004). Posttraumatic growth: Conceptual foundations and empirical evidence. *Psychological Inquiry, 15*, 1–18. http://dx.doi.org/10.1207/s15327965pli1501_01

Tedeschi, R. G., Cann, A., Taku, K., Senol-Durak, D. E., & Calhoun, L. G. (2017). The posttraumatic growth inventory: A revision integrating existential and spiritual change. *Journal of Traumatic Stress, 30*(1), 11–18. doi:10.1002/jts.22155

Tennen, H., & Affleck, G. (2002). Benefit-finding and benefit-reminding. In C. R. Snyder & S. J. Lopez (Eds.), *Handbook of positive psychology* (pp. 584–597). New York, NY, US: Oxford University Press.

Tofler, G. H., May, R., Bartrop, R., Kirkness, A., Glinatsis, H., & de Burgh, S. (2015). Acute coronary syndrome as a teachable moment for smoking cessation. *Journal of Smoking Cessation, 10*(1), 5–11.

Tomich, P. L., & Helgeson, V. S. (2004). Is finding something good in the bad always good? Benefit finding among women with breast cancer. *Health Psychology, 23*(1), 16–23. https://doi.org/10.1037/0278-6133.23.1.16

Trevino, K. M., Naik, A. D., & Moye, J. (2016). Perceived and actual change in religion/spirituality in cancer survivors: Longitudinal relationships with distress and perceived growth. *Psychology of Religion and Spirituality, 8*(3), 195–205. https://doi.org/10.1037/rel0000030

Wang, Y., Zhu, X., Yi, J., Tang, L., He, J., Chen, G., . . . Yang, Y. (2015). Benefit finding predicts depressive and anxious symptoms in women with breast cancer. *Quality of Life Research, 24*(11), 2681–2688. doi:10.1007/s11136-015-1001-z

Wilson, A. E., & Ross, M. (2001). From chump to champ: People's appraisals of their earlier and present selves. *Journal of Personality and Social Psychology, 80*(4), 572–584. https://doi.org/10.1037/0022-3514.80.4.572

Yanez, B. R., Stanton, A. L., Hoyt, M. A., Tennen, H., & Lechner, S. (2011). Understanding perceptions of benefit following adversity: How do distinct assessments of growth relate to coping and adjustment to stressful events?. *Journal of Social and Clinical Psychology, 30*(7), 699–721.

Zoellner, T., & Maercker, A. (2006). Posttraumatic growth in clinical psychology—A critical review and introduction of a two component model. *Clinical Psychology Review, 26*(5), 626–653.

3

Post-Traumatic Growth Interventions

ANN MARIE ROEPKE, ARETI ZIKOPOULOS, AND MARIE FORGEARD ■

Individuals who live through adverse experiences such as natural disasters, abuse, combat, and chronic illness have the potential to develop posttraumatic stress symptoms, which have been the target of various therapeutic interventions (e.g., Powers, Halpern, Ferenschak, Gillihan, & Foa, 2010; Resick & Schnicke, 1992). In the aftermath of adversity, individuals may also experience positive psychological changes attributed to their struggle with adversity; such changes are often referred to as *post-traumatic growth* (PTG) and can include a self-reported deeper appreciation for life, a sense of new possibilities, closer relationships, a feeling of greater personal strength, and a deeper understanding of spirituality (Calhoun & Tedeschi, 1999, 2001). Psychological research has begun to focus on interventions that may foster PTG in addition to or instead of aiming to decrease post-traumatic stress or other forms of psychopathology.

CHALLENGES AND CRITICISMS OF POST-TRAUMATIC GROWTH INTERVENTION RESEARCH

Efforts to foster PTG have not been uncontroversial. Criticisms of PTG intervention research and practice frequently center on two main themes (Harbin, 2015; Jayawickreme & Blackie, 2014). First, there are concerns about whether the most well-established approach to measuring PTG is valid. The Posttraumatic Growth Inventory (PTGI; Tedeschi & Calhoun, 1996), the most commonly used measure, has been regarded with skepticism because it requires the respondent to assess their current level of functioning (e.g., how close they are to other people), recall their past level of functioning, compare the two to assess any change, and decide how much of this change is a result of the struggle with adversity (Jayawickreme & Blackie, 2014). Evidence suggests that retrospective self-reports are not ideal predictors of actual change and may be influenced by our desire to see ourselves in a more positive or hopeful light (Frazier et al., 2009; Robins, Noftle, Trzesniewski, & Roberts, 2005). Thus, it is unclear to what extent the PTGI and similar measures are capturing genuine change or what has been called "illusory growth" (Boals & Schuler, 2018).

On the other hand, some empirical evidence supports the validity of such reports. A number of studies have shown that informants (e.g., loved ones) corroborate people's reports of growth, suggesting that these are not solely the product of subjective perceptions (Blackie et al., 2015; Shakespeare-Finch & Enders, 2008). In addition, measuring self-perceived growth may be valuable because positive reports (even inflated or biased) likely have an adaptive function. Research on self-enhancing beliefs suggests that not only is it common for individuals to believe they are better off than what may be realistic, but that this thought process can actually be helpful in promoting psychological health in the aftermath of adverse circumstances (Leedham, Meyerowitz, Muirhead, & Frist, 1995). Nonetheless, it is important to distinguish between self-perceptions of growth and other indicators of growth in order to better understand what changes do versus do not take place following adversity. Given the complexity inherent in discerning "genuine" growth versus "illusory" growth, PTG intervention research should ideally use a measurement strategy that aims to assess growth and well-being in multiple ways (as we discuss later). Without a nuanced measurement strategy, PTG intervention research can only tell us about what strategies help people to *believe* they have changed for the better and little about what strategies foster growth and change more broadly. Different interventions might be expected to impact one of these more than the other (e.g., self-perception vs. behavioral indicators of growth). Of note, nearly all of the studies herein assessed PTG using either the PTGI or a similar retrospective self-report measure (i.e., a measure of how much participants *believe* they have grown from adversity, looking back).

A second critique of PTG intervention research stems from concerns about potential negative consequences of intentionally targeting PTG in interventions: for instance, intervention participants might be induced to feel shame or discouragement if they seem to have "failed" at attaining personal growth while struggling to survive an unspeakably painful time in their lives. Harbin (2015) has highlighted ethical considerations relevant to developing and testing PTG interventions These include concerns about the status and effects of the ideal picture of post-traumatic health which are implicit in the account of growth-oriented therapies, concerns about the ethical implications of growth-oriented recommendations given to patients after trauma, and potential harm in implying to clients that they are in the process of—and in control of—their own growth. These are certainly valid issues and important considerations in the development and evaluation of PTG interventions. It is important that PTG-oriented interventions take care not to inadvertently pressure or shame people into attempts at personal growth, that they are sensitive to the vulnerabilities of people with recent trauma exposure, that they do not ignore individuals' distress nor include strategies that would foster growth but worsen distress, and that they are rigorously evaluated with attention to both growth and distress. In addition, care is needed in determining the appropriate time to provide a PTG-oriented intervention. There is no decisive evidence about the optimal timing for such approaches, but it is likely that in the immediate aftermath of a crisis most people would be better served by supports that address more immediate emotional distress and life disruption (Vernberg et al., 2008).

One thing is clear: despite ongoing controversy about some methodological and ethical dimensions of developing and testing PTG-oriented interventions, this work is well under way and deserves careful consideration. The proverbial horse has left the barn. To date, this area of research has both examined the impact of existing psychosocial interventions on PTG, and also involved the development and evaluation of novel interventions that more explicitly target PTG. We describe this literature here, having done our best to group the large quantity of interventions into reasonable categories.[1] Importantly, and as described later, the utility of the approaches described has primarily been tested using measures of retrospectively self-reported PTG (e.g., the PTGI), limiting the conclusions that can be drawn about their effects.

INTERVENTION APPROACHES

Existing Interventions Relevant to Post-Traumatic Growth

Cognitive-Behavioral Therapies

Several cognitive-behavioral therapy (CBT) approaches have established a solid evidence base in the treatment of post-traumatic stress disorder (PTSD; e.g., Powers et al., 2010; Resick & Schnicke, 1992). These may be relevant to fostering PTG as well, particularly given that traumatic events and trauma-focused therapies may lead individuals to modify their thoughts about themselves and their world—a process that may also be key for growth to occur (Sherman, 1998; Janoff-Bulman, 1989; Tedeschi & Calhoun, 2004). Although some CBT interventions may not explicitly discuss or target PTG, they may influence it regardless. A recent meta-analysis (Roepke, 2015) pointed to several CBT programs that appear to have the potential to foster PTG. We review here some of the main findings pointing to such gains, as documented by changes on retrospective measures of self-reported PTG.

For instance, gains in PTG were found after CBT for PTSD among individuals who survived car accidents (Zoellner, Rabe, Karl, & Maercker, 2011) and after CBT-oriented coping skills training provided to couples coping with cancer (Heinrichs et al., 2012). Another CBT program to produce a significant effect on PTG is Cognitive-Behavioral Stress Management (CBSM), a manualized therapy that assists participants in identifying and working with stressful and negative thoughts, as well as garnering social support and using coping skills (Antoni et al., 2006). Cognitive Behavioral Conjoint Therapy (CBCT) for PTSD has also yielded positive findings: compared to couples on a waiting list, couples who received CBCT showed increases in PTG, though the trial's secondary aim of identifying moderators of this effect yielded no findings (i.e., increases in PTG did not appear to be impacted by participants' symptomatology or relationship satisfaction) (Wagner et al., 2016). Another adaptation of CBT designed to target prolonged grief (PG-CBT) has also been shown to foster PTG: a randomized controlled trial (RCT) indicated that PG-CBT facilitated growth compared to a waiting list control, and the effect was maintained at the 1.5-year follow-up (Bartl, Hagl, Kotoučová, Pfou, & Rosner, 2018). Research on Gray et al.'s (2012) adaptive disclosure therapy has also offered corroborating evidence. This intervention, designed for active-duty service members, combines CBT techniques such as imaginal exposure and cognitive processing and adapts these to address moral injury (i.e., distress resulting from breaking one's moral code). In an open trial (i.e., one without a control group), participants reported higher PTG scores along with lower scores on PTSD, depression, and post-traumatic cognitions after taking part in AD (Gray et al., 2012). Finally, Knaevelsrud, Liedl, and Maercker (2010) found that even when CBT for PTSD symptoms or grief was delivered via the Internet or over the phone, PTG scores increased among adult participants.

Narrative-Based and Disclosure-Based Interventions

Processing traumatic or adverse events often involves disclosure to others in an environment that is safe and supportive (Tedeschi, Calhoun, & Groleau, 2015). This positive and empathic relationship is of course relevant across a range of psychotherapies, not just those explicitly centered on narrative or disclosure (Baldwin, Wampold, & Imel, 2007); likewise, opportunities for the client to form an adaptive explanation of their difficulties appears relevant across diverse types of therapy (Wampold, 2007).

A safe space for disclosure is also broadly relevant to social relationships, not just the therapist–client relationship. Individuals who lack support to facilitate the disclosure of challenging experiences are at heightened risk of dysphoria, trauma-related thoughts, and depression (Nolen-Hoeksema & Larson, 1999; Lepore & Helgeson, 1998; Lepore, Silver, Wortman, & Wayment, 1996). If an individual feels as though their story is unwanted or undesirable, productive cognitive processing might be inhibited; in contrast, PTG may be more likely if an individual experiences others as supportive and accepting (Tedeschi & Calhoun, 2004). Another factor is the individual's willingness and ability to engage with trauma-related memories; if an individual is highly avoidant of painful memories, feelings, and thoughts, PTG may be less likely (Kashdan & Kane, 2011).

A variety of disclosure- and narrative-based interventions have been examined to determine whether these approaches might foster PTG, again measured using retrospective self-report instruments. Unlike some of the forms of CBT just described, disclosure- and narrative-based interventions tend to put less focus on skill-building, psychoeducation, or other such structured therapeutic content. Instead, the interventions tend to emphasize the core process of disclosure (i.e., describing/sharing the experience) and/or narrative (i.e., making sense of our world and our lives through telling stories; Schauer, Neuner, & Elbert, 2011).

Disclosure, Expressive Writing, and Post-Traumatic Growth

Disclosure-based interventions are diverse but share the common emphasis on telling the experience to others or even just writing or recording it for oneself. Previous research on such interventions has been inconclusive, with some evidence that making a written disclosure of one's experience of an adverse event can foster PTG (Lutgendorf & Ullrich, 2002; Smyth, Hockemeyer, & Tulloch, 2008), along with null findings (e.g., Groleau, 2015), and even some evidence of *decreased* PTG after expressive writing (Gallagher, Long, Tsai, Stanton, & Lu, 2018). Research on narrative and disclosure-based interventions is inconclusive about the best format to use (writing vs. describing the trauma aloud) and about exactly how these methods work (Pennebaker, 2004). More research is therefore needed to understand the mechanisms underlying the benefits of disclosure and narrative formation.

Narrative Interventions and Post-Traumatic Growth

Narrative approaches to well-being emphasize the idea that the way people construe their life story is an important aspect of personality: one's "narrative identity," then, consists of a person's internalized and evolving life story, integrating the past and future to provide life with more unity and purpose (McAdams & McLean, 2013). Maintaining a coherent narrative identity after adversity may therefore be crucial to coping and growing. According to PTG theory (Tedeschi & Calhoun, 2004), PTG should be facilitated by interventions that support people in considering—and reconsidering—how challenging events fit into their life story. Creating and reworking a narrative to provide a coherent sense of meaning to traumatic events and their aftermath is therefore hypothesized to foster PTG. Alternatively, PTG itself might be considered a special type of narrative: one involving themes of transformation and redemption, especially in Western cultures (Pals & McAdams, 2004). These narratives, like PTG itself, may reflect the multifaceted nature of growth, including both our own perceptions of how our character has changed, as well as more observable/verifiable changes in our functioning.

Limited empirical evidence speaks to the usefulness of narrative approaches for PTG specifically. Narrative exposure therapy (NET) is a short-term treatment originally created for survivors of war and integrates elements of exposure therapy and testimony therapy (Schauer et al., 2011). Rather than requiring clients to identify a single traumatic event as a target, this therapy involves a narrative about the client's entire life. NET allows clients to reexamine their traumatic memories as well as their emotional responses to the event (Zang, Hunt, & Cox, 2013). In a study of the effectiveness of NET on adult survivors of the 2008 Sichuan earthquake, participants randomly assigned to the NET condition reported significant increases in PTG and decreases in PTSD symptoms, anxiety, depression, and general mental stress compared to a waiting list (Zang et al., 2013). Similar results were found when Chinese earthquake survivors were given NET or revised NET (NET-R), which involved reinforcement of the narration of a single traumatic event and a cancellation of the testimony sign-off phase (Zang, Hunt, & Cox, 2014). Participants in both NET and NET-R groups showed reductions in PTSD symptoms and increases in PTG, thus highlighting the value of oral narrative approaches in the context of natural disasters and low-income areas.

NET has also been adapted to a briefer, three-session version to address post-traumatic stress in an efficient, culturally sensitive way in Iraqi refugees in the United States (Hijazi et al., 2014). Individuals in the brief NET condition (compared to the waiting list control group) showed greater PTG and well-being, with effects lasting through to the 4-month follow-up. Brief NET also appeared to reduce PTSD and depression symptoms relative to the control group, though these results only persisted through the 2-month follow-up (Hijazi et al., 2014). This study highlighted that narrative approaches are particularly promising because they may be particularly well-suited to adaptation for varied cultural contexts (see also Lane, Myers, Hill, & Lane, 2016).

Other Established Interventions

Other well-known interventional approaches have also shown promise for fostering PTG and well-being after trauma and adversity. These include mindfulness-based programs, other trauma-focused psychotherapies (outside the realm of CBT as just described), and nonclinical interventions.

Mindfulness-based interventions. Mindfulness, sometimes defined as the intentional focus on present-moment experience in a nonjudgmental, open, and curious manner (Bishop et al., 2004), has played an increasingly large role in modern psychological research and practice. Mindfulness-based approaches have the potential to facilitate meaning-making, which is relevant to the PTG process (Garland, Farb, Goldin, & Fredrickson, 2015).

A recent meta-analysis of 11 studies examined the impact of short-term mindfulness training on self-reported PTG (Shiyko, Hallinan, & Naito, 2017). All participants included in studies had experienced a medical trauma, with 98.6% of these being cancer-related. Regardless of study design or intervention type, mindfulness-based interventions tended to produce a small, positive effect on PTG scores. Individual studies also provide more information about the potential usefulness of mindfulness for growth. Garland, Carlson, Cook, Landsdell, and Speca (2007) compared the effects of a Mindfulness-Based Stress Reduction (MBSR) program to a healing arts program on PTG, spirituality, stress, and mood, in cancer patients. Both programs led to a significant improvement in PTG, with the MBSR group additionally endorsing more improvement on measures of spirituality, anxiety, anger, stress, and mood. Similarly, Zhang et al. (2017) examined the efficacy of MBSR in a randomized control trial involving breast cancer patients in China. Participants in an 8-week MBSR group showed significantly higher levels of PTG after the intervention and at a 3-month follow-up than did participants in a "usual care" group (Zhang et al., 2017). Of note, although mindfulness practices may be helpful in fostering PTG after trauma, these approaches may be also particularly difficult for some to use after trauma. PTSD symptoms such as intrusive trauma-related thoughts or avoidance might negatively affect an individual's ability to practice or benefit from mindfulness (Vujanovic, Niles, Pietrefesa, Schmertz, & Potter, 2013).

Other trauma-focused psychotherapies. Other types of trauma-focused psychotherapies (not part of traditional CBT approaches described earlier) may also foster self-reported PTG. For example, Nijdam et al. (2018) conducted an RCT comparing Brief Eclectic Psychotherapy (BEPP) for PTSD (Gersons, Meewisse, & Nijdam, 2015) and Eye Movement Desensitization and Reprocessing (EMDR) therapy (Shapiro, 2017) for participants with PTSD. Participants in both groups showed significant increases in PTG scores, which also related to declines in PTSD symptoms. Similarly, Jeon et al. (2017) found that an 8-week course of EMDR led to significant increases in PTG in a small sample of 10 survivors of a maritime disaster in South Korea.

Other psychosocial programs. Clinical interventions are not the only means to potentially foster PTG. Other psychosocial supports and programs outside the therapy office may also produce similar results. We provide here two examples. First, the Health Partner Program, an 8-week intervention developed to train long-term cancer survivors to be health coaches by developing skills in health management, leadership, and coaching, led to significant increases in PTG scores compared to a control group (Yun et al., 2013). Second, Crawford, Vallance, Holt, Steed, and Courneya (2016) found that an 8-week wall-climbing intervention increased perceptions of new possibilities and personal strength (as measured by the PTGI) in a sample of gynecologic cancer survivors compared to a usual care group. These studies suggest that supportive programming outside the realm of psychotherapy may also influence self-reported PTG.

Newer Interventions Specifically Targeting PTG and Related Constructs

Researchers have recently begun developing and testing interventions that more specifically target PTG (or related variables such as meaning and resilience), in addition to or instead of targeting distress. We note here that this distinction—does an intervention aim to increase growth or decrease distress?—is a difficult one to make as many interventions are developed with multiple aims in mind. Indeed, it is helpful for interventions to include strategies for supporting participants in several ways and domains, and many do so. As such, our primary purpose in categorizing interventions is to facilitate their review. Although the interventions reviewed here share many features, we also group them by targeted populations to organize our summary of the evidence.

Interventions with Individuals Affected by Cancer

The largest literature concerning novel and targeted interventions for PTG has been conducted with cancer patients. Ramos et al. (2018) conducted an RCT with breast cancer patients to test the effectiveness of a group intervention designed to facilitate PTG specifically using principles proposed by Tedeschi and McNally (2011) including psychoeducation about the trauma response, emotion regulation training, self-disclosure, creation of a new narrative to include themes of growth, and a focus on developing new life principles. Compared to patients who received only standard medical care for cancer, patients who took part in this intervention reported higher gains in self-reported PTG, as well as improvements in intrusive rumination and challenges to core beliefs (Ramos et al., 2018).

Meaning-Centered Group Psychotherapy for Cancer Survivors (MCGP-CS) is another program that directly targets meaning-making. In this intervention, individuals with cancer are supported in exploring sources of meaning, examining how this has changed due to cancer, and exploring how to find meaning in one's life story (van der Spek et al., 2017). In a trial comparing MCGP-CS, supportive group psychotherapy (SGP), and care as usual, cancer survivors were randomly assigned to one of the three groups and completed the primary outcome measure, the Personal Meaning Profile (PMP), with secondary measures including the PTGI. Survivors who were a part of the MCGP-CS group showed significantly higher scores on personal meaning, goal orientation, positive relationships, purpose in life, and fighting spirit when compared to those in the CAU group. When compared to the SGP group, survivors in the MCGP-CS group reported higher scores on personal growth. These results were maintained at a 3-month follow-up (van der Spek et al., 2017).

Üzar-Özcetin and Hiçdurmaz (2019) also found promising results for a novel empowerment program designed to foster resilience and PTG in cancer survivors. Participants were randomly assigned to the empowerment program or a routine care control group; those who took part in the empowerment program showed significant increases in PTG and resilience compared to the control group, effects which lasted through the 1-month follow-up.

Managing Cancer and Living Meaningfully (CALM) is a brief manualized intervention developed for individuals with cancer, intended to treat and prevent depression and end-of-life distress in the context of advanced cancer (Rodin et al., 2018). In an RCT, CALM appeared effective for those goals because it produced improvements in depressive symptoms compared to a waiting list; however, it did not appear to impact PTG.

Finally, Positive Psychotherapy for Cancer (PPC) is a program designed for cancer survivors, and it aims to facilitate PTG as a means of reducing symptoms of emotional distress and post-traumatic stress (Ochoa, Casellas-Grau, Vives, Font, & Borràs, 2017). In a trial comparing PPC to a waiting list control, PPC resulted in increased PTG, reduced stress, and decreased post-traumatic symptoms, effects maintained at a 3- and 12-month follow-up. This trial is also notable for its thoughtful measurement strategy, which included a comparison of participants' own reports of PTG and their significant others' descriptions of that person's PTG; these two reports were correlated, suggesting that participants' gains in PTG went beyond a self-perception of having grown (Ochoa et al., 2017).

Interventions with Healthcare Professionals

A few studies have examined the usefulness of novel interventions targeting PTG with healthcare professionals who routinely encounter trauma during professional activities. One such intervention was conducted with healthcare workers in China (Xu et al., 2016). This intervention, which integrated positive psychology principles and elements from traditional Chinese culture, led to significantly higher PTG scores for participants who had taken part in an open trial (without a control group).

Second, Cieslack et al. (2016) designed an Internet-based self-efficacy intervention to support the mental health of professionals who are indirectly exposed to trauma through their clients. The intervention therefore aimed to influence both secondary traumatic stress (STS) and secondary PTG (SPTG). Those who were assigned to the four-session online intervention reported lower STS and higher self-efficacy compared to the education control group (who received information on stress and coping); however, individuals in the *control* group, not the intervention group, reported higher secondary PTG at the 1-month follow-up. These mixed findings highlight that more research is needed to understand the nature and timeline of the benefits of PTG interventions.

Interventions with Other Populations

Transforming Lives Through Resilience Education (TLTRE; Dolbier et al., 2010) is another newer program that directly targets resilience; this psychoeducation intervention includes cognitive restructuring, themes of personal responsibility, social support, and other strategies to enhance protective factors and coping abilities. In a randomized trial conducted with college students interested in learning to manage stress, TLTRE produced greater impact on PTG scores compared to a wait-list control group (Dolbier et al., 2010).

SecondStory is another newer group-format psychosocial intervention aimed at facilitating PTG by helping participants make meaning of the past and plan a purposeful future (Roepke, Tsukayama, Forgeard, Blackie, & Jayawickreme, 2018). In an RCT with bereaved adults, SecondStory was compared to an active control using expressive writing. The primary outcome, PTG, was measured using two contrasting methods (both involving self-reports): the PTGI, which asks participants retrospectively how much they believe they have changed due to struggling with adversity, and the Current-Standing Post-traumatic Growth Inventory (C-PTGI; Frazier et al., 2009), which tracks quantifiable change in participants' standing in PTG domains over time. SecondStory participants did not show significantly greater improvements than control participants on measures of PTG (with both groups showing increased PTGI scores), but they did show greater decreases in depression symptoms by the first follow-up (Roepke, Tsukayama et al., 2018).

Finally, Roepke, Benson, Tsukayama, and Yaden (2018) designed and tested a prospective writing intervention which aimed to facilitate PTG by inviting the individual to explore new possibilities following adversity. Participants were randomly assigned to one of three conditions: prospective writing, factual writing about daily life, or no writing. These writing exercises occurred weekly for 1 month, with PTG being measured through the original, retrospective PTGI (Tedeschi & Calhoun, 1996) and the current-standing PTGI measure (C-PTGI; Frazier et al., 2009). Participants in the prospective writing condition reported greater gains in PTG compared to the control group when the current-standing measure was used but not when the retrospective measure was used. In other words, intervention participants seemed to be functioning better in PTG domains but not necessarily *viewing* themselves as having grown from adversity.

WHAT HAVE WE LEARNED ABOUT FACILITATING PTG?

Taken as a whole, the PTG intervention literature suggests that a wide range of psychosocial interventions may influence individuals' beliefs or perceptions that they have grown from struggling with adversity. That is, various interventions tested in RCT designs have been found to raise scores on the PTGI or similar retrospective self-report measures. Several important questions remain unanswered, however. One set of questions arises from the difference between self-perceived PTG versus other indicators of PTG: Do our interventions only influence self-perceptions? Or do they also help people to grow and change in ways that might be reflected in behavior and observable to those around them? Do they impact personality traits and the expression of those traits in daily life (e.g., becoming more agreeable or more open to experience)? Do they change individuals' level of functioning in well-being domains and PTG-relevant domains (e.g., meaning in life, gratitude, or intimacy)?

The current PTG intervention literature provides no definitive answer because studies have overwhelmingly relied on self-reported PTG rather than the other indicators listed earlier. However, several studies indeed measured multiple indicators of PTG. For instance, Ochoa et al. (2017) reported congruence between self-perceptions and loved ones' perceptions of PTG. Roepke, Benson, et al. (2018) found that a future-oriented writing intervention did *not* impact PTGI scores but did impact C-PTGI scores; that is, individuals indeed improved in PTG-related domains, but did not report feeling a stronger sense of having grown from adversity. More research is needed to detect patterns (i.e., which intervention strategies specifically impact self-perceptions and narrative identity, and which intervention strategies specifically impact observable changes in personality, behavior, and well-being). It may be, for instance, that intervention strategies that involve reflecting on and reinterpreting the past lead to greater self-perceived PTG, whereas intervention strategies that focus on the future and help people to set specific implementation intentions to achieve their goals lead to greater behavioral or observable change (Hudson & Fraley, 2015). Relatedly, it is important to investigate whether interventions that effectively foster either self-perceptions of growth or observable changes actually prepare participants to then experience the other type of change (or not). For example, an intervention that increases individuals' self-perceptions of growth in the short to medium term may be crucial in predisposing them to then take action and implement relevant concrete changes in their lives in the long run (or vice versa). Examining this hypothesis would require that intervention studies assess multiple types of outcomes over a longer period of time to better tease out the timeline of various changes experienced by participants. Such knowledge would also help refine the optimal way to deliver PTG interventions to maximize benefits. It is, of course, also possible that both types of changes are unrelated at distinct time points and also over time.

Another set of questions is concerned with *how* and *why* interventions may produce increases in PTG. Do interventions primarily work through common factors shared by many therapeutic approaches (e.g., developing discrepancy between one's current state and desired state, activating one's strengths, increasing insight, and practicing behavior change) (Allemand & Flückiger, 2017)? Which interventions have specific efficacy for increasing PTG (i.e., which are more effective than other interventions, rather than only being more effective than being placed on a waiting list or receiving usual medical care)? It may be that common factors are responsible for various positive outcomes of psychosocial interventions, whether that is decreased distress, increased PTG, or intentional personality change (Allemand & Flückiger, 2017).

Next, we outline some methodological considerations for future PTG intervention research, which may help to answer these questions and deepen our understanding about how interventions may impact different indicators of growth.

METHODOLOGICAL CONSIDERATIONS FOR POST-TRAUMATIC GROWTH INTERVENTION TRIALS

Nuanced Measurement of Post-Traumatic Growth

The vast majority of studies reviewed so far in this chapter have measured PTG with a retrospective self-report instrument like the PTGI. Given that one of the primary goals of clinical psychologists is to understand and address people's beliefs about themselves and the world, the use of such measures is informative because they reflect how people understand their own experience and the effect of past adverse events on their lives. From a research perspective, however, and from the broader perspective of the scientific understanding of personality development, such measures have critical limitations that can only be addressed by using other complementary measures of growth. For instance, trials can include both the PTGI and the C-PTGI (which assesses someone's current level of functioning in PTG domains at a given point in time). As noted earlier, trials that have done so showed that these two manifestations of PTG may follow different patterns (Roepke, Benson et al., 2018; Roepke, Tsukayama et al., 2018). Whenever feasible, trials would also ideally include reports from participants' loved ones to determine whether self-perceived growth is corroborated by others (e.g., Ochoa et al., 2017). It would also be fruitful to measure aspects of PTG beyond the PTGI and its five domains, such as assessing changes in the big five personality traits, and changes in life story or narrative identity, character virtues, and/or daily behaviors (which can be measured through experience sampling methodology). Longer measurement timeframes are also ideal for determining whether gains are maintained and what types of gains occur within which timeframes.

Examining Growth, Distress, and Their Relationship

It is crucial to understand whether intervention strategies that alleviate suffering also promote growth, and vice versa. We need to better understand whether there are tradeoffs versus synergies in trying to address these dual aims. Additionally, we need a better understanding of how these dual aims might unfold over time and how these changes influence each other: Does lowered distress lead to increased growth? Does growth lead to later reductions in distress? Longitudinal research has suggested that higher PTG may be followed by lower distress, particularly in a higher impact context (e.g., more serious surgical intervention) but more work is needed to answer this crucial question (Wang et al., 2017). Likewise, cross-lagged designs have indicated that finding positive meaning (i.e., PTG) after cancer may lead to increases in positive coping strategies, but more work is needed to understand the ways that seeing oneself as having grown from adversity might impact coping strategies (Hamama-Raz, Pat-Horenczyk, Roziner, Perry, & Stemmer, 2019).

Minding Multiple Comparisons

In our enthusiasm for assessing all the outcomes that matter—diverse manifestations of growth as well as relevant forms of distress/difficulty—we must also be mindful of the risks of measuring so many constructs. This is even more true when investigators also analyze multiple subscales of each measure (e.g., five tests for the five domains of the PTGI). When a trial has many outcomes and this is not accounted for in statistical analyses and transparent reporting, the risk of Type I error (false positives) is inflated. This can be mitigated by transparent reporting of planned versus exploratory comparisons, preregistration of hypotheses, statistical corrections for multiple comparisons, and reporting of effect sizes in addition to tests of statistical significance.

Careful Selection of Control Groups

The reader may have noted in our literature review that many of the newer PTG-oriented interventions have been tested in comparison to waiting lists or standard care for a medical condition. These are not particularly rigorous control conditions, though they may be quite appropriate and useful in the initial tests of a new program. As research progresses, however, it will be important to compare PTG-oriented interventions to more active control groups. This will help to address whether these interventions have active ingredients that are specifically efficacious for fostering PTG or if more general factors such as social support and positive expectancies may account for benefits. In some cases where PTG interventions have been compared to active controls (i.e., other interventions), null findings have been reported: for instance, the RCT testing SecondStory compared it to expressive writing (known to foster PTG) and found that SecondStory did not yield greater effects on PTG, even though it did so with regard to depressive symptoms (Roepke, Tsukayama, et al., 2018). In cases where ethical considerations prevent researchers from using a no-treatment control, one useful strategy might be to use a control that is expected to yield benefits (such as reductions in stress) but not expected to yield increases in PTG—for instance, a relaxation training control group.

Mediation and Moderation

As PTG intervention research progresses, it will be especially useful to examine *how* and for *whom* these interventions foster PTG. The "how" can be addressed through tests of *mediation* (exploring which active ingredients seem to precede and account for beneficial outcomes) as well as through dismantling studies (testing the relative contributions of different modules/parts of an intervention program). The "for whom" can be addressed through tests of *moderation*, examining whether certain subgroups of people benefit more or less and whether certain types of adversity or trauma are more or less appropriate for these interventions. It may be quite necessary to tailor or change intervention content for different cultural contexts as well as for different types of events (e.g., bereavement vs. trauma involving victimization vs. stressful life transitions vs. moral injury).

Quality Standards for Conduct and Reporting of RCTs

To ensure high-quality intervention research that can answer the important questions at hand, PTG research efforts should strive to adhere to standards for the conduct and reporting of RCTs. Evidence suggests that this reporting has been suboptimal in medical and psychological research as a whole, which has led to the development of guides such as the CONSORT statement and accompanying checklist (Moher, Schulz, Altman, & Consort Group, 2001).

CONCLUSION

At this stage, the study of interventions' impact on PTG provides as many questions as answers. Research on this important topic should proceed, but cautiously, with thoughtful consideration of the relevant scientific and ethical issues, as well as the potential for adverse effects. Likewise, clinicians may find the concept of PTG to be highly relevant in their clinical work as they support individuals in coping with adversity and trauma, and it may be appropriate to discuss these topics by proceeding in a careful manner: discussions of PTG are perhaps more likely to be beneficial when the clinician follows the client's lead in elaborating on themes that arise organically. A more directive style—instructing clients to look for silver linings—might be more likely to backfire, leading to feelings of pressure, invalidation, guilt, or failure. It is important to avoid inadvertently romanticizing adversity or suggesting that it is the only means for personal growth. When working with individuals dealing with post-traumatic stress symptoms, clinicians should of course continue using interventions that have demonstrated empirical support for alleviating trauma and suffering rather than replace these with interventions that aim to target growth but lack solid evidence. Themes of growth can be integrated organically into existing trauma-focused treatments. For example, when a clinician and client discuss and process imaginal exposures (i.e., recounted trauma memories) in prolonged exposure (Foa, Hembree, & Rothbaum, 2007), the client may bring up lessons learned, new perspectives, and changed priorities, which the clinician may help them to elaborate and explore.

Psychological science has made significant contributions to our understanding of how to prevent and alleviate suffering in individuals who have experienced trauma, loss, and significant adversity. More recent undertakings have sought to complement our knowledge of alleviating suffering with knowledge of fostering growth. Though emerging research suggests that interventions may be able to foster growth following adversity, future scholarship is needed to provide further support for such interventions. Importantly, future studies need to clarify the degree to which interventions affect people's perceptions of growth versus observable changes in their personality and behavior (and the time frames within which such changes take place). In addition, research needs to shed light on the circumstances under which these PTG-oriented interventions may or may not be helpful. As this chapter suggests, researchers must attend to significant ethical and scientific complexities to meaningfully contribute to this area of applied research and advance our understanding of how to help individuals feel good and live well in the face of life's inevitable hardships.

NOTE

1.. Of note, however, a given intervention may have qualities of multiple categories, and/or it may have multiple aims (e.g., targeting distress as well as targeting PTG). We therefore encourage the reader to take an expansive view of these categories, and we also alert the reader to the existence of several interventions that have been evaluated for their effects on PTG but fall outside of the categories included in the present review: for instance, an integrative retreat for veterans and their partners, which appeared to potentially foster PTG among partners but not among veterans (Monk et al., 2017); CanChange, a health behavior change intervention for cancer survivors that was found to facilitate PTG compared to usual care (Hawkes et al., 2014); and a coping skills intervention for Chinese men who have sex with men and are HIV positive (Ye et al., 2018).

REFERENCES

Allemand, M., & Flückiger, C. (2017). Changing personality traits: Some considerations from psychotherapy process-outcome research for intervention efforts on intentional personality change. *Journal of Psychotherapy Integration, 27*(4), 476–488.

Antoni, M. H., Lechner, S. C., Kazi, A., Wimberly, S. R., Sifre, T., Urcuyo, K. R., . . . Carver, C. S. (2006). How stress management improves quality of life after treatment for breast cancer. *Journal of Consulting and Clinical Psychology, 74*, 1143–1152.

Baldwin, S. A., Wampold, B. E., & Imel, Z. E. (2007). Untangling the alliance-outcome correlation: Exploring the relative importance of therapist and patient variability in the alliance. *Journal of Consulting and Clinical Psychology*, 75(6), 842–854.

Bartl, H., Hagl, M., Kotoučová, M., Pfoh, G., & Rosner, R. (2018). Does prolonged grief treatment foster posttraumatic growth? Secondary results from a treatment study with long-term follow-up and mediation analysis. *Psychology and Psychotherapy: Theory, Research and Practice, 91*(1), 27–41.

Bishop, S. R., Lau, M., Shapiro, S., Carlson, L., Anderson, N. D., Carmody, J., . . . Devins, G. (2004). Mindfulness: A proposed definition. *Clinical Psychology Science and Practice, 11*(3), 230–241.

Blackie, L. E., Jayawickreme, E., Helzer, E. G., Forgeard, M. J., & Roepke, A. M. (2015). Investigating the veracity of self-perceived posttraumatic growth: A profile analysis approach to corroboration. *Social Psychological and Personality Science, 6*(7), 788–796.

Boals, A., & Schuler, K. L. (2018). Reducing reports of illusory posttraumatic growth: A revised version of the Stress-Related Growth Scale (SRGS-R). *Psychological Trauma: Theory, Research, Practice, and Policy, 10*(2), 190–198.

Calhoun, L. G., & Tedeschi, R. G. (1999). *Facilitating posttraumatic growth: A clinician's guide*. Mahwah, NJ: Lawrence Erlbaum Associates.

Calhoun, L. G., & Tedeschi, R. G. (2001). Posttraumatic growth: The positive lessons of loss. In R. A. Neimeyer (Ed.), *Meaning Re-Construction and the Experience of Loss* (pp. 157–172). Washington, DC: American Psychological Association.

Cieslak, R., Benight, C. C., Rogala, A., Smoktunowicz, E., Kowalska, M., Zukowska, K., . . . Luszczynska, A. (2016). Effects of internet-based self-efficacy intervention on secondary traumatic stress and secondary posttraumatic growth among health and human services professionals exposed to indirect trauma. *Frontiers in Psychology, 7*, 1–13.

Crawford, J. J., Vallance, J. K., Holt, N. L., Steed, H., & Courneya, K. S. (2016). A phase I/II pilot study assessing the preliminary efficacy of wall climbing for improving posttraumatic growth and quality of life in gynecologic cancer survivors. *Mental Health and Physical Activity, 11*, 60–66.

Dolbier, C. L., Jaggars, S. S., & Steinhardt, M. A. (2010). Stress-related growth: Preintervention correlates and change following a resilience intervention. *Stress and*

Health: Journal of the International Society for the Investigation of Stress, 26(2), 135–147.

Foa, E., Hembree, E., & Rothbaum, B. O. (2007). *Prolonged Exposure Therapy for PTSD: Emotional Processing of Traumatic Experiences Therapist Guide*. New York: Oxford University Press.

Frazier, P., Tennen, H., Gavian, M., Park, C., Tomich, P., & Tashiro, T. (2009). Does self-reported posttraumatic growth reflect genuine positive change? *Psychological Science, 20*, 912–919.

Gallagher, M. W., Long, L. J., Tsai, W., Stanton, A. L., & Lu, Q. (2018). The unexpected impact of expressive writing on posttraumatic stress and growth in Chinese American breast cancer survivors. *Journal of Clinical Psychology, 74*(10), 1673–1686.

Garland, E. L., Farb, N. A., Goldin, P., & Fredrickson, B. L. (2015). Mindfulness broadens awareness and builds eudaimonic meaning: A process model of mindful positive emotion regulation. *Psychological Inquiry, 26*(4), 293–314.

Garland, S. N., Carlson, L. E., Cook, S., Lansdell, L., & Speca, M. (2007). A non-randomized comparison of mindfulness-based stress reduction and healing arts programs for facilitating post-traumatic growth and spirituality in cancer outpatients. *Support Care Cancer, 15*, 949–961.

Gersons, P. R. B., Meewisse, M., & Nijdam, M. J. (2015). Brief Eclectic Psychotherapy for PTSD. In U. Schnyder & M. Cloitre (Eds.), *Evidence-based treatments for trauma-related psychological disorders*. Switzerland: Springer International Publishing.

Gray, M. J., Schorr, Y., Nash, W., Lebowitz, L., Amidon, A., Lansing, A., . . . Litz, B. T. (2012). Adaptive disclosure: An open trial of a novel exposure-based intervention for service members with combat-related psychological stress injuries. *Behavior Therapy, 43*, 407–415.

Groleau, J. M. (2015). The effects of an expressive writing intervention on facilitating posttraumatic growth. Doctoral dissertation, University of North Carolina at Charlotte.

Hamama-Raz, Y., Pat-Horenczyk, R., Roziner, I., Perry, S., & Stemmer, S. M. (2019). Can posttraumatic growth after breast cancer promote positive coping? A cross-lagged study. *Psycho-oncology, 28*(4), 767–774.

Harbin, A. (2015). Prescribing posttraumatic growth. *Bioethics, 29*(9), 671–679.

Hawkes, A. L., Pakenham, K. I., Chambers, S. K., Patrao, T. A., & Courneya, K. S. (2014). Effects of a multiple health behavior change intervention for colorectal cancer survivors on psychosocial outcomes and quality of life: A randomized controlled trial. *Annals of Behavioral Medicine, 48*(3), 359–370.

Heinrichs, N., Zimmermann, T., Huber, B., Herschbach, P., Russell, D. W., & Baucom, D. H. (2012). Cancer distress reduction with a couple-based skills training: A randomized controlled trial. *Annals of Behavioral Medicine, 43*, 239–252.

Hijazi, A. M., Lumley, M. A., Ziadni, M. S., Haddad, L., Rapport, L. J., & Arnetz, B. B. (2014). Brief narrative exposure therapy for posttraumatic stress in Iraqi refugees: A preliminary randomized clinical trial. *Journal of Traumatic Stress, 27*(3), 314–322.

Hudson, N. W., & Fraley, R. C. (2015). Volitional personality trait change: Can people choose to change their personality traits? *Journal of Personality and Social Psychology, 109*, 490.

Janoff-Bulman, R. (1989). Assumptive worlds and the stress of traumatic events: Applications of the schema construct. *Social Cognition, 7*, 113–136.

Jayawickreme, E., & Blackie, L. R. (2014). Post-traumatic growth as positive personality change: Evidence, controversies and future directions. *European Journal of Personality, 28*, 312–331.

Jeon, S. W., Han, C., Choi, J., Ko, Y. H., Yoon, H. K., & Kim, Y. K. (2017). Eye movement desensitization and reprocessing to facilitate posttraumatic growth: A prospective clinical pilot study on ferry disaster survivors. *Clinical Psychopharmacology and Neuroscience, 15*(4), 320.

Kashdan, T. B., & Kane, J. Q. (2011). Post-traumatic distress and the presence of post-traumatic growth and meaning in life: Experiential avoidance as a moderator. *Personality and Individual Differences, 50*(1), 84–89.

Knaevelsrud, C., Liedl, A., & Maercker, A. (2010). Posttraumatic growth, optimism and openness as outcomes of a cognitive-behavioural intervention for posttraumatic stress reactions. *Journal of Health Psychology, 15*, 1030–1038.

Lane, W. D., Myers, K. J., Hill, M. C., & Lane, D. E. (2016). Utilizing narrative methodology in trauma treatment with Haitian earthquake survivors. *Journal of Loss and Trauma, 21*(6), 560–574.

Leedham, B., Meyerowitz, B. E., Muirhead, J., & Frist, W. H. (1995). Positive expectations predict health after heart transplantation. *Health Psychology, 14*, 74–79.

Lepore, S. J., & Helgeson, V. S. (1998). Social constraints, intrusive thoughts, and mental health after prostate cancer. *Journal of Social and Clinical Psychology, 17*, 89–106.

Lepore, S. J., Silver, R. C., Wortman, C. B., & Waymant, H. A. (1996). Social constraints, intrusive thoughts, and depressive symptoms among bereaved mothers. *Journal of Personality and Social Psychology, 70*, 271–282.

Lutgendorf, S. K., & Ullrich, P. (2002). Cognitive processing, disclosure, and health: Psychological and physiological mechanisms. In S. J. Lepore & J. M. Smyth (Eds.), *The writing cure: How expressive writing promotes health and emotional well-being* (pp. 177–196). American Psychological Association. https://doi.org/10.1037/10451-009

McAdams, D. P., & McLean, K. C. (2013). Narrative identity. *Current Directions in Psychological Science,* 22(3), 233–238.

Moher, D., Schulz, K. F., Altman, D., & Consort Group. (2001). The CONSORT statement: Revised recommendations for improving the quality of reports of parallel-group randomized trials. *JAMA, 285*(15), 1987–1991.

Monk, J. K., Oseland, L. M., Nelson Goff, B. S., Ogolsky, B. G., & Summers, K. (2017). Integrative intensive retreats for veteran couples and families: A pilot study assessing change in relationship adjustment, posttraumatic growth, and trauma symptoms. *Journal of Marital and Family Therapy, 43*(3), 448–462.

Nijdam, M. J., van der Meer, C. A., van Zuiden, M., Dashtgard, P., Medema, D., Qing, Y., . . . Olff, M. (2018). Turning wounds into wisdom: Posttraumatic growth over the course of two types of trauma-focused psychotherapy in patients with PTSD. *Journal of Affective Disorders, 227*, 424–431.

Nolen-Hoeksema, S., & Larson, J. (1999). *Coping with Loss*. Mahwah, NJ: Erlbaum.

Ochoa, C., Casellas-Grau, A., Vives, J., Font, A., & Borràs, J. M. (2017). Positive psychotherapy for distressed cancer survivors: Posttraumatic growth facilitation reduces posttraumatic stress. *International Journal of Clinical and Health Psychology, 17*(1), 28–37.

Pals, J. L., & McAdams, D. P. (2004). The transformed self: A narrative understanding of posttraumatic growth. *Psychological Inquiry, 15*, 65–69.

Pennebaker, J. W. (2004). Theories, therapies, and taxpayers: On the complexities of the expressive writing paradigm. *Clinical Psychology: Science and Practice, 11*, 138–142.

Powers, M. B., Halpern, J. M., Ferenschak, M. P., Gillihan, S. J., & Foa, E. B. (2010). A meta-analytic review of prolonged exposure for posttraumatic stress disorder. *Clinical Psychology Review, 30*(6), 635–641.

Resick, P. A., & Schnicke, M. K. (1992). Cognitive processing therapy for sexual assault victims. *Journal of Consulting and Clinical Psychology, 60*(5), 748–759.

Robins, R. W., Noftle, E. E., Trzesniewski, K. H., & Roberts, B. W. (2005). Do people know how their personality has changed? Correlates of perceived and actual personality change in young adulthood. *Journal of Personality, 73*, 489–521.

Rodin, G., Lo, C., Rydall, A., Shnall, J., Malfitano, C., Chiu, A., . . . Li, M. (2018). Managing Cancer and Living Meaningfully (CALM): A randomized controlled trial of a psychological intervention for patients with advanced cancer. *Journal of Clinical Oncology, 36*(23), 2422.

Roepke, A. M. (2015). Psychosocial interventions and posttraumatic growth: A meta-analysis. *Journal of Consulting and Clinical Psychology, 83*(1), 129–142.

Roepke, A. M., Benson, L., Tsukayama, E., & Yaden, D. B. (2018). Prospective writing: Randomized controlled trial of an intervention for facilitating growth after adversity. *The Journal of Positive Psychology, 13*(6), 627–642.

Roepke, A. M., Tsukayama, E., Forgeard, M., Blackie, L., & Jayawickreme, E. (2018). Randomized controlled trial of SecondStory, an intervention targeting posttraumatic growth, with bereaved adults. *Journal of Consulting and Clinical Psychology, 86*(6), 518.

Schauer, M., Neuner, F., & Elbert, T. (2011). *Narrative Exposure Therapy: A Short-Term Treatment for Traumatic Stress Disorders*. Boston: Hogrefe Publishing.

Shakespeare-Finch, J., & Enders, T. (2008). Corroborating evidence of posttraumatic growth. *Journal of Traumatic Stress, 21*(4), 421–424.

Shapiro, F. (2017). *Eye movement Desensitization and Reprocessing (EMDR) Therapy: Basic Principles, Protocols, and Procedures*. New York: Guilford.

Sherman, J. J. (1998). Effects of psychotherapeutic treatments for PTSD: A meta-analysis of controlled clinical trials. *Journal of Traumatic Stress, 11*, 413–435.

Shiyko, M. P., Hallinan, S., & Naito, T. (2017). Effects of mindfulness training on posttraumatic growth: A systematic review and meta-analysis. *Mindfulness, 8*(4), 848–858.

Smyth, J. M., Hockemeyer, J. R., & Tulloch, H. (2008). Expressive writing and post-traumatic stress disorder: Effects on trauma symptoms, mood states, and cortisol reactivity. *British Journal of Health Psychology, 13*(1), 85–93.

Tedeschi, R. G., & Calhoun, L. G. (1996). The posttraumatic growth inventory: Measuring the positive legacy of trauma. *Journal of Traumatic Stress, 9*, 455–471.

Tedeschi, R. G., & Calhoun, L. G. (2004). Posttraumatic growth: Conceptual foundations and empirical evidence. *Psychological Inquiry, 15*(1), 1–18.

Tedeschi, R. G., Calhoun, L. G., & Groleau, J. M. (2015). Clinical applications of posttraumatic growth. In S. Joseph (Ed.), *Positive psychology in practice: Promoting human flourishing in work, health, education and everyday life* (pp. 503–518). Hoboken, NJ: Wiley.

Tedeschi, R. G., & McNally, R. J. (2011). Can we facilitate posttraumatic growth in combat veterans?. *American Psychologist, 66*(1), 19.

Üzar-Özçetin, Y. S., & Hiçdurmaz, D. (2019). Effects of an empowerment program on resilience and posttraumatic growth levels of cancer survivors: A randomized controlled feasibility trial. *Cancer Nursing, 42*(6), E1-E13.

van der Spek, N., Vos, J., van Uden-Kraan, C. F., Breitbart, W., Cuijpers, P., Holtmaat, K., . . . Verdonck-de Leeuw, I. M. (2017). Efficacy of meaning-centered group psychotherapy for cancer survivors: A randomized controlled trial. *Psychological Medicine, 47*(11), 1990–2001.

Vernberg, E. M., Steinberg, A. M., Jacobs, A. K., Brymer, M. J., Watson, P. J., Osofsky, J. D., . . . Ruzek, J. I. (2008). Innovations in disaster mental health: Psychological first aid. *Professional Psychology: Research and Practice, 39*(4), 381–391.

Vujanovic, A. A., Niles, B., Pietrefesa, A., Schmertz, S. K., & Potter, C. M. (2013). Mindfulness in the treatment of posttraumatic stress disorder among military veterans. *Spirituality in Clinical Practice, 1*(S), 15–25.

Wagner, A. C., Torbit, L., Jenzer, T., Landy, M. S., Pukay-Martin, N. D., Macdonald, A., . . . Monson, C. M. (2016). The role of posttraumatic growth in a randomized controlled trial of cognitive–behavioral conjoint therapy for PTSD. *Journal of Traumatic Stress, 29*(4), 379–383.

Wampold, B. E. (2007). Psychotherapy: The humanistic (and effective) treatment. *American Psychologist, 62*(8), 857–870.

Wang, A. W. T., Chang, C. S., Chen, S. T., Chen, D. R., Fan, F., Carver, C. S., & Hsu, W. Y. (2017). Buffering and direct effect of posttraumatic growth in predicting distress following cancer. *Health Psychology, 36*(6), 549–558.

Xu, X., Hu, M. L., Song, Y., Lu, Z. X., Chen, Y. Q., Wu, D. X., & Xiao, T. (2016). Effect of positive psychological intervention on posttraumatic growth among primary healthcare workers in China: A preliminary prospective study. *Scientific Reports, 6*(1), 1–7.

Ye, Z., Yu, N. X., Zhu, W., Chen, L., & Lin, D. (2018). A randomized controlled trial to enhance coping and posttraumatic growth and decrease posttraumatic stress disorder in HIV-Infected men who have sex with men in Beijing, China. *AIDS Care, 30*(6), 793–801.

Yun, Y. H., Lee, M. K., Bae, Y., Shon, E. J., Shin, B. R., Ko, H., . . . Kim, S. Y. (2013). Efficacy of a training program for long-term disease-free cancer survivors as health partners: A randomized controlled trial in Korea. *Asian Pacific Journal of Cancer Prevention, 14*(12), 7229–7235.

Zang, Y., Hunt, N., & Cox, T. (2013). A randomised controlled pilot study: The effectiveness of narrative exposure therapy with adult survivors of the Sichuan earthquake. *BMC Psychiatry, 13*, 41.

Zang, Y., Hunt, N., & Cox, T. (2014). Adapting narrative exposure therapy for Chinese earthquake survivors: A pilot randomised controlled feasibility study. *BMC Psychiatry, 14*(1), 262.

Zhang, J. Y., Zhou, Y. Q., Feng, Z. W., Fan, Y. N., Zeng, G. C., & Wei, L. (2017). Randomized controlled trial of mindfulness-based stress reduction (MBSR) on posttraumatic growth of Chinese breast cancer survivors. *Psychology, Health & Medicine, 22*(1), 94–109.

Zoellner, T., Rabe, S., Karl, A., & Maercker, A. (2011). Post-traumatic growth as outcome of a cognitive-behavioural therapy trial for motor vehicle accident survivors with PTSD. *Psychology and Psychotherapy: Theory, Research and Practice, 84*, 201–213.

4

Using Dynamic Personality Theories, Cognitive Neuroscience, and mHealth to Uncover the Process of Post-Traumatic Personality Change in Women with Breast Cancer

LARA M. BAEZ, MICHAEL H. ANTONI, AND AARON S. HELLER

POST-TRAUMATIC GROWTH, CHARACTER, AND PERSONALITY CHANGE

Overview

The role of the brain is to facilitate one's ontological capacity to learn from and adapt to life's events (Eibl-Eibesfeldt, 1979). Thus, following adverse and traumatic life events physical and psychological change inevitably occurs. Many experience debilitating psychiatric and health consequences (Maddox, Hartmann, Ross, & Ressler, 2019), yet there are also some who report positive psychological changes. After interviewing individuals who had experienced trauma, Tedeschi and Calhoun noted that many reported changes in the way they perceived themselves, the quality of their personal relationships, spiritual growth, and an enhanced appreciation for life coupled with a change in priorities (Tedeschi & Calhoun, 1996).

In other words, some trauma survivors reported that their character and personality was fundamentally altered as a result of these adverse experiences.

Tedeschi and Calhoun termed the concept of *post-traumatic growth* (PTG) as the process that can accompany perceived character change as individuals come to terms with their trauma (Tedeschi & Calhoun, 2004). Citing the experiences of individuals following bereavement, chronic disease (e.g., arthritis, HIV, cancer), acute disease (e.g., bone marrow transplantation, heart attacks), coping with medical problems of children, transportation accidents, house fires, abuse, combat, refugee experiences, and hostage experiences, Tedeschi and Calhoun (2004) argued that traumas challenge the individual's ways of understanding the world and their place in it. This process of coping with the trauma results in the individual restructuring their worldview. As such, PTG is often defined as "positive psychological change experienced as a result of the struggle with highly challenging life circumstances" (Tedeschi & Calhoun, 2004).

There is a large literature suggesting that PTG may occur. Research in this area has tended to use retrospective designs. Thus, work investigating PTG recruits survivors following trauma (often years afterward) and asks them to report on whether they have changed on the five dimensions assessed by the Post-Traumatic Growth Inventory (PTGI; Tedeschi & Calhoun, 1996): *personal strength* ("I discovered that I'm stronger than I thought I was"), *interpersonal relationships* ("I learned a great deal about how wonderful people are"), *spirituality* ("I have a stronger religious faith"), *new possibilities for one's life* ("New opportunities are available which wouldn't have been otherwise"), and *appreciation of life* ("An appreciation for the value of my own life") as a result of the trauma. Although not reviewed in this chapter, there is an ample body of evidence suggesting that individuals perceive salubrious character change following trauma (Jayawickreme & Blackie, 2014).

That such a thing as PTG occurs following adverse life events as individuals come to terms with trauma is appealing. However, there are several shortcomings with the extant literature (Jayawickreme & Blackie, 2014). The principal shortcomings of PTG research are that most of the work is (1) cross-sectional, (2) retrospective, and (3) gathered via subjective self-report. Thus, first, the vast majority of research on PTG does not have premorbid baseline measures of personality, character, well-being, or other traits. This makes evaluating the magnitude of character change or growth impossible without an assessment of functioning prior to or even during the adverse events. Second, PTG research asks survivors to retrospect to estimate the extent of change across the five PTG dimensions. The bias inherent to retrospection is well-documented (Kahneman & Riis, 2005) and may be even more germane to cumulative trait change, such as PTG. For instance, it was recently demonstrated that when individuals retrospectively report about their own mental health history, they substantially underestimate the prevalence of their own past psychiatric diagnoses (Takayanagi et al., 2014). Such a nonrandom ("rose-colored") bias in assessing one's own past functioning suggests that individuals who recover from adverse and traumatic events may overestimate their own amount of positive growth. Third, virtually all PTG research utilizes self-report. While self-report is a crucial tool in the psychological science toolbox, the degree to which PTG is associated with objective, measurable changes in behavior, affect, cognition, or character (e.g., gratitude, spirituality, prosociality, empathy) is unknown. It is equally possible that PTG simply reflects one's own self-perception and that this self-perception is uncorrelated with behavior. Assessing in vivo measures of behavior, affect, cognition, and character is critical to determine whether changes in self-reported PTG are linked to measurable changes in objective states.

Thus, in general, there is little prospective, longitudinal evidence that allow investigators to address fundamental questions such as (1) How much psychological growth occurs? It remains unclear what is a "normative" response to trauma (Almedom & Glandon, 2007; Galatzer-Levy, Huang, & Bonanno, 2018; Infurna & Luthar, 2016; Kessler et al., 2005): Is it post-traumatic stress disorder (PTSD)? A return to premorbid baseline? No response at all? Or PTG? (2) If PTG and/or personality change is to occur, what is the timeline by which this occurs? Does it tend to occur immediately following traumatic or stressful life events, or does the event need to resolve for PTG to begin? Most prospective research examining the impact of life events on personality change has not followed individuals for a sufficiently long time to address such questions (Bleidorn, Hopwood, & Lucas, 2018), and thus the timeline required to observe the emergence of PTG remains unknown. (3) Do changes in specific behaviors, affect, and cognitions parallel (or precede) trait change and PTG? Evidence from personality process research (Baumert et al., 2017; Fleeson & Jayawickreme, 2015) suggests that this would be necessary, but there is limited direct subjective or objective evidence for this hypothesis. And last, (4) Are there pre-trauma factors that predict who is most likely to experience psychological growth following major life stress? For instance, prospective PTSD research suggests that "resilience" to trauma (i.e., not developing PTSD) is predicted by specific pre-trauma cognitive styles including low levels of rumination, a sense of locus of control, and lower levels of inflammation (Bryant & Guthrie, 2005; Eraly et al., 2014; Heinrichs et al., 2005; Wild et al., 2016). Yet just as health is not simply the absence of disease (International Health Conference, 2002), one cannot assume that positive character change is simply resiliency to PTSD. The existing PTG literature does not address whether specific pre-trauma factors facilitate personality change or PTG.

Despite the shortcomings in the extant research demonstrating positive personality change following trauma, personality change is unquestionably possible. First, it is well-documented that personality changes across the life span (Damian, Spengler, Sutu, & Roberts, 2019; Donnellan, Hill, & Roberts, 2015). As one ages, the pattern of most trait change is in the direction of "maturation"; that is, a tendency toward increased conscientiousness, emotional stability, agreeableness, and the dominance aspects of extraversion (Roberts, Caspi, & Moffitt, 2001). Over a 50-year period, traits change on average half of a standard deviation, not an insubstantial amount. This indicates that personality and character change are not only possible, but occur normatively. Second, personality changes in response to targeted intervention. A recent meta-analysis indicates that over a period of months to years, individuals with psychiatric disorders who were motivated to change and who engaged in regular psychotherapy evidenced changes in emotional stability and conscientiousness (Roberts et al., 2017). Third, there is evidence for certain life events to be linked to changes in personality. Transitions into the first romantic relationship tends to increase Agreeableness and Extraversion while transitions from school to college/work increase agreeableness, conscientiousness, and openness and decrease neuroticism (Bleidorn et al., 2018). However, following single, restricted events, such as winning the lottery, the evidence for personality change is substantially more mixed, with meta-analyses indicating no significant mean level personality change following such events (Bleidorn et al., 2018). But what about events that have even more existential weight—like a life-threatening medical diagnosis?

Post-Traumatic Growth, Character Change, Breast Cancer

Breast cancer is the most common cancer among women and is the second leading cause of cancer-related deaths among women. That said, breast cancer mortality rates have decreased substantially over the past 30 years (currently around 1.3%), resulting in upward of 3.5 million survivors in the United States (DeSantis et al., 2019). Among breast cancer patients and survivors, fear of disease progression or recurrence as well as fear of early mortality is common (Simard et al., 2013). For these reasons, breast cancer diagnosis presents a particular life experience by which to examine the potential mechanisms of PTG.

There is a significant body of literature supporting the notion that PTG occurs in the wake of breast cancer diagnosis and treatment. Classic studies indicate that between 53% and 84% of women with breast cancer experience PTG (Collins, Taylor, & Skokan, 1990; Taylor, Lichtman, & Wood, 1984). PTG in this context is often operationalized as "benefit-finding" (BF, sometimes also called "meaning-making"), which is the ability to retrospectively identify positive change in oneself after a trauma (Helgeson, Reynolds, & Tomich, 2006). In essence, BF is a strategy some women use to cope with the shock of cancer diagnosis/treatment. Thus, BF is also a specific learning process—a way by which a woman can adapt to her new life circumstances.

BF has both psychological and biological correlates in women with breast cancer. Among postsurgical breast cancer patients, increases in BF can be achieved in cognitive behavioral treatment (Antoni et al., 2001), which in some cases is dependent on their baseline levels of traits such as dispositional optimism. From our perspective, this suggests that treatment may assist in the process of positive personality change by modulating the density distributions of various personality states (see the next two sections). BF is also associated with better general psychosocial adjustment, indicated by improved quality of life, more positive/less negative affect, less social disruption, and fewer cancer-related intrusive thoughts

(Lechner, Carver, Antoni, Weaver, & Phillips, 2006). Another study demonstrated that BF is associated with coping mechanisms such as positive reframing and increased religiosity, as well as the personality trait optimism (Urcuyo, Boyers, Carver, & Antoni, 2005). Moreover, BF at the time of initial breast cancer treatment is associated with lower levels of distress and depression up to 8 years later (Carver & Antoni, 2004). However, it is important to note that some studies have found negative (Tomich & Helgeson, 2004) or no (Cordova, Cunningham, Carlson, & Andrykowski, 2001; Sears, Stanton, & Danoff-Burg, 2003; Tomich & Helgeson, 2002; Widows, Jacobsen, Booth-Jones, & Fields, 2005) psychosocial implications for BF in women with breast cancer. In addition to the psychological consequences, BF may also be associated with biological processes relevant for positive physical health outcomes in breast cancer such as decreased adrenal stress hormone levels (Cruess et al., 2000) and improved immune function (McGregor et al., 2004).

These discrepant findings should be interpreted in light of the fact that the construct of BF, along with the ways it is measured, is flawed in the same ways discussed around PTG in the overview. Most studies are cross-sectional, and BF is by definition retrospective, subjective, and self-reported. Also, generally, only linear associations are examined, when some work suggests that nonlinear associations may be more likely (Lechner et al., 2006; Park, Lechner, Antoni, & Stanton, 2009). Measurement of BF is inconsistent, and the construct of BF may be even multidimensional in women with breast cancer (Weaver, Llabre, Lechner, Pendo, & Antoni, 2008).

What's more, the very concept of BF is amorphous, rendering it difficult to study in a rigorous way and determine whether it is redundant with the PTG construct. To determine whether PTG and BF are redundant, there are two important points to consider. One critical point of confusion is whether BF is an outcome or a process (Helgeson et al., 2006). The gerund in the name BF ("finding") implies that it is an ongoing process to be measured, but the extant literature has focused on BF as an outcome (cf. meta analysis by Helgeson et al., 2006). Thus, in the current literature, BF and PTG have been statistically modeled such that they are indistinguishable from one another. A second point of confusion is that BF is defined in purely subjective terms (e.g., "How much did I benefit from cancer and it's treatment?"), whereas PTG encompasses a much broader array including both subjective and objective outcomes. For example, while PTG does include subjective features like BF, it also encompasses objective behavioral measures of character change, which may include prosociality, exploration, and changes in affective functioning.

Here, we define BF as one process (indeed, a learning process) among many possible processes that result in PTG. We posit that there are specific features of a woman's experience at pre-cancer baseline, upon diagnosis, throughout treatment, and during recovery that facilitate BF along with its behavioral correlates and consequences and thus PTG. The nature and qualities of these specific features are not yet fully understood.

DYNAMIC THEORIES OF PERSONALITY

As has been widely noted, trait theories of personality, including the Big Five (John, Naumann, & Soto, 2008), while useful, highly replicated, and mostly consistent across cultures, do not provide a mechanistic explanation for how individual differences in traits manifest in affect, cognition, or behavior. Because of this basic limitation, research exploring the mechanisms of personality and personality change are mostly absent. Recent theoretical work, notably via whole-trait theory as well as other "dynamic personality theories" (DeYoung, 2015; Fleeson & Jayawickreme, 2015; Jayawickreme, Zachry, & Fleeson, 2019; Wrzus & Roberts, 2016), provide avenues for theorizing for how to bridge this gap.

The Distribution of States Represents One's Personality

Personality is typically defined as the patterns of cognition, affect, and behavior an individual normally experiences (Funder, 2001). Expanding from this definition, dynamic theories of personality, including whole-trait theory, posit that personality manifests in the distribution of moment-to-moment states. Thus, the density distribution (described by the mean, variance, skew, kurtosis, minimum, and maximum) of *states* largely accounts for one's personality *traits* (Jayawickreme et al., 2019). So, if a person tends to exist more frequently in an extraverted than introverted state, that person is, by definition, more extraverted. Work in this area finds that the mean of one's distribution of states tends to be strongly associated with their trait level on that trait (Fleeson, 2017; Fleeson & Gallagher, 2009). Other moments of one's state distribution (variance, skew, kurtosis) tend to be less strongly associated with one's trait level, although there is some suggestive evidence for skew of the state distribution to be linked to trait.

The Accumulation of States Explains One's State Distribution

But how do individuals come to differ in the distribution of their states? From the perspective of dynamic personality theories, individuals come to their own idiographic state distribution as a result of an accumulation of experiences—in other words as adaptations to their own unique lives. Adaptations (or learning) from life experiences manifest in one's goals, beliefs, values, and expectations (Jayawickreme et al., 2019) and, by extension, the density distribution of one's affective, cognitive, and behavioral states. Via this normative process of adaptation, the density distribution of one's states can gradually shift. Thus, adaptations to life experiences are the fundamental process by which any personality change (PTG included) may occur.

USING COGNITIVE AND BEHAVIORAL NEUROSCIENCE TO CONSIDER THE FACTORS THAT COULD CONTRIBUTE TO POST-TRAUMATIC GROWTH THROUGH THE LENS OF DYNAMIC THEORIES OF PERSONALITY

Thus, dynamic personality theories provide a useful framework to posit clear hypotheses surrounding why and how PTG may occur. Stressful life events, the types of events that putatively engender PTG, cause learning and adaptation. The idea that learning is the core mechanism of personality change is inherent to the writings of Freud, Horney, Rogers, Beck, and also the Behaviorists, such as Skinner and Tolman, among others (Heller, 2020). Thus, in some cases these events do not lead to PTG but lead to psychopathology, including depression, anxiety, and PTSD. A large psychiatric literature demonstrates this conclusively.

So, when applying the lens of dynamic theories of personality—that the accumulation of states explains one's current state density distribution—what are the experiential features following stressful life events that might facilitate a return to normal functioning or even character growth? From the field of behavioral neuroscience and learning theory, another way to ask this question is, given conditioning to some set of stressors or contexts, what are the environmental features that promote extinction learning (Dunsmoor, Niv, Daw, & Phelps, 2015)? One perspective is that learning that one's environment is safe for engagement and exploration is a pathway by which beliefs such as PTG may emerge.

Applying learning theory to PTG concepts leads to several strands of evidence typically unexplored in the PTG literature. First, a long-standing literature indicates that experiencing unpredictable and uncontrollable stress enhances threat learning, makes extinction more challenging, and leads to a depressed phenotype in rodents and primates (Seligman, 1972). Conversely, if stress is subjectively perceived as controllable (e.g., unconditioned aversive stimuli such as electric shocks are escapable), extinction learning is more effective and robust (Baratta et al., 2007; Hartley, Gorun, Reddan, Ramirez, & Phelps, 2014; Maier & Seligman, 1976). Similarly, psychiatric research indicates that the cognitive factors that most strongly predict resilience to stressful life and traumatic events include a sense of perceived control over the event outcome (Wild et al., 2016). Second, exploration in general, and exposure to novel stimuli and contexts in particular, have beneficial psychological and neurobiological consequences. In studies of both humans (Dunsmoor, Ahs, Zielinski, & LaBar, 2014) and nonhumans (Myskiw, Benetti, & Izquierdo, 2013), exploration of novel environments facilitates learning generally but also promotes neural plasticity in regions responsible for stress regulation (McEwen & Gianaros, 2011). In line with this, if rodents explore novel environments (e.g., new cages) after being threat-conditioned, the quality of extinction on a following day is longer lasting and more robust than if the rodent did not explore novel environments in the interstitial period. Thus, one way to promote personality change may be by increasing one's exposure to novel situations, environments, and experiences.

These examples suggest that, following stressful life events, an accumulation of rewarding novel experiences or circumstances in which one perceives a level of efficacy and control could lead to fundamental positive changes in personality. Furthermore, these lines of evidence strongly suggest that assessing cognition, emotion, and behavior in the moment in everyday life using so-called idiographic and longitudinal mobile Health (mHealth) methods will be critical to determine whether PTG occurs and, if so, what are the factors that precede, facilitate, and result from it.

USING MHEALTH TO MEASURE STATES IN VIVO (OBJECTIVE AND SUBJECTIVE MEASURES)

mHealth (also referred to as *ambulatory assessment*) methods refer to a set of methods for collecting data "in the field" as individual's traverse everyday life. Today, mHealth methods typically use one's own smartphone, and data collection can be either passive (requiring no response from the participant) or active. Typical methods include (1) *ecological momentary assessment* (EMA), which often sends an SMS message containing a URL which leads to a self-report survey; (2) *geolocation*, which passively tracks an individual's movements; and (3) other movement (pedometer/accelerometer) data. This field is exploding, with new papers emerging weekly. Thus, what is presented here is necessarily selective.

Ecological Momentary Assessment

EMA is the most common way to assay subjective real-world experiences as they occur. In EMA paradigms, participants are prompted at regular intervals to respond to a set of questions about their current thoughts, feelings, contexts, and behavior.

Linking the idiographic density distribution of states to traits using EMA has been done in both personality and psychopathology research arenas (Fleeson & Gallagher, 2009; Houben, Van Den Noortgate, & Kuppens, 2015), while continued theoretical and empirical work is attempting to integrate these arenas (Widiger et al., 2018). To date, EMA research has primarily focused on individuals' subjective emotional feelings. Now more than 10 years ago, Ebner-Preimer and Trull (2009) reviewed the literature on the relationship between momentary affect and more stable states of mood dysregulation (e.g., mood disorders). They found that various features of the distribution of an individual's day-to-day affect (specifically, the mean and variance) may reflect some underlying dysfunction, manifested as borderline personality disorder, major depressive disorder, or bipolar disorder. As the EMA literature has further developed, a plethora of metrics of one's state affect, including the mean, standard deviation, "instability" (mean square of successive differences), "inertia" (first-order autoregression), and emotional diversity (within assessment entropy, or Gini coefficient) have been used (Houben et al., 2015). Currently, one can find studies demonstrating that any and all of these metrics are linked to psychiatric symptoms or personality traits.

What has been lacking in the EMA literature is a unified theoretical and statistical framework for determining the relative and unique variance each EMA-derived metric accounts for in one's trait. Recently, this has begun to change. Expanding on earlier EMA work done in the personality domain (Fleeson & Gallagher, 2009), the EMA psychopathology literature has begun to suggest more principled approaches to determining which features of the distribution of one's states are linked to traits (Dejonckheere, Mestdagh, Houben, et al., 2019). First, the mean—the first statistical "moment" of a distribution—of one's EMA responses is commonly the most robust predictor of one's trait. For example, in the clinical literature the mean of one's negative affect (derived from EMA) nearly always predicts one's level of depression (Dejonckheere, Mestdagh, Houben, et al., 2019), anxiety (Walz, Nauta, & aan het Rot, 2014), and borderline personality (Trull et al., 2008). Similarly, in the personality literature, mean negative affect predicts neuroticism (Kalokerinos et al., 2020), whereas mean positive affect predicts levels of extraversion (Ching et al., 2014; Wilson, Thompson, & Vazire, 2017).

Thus, the simplest and most parsimonious description of one's EMA-derived affect distribution (the mean) predicts a myriad of outcomes. As a result, what is now emerging in the literature is that a step-wise statistical approach is required. What this means is that the mean of one's affective (or cognitive) distribution must first be tested and controlled for when examining any more complex EMA metrics (Dejonckheere, Mestdagh, Houben, et al., 2019). When approaching statistical models in this fashion, there is often insignificant variance in the outcome that is accounted for by the more complex metrics, in particular, instability, inertia, or emotional diversity. One recent finding, using a higher order confirmatory factor analytic approaches to model psychiatric symptoms, like the Hierarchical Taxonomy of Psychopathology (HiTOP) system (Kotov et al., 2017), found that while mean negative affect was linked to nearly all psychiatric phenomena, additional positive and negative affective distributional moments (standard deviation and skew, specifically) further distinguished internalizing and externalizing symptoms above and beyond simply mean levels of negative and positive affect (Heller, Stamatis, Puccetti, & Timpano, 2021).

Thus, although the literature linking momentary states to personality traits and the literature linking momentary states with psychopathology have emerged separately, common findings are apparent. The distribution of one's set of states, and in particular one's mean level of that state, strongly predicts one's standing on that trait. This is perhaps not all that surprising (Dohrenwend, Link, Kern, Shrout, & Markowitz, 1990; Finnigan & Vazire, 2018) and may reflect shared method variance as both approaches rely on subjective self-report. Thus, it remains to be determined which specific distributional measures above the mean should be considered. Furthermore, examining how and why subjective affect changes over time may have implications for concomitant changes in well-being and personality.

Geolocation Tracking

Geospatial movement, as measured by GPS tracking devices, represents the extent to which an individual moves around in or explores their environment. Geospatial movement can be related to physical movement (i.e., activity), but is broader because it can reflect movement via car, public transportation, airplane, etc. Recent work has demonstrated that humans tend to follow some set of mobility patterns (González, Hildago, & Barabási, 2008; Kraemer et al., 2020). An individual's deviations from their specific pattern may be an objective indicator of personality change.

For example, reductions in geolocation-based measures of location-based exploration, so-called *roaming entropy*, has been linked to depression in small samples (Saeb et al., 2015; Saeb, Lattie, Schueller, Kording, & Mohr, 2016). Furthermore, a recent finding from our group demonstrated that within persons, on days when an individual demonstrated greater levels of exploration, they reported higher levels of positive emotion, indicating an association between exploration and affective states (Heller et al., 2020). Tying these findings to the learning models of extinction described earlier, the features of daily exploration that shared the strongest effect size with variation in positive emotion was the degree to which an individual explored novel locations that day (locations they had not previously visited in the recording period). This suggests that exploration in general, and experiences of novelty in particular, are linked with momentary affective states. Although this study is correlational, an intriguing hypothesis is that sustained changes in levels of exploration following stressful life events could facilitate improvements in psychological well-being, positive personality change, and PTG.

Pedometer/Accelerometer Data

Other wearable technology, such as accelerometers and pedometers, are a relatively simple and low-burden way to measure an individual's daily physical activity patterns. Data from accelerometers are analyzed to estimate the type and amount of movement, and data from pedometers estimate the quantity of steps. Although these data can be mostly gathered from smartphone-based geolocation applications, people sometimes do not keep their phones on them, whereas wearables may be more likely to be worn throughout a tracking period. Several years of research have demonstrated that objective measures of activity are associated with mood and energy (Merikangas et al., 2019; Vallance et al., 2011). Day-to-day physical activity may also be associated with personality characteristics. Several studies have examined how Big Five traits are related to physical activity. In general, extraversion and conscientiousness are associated with higher levels of activity, while neuroticism is associated with lower levels of activity (Artese, Ehley, Sutin, & Terracciano, 2017). These associations may be sample- or context-dependent. For example, among college students, neuroticism was associated with increased accelerometer-measured physical activity.

It remains to be studied whether changes in activity levels are associated with changes in personality.

TIMING ASSESSMENTS TO AFFECTIVELY MEANINGFUL EVENTS IS CRITICAL

Most research linking the distribution of states to traits samples one's state at random intervals. However, when states are sampled randomly, researchers have limited information surrounding the context in which a state occurred. It is not surprising then that the mean of one's randomly sampled state is the most consistent metric of the state that predicts the trait (Lapate & Heller, 2020). The context (or "situation") in which affect, cognition, or behavior is sampled matters enormously for determining associations between states and traits. This, of course, is not a new idea in personality research (Mischel, 1996). Yet the integrity of various systems—from zooplankton to economic markets, from tropical forests to human emotional and physical health—is perhaps most evident in the temporal dynamics in the anticipation of and aftermath from affectively impactful events (Scheffer et al., 2018). Specifically, the temporal dynamics surrounding how long it takes a system to return to baseline following a meaningful event is a core feature of the health and makeup of different systems.

Much of the research indicating how critical it is to precisely time-lock assessments of emotion, cognition, and behavior to affective events has been done in controlled settings in the lab. For instance, when rodents, non-human primates, and humans encounter a perceived threat or even an ambiguous, novel stimulus, those at higher risk for anxiety disorders demonstrate more prolonged freezing (Fox & Kalin, 2014; Kagan, Reznick, & Snidman, 1987; Nestler & Hyman, 2010). This prolonged freezing reflects a slower recovery from the affective event. Similarly, conscientiousness is associated with a faster return to baseline at several seconds following negative-stimulus processing as indexed by the duration of corrugator supercilii facial electromyography activation (the muscles comprising the furrowing of the brow)—with no such association during the reactivity epoch (Javaras et al., 2012). In the brain, such individual differences in the recovery period may be particularly dependent on prolonged representations of affective events in the amygdala (Puccetti et al., 2021). In fact, following negative affective events, individuals whose amygdala maintains those representations for longer periods report less frequent positive and more frequent negative emotion in their daily lives (assessed via daily diaries).

In the personality and clinical EMA literatures to date, most research timing assessments to specific events ask the participants themselves to self-report when a specific situation occurred (e.g., social interaction; Himmelstein, Woods, & Wright, 2019; Wilson et al., 2017). This type of approach, while convenient, has drawbacks due to individual differences in the likelihood of remembering to spontaneously self-report that one is in a relevant situation or to select certain situations. Thus, while understudied to date, it is essential to precisely time-lock assessments to the onset of salient events without relying on the individuals themselves to identify them.

When research explicitly considers context and time-locks assessment to the onset of affective events, emotional dynamics appear more critical to account for personality and psychopathology (Lapate & Heller, 2020). Early EMA research demonstrated that, in response to exam feedback, when getting poor grades on midterm exams, a sustained spike in depressive symptoms (over a period of days) was strongly associated with depressogenic cognitive styles. This lack of recovery was more strongly linked to risk for depression than the mean spike in symptoms (Metalsky, Joiner, Hardin, & Abramson, 1993). More modern forthcoming work is starting to return to this work of the early 1990s and is taking similar approaches (Dejonckheere, Mestdagh, Verdonck, et al., 2019; Shrout et al., 2010; Villano, Otto, Ezrie, Gillis, & Heller, 2020) demonstrating, for example, that the degree to which an outcome differs from the outcome one expected (a so-called *prediction error*) appears to drive emotional responses more strongly than the outcome itself.

As described previously, the distributional metrics of myriad types of states (location, affect, etc.) contribute to one's personality. The timing of assessment of these states puts limits on the interpretation of their distributional metrics. Standard deviation of negative affect over the day represents something very different from standard deviation of negative affect over the year. Within-day standard deviation is inherently more error-prone (simply because there are fewer measurements) but perhaps more sensitive to the environment. While the sampling scheme may be critical to determining which distributional metrics of affect are linked to PTG, we hypothesize that changes in state distributional metrics may signal the emergence of PTG. For example, a more flexible response to a stressful event (operationalized perhaps as lower negative affect and greater variability in affect) may reflect more effective emotion regulation, which is one psychological correlate of PTG.

MHEALTH AND RESEARCH WITH BREAST CANCER PATIENTS

To our knowledge, few studies have employed mHealth methods in the context of breast cancer. In general, these studies were exploratory and focused on determining the feasibility of a particular intervention delivered via mobile application. The earliest study followed 30 women with breast cancer for 90 days during chemotherapy and assessed sleep quality via mobile app (Min et al., 2014). The next study offered mobile counseling on diet and exercise to 50 women with breast cancer and measured their self-reported food intake and activity levels (McCarroll et al., 2015). A similar study evaluated a weight-loss application in 356 women with breast cancer using a pedometer and daily measures of quality of life (Uhm et al., 2017). Kim et al. (2016) was the first study to specifically examine day-to-day changes in mood in women with breast cancer in an effort to determine the efficacy of an mHealth depression screening tool. Results from these first four studies demonstrated the overall acceptability of mHealth and the feasibility of using this tool in women with breast cancer. However, compliance rates and overall study quality (sample size, homogeneity, inconsistent methods) were marginal.

Most recently, some researchers have focused specifically on how to increase engagement in mobile mental health interventions in women with breast cancer. Chow et al. (2020) were recently successful in demonstrating the ability to recruit and retain a sample of women in an mHealth study ($N = 23$). They demonstrated that the use a cognitive-behavioral therapy app, along with short coaching sessions from a therapist, was effective in reducing anxiety, depression, and stress. Women generally found this mode of service delivery easy to use, although upward of 40% of women dropped out of the trial prior to the end of the study.

All of these studies demonstrated that women diagnosed with and/or in treatment for breast cancer are amenable to utilizing mHealth applications in the context of research studies. In tandem, all of the apps were effective in improving the well-being of their users. Compliance rates were generally marginal, which may have been because the apps were not specifically designed for or tailored to women with breast cancer. Compliance may also have been impacted by the interventional (as opposed to the simpler observational) nature of the studies. The quality of these studies was also limited by their small, homogeneous samples. A recent review of mHealth interventions for a variety of cancers echoed these findings and highlighted the utility of mHealth specifically to improve the psychological well-being of cancer patients (Penedo et al., 2020). Using mHealth in women with breast cancer is clearly feasible and useful, but the studies thus far have not begun to scratch the surface of investigating personality change with mHealth methods.

mHealth studies in breast cancer patients present unique challenges. First, our research group has found that in recruiting for the Pathways study (described later), women had many concerns about privacy. Some women declined to participate because they felt uncomfortable having their geolocation tracked and/or completing surveys on their personal mobile device—even when data are collected and stored anonymously. Second, mHealth observational studies can be burdensome to participants. As described in the preceding section, the frequency and duration of assessment is key. Typically, studies are either of high-frequency and short-duration (e.g., EMA four times per day for 2 weeks) or low-frequency and long-duration (e.g., every 3 days for a year). It is currently unknown which of these designs is best suited for the study of PTG. To obtain the most valid results possible it is of course best to sample participants for as frequently and as long as possible, but this puts a burden on participants and may contribute to study dropout. In the Pathways study, we attempted to tailor the frequency of assessments to participants' unique needs to some degree while maintaining the study protocol. For one participant, this reduced the overall number of assessments (from one EMA every 3 days to one EMA every 20 days) but allowed us to retain her for the duration of the study.

An important direction for future mHealth research in breast cancer patients will be to discover new ways to sustain study buy-in and reduce burden over the course of the study. To that end we are considering ways to make participants stakeholders in the study by offering them some benefits, even in an observational design. This might include offering participants an analysis or summary of their mobile data that they could discuss with their physician. While providing participants feedback is an intervention in and of itself, which could have unknown consequences to PTG, the benefit in compliance would likely outweigh this cost.

STATISTICAL MODELS FOR CAPTURING WITHIN-PERSON AND GROUP-LEVEL CHANGES IN PERSONALITY

Myriad statistical techniques are germane to the analysis of personality change. Classic techniques might utilize summary statistics to examine cross-sectional associations between EMA data and personality traits. Multilevel modeling and network analysis are of particular interest for their ability to specifically model within- and between-person changes in personality characteristics.

Multilevel Models

Multilevel modeling, also commonly referred to as *hierarchical linear modeling*, is a statistical technique designed to handle nested data structures organized into levels (Raudenbush & Bryk, 2002). Accounting for the nested structure of the data is advantageous for multiple reasons. First, nested data do not meet the assumptions required for linear regression, most notably that observations (and errors) are not independent of one another. Violation of these assumptions can lead to significantly biased parameter estimates and therefore incorrect statistical inferences. Multilevel models account for the nested structure and avoid this kind of parameter bias. Second, accounting for the hierarchical nature of the data allows the researcher to examine within- and between-person effects simultaneously. Predictors can also be included in multilevel models to explain individual variation and individual differences. Third, in multilevel models, individuals are treated as a random sample; therefore, inferences can be made about the population in question.

In data collected using EMA techniques, observations are generally nested within individuals. More complex EMA data structures may include additional levels—for example, observations nested within days, days within weeks, and weeks within individuals. More specifically, women with breast cancer could be recruited pre-diagnosis and followed using mHealth methods throughout treatment. Women could be asked several times per day, for a couple weeks, several times per year, about how they are experiencing various personality states.

A within-person analysis might examine how the trajectory of a certain personality state, for example stress, changes over time. A between-person analysis might examine how these trajectories vary across people (i.e., individual differences in stress trajectories). Predictor variables of interest can be at the level of the individual (e.g., age, sex, diagnostic status, etc.) or at the level of the observation (e.g., social interactions that day, the weather that day, etc.). Multilevel modeling is an exciting way to measure change in personality because it provides a flexible toolbox for discovering the evolution of individual differences.

Network Models

The network perspective is a novel way to conceptualize and visualize changes in personality over time (Borsboom, 2017). From the network perspective, it is the dynamics among the states described earlier that give rise to an individual's personality. Different states are causally connected by some mechanism (known or unknown). In network theory, the causal connections between states are modeled using partial correlations—the unique association between two states, net of any associations with other states. In the visual depiction of the model, the states are represented by nodes, and the associations between the states are represented by edges (Epskamp & Fried, 2018).

Longitudinal network models (models that allow for repeated measures within person) establish how states are related to one another over time (Bringmann et al., 2013). A state can predict itself over time (represented by a self-loop). One state can also predict another state over time (represented by an arrow pointing from State 1 to State 2). These relationships are *lagged partial regression coefficients*—the associations between states at time t − 1 and time t, net of any associations between any other states at time t. The resulting networks depict how overall personality arises from individual causal relationships between relevant states.

Longitudinal networks are estimated in a multilevel framework—between- and within-person are visualized. Between-person networks depict the associations between states, on average, over time. Within-person networks depict an individual's unique associations between states over time. Between-person networks can be leveraged to make inferences about how personality is expressed, generally, in the sample studied. Within-person networks are person-specific and can be situated in the context of other individual differences to determine how a particular individual's personality manifests in daily life.

The networks we've described so far assume that the relationships between states are stable over time. However, it is possible (and even probable) that states interact in a dynamic way, for example, in response to environmental perturbations. These kinds of changes can be estimated using *time-varying network models* (Haslbeck & Waldorp, 2015). Changes in the strength of the relationships between states are plotted as a function of time and can be linked to naturalistic events that could impact personality change.

Network theory is a promising avenue for future research on personality development and change, but is not without limitations. First, longitudinal networks model linear relationships between states, though this may not always be the case. Research including higher order relationships between variables may be warranted. Second, to propose a comprehensive theory for how changing states are related to personality assumes that all possible relevant states are included in the network model. This is currently not possible, as prior research has not definitively determined which states are important. Any theory derived from a network model is limited by the nodes the network includes.

To summarize thus far, we have made a case for using mHealth methods within the cognitive neuroscience and dynamic personality theory frameworks to study post-traumatic personality change in women with breast cancer. Next, we propose a study that addresses many of the shortcomings in the literature thus far and is well-suited to enhance our understanding of post-traumatic personality change.

PATHWAYS STUDY AND FUTURE DIRECTIONS

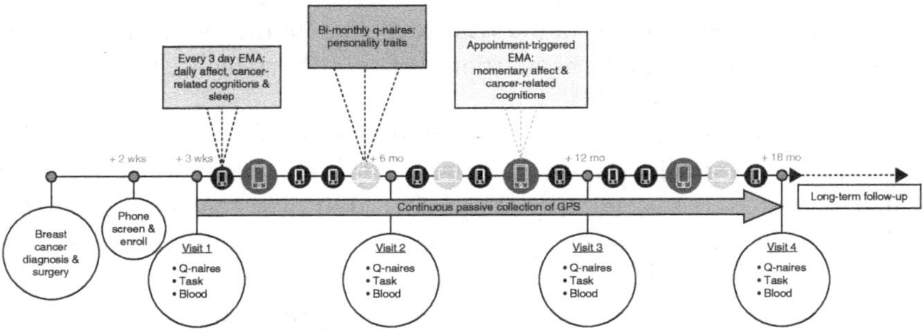

The Pathways to Resilience in Breast Cancer study at the University of Miami (Pathways) was designed with an eye on the shortcomings of the PTG literature raised thus far. These include the reliance on cross-sectional and retrospective subjective self-reports. The use of mHealth methods, and particularly mHealth methods informed by context, has the capacity to identify whether changes in one's distributions of emotion, cognition, and behavior precede personality change and specifically PTG. Thus, using mHealth methods, our project follows women for 18 months during and then after cancer treatment to determine whether changes in patterns of everyday emotions, cognitions, and behaviors predict PTG outcomes.

We chose breast cancer diagnosis and treatment because breast cancer is a stressful life event that has previously been associated with PTG. However, another advantage of using cancer is that it tends to be treatable. Today, breast cancer treatment is often successful, with 10-year survival rates now around 84% for malignant tumors (American Cancer Society, 2019). Breast cancer diagnosis is no longer a "death sentence," and many women find substantial personal meaning and purpose in the process of treatment and subsequently as a survivor (Helgeson et al., 2006; Taylor et al., 1984).

Four times during the 18-month period (0 6, 12, 18 months), we collect standard measures of personality, character, psychopathology (depression/anxiety), and PTG. These measures are used as the outcomes, or the consequences of experience of breast cancer diagnosis and treatment. Critically, as primary (curative) treatment for breast cancer typically lasts around 1 year, we are able to sample these outcomes 6 months after the typical course of treatment has concluded.

Applying the principles of whole-trait theory to our study design, we are measuring the so-called descriptive aspects of functioning via mHealth. One mHealth method is EMA. By measuring EMA regularly over the 18-month study period, we are constructing a density distribution of one's affective, cognitive, and behavioral states reflecting the current levels of traits without the reliance on single, cross-sectional, or retrospective assessments. A second mHealth method we are measuring is geolocation as an objective metric of exploration. Operationalizing exploration as "roaming entropy" (Freund et al., 2013), or the distribution of one's time spent over locations in a day, days with greater exploration have higher levels of roaming entropy. Both the EMA and geolocation measures provide indices of in-the-moment and in vivo measures of functioning over time.

Furthermore, because randomly sampled EMAs are insensitive to the circumstance and situation the individual is experiencing when they complete the assessment, we are triggering specific EMA sampling surrounding stressful events. Instead of asking participants to indicate during an EMA if they are currently experiencing a stressful event, we are preselecting and timing EMAs of emotion and cognition to occur surrounding likely stressful events: oncological visits. These visits are particularly stressful events as the patient often learns about her prognosis. Similarly, the concept of "scanxiety" has emerged as a real and important psychosocial feature of the cancer treatment experience as women undergo and learn information derived from bodily scans of underlying tissue changes (Bauml et al., 2016). Thus, instead of relying solely on context-insensitive assessments of emotion, cognition, and behavior, we are able to examine the distribution of emotion and cognition surrounding stressful phasic events.

Furthermore, the distributions of context-insensitive mHealth assessments of emotion, cognition, or behavior; geolocation assessments of exploration; or event-triggered assessments of emotion and cognition may change over the 18-month sampling period. Changes in the distributions of these measures may be indicative of personality or character change, or PTG. Thus, increases in exploration assessed via geolocation may be a vital indicator of personality change. Similarly, changes in the dynamics of emotion and cognition leading up to and following oncological visits may represent successful adaptation and learning, which may be indicative of personality change and PTG.

Data from the Pathways study will be analyzed using the novel methods described earlier. We will use hierarchical linear models to capture individual differences in the trajectories of positive/negative affect and roaming entropy. We will select time-variant variables, such as levels of intrusive cancer-related thoughts, as moderators of individual slopes. We will also use subjective personality change (e.g., change in subjective reports of empathy) as moderators of individuals' trajectories. We plan to use network models to examine how personality and affect items are related to one another over the course of the study. We will use time-varying network models to identify state shifts that could be indicators of personality change.

Personality change undoubtedly occurs. It is likely that personality change occurs via transformations to the types of emotions, thoughts, and behaviors one has day-in and day-out. However, it remains unknown whether, in response to stressful life events, PTG occurs, and, if it does, what are the mechanisms by which this happens. Retrospective introspection, answering the question, "Have I changed?" addresses the subjective feeling of change but not whether one's actions and experiences have transformed in any objective sense. Using a longitudinal and prospective design while collecting momentary and in vivo measures, this project hopes to address these precise questions.

The term "post-traumatic growth" seems to imply there is some end-point at which the individual has reached their maximum personal post-traumatic "height." Unfortunately, there is no specified time course for achieving such a peak. Short of studying people for their entire lives, the Pathways study seeks to measure and model growth (statistically defined, as we may actually see no change or decay under certain circumstances) in the year and a half following a breast cancer diagnosis. Pathways is a prospective, longitudinal study that was designed to test and challenge a variety of mechanistic models for the emergence of PTG. Based on what we know about the distributional attributes of personality states in the realm of psychopathology, we expect that PTG will emerge with increased flexibility in responses to the stress of cancer treatment, recovery, and remission.

REFERENCES

Almedom, A. M., & Glandon, D. (2007). Resilience is not the absence of PTSD any more than health is the absence of disease. *Journal of Loss and Trauma, 12*(2), 127–143. https://doi.org/10.1080/15325020600945962

American Cancer Society. (2019). *Breast Cancer Facts & Figures 2019—2020*. Atlanta: American Cancer Society, 44.

Antoni, M. H., Lehman, J. M., Kilbourn, K. M., Boyers, A. E., Culver, J. L., Alferi, S. M., . . . Carver, C. S. (2001). Cognitive-behavioral stress management intervention decreases the prevalence of depression and enhances benefit finding among women under treatment for early-stage breast cancer. *Health Psychology, 20*(1), 20–32. https://doi.org/10.1037//0278-6133.20.1.20

Artese, A., Ehley, D., Sutin, A. R., & Terracciano, A. (2017). Personality and actigraphy-measured physical activity in older adults. *Psychology and Aging, 32*(2), 131–138. https://doi.org/10.1037/pag0000158

Baratta, M. V., Christianson, J. P., Gomez, D. M., Zarza, C. M., Amat, J., Masini, C. V., Watkins, L. R., & Maier, S. F. (2007). Controllable versus uncontrollable stressors bi-directionally modulate conditioned but not innate fear. *Neuroscience, 146*(4), 1495–1503. https://doi.org/10.1016/j.neuroscience.2007.03.042

Baumert, A., Schmitt, M., Perugini, M., Johnson, W., Blum, G., Borkenau, P., . . . Wrzus, C. (2017). Integrating personality structure, personality process, and personality development. *European Journal of Personality, 31*(5), 503–528. https://doi.org/10.1002/per.2115

Bauml, J. M., Troxel, A., Epperson, C. N., Cohen, R. B., Schmitz, K., Stricker, C., . . . Langer, C. J. (2016). Scan-associated distress in lung cancer: Quantifying the impact of "scanxiety." *Lung Cancer, 100*, 110–113. https://doi.org/10.1016/j.lungcan.2016.08.002

Bleidorn, W., Hopwood, C. J., & Lucas, R. E. (2018). Life events and personality trait change. *Journal of Personality, 86*(1), 83–96. https://doi.org/10.1111/jopy.12286

Borsboom, D. (2017). A network theory of mental disorders. *World Psychiatry, 16*(1), 5–13. https://doi.org/10.1002/wps.20375

Bringmann, L. F., Vissers, N., Wichers, M., Geschwind, N., Kuppens, P., Peeters, F., . . . Tuerlinckx, F. (2013). A network approach to psychopathology: New insights into clinical longitudinal data. *Plos One, 8*(4), e60188. https://doi.org/10.1371/journal.pone.0060188

Bryant, R. A., & Guthrie, R. M. (2005). Maladaptive appraisals as a risk factor for posttraumatic stress: A study of trainee firefighters. *Psychological Science, 16*(10), 749–752. https://doi.org/10.1111/j.1467-9280.2005.01608.x

Carver, C. S., & Antoni, M. H. (2004). Finding benefit in breast cancer during the year after diagnosis predicts better adjustment 5 to 8 years after diagnosis. *Health Psychology, 23*(6), 595–598. https://doi.org/10.1037/0278-6133.23.6.595

Ching, C. M., Church, A. T., Katigbak, M. S., Reyes, J. A. S., Tanaka-Matsumi, J., Takaoka, S., . . . Ortiz, F. A. (2014). The manifestation of traits in everyday behavior and affect: A five-culture study. *Journal of Research in Personality, 48*, 1–16. https://doi.org/10.1016/j.jrp.2013.10.002

Chow, P. I., Showalter, S. L., Gerber, M., Kennedy, E. M., Brenin, D., Mohr, D. C., . . . Cohn, W. F. (2020). Use of mental health apps by patients with breast cancer in the United States: Pilot pre-post study. *JMIR Cancer, 6*(1), e16476. https://doi.org/10.2196/16476

Collins, R. L., Taylor, S. E., & Skokan, L. A. (1990). A better world or a shattered vision? Changes in life perspectives following victimization. *Social Cognition, 8*(3), 263–285. https://doi.org/10.1521/soco.1990.8.3.263

Cordova, M. J., Cunningham, L. L. C., Carlson, C. R., & Andrykowski, M. A. (2001). Social constraints, cognitive processing, and adjustment to breast cancer. *Journal of Consulting and Clinical Psychology, 69*(4), 706–711. https://doi.org/10.1037/0022-006X.69.4.706

Cruess, D. G., Antoni, M. H., McGregor, B. A., Kilbourn, K. M., Boyers, A. E., Alferi, S. M., . . . Kumar, M. (2000). Cognitive-behavioral stress management reduces serum cortisol by enhancing benefit finding among women being treated for early stage breast cancer. *Psychosomatic Medicine, 62*(3), 304–308. https://doi.org/10.1097/00006842-200005000-00002

Damian, R. I., Spengler, M., Sutu, A., & Roberts, B. W. (2019). Sixteen going on sixty-six: A longitudinal study of personality stability and change across 50 years. *Journal of Personality and Social Psychology, 117*(3), 674–695. https://doi.org/10.1037/pspp0000210

Dejonckheere, E., Mestdagh, M., Houben, M., Rutten, I., Sels, L., Kuppens, P., & Tuerlinckx, F. (2019). Complex affect dynamics add limited information to the prediction of psychological well-being. *Nature Human Behaviour, 3*(5), 478–491. https://doi.org/10.1038/s41562-019-0555-0

Dejonckheere, E., Mestdagh, M., Verdonck, S., Lafit, G., Ceulemans, E., Bastian, B., & Kalokerinos, E. K. (2021). The relation between positive and negative affect becomes more negative in response to personally relevant events. *Emotion, 21*(2), 326–336. https://doi.org/10.1037/emo0000697

DeSantis, C. E., Ma, J., Gaudet, M. M., Newman, L. A., Miller, K. D., Sauer, A. G., . . . Siegel, R. L. (2019). Breast cancer statistics, 2019. *CA: A Cancer Journal for Clinicians, 69*(6), 438–451. https://doi.org/10.3322/caac.21583

DeYoung, C. G. (2015). Cybernetic Big Five theory. *Journal of Research in Personality, 56*, 33–58. https://doi.org/10.1016/j.jrp.2014.07.004

Dohrenwend, B. P., Link, B. G., Kern, R., Shrout, P. E., & Markowitz, J. (1990). Measuring life events: The problem of variability within event categories. *Stress Medicine, 6*(3), 179–187. https://doi.org/10.1002/smi.2460060303

Donnellan, M. B., Hill, P. L., & Roberts, B. W. (2015). Personality development across the life span: Current findings and future directions. In M. Mikulincer, P. R. Shaver, M. L. Cooper, & R. J. Larsen (Eds.), *APA handbooks in psychology®. APA handbook of personality and social psychology, Vol. 4. Personality processes and individual differences* (pp. 107–126). American Psychological Association. https://doi.org/10.1037/14343-005

Dunsmoor, J. E., Ahs, F., Zielinski, D. J., & LaBar, K. S. (2014). Extinction in multiple virtual reality contexts diminishes fear reinstatement in humans. *Neurobiology of Learning and Memory, 113*, 157–164. https://doi.org/10.1016/j.nlm.2014.02.010

Dunsmoor, J. E., Niv, Y., Daw, N., & Phelps, E. A. (2015). Rethinking extinction. *Neuron, 88*(1), 47–63. https://doi.org/10.1016/j.neuron.2015.09.028

Ebner-Priemer, U. W., & Trull, T. J. (2009). Ecological momentary assessment of mood disorders and mood dysregulation. *Psychological Assessment, 21*(4), 463–475. https://doi.org/10.1037/a0017075

Eibl-Eibesfeldt, I. (1979). Human ethology: Concepts and implications for the sciences of man. *Behavioral and Brain Sciences, 2*(1), 1–26. https://doi.org/10.1017/S0140525X00060416

Epskamp, S., & Fried, E. I. (2018). A tutorial on regularized partial correlation networks. *Psychological Methods, 23*(4), 617–634. https://doi.org/10.1037/met0000167

Eraly, S. A., Nievergelt, C. M., Maihofer, A. X., Barkauskas, D. A., Biswas, N., Agorastos, A., . . . Baker, D. G. (2014). Assessment of plasma c-reactive protein as a biomarker of posttraumatic stress disorder risk. *JAMA Psychiatry, 71*(4), 423–431. https://doi.org/10.1001/jamapsychiatry.2013.4374

Finnigan, K. M., & Vazire, S. (2018). The incremental validity of average state self-reports over global self-reports of personality. *Journal of Personality and Social Psychology, 115*(2), 321–337. https://doi.org/10.1037/pspp0000136

Fleeson, W. (2017). The production mechanisms of traits: Reflections on two amazing decades. *Journal of Research in Personality, 69*, 4–12. https://doi.org/10.1016/j.jrp.2017.07.003

Fleeson, W., & Gallagher, P. (2009). The implications of Big Five standing for the distribution of trait manifestation in behavior: Fifteen experience-sampling studies and a meta-analysis. *Journal of Personality and Social Psychology, 97*(6), 1097–1114. https://doi.org/10.1037/a0016786

Fleeson, W., & Jayawickreme, E. (2015). Whole trait theory. *Journal of Research in Personality, 56*, 82–92. https://doi.org/10.1016/j.jrp.2014.10.009

Fox, A. S., & Kalin, N. H. (2014). A translational neuroscience approach to understanding the development of social anxiety disorder and its pathophysiology. *American Journal of Psychiatry, 171*(11), 1162–1173. https://doi.org/10.1176/appi.ajp.2014.14040449

Freund, J., Brandmaier, A. M., Lewejohann, L., Kirste, I., Kritzler, M., Krüger, A., . . . Kempermann, G. (2013). Emergence of individuality in genetically identical mice. *Science (New York, N.Y.), 340*(6133), 756–759. https://doi.org/10.1126/science.1235294

Funder, D. C. (2001). Personality. *Annual Review of Psychology, 52*(1), 197–221. https://doi.org/10.1146/annurev.psych.52.1.197

Galatzer-Levy, I. R., Huang, S. H., & Bonanno, G. A. (2018). Trajectories of resilience and dysfunction following potential trauma: A review and statistical evaluation. *Clinical Psychology Review, 63*, 41–55. https://doi.org/10.1016/j.cpr.2018.05.008

González, M. C., Hidalgo, C. A., & Barabási, A.-L. (2008). Understanding individual human mobility patterns. *Nature, 453*(7196), 779–782. https://doi.org/10.1038/nature06958

Hartley, C. A., Gorun, A., Reddan, M. C., Ramirez, F., & Phelps, E. A. (2014). Stressor controllability modulates fear extinction in humans. *Neurobiology of Learning and Memory, 113*, 149–156. https://doi.org/10.1016/j.nlm.2013.12.003

Haslbeck, J. M. B., & Waldorp, L. J. (2015). MGM: Estimating time-varying mixed graphical models in high-dimensional data. ArXiv:1510.06871 [Stat]. http://arxiv.org/abs/1510.06871

Heinrichs, M., Wagner, D., Schoch, W., Soravia, L. M., Hellhammer, D. H., & Ehlert, U. (2005). Predicting posttraumatic stress symptoms from pretraumatic risk factors: A 2-year prospective follow-up study in firefighters. *American Journal of Psychiatry, 162*(12), 2276–2286. https://doi.org/10.1176/appi.ajp.162.12.2276

Helgeson, V. S., Reynolds, K. A., & Tomich, P. L. (2006). A meta-analytic review of benefit finding and growth. *Journal of Consulting and Clinical Psychology, 74*(5), 797–816. https://doi.org/10.1037/0022-006X.74.5.797

Heller, A. S. (2020). From conditioning to emotion: Translating animal models of learning to human psychopathology. *Neuroscientist, 26*(1), 43–56. https://doi.org/10.1177/1073858419866820

Heller, A. S., Shi, T. C., Ezie, C. E. C., Reneau, T. R., Baez, L. M., Gibbons, C. J., & Hartley, C. A. (2020). Association between real-world experiential diversity and positive affect relates to hippocampal–striatal functional connectivity. *Nature Neuroscience*, 1–5. https://doi.org/10.1038/s41593-020-0636-4

Heller, A. S., Stamatis, C. A., Puccetti, N. A., & Timpano, K. R. (2021). The distribution of daily affect distinguishes internalizing and externalizing spectra and subfactors. *Journal of Abnormal Psychology.* Advance online publication. https://doi.org/10.1037/abn0000670

Himmelstein, P. H., Woods, W. C., & Wright, A. G. C. (2019). A comparison of signal- and event-contingent ambulatory assessment of interpersonal behavior and affect in social situations. *Psychological Assessment, 31*(7), 952–960. https://doi.org/10.1037/pas0000718

Houben, M., Van Den Noortgate, W., & Kuppens, P. (2015). The relation between short-term emotion dynamics and psychological well-being: A meta-analysis. *Psychological Bulletin, 141*(4), 901–930. https://doi.org/10.1037/a0038822

Infurna, F. J., & Luthar, S. S. (2016). Resilience to major life stressors is not as common as thought. *Perspectives on Psychological Science, 11*(2), 175–194. https://doi.org/10.1177/1745691615621271

International Health Conference. (2002). Constitution of the World Health Organization. 1946. *Bulletin of the World Health Organization, 80*(12), 983–984.

Javaras, K. N., Schaefer, S. M., van Reekum, C. M., Lapate, R. C., Greischar, L. L., Bachhuber, D. R., . . . Davidson, R. J. (2012). Conscientiousness predicts greater recovery from negative emotion. *Emotion (Washington, D.C.), 12*(5), 875–881. https://doi.org/10.1037/a0028105

Jayawickreme, E., & Blackie, L. E. R. (2014). Post-traumatic growth as positive personality change: Evidence, controversies and future directions. *European Journal of Personality, 28*(4), 312–331. https://doi.org/10.1002/per.1963

Jayawickreme, E., Zachry, C. E., & Fleeson, W. (2019). Whole trait theory: An integrative approach to examining personality structure and process. *Personality and Individual Differences, 136*, 2–11. https://doi.org/10.1016/j.paid.2018.06.045

John, O. P., Naumann, L. P., & Soto, C. J. (2008). Paradigm shift to the integrative Big Five trait taxonomy: History, measurement, and conceptual issues. In O. P. John, R. W. Robins, & L. A. Pervin (Eds.), *Handbook of personality: Theory and research* (pp. 114–158). The Guilford Press.

Kagan, J., Reznick, J. S., & Snidman, N. (1987). The physiology and psychology of behavioral inhibition in children. *Child Development, 58*(6), 1459–1473.

Kahneman, D., & Riis, J. (2005). Living, and thinking about it: Two perspectives on life. *Science of Well-Being, 1*, 285–304.

Kalokerinos, E. K., Murphy, S. C., Koval, P., Bailen, N. H., Crombez, G., Hollenstein, T., . . . Bastian, B. (2020). Neuroticism may not reflect emotional variability. *Proceedings of the National Academy of Sciences, 117*(17), 9270–9276. https://doi.org/10.1073/pnas.1919934117

Kessler, R. C., Berglund, P., Demler, O., Jin, R., Merikangas, K. R., & Walters, E. E. (2005). Lifetime prevalence and age-of-onset distributions of DSM-IV disorders in the National Comorbidity Survey Replication. *Archives of General Psychiatry, 62*(6), 593–602. https://doi.org/10.1001/archpsyc.62.6.593

Kim, J., Lim, S., Min, Y. H., Shin, Y.-W., Lee, B., Sohn, G., . . . Lee, J. W. (2016). Depression screening using daily mental-health ratings from a smartphone application for breast cancer patients. *Journal of Medical Internet Research, 18*(8), e216. https://doi.org/10.2196/jmir.5598

Kotov, R., Krueger, R. F., Watson, D., Achenbach, T. M., Althoff, R. R., Bagby, R. M., . . . Zimmerman, M. (2017). The Hierarchical Taxonomy of Psychopathology (HiTOP): A dimensional alternative to traditional nosologies. *Journal of Abnormal Psychology, 126*(4), 454–477. https://doi.org/10.1037/abn0000258

Kraemer, M. U. G., Sadilek, A., Zhang, Q., Marchal, N. A., Tuli, G., Cohn, E. L., . . . Brownstein, J. S. (2020). Mapping global variation in human mobility. *Nature Human Behaviour*, 1–11. https://doi.org/10.1038/s41562-020-0875-0

Lapate, R. C., & Heller, A. S. (2020). Context matters for affective chronometry. *Nature Human Behaviour, 4(7)*, 688-689.

Lechner, S. C., Carver, C. S., Antoni, M. H., Weaver, K. E., & Phillips, K. M. (2006). Curvilinear associations between benefit finding and psychosocial adjustment to breast cancer. *Journal of Consulting and Clinical Psychology, 74*(5), 828–840. https://doi.org/10.1037/0022-006X.74.5.828

Maddox, S. A., Hartmann, J., Ross, R. A., & Ressler, K. J. (2019). Deconstructing the gestalt: Mechanisms of fear, threat, and trauma memory encoding. *Neuron, 102*(1), 60–74. https://doi.org/10.1016/j.neuron.2019.03.017

Maier, S. F., & Seligman, M. E. (1976). Learned helplessness: Theory and evidence. *Journal of Experimental Psychology: General, 105*(1), 3–46. https://doi.org/10.1037/0096-3445.105.1.3

McCarroll, M. L., Armbruster, S., Pohle-Krauza, R. J., Lyzen, A. M., Min, S., Nash, D. W., . . . von Gruenigen, V. E. (2015). Feasibility of a lifestyle intervention for overweight/obese endometrial and breast cancer survivors using an interactive mobile application. *Gynecologic Oncology, 137*(3), 508–515. https://doi.org/10.1016/j.ygyno.2014.12.025

McEwen, B. S., & Gianaros, P. J. (2011). Stress- and allostasis-induced brain plasticity. *Annual Review of Medicine, 62*, 431–445. https://doi.org/10.1146/annurev-med-052209-100430

McGregor, B. A., Antoni, M. H., Boyers, A., Alferi, S. M., Blomberg, B. B., & Carver, C. S. (2004). Cognitive-behavioral stress management increases benefit finding and immune function among women with early-stage breast cancer. *Journal of Psychosomatic Research, 56*(1), 1–8. https://doi.org/10.1016/S0022-3999(03)00036-9

Merikangas, K. R., Swendsen, J., Hickie, I. B., Cui, L., Shou, H., Merikangas, A. K., . . . Zipunnikov, V. (2019). Real-time mobile monitoring of the dynamic associations among motor activity, energy, mood, and sleep in adults with bipolar disorder. *JAMA Psychiatry, 76*(2), 190–198. https://doi.org/10.1001/jamapsychiatry.2018.3546

Metalsky, G. I., Joiner, T. E., Hardin, T. S., & Abramson, L. Y. (1993). Depressive reactions to failure in a naturalistic setting: A test of the hopelessness and self-esteem theories of depression. *Journal of Abnormal Psychology, 102*(1), 101–109. https://doi.org/10.1037/0021-843X.102.1.101

Min, Y. H., Lee, J. W., Shin, Y.-W., Jo, M.-W., Sohn, G., Lee, J.-H., . . . Ahn, S. H. (2014). Daily collection of self-reporting sleep disturbance data via a smartphone app in breast cancer patients receiving chemotherapy: A feasibility study. *Journal of Medical Internet Research, 16*(5), e135. https://doi.org/10.2196/jmir.3421

Mischel, W. (1996). *Personality and Assessment*, 1st ed. New York: Lawrence Erlbaum.

Myskiw, J. de C., Benetti, F., & Izquierdo, I. (2013). Behavioral tagging of extinction learning. *Proceedings of the National Academy of Sciences, 110*(3), 1071–1076. https://doi.org/10.1073/pnas.1220875110

Nestler, E. J., & Hyman, S. E. (2010). Animal models of neuropsychiatric disorders. *Nature Neuroscience, 13*(10), 1161–1169. https://doi.org/10.1038/nn.2647

Park, C. L., Lechner, S. C., Antoni, M. H., & Stanton, A. L. (Eds.). (2009). *Medical Illness and Positive Life Change: Can Crisis Lead to Personal Transformation?* Washington, DC: American Psychological Association.

Penedo, F. J., Oswald, L. B., Kronenfeld, J. P., Garcia, S. F., Cella, D., & Yanez, B. (2020). The increasing value of eHealth in the delivery of patient-centred cancer care. *Lancet. Oncology, 21*(5), e240–e251. https://doi.org/10.1016/S1470-2045(20)30021-8

Puccetti, N. A., Schaefer, S. M., Van Reekum, C. M., Ong, A. D., Almeida, D. M., Ryff, C. D., . . . Heller, A. S. (2021). Linking Amygdala Persistence to Real-World Emotional Experience and Psychological Well-Being. *Journal of Neuroscience, 41*(16), 3721–3730.

Raudenbush, S. W., & Bryk, A. S. (2002). *Hierarchical Linear Models: Applications and Data Analysis Methods*. Los Angeles: Sage.

Roberts, B. W., Luo, J., Briley, D. A., Chow, P. I., Su, R., & Hill, P. L. (2017). A systematic review of personality trait change through intervention. *Psychological Bulletin, 143*(2), 117–141. https://doi.org/10.1037/bul0000088

Roberts, B. W., Caspi, A., & Moffitt, T. E. (2001). The kids are alright: Growth and stability in personality development from adolescence to adulthood. *Journal of Personality and Social Psychology, 81*(4), 670–683. https://doi.org/10.1037/0022-3514.81.4.670

Saeb, S., Lattie, E. G., Schueller, S. M., Kording, K. P., & Mohr, D. C. (2016). The relationship between mobile phone location sensor data and depressive symptom severity. *PeerJ, 4*. https://doi.org/10.7717/peerj.2537

Saeb, S., Zhang, M., Karr, C. J., Schueller, S. M., Corden, M. E., Kording, K. P., & Mohr, D. C. (2015). Mobile phone sensor correlates of depressive symptom severity in daily-life behavior: An exploratory study. *Journal of Medical Internet Research, 17*(7), e175. https://doi.org/10.2196/jmir.4273

Scheffer, M., Bolhuis, J. E., Borsboom, D., Buchman, T. G., Gijzel, S. M. W., Goulson, D., . . . Rikkert, M. G. M. O. (2018). Quantifying resilience of humans and other animals. *Proceedings of the National Academy of Sciences, 115*(47), 11883–11890. https://doi.org/10.1073/pnas.1810630115

Sears, S. R., Stanton, A. L., & Danoff-Burg, S. (2003). The yellow brick road and the emerald city: Benefit finding, positive reappraisal coping and posttraumatic growth in women with early-stage breast cancer. *Health Psychology, 22*(5), 487–497. https://doi.org/10.1037/0278-6133.22.5.487

Seligman, M. E. P. (1972). Learned helplessness. *Annual Review of Medicine, 23*(1), 407–412. https://doi.org/10.1146/annurev.me.23.020172.002203

Shrout, P. E., Bolger, N., Iida, M., Burke, C. T., Gleason, M. E. J., & Lane, S. P. (2010). The effects of daily support transactions during acute stress: Results form a diary study of bar exam preparation. In K. T. Sullivan & J. Davila (Eds.), *Support processes in intimate relationships* (pp. 175–199). New York, NY: Oxford University Press.

Simard, S., Thewes, B., Humphris, G., Dixon, M., Hayden, C., Mireskandari, S., & Ozakinci, G. (2013). Fear of cancer recurrence in adult cancer survivors: A systematic review of quantitative studies. *Journal of Cancer Survivorship, 7*(3), 300–322. https://doi.org/10.1007/s11764-013-0272-z

Takayanagi, Y., Spira, A. P., Roth, K. B., Gallo, J. J., Eaton, W. W., & Mojtabai, R. (2014). Accuracy of reports of lifetime mental and physical disorders: Results from the Baltimore epidemiological catchment area study. *JAMA Psychiatry, 71*(3), 273–280. https://doi.org/10.1001/jamapsychiatry.2013.3579

Taylor, S. E., Lichtman, R. R., & Wood, J. V. (1984). Attributions, beliefs about control, and adjustment to breast cancer. *Journal of Personality and Social Psychology, 46*(3), 489–502. https://doi.org/10.1037/0022-3514.46.3.489

Tedeschi, R. G., & Calhoun, L. G. (1996). The Posttraumatic Growth Inventory: Measuring the positive legacy of trauma. *Journal of Traumatic Stress, 9*(3), 455–472. https://doi.org/10.1002/jts.2490090305

Tedeschi, R. G., & Calhoun, L. G. (2004). Target article: "Posttraumatic growth: Conceptual foundations and empirical evidence." *Psychological Inquiry, 15*(1), 1–18. https://doi.org/10.1207/s15327965pli1501_01

Tomich, P. L., & Helgeson, V. S. (2004). Is finding something good in the bad always good? Benefit finding among women with breast cancer. *Health Psychology, 23*(1), 16–23. https://doi.org/10.1037/0278-6133.23.1.16

Tomich, P. L., & Helgeson, V. S. (2002). Five years later: A cross-sectional comparison of breast cancer survivors with healthy women. *Psycho-Oncology, 11*(2), 154–169. https://doi.org/10.1002/pon.570

Trull, T. J., Solhan, M. B., Tragesser, S. L., Jahng, S., Wood, P. K., Piasecki, T. M., & Watson, D. (2008). Affective instability: Measuring a core feature of borderline personality disorder with ecological momentary assessment. *Journal of Abnormal Psychology, 117*(3), 647–661. https://doi.org/10.1037/a0012532

Uhm, K. E., Yoo, J. S., Chung, S. H., Lee, J. D., Lee, I., Kim, J. I., . . . Hwang, J. H. (2017). Effects of exercise intervention in breast cancer patients: Is mobile health (mHealth) with pedometer more effective than conventional program using brochure? *Breast Cancer Research and Treatment, 161*(3), 443–452. https://doi.org/10.1007/s10549-016-4065-8

Urcuyo, K. R., Boyers, A. E., Carver, C. S., & Antoni, M. H. (2005). Finding benefit in breast cancer: Relations with personality, coping, and concurrent well-being. *Psychology & Health, 20*(2), 175–192. https://doi.org/10.1080/08870440512331317634

Vallance, J. K., Winkler, E. A. H., Gardiner, P. A., Healy, G. N., Lynch, B. M., & Owen, N. (2011). Associations of objectively-assessed physical activity and sedentary time with depression: NHANES (2005–2006). *Preventive Medicine, 53*(4), 284–288. https://doi.org/10.1016/j.ypmed.2011.07.013

Villano, W. J., Otto, A. R., Ezie, C. E. C., Gillis, R., & Heller, A. S. (2020). Temporal dynamics of real-world emotion are more strongly linked to prediction error than outcome. *Journal of Experimental Psychology: General, 149*(9), 1755–1766. https://doi.org/10.1037/xge0000740

Walz, L. C., Nauta, M. H., & aan het Rot, M. (2014). Experience sampling and ecological momentary assessment for studying the daily lives of patients with anxiety disorders: A systematic review. *Journal of Anxiety Disorders, 28*(8), 925–937. https://doi.org/10.1016/j.janxdis.2014.09.022

Weaver, K. E., Llabre, M. M., Lechner, S. C., Penedo, F., & Antoni, M. H. (2008). Comparing unidimensional and multidimensional models of benefit finding in breast and prostate cancer. *Quality of Life Research, 17*(5), 771–781. https://doi.org/10.1007/s11136-008-9348-z

Widiger, T. A., Sellbom, M., Chmielewski, M., Clark, L. A., DeYoung, C. G., Kotov, R., . . . Wright, A. G. C. (2018). Personality in a hierarchical model of psychopathology. *Clinical Psychological Science*. https://doi.org/10.1177/2167702618797105

Widows, M. R., Jacobsen, P. B., Booth-Jones, M., & Fields, K. K. (2005). Predictors of posttraumatic growth following bone marrow transplantation for cancer. *Health Psychology, 24*(3), 266–273. https://doi.org/10.1037/0278-6133.24.3.266

Wild, J., Smith, K. V., Thompson, E., Béar, F., Lommen, M. J. J., & Ehlers, A. (2016). A prospective study of pre-trauma risk factors for post-traumatic stress disorder and depression. *Psychological Medicine, 46*(12), 2571–2582. https://doi.org/10.1017/S0033291716000532

Wilson, R. E., Thompson, R. J., & Vazire, S. (2017). Are fluctuations in personality states more than fluctuations in affect? *Journal of Research in Personality, 69*, 110–123. https://doi.org/10.1016/j.jrp.2016.06.006

Wrzus, C., & Roberts, B. W. (2016). Processes of personality development in adulthood: The TESSERA framework. *Personality and Social Psychology Review*. https://doi.org/10.1177/1088868316652279

5

Using Methods from Personality Psychology to Study Post-Traumatic Growth

ERANDA JAYAWICKREME AND SARA ETZ MENDONÇA

EMPLOYING METHODS FROM PERSONALITY PSYCHOLOGY TO STUDY POST-TRAUMATIC GROWTH

Post-traumatic growth (PTG) has been defined as enduring positive change or improvements in psychological functioning following adversity (Tedeschi & Calhoun, 2004). While theories of PTG stipulate that people experience *enduring* changes in their characteristic patterns of thoughts, feelings, and behaviors (Jayawickreme & Blackie, 2014; Jayawickreme & Zachry, 2018), research on this topic has heavily relied on cross-sectional studies utilizing retrospective measures of self-perceived growth (Infurna & Jayawickreme, 2019). While concerns about the validity of this research program have been repeatedly raised over the past two decades (Frazier et al., 2009; Jayawickreme & Blackie, 2014; Tennen & Affleck, 2002, 2009), retrospective measures of self-perceived growth have remained the dominant paradigm (e.g., Kunz, Joseph, Geyh, & Peter, 2019). While self-perceptions of growth may have functional utility (especially when examined using narrative methods or as changes in secondary control; Blackie, Jayawickreme, Hitchcott, & Joseph, 2017; Jayawickreme, Rivers & Rauthmann, 2018), future research on PTG needs to clearly distinguish such perceptions from veridical prospective change (see Jayawickreme et al., 2021, for a consensus description of this argument).

In this chapter, we provide a primer on selected research designs and methods prominent in personality psychology that researchers may consider when examining whether the experience of adversity leads to meaningful and enduring change. Specifically, we discuss the importance (and current paucity) of longitudinal assessments of personality to examine the ubiquity of personality change in the wake of adversity, the importance of clearly theorizing and operationalizations of adversity, trauma and other types of life events, the value and limitations of informant reports of PTG, methodological considerations when examining trajectories of change, and the potential value of methods beyond global self-report trait measures, such as intensive longitudinal methods, in both corroborating personality change and uncovering the mechanisms behind such change. We recommend that readers interested in further details about the value of these methods also review Jayawickreme et al. (2021) and Jayawickreme and Blackie (2014, chap. 3).

LONGITUDINAL ASSESSMENTS OF POST-TRAUMATIC GROWTH

To examine the degree to which growth occurs following adversity, prospective longitudinal data is vital (Tennen & Affleck, 2009). Helgeson (2010) noted that researchers should collect both reports of PTG as well as objective indices of the outcomes associated with growth both before and after an adverse event occurred. Such a method offers the only truly objective way to determine whether participants have actually changed in domains associated with PTG from pre to post-adversity (Jayawickreme & Blackie, 2016, chap. 3). These designs are unfortunately rare in the field, in part due to the challenges and expenses associated with surveying a large sample over time under the assumption that a small percentage will experience an adverse event during the period of assessment (Jayawickreme & Blackie, 2016).

In one of the first prospective examinations of PTG, Frazier and colleagues (2009) found that perceived change does not typically translate to actual change. This study was instrumental because it had closely spaced prospective data, which allowed for the examination of short-term changes over a 2-month period. Along similar lines, a prospective study by Owens and Fowers (2019) found that retrospective reports of PTG as measured by the Post-Traumatic Growth Index (PTGI) may not reflect actual personal growth measured before and after an event. They did not find a relationship between PTGI scores and actual changes in related domains before and after a relationship break-up. While these studies focused on PTG with only two assessment points, other work has evaluated whether change is possible using multiple assessments prior to and after the onset of adversity, although these studies have not directly examined domains of PTG (e.g., Bleidorn, Hopwood, & Lucas, 2018; Luhmann, Orth, Specht, Kandler, & Lucas, 2014).

Of note, a recent systematic review and meta-analysis conducted by Mangelsdorf and colleagues (2019) did not find conclusive evidence that negative life events can lead to growth across outcomes that commonly map onto the PTGI. Focusing on positive relationships, experiencing major life events led to an initial decline in relationship quality, irrespective of the event's valence, and this effect was strongest for positive events. However, after an initial decline, there was a significant positive trend. This suggests that the experience of major life events is related to deeper relationships after an initial phase of impairment. There were, however, no significant changes following major life events for meaning in life, spirituality, personal strengths, and self-acceptance. Focusing on environmental mastery, after an initial decline following the event, there was a significant increase over time, whereas self-esteem showed evidence to suggest an increase after major life events, especially during the first 4 years following the event.

USING PANEL STUDIES TO EXAMINE TRAJECTORIES OF GROWTH BEFORE AND AFTER ADVERSITY

The past few decades have seen a proliferation of research employing longitudinal panel surveys to prospectively examine the extent to which major life events impact life satisfaction and other indicators of well-being (Diener, Lucas, & Scollon, 2006; Lucas, 2007). Lucas (2007) in particular utilized longitudinal panel surveys, such as the German Socio-Economic Panel Survey, British Household Panel Survey, Household Income and Labour Dynamics of Australia Study, and Swiss Longitudinal Panel Survey. These surveys have the advantage of annually assessing a large number of participants from across the nation in which the panel survey is housed. In each panel survey, participants are assessed annually on a wide range of outcomes, ranging from life events, to well-being, health, and economic and labor force indicators. From this wealth of data that participants provide on an annual basis, researchers are able to identify participants who had experienced various types of adversities or traumas and "re-align" their time metric from the study year to before and after an adversity. For example, the German Socio-Economic Panel Survey began in 1984 and is continually assessing individuals on an annual basis; for illustration purposes, if someone who began the study in 1984 experienced spousal loss in 1992, instead of assessing them from the time of entry, researchers can align the time metric to the year of spousal loss. Therefore, researchers would have up to seven assessments before spousal loss and all the assessments thereafter to examine the extent to which life satisfaction or other indicators changed because of spousal loss. Empirical examples for spousal loss can be found by Infurna and Luthar (2017) and Lucas, Clark, Georgellis, and Diener (2003). This approach has been extended to various life events of unemployment, childbirth, marriage, divorce, and disability. Examining ipsative change in traits within persons can be also facilitated by such longitudinal designs. Specifically, intra-individual shifts in the structure of personality traits may occur in response to adversity (Bleidorn et al., 2018; Lönnqvist, Makinen, Paunonen, Henriksson, & Verkasalo, 2008). In other words, the experience of adversity may impact the degree of prominence in a person's personality of various traits. Of note, these individual developmental patterns may be different from mean-level developmental trajectories (Jayawickreme & Blackie, 2014).

Of relevance to PTG research, panel studies can also be utilized to examine how specific life events are associated with changes on specific personality traits.

One substantive advantage of these studies is that they allow for the prospective assessment of personality prior to the life event as well as the possibility of examining the long-term impact of that event depending on the number of waves in the study post-event. However, one limitation is that analyses are necessarily restricted to the existing assessments, which means that specific questions of theoretical importance (e.g., subjective impact and perceived characteristics of the event) cannot be tested in such samples (see Jayawickreme et al., 2021, for an extended discussion of the value and limitations of using panel data).

INFORMANT REPORTS AND POST-TRAUMATIC GROWTH

Collecting prospective data may not always be an option, particularly in specific populations (e.g., refugees; Demaske, Blackie, Jayawickreme, & Jayawickreme, in press). Helgeson (2010) has noted that researchers should employ alternative methods to study the possible occurrence of PTG, including (1) examining whether there are actual improvements to individual health for those who report PTG as opposed to those who do not report PTG, (2) using a variety of measures to determine the effect of PTG on a single PTG construct (Frazier, Coyne, & Tennen, 2014), or (3) using informant reports to assess whether reports of PTG are corroborated by the individual's close others such as spouse, family, and friends. We focus here on the last method, informant reports, because of its widespread use in personality assessment (Vazire, 2006; Vazire & Carlson, 2010).[1]

Informant reports of recent behavior are an important way to study actual behavior (Furr, 2009) and therefore may provide the best option to gain information in studies where baseline data have not been collected. Undoubtedly, when reports are substantiated by others besides the target individual, researchers may feel more assured that reports of PTG reflect actual change. However, the level of agreement between self-reports and informant reports, among informant reports, and the particular domains for which PTG is corroborated has differed across studies. An early study of informant reports of PTG conducted by Park, Cohen, and Murch (1996) determined there was significant yet modest agreement ($r = 0.21$) between the participants' self-ratings of PTG and the PTG ratings reported for target participants by their family and friends. When the analysis was restricted to only those informants who reported being very close to the participants, the level of agreement increased to $r = 0.31$ (Park et al., 1996). Despite lower levels of agreement found in earlier research, more recent studies have demonstrated higher correlations, ranging from 0.40 to 0.69 (see Shakespeare-Finch & Enders, 2008; McMillen & Cook, 2003; Weiss, 2002). Furthermore, researchers such as Weiss (2002) and Shakespeare-Finch and Enders (2008) found that, for all domains of PTG as measured by the PTGI (Tedeschi & Calhoun, 1996), there were significant levels of agreement. The stronger agreement found in the later studies could be the result of the level of trauma experienced—for example, participants' events fulfilled clinical criteria for traumatic experiences in those studies; in contrast,

Park and colleagues (1996) included a wider range of events, including romantic break-ups and academic issues.

Contrary to these positive results, Helgeson (2010) found no evidence of agreement between survivors of breast cancer and their chosen informants 10 years after receiving their diagnosis based on the commonly used and well-established PTGI. Importantly, informants chosen by all participants were involved in the participants' lives at the time of diagnosis and were still in contact at the time of the follow-up assessment. When an open-ended format was used, Helgeson (2010) discovered that informants did corroborate some of the continuing effects of the cancer diagnosis. Yet changes agreed upon by both participants and their informants were detrimental to participants' health, self-image, and emotions. The one positive change noted by both survivors and informants since the diagnosis as a lasting change was an increase in aiding others battling cancer. Considering the other evidence, this study suggests that the positive effects of withstanding difficult life challenges may not necessarily endure over an extended period of time. It is compelling that the only positive change that was corroborated between sources at the 10-year follow up was behavioral, which makes it more easily observable by others.

Despite evidence demonstrating that very close others corroborate participants' reports of PTG, the majority of research has focused on trait-level agreement alone and thus has examined one domain of PTG at a time. Both Weiss (2002) and Shakespeare-Finch and Enders (2008) chose to examine agreement between participants' and informants' ratings, construct by construct, for all of the five PTG domains assessed by the PTGI. It is undoubtedly valuable to show that others are observing that the participant has changed in each of the domains associated with PTG (Tedeschi & Calhoun, 2004); however, it is also essential to consider that all of the changes were brought about by the occurrence of the same negative event. For example, a woman battling a breast cancer diagnosis may report experiencing some PTG, in so far as she feels closer to her family and God and has realized the importance of making time for the small things. She may also feel vulnerable and in less control of her life. If we were to plot this woman's profile, we would see that she reports greater positive change in the domains of relationships, spirituality, and appreciation of life and depreciation in the domain of personal strength.

After examining averaged scores on the PTGI, Blackie, Jayawickreme, Helzer, Forgeard, and Roepke (2015) found agreement only for post-traumatic depreciation (self-perceived negative changes as the result of trauma) among a clinical sample recruited in the south-eastern United States. However, using a profile analysis procedure that detects the level to which participants and informants agree on the extent to which the informant's impressions correspond with the target participant's unique ordering of traits, such as whether they are more religious than open to new possibilities (Furr, 2008), they discovered significant participant–informant agreement on those domains of change that had relatively higher scores in the target's profile than those that had relatively lower scores. It could be that informants were able to see that targets were not the same and were conscious of the idiosyncratic ways in which these changes had revealed themselves in targets' behavior. This allowed them to discriminate between domains of PTG in making their judgments.

LIMITATIONS OF INFORMANT REPORTS

Informant reports have potential, yet there is significant need for caution when employing them to study PTG. Targets may share reports of their own growth with informants, thus influencing their reports (Frazier et al., 2014). Moreover, targets may feel the need to shut close others off from knowledge that contradicts their "growth-oriented" self-concept based on self-confirming relationship dynamics (see Swann, Rentfrow, & Guinn, 2003). Additionally, it is not clear which dimensions of PTG may be most accurately corroborated by informants (Vazire, 2010). As discussed by Vazire (2010), observable behavioral trait in contrast to internal states (e.g., thoughts and feelings) may contribute to variations in the ability of the informant to correctly report on the outcome of interest.

Regardless of these possible limitations, we have noted two arguments for why evidence of agreement between participants and informants casts doubt on the assertion that self-perceived PTG is *absolutely* illusory (Blackie et al., 2015; Jayawickreme & Blackie, 2016; Helzer et al., 2014). First, it is probable that even with their preconceived biases and prejudices, informants will arrive at the same conclusions when assessing target participants, thus implying a greater likelihood that something objective exists to observe in the targets' behavior (Allport, 1937; Blackie et al., 2015, p. 789). Second and importantly, finding evidence of agreement across various judges illustrates the behavioral stability of PTG and the way that positive changes are demonstrated to manifest in various situations with a variety of people (Blackie et al., 2015; Helzer et al., 2014). Finding agreement between targets and participants therefore supports the argument that self-perceived PTG is not merely a reflection of the target's false impressions, and this method can be useful for investigating this question (Kenny & West, 2010; Vazire & Carlson, 2010).

In spite of this, the study of PTG presents singular challenges that may create difficulties in finding evidence of agreement. Informant reports may certainly provide unique information over and above self-reports with regard to an individual's personality (Infurna & Luthar, 2018; Vazire, 2006), but those same informants may be prone to shared biases based on the character of their relationship with the targets (Leising, Erbs, & Fritz, 2010). For example, it may be that informants corroborated target participants' reports because they were repeating what they had been told by participants (Frazier et al., 2014). Another related concern is a shared "positivity bias" created by the wish of both the target participant and the informant to believe in the target's successful coping after adversity. Nevertheless, it is essential to note that this inflation of agreement levels is improbable because it will only occur in an unlikely circumstance. Helzer et al. (2014) noted that evaluative processes will generate artificial agreement only when the same bias is shared between each pair of raters, and this bias differs from a shared bias of a different pair of raters about the same target.

THE VALUE OF INTENSIVE LONGITUDINAL METHODS FOR ASSESSING POST-TRAUMATIC GROWTH

Experiencing PTG at the daily level may have value on its own, principally when it is conceptualized as positive personality change. Fleeson (2014) has argued that an essential test of whether PTG following trauma or adversity is "real" is experiencing day-to-day changes in PTG. Thus, the extensive changes people report at the trait level should ideally be instantiated in daily beliefs, behaviors, and emotions. Although individuals may assert that they have changed in their relationships, their attitudes, and in their emotions when answering summary assessments, it may not actually reflect what people engage in day to day. This type of disconnect casts doubt on the value of interventions that changed only self-perceived PTG as opposed to growth-relevant thoughts, feelings, and behaviors arising in real-life situations.

What benefits may exist from experiencing state PTG on a day-to-day or even a moment-to-moment basis? It is beneficial to examine first what we currently know about trait PTG (Jayawickreme & Blackie, 2014). People easily report PTG in the aftermath of traumatic life events (Joseph & Linley, 2005), suggesting that it is quite typical for one to *believe* that she or he has experienced positive personality change, and it may be that this belief has value and merit in and of itself. Trait PTG assessed with retrospective self-perceived measures does in fact predict improved psychological and physical health, although across studies this finding is inconsistent (Helgeson, Reynolds, & Tomich, 2006). Interestingly, Frazier et al. (2009) found compatible results examining different types of measures such that retrospective self-perceived PTG predicted more effective coping, while prospectively assessed scores on PTG before and after the traumatic event were associated with lower distress.

PTG can be measured at the state level through intensive longitudinal assessments such as *experience sampling* (ESM; Conner, Tennen, Fleeson, & Barrett, 2009; Fleeson, 2007a). For example, in ESM, each participant reports on his or her current behavior, thoughts, and feelings several times daily over a period of several days using a device (such as a smartphone). ESM has many unique benefits, such as high ecological validity, over alternative methods that use self-report assessment (Furr, 2009; Scollon, Prieto, & Diener, 2009). Moreover, it avoids memory biases found with retrospective methods of behavioral measurement (such as the PTGI) by asking respondents to report on their immediate or recent experiences (Shiffman, Stone, & Hufford, 2008).

Employing methods such as ESM can determine the degree to which the wide-ranging, more existential beliefs that characterize PTG actually translate into observable differences in daily life. With the use of ESM, researchers can additionally begin to comprehend the daily processes underlying PTG. Such methods have the added benefit of placing research on PTG in line with current innovations occurring in personality psychology (e.g., DeYoung, 2015; Fleeson & Jayawickreme, 2021). Traditionally, personality has been conceptualized as the *typical* way that individuals think, feel, and act. This manner of study has had significant advantages. For example, summarizing general tendencies has allowed personality psychologists to successfully explain past behavior as well as predict future behavior and a broad range of significant life outcomes (Jayawickreme, Meindl, Helzer, Furr, & Fleeson, 2014). Nevertheless, Fleeson's (2001) *density distribution approach* to personality has demonstrated that people's characterization of personality actually reflects summary descriptions of subtly different distributions of personality states. Moreover, Fleeson (2001, 2004, 2007b) has repeatedly demonstrated that the overall majority of people engage in almost all levels of a particular personality trait over the course of a week: in other words, they manifest significant within-person variability. This within-person variability is an important and robust individual difference (Fleeson & Jayawickreme, 2015; Wilson & Vazire, 2015).

Compellingly, using this baseline information, Blackie et al. (2016) developed a daily measure of PTG. An important first step in creating this daily measure involved determining appropriate state analogues of PTG dimensions that capture the construct at a daily or hourly level. Following Whole Trait Theory (Fleeson & Jayawickreme, 2015), a "state" is defined as having the same content as a corresponding trait, but applied to a shorter period of time. States are qualitatively similar to traits, and both states and traits are descriptive of a person's behavior, feelings, and thoughts. A state measure of PTG evaluates what individuals are concretely doing, thinking, or feeling at the moment they are doing it, in real time, using the same information and numeric rating scales found on measures used to examine the PTG constructs at the global "trait" level.

Notably, the process of designing state versions of broad PTG items was more complicated than constructing state measures for Big Five traits, which in many cases involved adapting trait adjectives such as "bold" or "assertive" for state measures (Blackie et al., 2016; Fleeson, 2001). Measuring PTG in daily life encompasses studying the degree to which individuals who have lived through a traumatic or stressful adverse life event may perceive greater appreciation of life, improved relationships, increased personal strength, identification of new possibilities, and spiritual change *in daily life, moment to moment* (Blackie & Jayawickreme, 2014, 2015; Fleeson, 2014). To determine whether individuals have gained "personal strength," for example, researchers can track the frequency and duration of certain thoughts and feelings associated with effective coping with daily stressors (in this case, "I stayed calm" or "I felt overwhelmed and unable to cope").

Blackie et al. (2015) tested this new measure in an ESM study conducted with a college sample and found that, following adversity, the five domains of PTG assessed retrospectively (and as repeatedly measured in the literature) were not associated with the assessments of the experience of these domains from day to day (with the single exception of spirituality). These findings provide support for the idea that self-perceived retrospective growth does not convert into its manifestation in daily life. Furthermore, this highlights the significance and value of measuring change following adversity using appropriate methods and assessment.

The cumulative effect of daily stress may not be as easily examined, but we note that continuous reports of daily stress likely predict key outcomes. Schilling and Diehl (2014) explored this cumulative effect in a study using 30-day daily survey data from participants aged 18–89. Participants completed daily surveys for a period of 30 days, and, rather than analyzing the degree to which daily stressors themselves impact positive and negative affect, the researchers investigated whether the accumulation of daily stressors impacted daily positive and negative affect. In other words, researchers created lagged variables to index the number and severity of stressors over the 7-day period. This measure affords the possibility of measuring dynamic processes over a certain time span, with it changing intra-individually over time. This method is flexible in its approach, such that it is not restricted to only using daily survey data, but instead the chosen variable used at the time of assessments could be days, weeks, months, or years.

USING CURRENT THEORIZING ON PERSONALITY DYNAMICS TO IDENTIFY MECHANISMS OF GROWTH

While much work on personality has focused on uncovering the content or structure of personality traits (Fleeson & Jayawickreme, 2019), the thoughts, feelings, motivation, and behavior that make up discrete traits also vary within individuals, and this variability is meaningful (Jayawickreme, Zachry, & Fleeson, 2019; Fleeson & Jayawickreme, 2021). Explaining these dynamics can help us both understand why people differ from each other and how people can improve their lives by shifting these dynamics.

Current theories of personality dynamics (e.g., DeYoung, 2015; DeYoung & Krueger, 2018; Fleeson & Jayawickreme, 2015; Jayawickreme, Zachry, & Fleeson, 2019; Wrzus & Roberts, 2016; see Kuper, Modersitzki, Phan, & Rauthman., 2021 for an overview of these theories) focus on identifying the mechanism underlying the patterns of thoughts, feelings, motivation, and behavior (i.e., states) through which personality characteristics (i.e., traits) manifest in particular contexts. For example, Whole Trait Theory (Fleeson & Jayawickreme, 2021; Jayawickreme & Fleeson, 2017) stipulates a link between density distributions of Big Five-relevant personality states (Fleeson, 2001) and relevant social-cognitive mechanisms that explain those distributions. On this view, behavior in daily life takes a form predicted by social-cognitive explanations, and patterns of behavior, while varying meaningfully from context to context, are nevertheless consistent with structural accounts of traits such as the Big Five (Fleeson & Gallagher, 2009; Fleeson, 2001). Relatedly, Wrzus and Roberts (2017) have proposed a theoretical framework of recursive sequences of Triggering situations, Expectancies, State/State expressions, and ReActions (TESSERA) that explain personality development. Specific short-term processes of how life events translate into repeated daily experiences and situations lead to changes in behavioral patterns and personality representations.

One implication of these theoretical accounts is that enacting behaviorally based personality states may effectively facilitate positive psychological change in the wake of adversity, struggle, or failure (Blackie et al., 2014). For example, the personality traits of openness to experience and extraversion have been associated with PTG (Jayawickreme & Blackie, 2014; Jayawickreme et al., 2021). Thus, promoting specific (e.g., open, extraverted) states could lead to positive psychological change following personal adversity. Such interventions, were they to be carefully evaluated, may help individuals to behaviorally enact these traits in relevant life domains in the wake of the experience of adversity (see Hudson, Briley, Chopik, & Derringer, 2019, for a relevant example).

Examining the extent to which PTG states manifest in daily life and understanding their dynamics, as discussed earlier, could additionally increase our understanding of how different forms of adversity impact the individual and lead to changes in personality over the short- and long-term. Building on recent innovative work examining processes involved in trait change (e.g., self-esteem; Hutteman, Nestler, Wagner, Egoff, & Back, 2015), future work could examine whether the experience of adversity moderates the impact of state manifestations of PTG states on overall PTG trait change. Additionally, such research designs afford the testing of whether changes in specific contextual factors (such as changes in perceived social support; Mancini, 2019) lead to changes in PTG-relevant domains.

Finally, interventions that focus on changing individuals' narratives about the adverse life event may also lead to enduring personality change (Blackie et al., 2017; Jayawickreme et al., 2021; Roepke, Tsukayama, Forgeard, Blackie, & Jayawickreme, 2018). Narrative theories of personality have highlighted changes in narrative identity as a potentially powerful tool for promoting personality change through the process of strategically suggesting specific stories (potentially utilizing stories of role models and exemplars; Mischinski & Jayawickreme, 2019). When reflecting on adversity, a person can use the same facts to tell different stories: for example, the same information can inform a story of ruin and despair versus a story of pain and subsequent redemption (Roepke et al., 2018). Such strategies represent a potent personality mechanism to target in interventions.

CONCLUSION

Given that PTG was originally conceptualized as positive changes in people's enduring characteristics following adversity, it should not be surprising that recent innovations in personality theory and assessment hold the potential for systematic research examining the possibilities for growth following adversity. Future research that employs multiple methods and is founded on theoretical insights on personality dynamics holds the potential to uncover new insights on the possibilities for growth following adversity.

ACKNOWLEDGMENTS

This publication was made possible through the support of a grant from the John Templeton Foundation awarded to Eranda Jayawickreme. The opinions expressed in this publication are those of the authors and do not necessarily reflect the views of the John Templeton Foundation. Correspondence should be addressed to Eranda Jayawickreme, Department of Psychology & Program for Leadership and Character, Wake Forest University, PO Box 7778, Winston-Salem, NC 27104. Email: jayawide@wfu.edu.

NOTE

1. This section is adapted from Jayawickreme and Blackie (2014), chap. 3.

REFERENCES

Allport, G. W. (1937). *Personality*. New York: Holt.

Blackie, L. E. R., & Jayawickreme, E. (2014). Promoting change in posttraumatic growth research: Response to commentaries. *European Journal of Personality, 28*, 351–361.

Blackie, L. E. R., & Jayawickreme, E. (2015). The example of adverse life experiences as unique situations. *European Journal of Personality, 29*, 385–386.

Blackie, L. E. R., Jayawickreme, E., Helzer, E. G., Forgeard, M. J., & Roepke, A. M. (2015). Investigating the veracity of self-perceived posttraumatic growth: A profile analysis approach to corroboration. *Social Psychological and Personality Science*, 6, 788–796. doi:1948550615587986.

Blackie, L. E. R., Jayawickreme, E., Hitchcott, N., & Joseph, S. (2017). Distinguishing post-traumatic growth from psychological adjustment among Rwandan genocide survivors. In D. Carr (Ed.), *Varieties of Virtue Ethics* (pp. 299–317). London: Palgrave Macmillan.

Blackie, L. E. R., Jayawickreme, E., Tsukayama, E., Forgeard, M. J., Roepke, A. M., & Fleeson, W. (2016). Posttraumatic growth as positive personality change: Developing a measure to assess within-person variability. *Journal of Research in Personality*. http://dx.doi.org/10.1016/j.jrp.2016.04.001

Blackie, L. E. R., Roepke, A. M., Forgeard, M. J. C., Jayawickreme, E., & Fleeson, W. (2014). Act well to be well: The promise of changing personality states to promote well-being. In A. C. Parks & S. M. Schueller (Eds.), *Handbook of positive psychological interventions* (pp. 462–474). Oxford: Wiley-Blackwell.

Bleidorn, W., Hopwood, C. J., & Lucas, R. E. (2018). Life events and personality trait change. *Journal of Personality, 86*, 83–96.

Conner, T. S., Tennen, H., Fleeson, W., & Barrett, L. F. (2009). Experience sampling methods: A modern idiographic approach to personality research. *Social and personality psychology compass, 3*(3), 292–313.

Demaske, A., Blackie, L. E., Jayawickreme, N., & Jayawickreme, E. (in press). Examining the functional utility of personal growth initiative in a war-affected Sri Lankan Tamil sample. *Asian American Journal of Psychology*.

DeYoung, C. G. (2015). Cybernetic big five theory. *Journal of Research in Personality, 56*, 33–58.

DeYoung, C. G., & Krueger, R. F. (2018). A cybernetic theory of psychopathology. *Psychological Inquiry, 29(3)*, 117–138.

Diener, E., Lucas, R. E., & Scollon, C. (2006). Beyond the hedonic treadmill: Revising the adaptation theory of well-being. *American Psychologist, 61*, 305–314.

Fleeson, W. (2001). Toward a structure- and process-integrated view of personality: Traits as density distributions of states. *Journal of Personality and Social Psychology, 80*, 1011–1027.

Fleeson, W. (2004). Moving personality beyond the person-situation debate. The challenge and the opportunity of within-person variability. *Current Directions in Psychological Science, 13*, 83–87.

Fleeson, W. (2007a). Situation-based contingencies underlying trait-content manifestation in behavior. *Journal of Personality, 75*(4), 825–862.

Fleeson, W. (2007b). Studying personality processes: Explaining change in between-persons longitudinal and within-person multilevel models. In Richard W. Robins, R. Chris Fraley, & Robert F. Krueger (Eds.), *Handbook of* Research Methods in *Personality Psychology* (pp. 523–542). New York: Guilford.

Fleeson, W. (2014). Four ways of (not) being real and whether they are essential for posttraumatic growth. *European Journal of Personality, 28*, 336–337.

Fleeson W., & Gallagher, P. (2009). The implications of big five standing for the distribution of trait manifestation in behavior: Fifteen experience-sampling studies and a meta-analysis. *Journal of Personality and Social Psychology, 97*(6), 1097–1114. doi:10.1037/a0016786

Fleeson, W., & Jayawickreme, E. (2015). Whole trait theory. *Journal of Research in Personality, 56*, 82–92.

Fleeson, W., & Jayawickreme, E. (2019). Perspectives on the person: Rapid growth and opportunities for integration. In K. Deaux & M. Snyder (Eds.), *The Oxford Handbook of Personality and Social Psychology* (pp. 35–65). New York: Oxford University Press.

Fleeson, W., & Jayawickreme, E. (2021). Whole traits: Revealing the social-cognitive mechanisms constituting personality's central variable. *Advances in Experimental Social Psychology, 63*, 69–128.

Frazier, P., Coyne, J., & Tennen, H. (2014). Posttraumatic growth: A call for less, but better, research. *European Journal of Personality, 28*, 337–338.

Frazier, P., Tennen, H., Gavian, M., Park, C., Tomich, P., & Tashiro, T. (2009). Does self-reported posttraumatic growth reflect genuine positive change? *Psychological Science, 20*(7), 912–919. doi:10.1111/j.1467-9280.2009.02381.x

Furr, R. M. (2008). A framework for profile similarity: Integrating similarity, normativeness, and distinctiveness. *Journal of Personality, 76*, 1267–1316. doi:10.1111/j.1467-6494.2008.00521.x

Furr, R. M. (2009). Personality psychology as a truly behavioural science. *European Journal of Personality, 23*(5), 369–401.

Helgeson, V. S. (2010). Corroboration of growth following breast cancer: Ten years later. *Journal of Social and Clinical Psychology, 29*(5), 546–574.

Helgeson, V. S., Reynolds, K. A., & Tomich, P. L. (2006). A meta-analytic review of benefit finding and growth. *Journal of Consulting and Clinical Psychology, 74*(5), 797–816. doi:10.1037/0022-006X.74.5.797

Helzer, E. G., Furr, R. M., Hawkins, A., Barranti, M., Blackie, L. E., & Fleeson, W. (2014). Agreement on the perception of moral character. *Personality and Social Psychology Bulletin, 40*, 1698–710, doi:0146167214554957.

Helzer, E. G., & Jayawickreme, E. (2015). Control and the "good life" primary and secondary control as distinct indicators of well-being. *Psychological and Personality Science, 6*(6), 653–660.

Hudson, N. W., Briley, D. A., Chopik, W. J., & Derringer, J. (2019). You have to follow through: Attaining behavioral change goals predicts volitional personality change. *Journal of Personality and Social Psychology, 117*(4), 839–857.

Hutteman, R., Nestler, S., Wagner, J., Egloff, B., & Back, M. D. (2015). Wherever I may roam: Processes of self-esteem development from adolescence to emerging adulthood in the context of international student exchange. *Journal of Personality and Social Psychology, 108*(5), 767–783. doi:10.1037/pspp0000015

Infurna, F. J., & Jayawickreme, E. (2019). Fixing the growth illusion: New directions for research, resilience and posttraumatic growth. *Current Directions in Psychological Science, 28*(2), 152–158. http://doi.org/10.1177/0963721419827017

Infurna, F. J., & Luthar, S. S. (2017). The multidimensional nature of resilience to spousal loss. *Journal of Personality and Social Psychology, 112*, 926–947.

Infurna, F. J., & Luthar, S. S. (2018). Re-evaluating the notion that resilience is commonplace: A review and distillation of directions for future research, practice, and policy. *Clinical Psychology Review, 65*, 43–56.

Jackson, J. J., & Roberts, B. W. (2017). Conscientiousness. In T. A. Widiger (Ed.), *The Oxford handbook of the five factor model* (pp. 133–147). New York, NY: Oxford University Press.

Jayawickreme, E., & Blackie, L. E. R. (2014). Posttraumatic growth as positive personality change: Evidence, controversies and future directions. *European Journal of Personality, 28*, 312–331.

Jayawickreme, E., & Blackie, L. E. R. (2016). *Exploring the Psychological Assessment of Posttraumatic Growth*. New York: Springer Science + Business Media. http://doi.org/10.1007/978-3-319-47989-7

Jayawickreme, E., & Fleeson, W. (2017). Does whole trait theory work for the virtues? In W. Sinnott-Armstrong & C. B. Miller (Eds.), *Moral Psychology, Virtue and Happiness, Vol. V* (pp. 75–103). Cambridge, MA: MIT Press.

Jayawickreme, E., Infurna, F. J., Alajak, K., Blackie, L. E. R., Chopik, W. J., Chung, J., . . . Zonneveld, R. (2021). Post-traumatic growth as positive personality change: Challenges, opportunities and recommendations. *Journal of Personality, 89(1)*, 145–165.

Jayawickreme, E., Meindl, P., Helzer, E. G., Furr, R. M., & Fleeson, W. (2014). Virtuous states and virtuous traits: How the empirical evidence regarding the existence of broad traits saves virtue ethics from the situationist challenge. *Theory and Research in Education, 12*(3), 1–26.

Jayawickreme, E., Rivers, J., & Rauthmann, J. M. (2018). Do we know how adversity impacts human development? *Research in Human Development, 15*(3–4), 294–316. doi:10.1080/15427609.2018.1495515

Jayawickreme, E., & Zachry, C. E. (2018). Positive personality change following adversity. In V. Zeigler-Hill & T. K. Shackelford (Eds.), *The SAGE Handbook of Personality and Individual Differences: Origins of Personality and Individual Differences* (pp. 450–464). Los Angeles: Sage Reference. doi:10.4135/9781526451200.n24

Jayawickreme, E., Zachry, C. E., & Fleeson, W. (2019). Whole trait theory: An integrative approach to examining personality structure and process. *Personality and Individual Differences, 136*, 2–11.

Joseph, S., & Linley, P. A. (2005). Positive adjustment to threatening events: An organismic valuing theory of growth through adversity. *Review of General Psychology, 9*(3), 262–280. https://doi.org/10.1037/1089-2680.9.3.262

Kenny, D. A., & West, T. V. (2010). Similarity and agreement in self-and other perception: A meta-analysis. *Personality and Social Psychology Review, 14*, 196–213.

Kunz, S., Joseph, S., Geyh, S., & Peter, C. (2019). Perceived posttraumatic growth and depreciation after spinal cord injury: Actual or illusory? *Health Psychology, 38*(1), 53–62. doi:10.1037/hea0000676

Kuper, N., Modersitzki, N., Phan, L. V., & Rauthmann, J. F. (2021). The dynamics, processes, mechanisms, and functioning of personality: An overview of the field. *British Journal of Psychology, 112*(1), 1–51. https://doi.org/10.1111/bjop.12486

Leising, D., Erbs, J., & Fritz, U. (2010). The letter of recommendation effect in informant ratings of personality. *Journal of Personality and Social Psychology, 98*(4), 668–682.

Lönnqvist, J. E., Makinen, S., Paunonen, S. V., Henriksson, M., & Verkasalo, M. (2008). Psychosocial functioning in young men predicts their personality stability over 15 years. *Journal of Research in Personality, 42*(3), 599–621. doi:10.1016/j.jrp.2007.08.006

Lucas, R. E. (2007). Personality and the pursuit of happiness. *Social and Personality Psychology Compass, 1*(1)168–182. doi:10.1111/j.1751-9004.2007.00009.x

Lucas, R. E., Clark, A. E., Georgellis, Y., & Diener, E. (2003). Reexamining adaptation and the set point model of happiness: Reactions to changes in marital status. *Journal of Personality and Social Psychology, 84*, 527–539.

Luhmann, M., Orth, U., Specht, J., Kandler, C., & Lucas, R. E. (2014). Studying changes in life circumstances and personality: It's about time. *European Journal of Personality, 28*(3), 256–266. doi:10.1002/per.1951

Mancini, A. D. (2019). When acute adversity improves psychological health: A social–contextual framework. *Psychological Review, 126*(4), 486–505.

Mangelsdorf, J., Eid, M., & Luhmann, M. (2019). Does growth require suffering? A systematic review and meta-analysis on genuine posttraumatic and postecstatic growth. *Psychological Bulletin, 145*(3), 302–338. https://doi.org/10.1037/bul0000173

McMillen, J. C., & Cook, C. L. (2003). The positive by-products of spinal cord injury and their correlates. Rehabilitation Psychology, *48*(2), 77–85.

Mischinski, M., & Jayawickreme, E. (2019). Can moral exemplars promote wisdom? In R. J. Sternberg, H. C. Nusbaum, & J. Glück (Eds.), *Applying Wisdom to Contemporary*

World Problems (pp. 173–200). Cham: Switzerland. doi:10.1007/978-3-030-20287-3_7

Mogle, J., Almeida, D. M., & Stawski, R. S. (2015). Psychometric properties of micro-longitudinal assessments: Between-and within-person reliability, factor structure and discriminate validity of cognitive interference. In *Handbook of Intraindividual Variability Across the Lifespan*, 293–306.

Owens, M., & Fowers, B. J. (2109). Perceived post-traumatic growth may not reflect actual positive change: A short-term prospective study of relationship dissolution. *Journal of Social and Personal Relationships, 36*, 3098–3116. doi:10.1177/0265407518811662

Park, C. L., Cohen, L. H., & Murch, R. L. (1996). Assessment and prediction of stress-related growth. *Journal of Personality, 64*(1), 71–105. doi:10.1111/j.1467-6494.1996.tb00815.x

Roepke, A. M., Tsukayama, E., Forgeard, M., Blackie, L., & Jayawickreme, E. (2018). Randomized control trial of Second Story, an intervention targeting posttraumatic growth, with bereaved adults. *Journal of Consulting and Clinical Psychology, 86*(6), 518–532.

Schilling, O. K., & Diehl, M. (2014). Reactivity to stressor pile-up in adulthood: Effects on daily negative and positive affect. *Psychology and Aging, 29*, 72–83. doi:10.1037/a0035500

Scollon, C. N., Kim-Prieto, C., & Diener, E. (2009). Experience sampling: Promises and pitfalls, strengths and weaknesses. In E. Diener (Ed.), *Social indicators research series: Vol. 39. Assessing well-being: The collected works of Ed Diener* (pp. 157–180). Springer Science + Business Media. https://doi.org/10.1007/978-90-481-2354-4_8

Shakespeare-Finch, J. E., & Enders, T. (2008). Corroborating evidence of posttraumatic growth. *Journal of Traumatic Stress, 21*(4), 421–424.

Shiffman, S., Stone, A. A., & Hufford, M. R. (2008). Ecological momentary assessment. *Annual Review of Clinical Psychology, 4*, 1–32.

Swann, W. B., Jr., Rentfrow, P. J., & Guinn, J. S. (2003). Self-verification: The search for coherence. In M. R. Leary & J. P. Tangey (Eds.), *Handbook of Self and Identity* (pp. 367–383). New York: Guilford.

Tedeschi, R. G., & Calhoun, L. G. (1996). The Posttraumatic Growth Inventory: Measuring the positive legacy of trauma. *Journal of Traumatic Stress, 9*(3), 455–471. doi:10.1007/BF02103658

Tedeschi, R. G., & Calhoun, L. G. (2004). Posttraumatic growth: Conceptual foundations and empirical evidence. *Psychological Inquiry, 15*(1), 1–18. doi:10.1207/s15327965pli1501_01

Tennen, H., & Affleck, G. (2002). Benefit-finding and benefit-reminding. In C. R. Snyder & S. J. Lopez (Eds.), Handbook of Positive Psychology (pp. 584–597). New York: Oxford University Press.

Tennen, H., & Affleck, G. (2009). Assessing positive life change: In search of meticulous methods. In C. L. Park, S. C. Lechner, M. H. Antoni, & A. L. Stanton (Eds.), *Medical Illness and Positive Life Change: Can Crisis Lead to Personal Transformation?* (pp. 31–49). Washington, DC: American Psychological Association.

Vazire, S. (2006). Informant reports: A cheap, fast, and easy method for personality assessment. *Journal of Research in Personality, 40*(5), 472–481.

Vazire, S. (2010). Who knows what about a person? The self–other knowledge asymmetry (SOKA) model. *Journal of Personality and Social Psychology, 98(2)*, 281–300. https://doi.org/10.1037/a0017908

Vazire, S., & Carlson, E. N. (2010). Self-knowledge of personality: Do people know themselves? *Social and Personality Psychology Compass, 4*(8), 605–620.

Weiss, T. (2002). Posttraumatic growth in women with breast cancer and their husbands: An intersubjective validation study. *Journal of Psychosocial Oncology, 20*(2), 65–80.

Wilson, R. E., Vazire, S. (2015). Taking personality to the next level: What does it mean to know a person? In R. A. Scott (Ed.), *Emerging trends in the social and behavioral sciences: An interdisciplinary, searchable, and linkable resource.* Retrieved from https://onlinelibrary.wiley.com/doi/abs/10.1002/9781118900772.etrds0327

Wrzus, C., & Roberts, B. W. (2017). Development in adulthood: The TESSERA framework. *Personality and Social Psychology Review, 21*(3), 253–277. doi:10.1177/1099969316652279

6

Emotions and Positive Personality Change in Syrian-Origin Young Adults Who Have Recently Resettled in the Netherlands

ODILIA M. LACEULLE, KINAN ALAJAK, EVA ALISIC, ZEINA AL SAWAF, HAZA F. RAHIM, RENÉE ZONNEVELD, AND JOANNE M. CHUNG ■

Around the world, the number of people who seek or have refugee status continues to increase. More than 500,000 individuals sought asylum in Europe in 2014, and this number increased to more than 1.2 million in 2016 (Eurostat, 2017). Within the Netherlands, there are at least 200,000 people with refugee status, many of whom are young adults of Syrian origin (Statistics Netherlands, 2017). This poses both a challenge and a responsibility for receiving societies due to the social and financial complexities of integrating asylum-seeking people into their new communities (Fazel, Wheeler, & Danesh, 2005; Kehoe, Alisic, & Heijlinger, 2019). Young adults who seek or have refugee status are likely to come from places where they have been exposed to major, life-changing hardships affecting their mental health and well-being. In addition, people with refugee backgrounds are likely to be at risk for new adverse experiences (Schick et al., 2016). Despite the suffering and challenges that come with facing adversity, adversity is thought to promote positive personality change or character more generally (Tedeschi & Calhoun, 2004). Therefore, obtaining a better understanding of people who seek or have refugee status provides a rare and valuable opportunity to gain insights into pathways to character.

LONGITUDINAL AND MULTIMETHOD APPROACHES TO EXAMINE POSITIVE PERSONALITY CHANGE IN REFUGEE SYRIAN-ORIGIN YOUTH IN THE NETHERLANDS

In the current research, we examine the link between adversity and personality change in Syrian-origin young adults who have recently resettled in the Netherlands. The challenges surrounding the integration of people who seek or have refugee status into receiving societies is not new, but recent events have made it a timely topic worldwide. The Syrian conflict has been ongoing since 2011, and it has been referred to as "the biggest humanitarian and refugee crisis of our time" (United Nations High Commissioner for Refugees, 2017). Unsurprisingly, recent research has sought to better understand the functioning of people with refugee background. Importantly, the current research joins a growing literature that broadens the scope from a deficit-based perspective focused on poor psychological functioning to a more balanced approach examining factors that may promote positive personality change for people who seek or have refugee status.

Post-traumatic growth (PTG) refers to the experience of positive psychological changes after encountering exceptionally difficult life circumstances (Tedeschi & Calhoun, 2004). Yet the majority of the work in this area is cross-sectional, with a typical study asking participants to provide retrospective reports regarding the extent to which they experienced positive changes in response to adverse life events. One drawback of this approach is that while it may pick up on one's *perceptions* of personality change, it does not detect actual changes over time (Joseph & Linley, 2008; Jayawickreme & Blackie, 2014). Here, we used a longitudinal approach to empirically examine the extent to which positive personality change follows adversity pre-, peri-, and post-flight. People who seek or have refugee status were followed for 13 months. During these months, they were invited to participate in four assessments, each including a questionnaire (1 hour, during a face-to-face session), daily assessments with experience sampling methodology (ESM; 7 days, 5 times a day; only following the first three face-to-face sessions), and naturalistic audio recordings (in a subsample of participants). More information on the assessments follows.

Adversity Pre-, Peri, and Post-Flight

For most people who seek or have refugee status, adversity can be considered in relation to flight in three different ways. Informed by earlier research efforts, we differentiated experiencing adversity (1) pre-flight, before coming to the Netherlands; (2) peri-flight, during the flight; and (3) post-flight, after arriving in the Netherlands (Brugha, 2004; Sleijpen, Haagen, Mooren, & Kleber, 2016). With regard to pre-flight adversity, people may experience such difficulties as interpersonal violence including torture, loss of family members, bombardment, and deprivation of food, healthcare, and shelter (Schweitzer, Melville, Steel, & Lacharez, 2006; Silove, Sinnerbrink, Field, Manicavasagar, & Steel, 1997) as well as loss of jobs or (social) status and fear of getting arrested. Importantly, these adversities may directly concern oneself, but also may be experienced on behalf of relatives and close others.

Regarding peri-flight adversity, individuals have been found to be at risk for a range of adverse experiences depending on the characteristics of the flight (Kehoe et al., 2019). For example, individuals may be subject to human trafficking involving high rates of sexual and physical violence (Kingsley, 2016). Additionally, people may experience stressors specific to daily living in refugee camps (Miller & Rasmussen 2010); losses experienced due to separation from family, communities, and social networks (Miller et al., 2002); and difficulties with language. However, it may not always be correct to assume that experiences are uniformly negative across individuals. In particular, while many researchers might classify the flight from Syria as an adverse life event, the flight may be experienced in different ways, with some individuals experiencing leaving Syria as a major, but strongly positive life event. This is likely due to a combination of factors, such as one's country of origin, the country that the person is resettling in, financial resources, and social capital. In general, individuals from advantaged backgrounds tend to have both financial and social capital to organize a safer flight than do individuals from disadvantaged backgrounds (Sempértegui, Knipscheer, & Bekker, 2018). Relatedly, heterogeneity may also reflect characteristics of the flight (e.g., the country they are resettling in), but also may reflect individual differences in both background factors (e.g., age, gender, location of family members) and personality (e.g., emotional stability). Moreover, and in line with the intersectionality model, these characteristics may not just have unique or accumulative effects, but also interact to determine the position and development process of an individual in (a new) society and shape their experiences in life (Sempértegui et al., 2018).

The preceding factors were of particular interest in the context of the current study because they can help shape an individual's narrative. *Narratives* are the evolving stories people construct about themselves, that provide the individual with a sense of unity and purpose and, as such, are an important aspect of the individual's identity (McAdams & McLean, 2013). As such, in addition to asking the participants to quantify their peri- and post-flight adverse experiences, the current research asked participants to construct their own story about the time between leaving Syria and coming to the Netherlands, including what the event says about who they are and how they have developed over time. Repeating this task over four study assessments will allow us to explore how changes in narratives may indicate positive personality change in Syrian-origin young adults. For an example of two assessments from this task for one of our participants, see Box 6.1.

In addition to obtaining participant accounts of experiences of adversity and life events before and during the transition to the Netherlands, the current research also assesses post-flight experiences. There has been increasing empirical support that individuals with refugee backgrounds have an increased vulnerability for post-migration difficulties (Bhugra & Becker, 2005; Porter & Haslam, 2005). These include but are not limited to difficulties with language, loss of occupation or social status, experiences of discrimination, sudden loss of social and family ties, unstable

Box 6.1

One Participant's Account of the Time Between Leaving Syria and Arriving in the Netherlands

At the beginning of the study. The idea started when I was in my last year of university, and what was going to happen next (which is joining the military service). My father decided to travel alone to Europe so he could then make a family reunion for me, my mother, and my sister. His basic motivation was about his concerns over my and my sister's physical and mental safety. So, he traveled to the Netherlands and started the family reunion procedures. For me and my sister, thinking about it was not that difficult—in fact we were excited! While my mother felt some fear and anxiety about it, the fear of feeling lonely far away from her family and social community was her primary obsession. But, for me it was not that complicated, as the majority of my friends were out of Syria already.

I find that moving to the Netherlands is one of the most important things that happened to me in my life. It is the event that will smooth the way for my strange dreams, as the Syrian society would consider them, until they will come true.

Four months later. I came to the Netherlands with my mother and sister by plane, after my father completed a family reunion request and it was approved by the Dutch government.

I felt a little bit scared, but it was a beautiful kind of fear combined with the excitement to travel and see new places. It was my dream since I was a child, and now that I am here, it's not impossible anymore.

I find that the event (me coming to the Netherlands) is the second important event that happened in my life after my graduation, as here I can feel that my dreams became much broader than they were in my homeland. Simply, my silly childhood dreams turned into something possible.

housing, lack of privacy, lack of sense of belonging, and stress related to obtaining refugee status. Even though post-migration difficulties may be less severe in nature than the traumatic events participants experienced in their home country, they may delay or interfere with the start of a new life in the Netherlands. Of note, although it is difficult to conduct research assessing adversity before and after flight, post-migration difficulties can be more easily assessed. Conducting longitudinal research on post-migration difficulties provides a methodologically robust way to disentangle how adversity that happens between subsequent assessments is linked to individual differences in positive personality change over time.

Longitudinal Assessments

The current study involved four measurement occasions over 13 months. This allowed for the examination of (1) how individual differences in reports of past adversity are related to ongoing changes in personality, (2) how current experiences of adversity are linked to positive personality change, and (3) the emotional experiences that may contribute to positive personality change.

It is important to note that the current research suffers from the limitation that we rely on retrospective assessments of both pre- and peri-flight adversity. However, the current approach contributes to our knowledge on how adverse experiences contribute to the *development* of positive personality traits and allows us to capture positive personality changes that are likely to occur. For instance, as individuals begin to settle in and engage in the process of building a new life, they are likely to encounter new challenges and opportunities in the social, academic, and occupational domains. Also, in the current study, we captured post-flight adversity, and post-migration difficulties in particular, occurring *in between* subsequent assessments of personality. This allowed to examine how post-flight adversity is related to personality while controlling for initial levels of the personality traits.

Multiple Levels of Analyses

Moreover, in the current research, we incorporated methodologies allowing us to explore three different levels at which adversity and positive personality change may occur. Participants were invited to participate in four assessments waves within 13 months (every 4 months). At the *macro* level, participants completed questionnaires that assessed their general characteristics, adverse experiences before and during the study (see below), mental health, positive personality traits (e.g., resilience, relatedness, empathy), and emotional dispositions (e.g., awe, compassion, gratitude). The first three assessments took place during face-to-face sessions; the fourth was online with research assistants being available in case the participant had any questions or concerns. At the *meso* level, participants completed daily questionnaires administered with ESM via a smartphone application, up to 5 times a day for 1 week, immediately following the first three macro-level assessments. For reasons of feasibility, the fourth macro-level assessment was not followed by the daily questionnaires. The meso-level questionnaire included items regarding situational characteristics (e.g., one's location; one's perceptions of the extent that the situation was pleasant), stressful and uplifting events in the past hour (i.e., the nature of both negative and positive events experienced in the past hour), character states (e.g., how humble a person felt and behaved in the past hour), and emotion experiences (e.g., how much compassion a person felt in the past hour). On the *micro* level, behavior was assessed for a subsample of participants through naturalistic audio recordings using an electronically activated recorder (EAR; Mehl, 2017). These assessments occurred in tandem with the meso-level portion of the study (after the first three macro-level questionnaires). These audio recordings can be coded with regard to emotion displays (e.g., laughing, crying), personality experiences (e.g., displays of affection), tone (e.g., using a loving tone of voice); topic (e.g., education, employment), and other contextual information (e.g., being alone or in the presence of others).

Cultural Sensitivity and Co-Creation

The current research also includes an objective to foster a partnership with young adults of Syrian origin in the Netherlands in the form of participatory research that focuses on the sharing of knowledge, community, and personal experiences. This objective has substantial consequences for the ways in which the research was designed, conducted, and disseminated. Although challenging, we attempted to take steps to address limitations of earlier research conducted with people with refugee backgrounds by focusing on cultural sensitivity.

We first organized a cultural advisory board that included people with Syrian heritage or who held expertise in interacting with Syrian youth in the Netherlands from relevant organizations, such as asylum seeker centers, language schools, and community centers. Members of this board provided feedback on the procedures, design, and materials of the study prior to data collection; assisted with recruitment; were available during the course of data collection; and helped brainstorm participatory research activities.

Relatedly, we took care to optimize study materials by presenting them in Arabic. It is worth noting that many of the questionnaires we used in the current research were originally constructed in English and therefore have limitations that come with importing Western measures into different cultural contexts. However, we employed a translation process over several months such that a large team of people fluent in both Arabic and English worked on the materials. Specifically, four bilingual people translated questionnaires from English to Arabic. Then, four additional bilingual people translated the Arabic to English without seeing the original English materials. Finally, two additional bilingual people examined discrepancies in these translations with members of the research team and then collectively decided on the definitive Arabic translations.

As we delved further into preparing our study, we recognized that not only did we need to have cultural informants on our advisory board but also as central members of our research team. This allowed continued awareness of cultural sensitivity issues, rather then incidental feedback to materials and procedures. Additionally, having Syrian researchers on the team helped foster communication with participants during all stages of the research, including recruitment and data collection. For example, many of our participants mentioned that meeting a Syrian researcher at the data collection appointments made it easier for them to share their experiences.

Furthermore, we had originally planned to recruit primarily from asylum seeker centers across the Netherlands and therefore envisioned conducting data collection sessions with groups of participants. Yet, as we began recruitment, it soon became apparent that this was not a feasible option and thus we turned to conducting data collection appointments that were typically with one participant. At the first assessment, a pair of researchers (one of whom was Syrian), were present to explain the study procedure, help answer additional questions that participants had, and be supportive during the data collection appointment. Perhaps one unexpected byproduct of having two different researchers at the first assessment was that participants were able to interact with a researcher who shared their heritage and share hospitality with someone from a different background. For example, it was common for participants to share food or drink with the researchers during a home visit.

EMOTIONS AS A MECHANISM IN THE CONTEXT OF POSITIVE PERSONALITY CHANGE FOLLOWING ADVERSITY

In the current research, we examined the link between adversity and positive personality change in a longitudinal study, with an emphasis on everyday emotional experiences. Positive personality traits—also referred to as *character strengths*—comprise virtues that are seen as valuable for the self and society (Peterson & Seligman, 2004). These virtues are found within philosophical and religious traditions across many cultures and offer one consistent theme: they promote a greater focus on others and reduce egoistic tendencies (Tangney, 2000). In addition, they are associated with better physical health (Hill, Allemand, & Roberts, 2013) and well-being (Park, Peterson, & Seligman, 2004; Wood, Froh, & Geraghty, 2010). Scholars have identified and conceptualized important traits such as being humble, thankful, honest, and kind (Peterson & Seligman, 2004). Over the past decade, the concept of positive personality change and specifically PTG has been studied in a range of different contexts and samples (Alisic, van de Schoot, van Ginkel, & Kleber, 2008; Nolen-Hoeksema & Davis, 2004; Tedeschi & Calhoun, 2004). Recently, studies on growth and adaptation have also included individuals who seek or have refugee status (Chan, Young, & Sharif, 2016; Sleijpen et al., 2016). For example, Sleijpen and colleagues (2016) demonstrated that adolescent refugees and asylum seekers experience growth in response to multiple post-traumatic experiences and ongoing post-migration difficulties, lending support to theoretical assertions that traumatic experiences may lead to the onset of a search for meaning and a fundamental reconfiguration of a person's life goals (Tedeschi & Calhoun, 2004). It is unknown, however, whether and how these findings generalize to changes in positive personality traits such as selflessness, empathy, or humility over a longer time span. Such research is important because it helps us gain insights into pathways to character, but it also has important implications for promoting the prosperity of a group that has experienced life-changing adversity (Tennen, Affleck, Armeli, & Carney, 2000), such as young adults of Syrian origin who are resettling in the Netherlands.

Young Adulthood as a Unique Window of Opportunity for Positive Personality Growth

Young adulthood, beginning at around the age of 18 and continuing into the 30s, is a period of challenge and opportunity. Those interested in development and personality have emphasized the importance of this period, illustrating the challenges that young adults face and the adaptations that follow (Arnett, 2011). Becoming an adult requires a questioning of one's identity (Kroger, Martinussen, & Marcia, 2010) and a reformulation of conceptions and evaluations of oneself (Bleidorn, 2015; Chung et al., 2014). Moreover, as young adults settle into new relationships and roles, their personalities may also change (Bleidorn, 2015). Finally, studies suggest that change can occur not only in response to normative life transitions, but also in response to major idiosyncratic life events (Caspi & Roberts, 2001) including adversity (Laceulle, Nederhof, Karreman, Ormel, & van Aken, 2012; Laceulle, van Aken, Ormel, & Nederhof, 2015; Shiner, Allen, & Masten, 2017). These findings suggest that early adulthood may be of special importance when examining positive personality change in people with refugee backgrounds. The normative challenges typical for these years and the unique experiences that individuals may encounter in the context of seeking refugee status may accumulate and collectively have a profound impact on an individual's development. Moreover, the extent to which young adults with refugee backgrounds experience positive personality change following adversity may set the stage for their future adult life in terms of social, professional, and personal life outcomes. As such, young adulthood can be considered a unique and important developmental window through which to study positive personality change in people who seek or have refugee status.

Emotions as a Mechanism in Young Adult Positive Personality Change

We propose that one understudied but important pathway from adversity to positive personality is through emotions. Emotions are "acute, intense, and typically brief psychophysiological changes that result from a response to a meaningful situation in one's environment" (Rosenberg, 1998). Emotions are multifaceted states, consisting of cognitive appraisals, physiological arousal, expressive behaviors, action tendencies, and phenomenology (Izard, 2010). They focus our attention and provide information that helps us reach personal goals (Keltner & Haidt, 1999).

Emotions are integral to the self (Kristjánsson, 2010) and can promote positive personality traits (Starkey, 2015), but empirical studies of the relation between them are rare. Research on emotion dispositions provides some indirect evidence for a relationship between the two. While emotions are states, *emotion dispositions* represent the tendency and frequency with which individuals typically experience a particular emotional state (Schriber, Chung, Sorensen, & Robins, 2017). For instance, dispositional compassion is associated with selflessness, and dispositional awe with humility (Cohen, Panter, & Turan, 2012; Stellar et al., 2017). Some emotion dispositions appear to be closely linked to factors important for PTG. For example, someone who has experienced growth after adversity is also likely to be high in dispositional compassion (Lim & DeSteno, 2016), and someone who shows a great appreciation for life is also likely to be high in dispositional gratitude (Wood, Maltby, Steward, & Joseph, 2008). Research that examines emotions in daily life (Smith, Ryan, Queen, Becker, & Gonzalez, 2014; Trampe, Quoidbach, & Taquet, 2015) suggests that investigating emotions as they naturally unfold, especially following (adverse) turning points in one's life, is a particularly compelling approach to understanding positive personality growth.

Additionally, emotions appear to be central to PTG. For example, Tedeschi and Calhoun (2004) put forward that "the psychological processing of the crisis events has a highly emotional element connected to it. What makes these experiences transformative seems to be that they have this affective component, so that the lessons learned are not merely intellectual reflections." Young adults who seek or have refugee status recount experiences that are laden with emotion in response to the hardships they have faced (United Nations High Commissioner for Refugees, 2017). Some recall feelings of anger for being forced to flee their homelands, guilt for surviving violence, sadness for having to let go of dreams for the future, or boredom from waiting for the next chapter of their life to begin (Lerner & Callina, 2014). Others recollect feelings of pride for self-improvement, determination to connect with others, gratitude for the aid they have received in their new communities, or awe toward a higher power for finding safety amid adverse surroundings (United Nations High Commissioner for Refugees, 2017). If the accumulation of emotion in one's life can result in positive personality change, and vice versa, it is worthwhile to examine how everyday experiences of emotions can shed light on the development and maintenance of positive personality traits.

We think that emotions may influence the formation and maintenance of positive personality traits following adversity in two ways. First, emotions likely prevent *axiological entropy*, when what we value loses importance over time (Starkey, 2015). Specifically, emotions highlight ideas and matters that we care about. For example, experiencing repeated instances of anger and compassion after witnessing a string of social injustices can inspire a person to protest for justice and provide aid to those in need. Enacting such behaviors could influence one's character development, and, without emotions to reinforce what we value by keeping them vivid in our minds, their importance would diminish, weakening character strengths. Second, it is also likely that possessing a specific character strength influences one's emotional repertoire, or set of emotional experiences. For example, someone who is high in the character strength of humility might have more frequent experiences of awe, gratitude, and guilt, but rarely experience emotions like contempt. Finally, processes or stages of emotional experiences over time may be of particular relevance for positive personality change in people with a refugee background. That is, it is likely that the cultural values, norms, and traditions people have adopted in their home country are challenged when confronted with substantially different values, norms, and traditions in the new country they are settling in. Discrepancies may contribute to the experience of emotions such as guilt, regret, loss of faith, anger, and sadness. Over time, however, this may trigger development of new beliefs and values reflective of what is most important for the person and, as such, cause positive personality change. Thus, in the current research, we explored the idea of emotional character—that the range of emotions we experience in everyday life, and the occasions in which they arise shape our interpretations of the world around us, and how they are connected to our positive personality traits.

KARAKTER IS A FIRST STEP, BUT MORE LONGITUDINAL RESEARCH IS NEEDED

The current research yields important outcomes that can guide future work in multiple ways. First, by taking a developmental perspective and using a longitudinal research design, this research will provide a better understanding of positive personality change following major, life-changing events. Moreover, the current project sheds light on how personality may develop following adversity from different time perspectives and using multiple methodologies. Furthermore, by assessing behavioral manifestations of character using the EAR, we can explore how personality change extends beyond self-perceptions and whether or not it manifests in actual behavior. With regard to the conceptualization and operationalization of adversity, while we are limited to retrospective assessments of adversity prior to arriving in the Netherlands, the design enables assessments of the post-flight adversity that people experience that occur between assessment instances. Given the substantial effects of post-migration difficulties on development and adjustment found in previous research and the individual differences in adverse experiences prior and during people's flight to the Netherlands, diverging trajectories of development can be expected. Moreover, the current focus on individual differences and processes is important for understanding recovery and growth. Future studies may extend this approach by examining development for an even longer period of time. One idea is to start with short, basic assessments after people's arrival in the Netherlands and expand with more detailed assessments over multiple years to shed light on longer term development as people settle in and progress personally, socially, and professionally. Moreover, larger scale studies might also include important others such as partners, children, extended family, or friends. For example, about 50% of all refugees are children (Abbara et al., 2016; United Nations High Commissioner for Refugees, 2017); in our sample, several participants were living with their partner and one or more children. Taking into account people's social networks more explicitly could help to further disentangle factors contributing to long-term positive personality change.

Second, the current project provides insights on the personal growth of young adults of Syrian origin who seek or have refugee status in the Netherlands. As the number of individuals who seek or have refugee status increases, it is necessary to advance our understanding of adaptation and growth following exposure to trauma and daily stress. Many of our participants expressed appreciation for the current study's focus on positive factors and cited it as a reason for participating. One suggestion that our participants had was to include educational and career outcomes in future studies. In addition, the current project may guide future work that will yield a better understanding of individuals who will become part of the social and economic fabric of their host societies, and such work has the potential of creating and changing interventions and policy for those who have faced major adversity in their lives.

Finally, Karakter can provide a model for future research that aims to integrate scientific goals with societal objectives. This is in line with earlier work by Ellis and colleagues, for example, on building community resilience (2015, 2016, 2017). As described earlier, the current project attempted to incorporate participatory research, albeit in the later stages. For example, our team collaborated to create newsletters to distribute to all participants. These newsletters included updates about the study as well as information about relevant organizations that may be of interest for the participants (see Figure 6.1). Also, we developed an experience survey asking participants to tell us what their experiences were like while participating in the study and how participating might have affected them. Finally, participatory research activities were organized, including an e-book, seminar series, and an end-of-project community event. Specifically, the electronic book is meant to give our participants a creative opportunity to share their visual, musical, and literary work with different communities, including Syrian, Dutch, and international audiences. The seminar series is designed to give our participants a chance to learn more about topics in psychology in a university setting and to receive a certificate of participation. The end-of-project community event is meant to allow us to discuss findings from the study with participants and the community and also celebrate with food and music. Taken together, Karakter contributes to research by taking a collaborative approach that involves co-creation between academics, newcomers, and bridge-builders (e.g., Syrian researchers, cultural brokers). This may have several advantages, including attending to a human rights focus by giving the participants of the research a say in what is studied, which may lead to deeper insights because the quality of the research is likely to be higher. Future research could take this further and explore additional ways to conduct

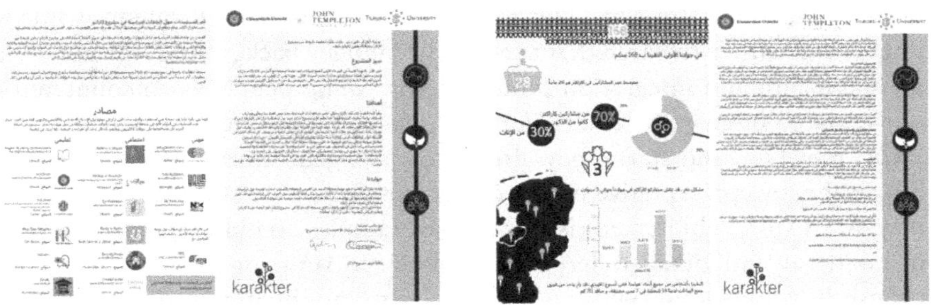

Figure 6.1 Examples of two newsletters that were sent to participants.

participatory research, particularly in the earlier stages of research. For example, researchers may decide on relevant research topics together with Syrian young adults. Also, future projects may invest in collaboration with policy-makers and practitioners to increase the societal impact of the research.

CONCLUSION

In summary, Karakter sheds light on pathways to character and positive personality change in the aftermath of adversity by placing an emphasis on emotions in everyday life. Karakter also joins a growing body of research focusing on positive personality development, and, in doing so, the current project advances representations of Syrian people in the Netherlands. This approach also brings us closer to examining the "whole person," which is an important objective for personality psychologists (McAdams, 2013). Moreover, obtaining a glimpse of the lives of Syrian-origin young adults over 13 months as they settle into the Netherlands allows us to explore and document what is associated with changes in positive personality over time. Critically, the current project required a participatory research component. Continued efforts for co-creation by team members were needed to understand similarities and differences in language, culture, and daily practices. This knowledge, in turn, was used to inform each part of the research process. Specifically, co-creation had an impact on the instruments, procedures, communication with participants, interpretation of our research findings, and dissemination of results.

Our efforts to take a culturally sensitive approach and attempts to conduct the study with co-creation in mind enabled us to better connect with our participants. By doing so, we were reminded of how different people can be and how important it is to take individual differences into account when conducting research. For example, the narratives we asked participants to construct in relation to leaving Syria and then resettling in the Netherlands seem to indicate variability in how people experienced this event. Although these data are to be coded and analyzed, the example in Box 6.1 suggests that a part of the young adult Syrian population in the Netherlands may see their experiences differently. Interestingly, events related to settling in the Netherlands (e.g., concerns about people left in Syria, housing, professional development, etc.) may be relatively more of a cause of stress and concern than the actual flight. Relatedly, while we know from earlier research that people with refugee backgrounds are at risk for mental health and integration problems, the young people we encountered in our research often expressed to our research team how motivated they were to settle, move on, and start a new life. Of course, generalizability is constrained due to the unrepresentative nature of our sample, and caution is needed not to play down vulnerability and risk, but these examples do indicate the importance of taking an individual differences approach to studying positive personality change in young adults with a refugee background. By doing so, we will better understand the developmental trajectories and specific needs of individual

Syrian-origin young adults who have recently resettled in the Netherlands as they continue to grow and build communities.

REFERENCES

Abbara, A., Coutts, A., Fouad, F. M., Ismail, S. A., Orcutt, M., & the Syria Public Health Network. (2016). Mental health among displaced Syrians: Findings from the Syria Public Health Network. *Journal of the Royal Society of Medicine, 109*(3), 88–90. doi:10.1177/ 0141076816629765

Alisic, E., Van der Schoot, T., van Ginkel, J. R., & Kleber, R. J. (2008). Looking beyond posttraumatic stress disorder in children: Posttraumatic stress reactions, posttraumatic growth, and quality of life in a general population sample. *Journal of Clinical Psychiatry, 69*, 1455–1461.

Arnett, J. J. (2011). *Debating Emerging Adulthood: Stage or Process?* New York: Oxford University Press.

Brugha, D. (2004). Migration and mental health. *Acta Psychiatrica Scandinavica, 109*(4), 243–258.

Bhugra, D., & Becker, M. A. (2005). Migration, cultural bereavement and cultural identity. *World Psychiatry, 4*(1), 18.

Bleidorn, W. (2015). What accounts for personality maturation in early adulthood? *Current Directions in Psychological Science, 24*(3), 245–252.

Caspi, A., & Roberts, B. W. (2001). Personality development across the life course: The argument for change and continuity. *Psychological Inquiry, 12*(2), 49–66.

Chan, K. J., Young, M. Y., & Sharif, N. (2016). Well-being after trauma: A review of posttraumatic growth among refugees. *Canadian Psychology/Psychologie Canadienne, 57*(4), 291–299.

Chung, J. M., Robins, R. W., Trzesniewski, K. H., Noftle, E. E., Roberts, B. W., & Widaman, K. F. (2014). Continuity and change in self-esteem during emerging adulthood. *Journal of Personality and Social Psychology, 106*(3), 469–483.

Cohen, T. R., Panter, A. T., & Turan, N. (2012). Guilt proneness and moral character. *Current Directions in Psychological Science, 21*(5), 355–359.

Ellis, B. H., Abdi, S. M., Horgan, J., Miller, A. B., Saxe, G. N., & Blood, E. (2015). Trauma and openness to legal and illegal activism among Somali refugees. *Terrorism and Political Violence, 27*(5), 857–883.

Ellis, B. H., Abdi, S. M., Lazarevic, V., White, M. T., Lincoln, A. K., Stern, J. E., & Horgan, J. G. (2016). Relation of psychosocial factors to diverse behaviors and attitudes among Somali refugees. *American Journal of Orthopsychiatry, 86*(4), 393.

Ellis, B. H., & Abdi, S. (2017). Building community resilience to violent extremism through genuine partnerships. *American Psychologist, 72*(3), 289.

Eurostat. (2017). *Your key to European* Statistics. http://ec.europa.eu/eurostat

Fazel, M., Wheeler, J., & Danesh, J. (2005). Prevalence of serious mental disorder in 7000 refugees resettled in western countries: A systematic review. *Lancet, 365*(9467), 1309–1314.

Hill, P. L., Allemand, M., & Roberts, B. W. (2013). Examining the pathways between gratitude and self-rated physical health across adulthood. *Personality and Individual Differences, 54*(1), 92–96.

Izard, C. E. (2010). The many meanings/aspects of emotion: Definitions, functions, activation, and regulation. *Emotion Review, 2*(4), 363–370.

Jayawickreme, E., & Blackie, L. E. (2014). Post-traumatic growth as positive personality change: Evidence, controversies and future directions. *European Journal of Personality, 28*(4), 312–331.

Joseph, S., & Linley, P. A. (Eds.). (2008). *Trauma, Recovery, and Growth: Positive Psychological Perspectives on Posttraumatic Stress*. New York: John Wiley & Sons.

Kehoe, S. K., Alisic, E., & Heilinger, J. C. (Eds.). (2019). *Responsibility for Refugee and Migrant Integration*. Berlin: De Gruyter

Keltner, D., & Haidt, J. (1999). Social functions of emotions at four levels of analysis. *Cognition & Emotion, 13*(5), 505–521.

Kingsley, P. (2016). *The New Odyssey: The Story of Europe's Refugee Crisis*. London: Guardian Faber Publishing.

Kristjánsson, K. (2010). *The Self and Its Emotions*. Cambridge: Cambridge University Press.

Kroger, J., Martinussen, M., & Marcia, J. E. (2010). Identity status change during adolescence and young adulthood: A meta-analysis. *Journal of Adolescence, 33*(5), 683–698.

Laceulle, O. M., Nederhof, E., Karreman, A., Ormel, J., & Aken, M. A. G. (2012). Stressful events and temperament change during early and middle adolescence: The TRAILS study. *European Journal of Personality, 26*(3), 276–284.

Laceulle, O. M., van Aken, M. A., Ormel, J., & Nederhof, E. (2015). Stress-sensitivity and reciprocal associations between stressful events and adolescent temperament. *Personality and Individual Differences, 81*, 76–83.

Lerner, R. M., Callina, K. S. (2014). The study of character development: Towards tests of a relational developmental systems model. *Human Development, 57*, 322–346

Lim, D., & DeSteno, D. (2016). Suffering and compassion: The links among adverse life experiences, empathy, compassion, and prosocial behavior. *Emotion, 16*(2), 175.

McAdams, D. P. (2013). Personality psychology. In A. L. C. Runehov & L. Oviedo (Eds.), *Encyclopedia of Sciences and Religions* (pp. 1634–1641). Dordrecht: Springer.

McAdams, D. P., & McLean, K. C. (2013). Narrative identity. *Current Directions in Psychological Science, 22*(3), 233–238.

Mehl, M. R. (2017). The Electronically Activated Recorder (EAR): A method for the naturalistic observation of daily social behavior. *Current Directions in Psychological Science, 26*(2), 184–190. doi:10.1177/0963721416680611

Miller, K. E., & Rasmussen, A. (2010). War exposure, daily stressors, and mental health in conflict and post-conflict settings: Bridging the divide between trauma-focused and psychosocial frameworks. *Social Science & Medicine, 70*(1), 7–16.

Miller, K. E., Weine, S. M., Ramic, A., Brkic, N., Bjedic, Z. D., Smajkic, A., . . . Worthington, G. (2002). The relative contribution of war experiences and exile-related stressors to levels of psychological distress among Bosnian refugees. *Journal of Traumatic Stress, 15*(5), 377–387.

Nolen-Hoeksema, S., & Davis, C. G. (2004). Theoretical and methodological issues in the assessment and interpretation of posttraumatic growth. *Psychological Inquiry, 15*(1), 60–64.

Park, N., Peterson, C., & Seligman, M. E. (2004). Strengths of character and well-being. *Journal of Social and Clinical Psychology, 23*(5), 603–619.

Peterson, C., & Seligman, M. E. (2004). *Character Strengths and Virtues: A Handbook and Classification* (Vol. 1). New York: Oxford University Press

Porter, M., & Haslam, N. (2005). Predisplacement and postdisplacement factors associated with mental health of refugees and internally displaced persons: A meta-analysis. *JAMA, 294*(5), 602–612.

Rosenberg, E. L. (1998). *Levels of Analysis and the Organization of Affect* (Vol. 2, No. 3). Washington, DC: Educational Publishing Foundation.

Schick, M., Zumwald, A., Knöpfli, B., Nickerson, A., Bryant, R. A., Schnyder, U., . . . Morina, N. (2016). Challenging future, challenging past: The relationship of social integration and psychological impairment in traumatized refugees. *European Journal of Psychotraumatology, 7*(1), 28057.

Shiner, R. L., Allen, T. A., & Masten, A. S. (2017). Adversity in adolescence predicts personality trait change from childhood to adulthood. *Journal of Research in Personality, 67*, 171–182.

Silove, D., Sinnerbrink, I., Field, A., Manicavasagar, V., & Steel, Z. (1997). Anxiety, depression and PTSD in asylum-seekers: Associations with pre-migration trauma and post-migration stressors. *British Journal of Psychiatry, 170*(4), 351–357.

Sleijpen, M., Haagen, J., Mooren, T., & Kleber, R. J. (2016). Growing from experience: An exploratory study of posttraumatic growth in adolescent refugees. *European Journal of Psychotraumatology, 7*(1), 28698.

Schriber, R. A., Chung, J. M., Sorensen, K. S., & Robins, R. W. (2017). Dispositional contempt: A first look at the contemptuous person. *Journal of Personality and Social Psychology, 113*(2), 280–309.

Schweitzer, R., Melville, F., Steel, Z., & Lacherez, P. (2006). Trauma, post-migration living difficulties, and social support as predictors of psychological adjustment in resettled Sudanese refugees. *Australian & New Zealand Journal of Psychiatry, 40*(2), 179–187.

Sempertegui, G. A., Knipscheer, J. W., & Bekker, M. H. (2018). Development and evaluation of diversity-oriented competence training for the treatment of depressive disorders. *Transcultural Psychiatry, 55*(1), 31–54.

Smith, J., Ryan, L. H., Queen, T. L., Becker, S., & Gonzalez, R. (2014). Snapshots of mixtures of affective experiences in a day: Findings from the Health and Retirement Study. *Journal of Population Ageing, 7*(1), 55–79

Starkey, C. (2015). Emotion and character. In C. B. Miller, R. M. Furr, A. Knobel, W. Fleeson, C. B. Miller, R. M. Furr, . . . W. Fleeson (Eds.), *Character: New Directions from Philosophy, Psychology, and Theology* (pp. 192–211). New York: Oxford University Press.

Stellar, J. E., Gordon, A. M., Piff, P. K., Cordaro, D., Anderson, C. L., Bai, Y., . . . Keltner, D. (2017). Self-transcendent emotions and their social functions: Compassion, gratitude, and awe bind us to others through prosociality. *Emotion Review, 9*(3), 200–207.

Statistics Netherlands. (2017). Centraal Bureau voor de Statistiek. https://www.cbs.nl/en-gb

Tangney, J. P. (2000). Humility: Theoretical perspectives, empirical findings and directions for future research. *Journal of Social and Clinical Psychology, 19*(1), 70–82.

Tedeschi, R. G., & Calhoun, L. G. (2004). Posttraumatic growth: Conceptual foundations and empirical evidence. *Psychological Inquiry, 15*(1), 1–18.

Tennen, H., Affleck, G., Armeli, S., & Carney, M. A. (2000). A daily process approach to coping: Linking theory, research, and practice. *American Psychologist, 55*(6), 626–636.

Trampe, D., Quoidbach, J., & Taquet, M. (2015). Emotions in everyday life. *PloS One, 10*(12), e0145450.

United Nations High Commissioner for Refugees. (2017). Europe. http://www.unhcr.org/pages/4a02d9346.html

Wood, A. M., Froh, J. J., & Geraghty, A. W. (2010). Gratitude and well-being: A review and theoretical integration. *Clinical Psychology Review, 30*(7), 890–905.

Wood, A. M., Maltby, J., Stewart, N., & Joseph, S. (2008). Conceptualizing gratitude and appreciation as a unitary personality trait. *Personality and Individual Differences, 44*(3), 621–632.

7

Post-Traumatic Growth in Later Adulthood

Disentangling Shorter and Longer Term Changes Following Transitions into Senior Housing Facilities

GLORIA LUONG, J. DOUG COATSWORTH, AND SY-MIIN CHOW

Character virtues (CVs), such as altruism, humility, gratitude, relatedness, empathy, spirituality, and open-mindedness, show relative stability similar to personality traits and have been linked to a meaningful life and adaptive psychosocial functioning, including affective well-being, life satisfaction, and greater social support and integration (e.g., Aghababaei, Mohammadtabar, & Saffarinia, 2014; Ciarrocchi & Deneke, 2005; Post, 2005; Shimai, Otake, Park, Peterson, & Seligman, 2006). Thus, in recent decades, there has been a growing interest in understanding how CVs may show positive development, particularly in the face of adversity (Hamby, Grych, & Banyard, 2018). Some research suggests that unexpected benefits can arise from adverse events. People report, for example, experiencing personal growth, a deeper appreciation for life, and a reprioritization of life goals following traumatic or stressful experiences (e.g., post-traumatic growth [PTG]; Tedeschi & Calhoun, 2004). These findings suggest that CVs may grow following adversity, even during adulthood and into later life. Yet it is still unclear which CVs may change (and in which direction) following adversity and how and why such changes are possible (i.e., mechanisms of change).

This chapter illustrates how an exemplary research study, the Relocation and Transitional Experiences (RELATE) project, leverages a multimethod multi-time scale design with community participatory research to address these open questions and understand how these processes may change on shorter or longer term time intervals. We demonstrate how the RELATE project uses design and quantitative methods that allow us to better understand the prospective longitudinal patterns of PTG of psychological states and traits. Moreover, our work engages with community partners to collect more ecologically valid data to understand how older adults may navigate the transition to senior housing facilities.

LIMITATIONS OF PREVIOUS RESEARCH ON POST-TRAUMATIC GROWTH AND PERSONALITY CHANGE

To better appreciate how our RELATE project builds on the scientific literature to address previously unanswered questions, it is important to understand the methodological approaches and limitations of past studies. In particular, this literature includes a number of limitations and inconclusive results, in part because previous research (1) has relied heavily on retrospective self-reports and (2) in the few existing longitudinal studies, assessments were rarely prospective and included assessments spaced widely apart, such that they may not have had the temporal specificity to capture shorter term changes that are observed in daily behaviors rather than in more stable or longer term trait changes (see reviews by Cohen, Hettler, & Pane, 1998; Jayawickreme & Blackie, 2014; Park & Lechner, 2006). Finally, past research has been generally descriptive of changes but has not focused on mechanisms or underlying processes that may explain *why* changes in CVs may occur following adversity. Each of these issues will be discussed in turn, and we will explain how the RELATE study addresses these problems.

Retrospective Self-Reports

One of the most common methods to assess PTG has been to ask people to reflect back on how they believe they have changed for the better after experiencing an adverse, stressful, or challenging experience (Jayawickreme & Blackie, 2014). This work has often relied on self-report measures that cue participants to think about ways that they may have improved or grown with the experience, even if they may not have grown or may have even exhibited declines following the stressor. These types of retrospective reports appear to have greater demand characteristics that cue participants to provide socially desirable responses. For example, participants may be more inclined to report PTG with these measures because they believe this is what researchers want them to report. Additionally, with respect to retrospective self-reports of change, it is known that such tasks require some level of introspection, and there are individual differences in the ability to introspect about internal states and the changes therein (Nisbett & Wilson, 1977). Not all people will be able to make these types of complex judgments accurately. Moreover, human memory is subject to distortions and reconstructions over time, which often serve in the interest of helping people recall and create schemas of themselves as good, self-efficacious people who are constantly improving (e.g.,

Walker, Skowronski, & Thompson, 2003). With greater time elapsed since the events have occurred, recall biases can set in, and people may reconstruct self-enhancing memories without consciously or deliberately trying to do so (e.g., Luong, Arredondo, & Charles, 2020; Luong, Charles, Rook, Reynolds, & Gatz, 2015; Ptacek, Smith, Espe, & Raffety, 1994; Thomas & Diener, 1990).

Cross-Sectional Assessments

Methodological and statistical advances have allowed for the modeling of complex change trajectories, but if assessments only occur once (cross-sectionally), it is difficult, if not impossible, to infer changes in personality and CVs over time, especially if it is hypothesized that trajectories before and after a major life event would be different. It may also be the case that change may occur on multiple time scales, with short-term fluctuations (e.g., over minutes, hours, and days) embedded within longer term changes of CVs (e.g., over weeks, months, or even years; Helm, Ram, Cole, & Chow, 2016). Yet much of the research in this literature has primarily taken assessments of a single report of PTG and inferred changes because people have reported that they believed they changed (Jayawickreme & Blackie, 2014). In these study designs, *actual* change is not assessed, only perceptions of change. Thus, given the limitations of prior studies, it is unknown how and to what extent CVs may change following a major life event.

Mechanisms

Related to the preceding discussions, it is important to not only document what changes in CVs are occurring, but also how and why they occur following a major life event. That is, are there concomitant changes in related psychological processes (e.g., in appraisals of the stressor, mindsets, or daily behaviors) that facilitate change over longer time periods? More research is needed to uncover these mechanisms, which will allow us to better understand how to develop prevention and intervention programs that may promote positive change in CVs, especially for vulnerable populations coping with major life stressors.

THE RELOCATION AND TRANSITIONAL EXPERIENCES (RELATE) PROJECT

Background and Rationale for the Study

The RELATE project addresses the limitations of previous studies on PTG and personality changes following life stressors in a number of ways. First, multimethod, prospective, longitudinal studies are necessary to track CVs before and after adverse events occur to be able to examine associated changes in CVs. The RELATE study builds on previous research by strategically selecting theoretically relevant study populations and adverse events. First, with respect to the study population, we chose to study older adults because this is one of the fastest growing segments of the US and world population (Pruchno, 2012). Thus, as individuals live longer lives and need to learn to adapt to functional limitations and situational constraints (e.g., relocation to assisted living), there is a need to understand whether CVs and adaptive psychological processes may continue to change in positive directions and how they might contribute to adaptation during this life phase (e.g., Infurna, Gerstorf, & Zarit, 2013). Second, although plasticity (the capacity for change) decreases in very late life, studies have demonstrated that this capacity still exists and is malleable into later adulthood (Kliegl, Smith, & Baltes, 1989; Yang, Krampe, & Baltes, 2006). Thus, as a proof of concept, demonstrating that positive CV changes are possible among older adults undergoing a major life stressor should extrapolate to relatively younger (adult) populations, given the greater plasticity, personal control, and flexibility of their social and personal environments (Infurna, Gerstorf, Ram, Schupp, & Wagner, 2011; Luong, Charles, & Fingerman, 2011; Roisman, Masten, Coatsworth, & Tellegen, 2004).

Additionally, with respect to the adverse event, we chose to examine transitions into a senior housing facility (e.g., independent living, assisted living, skilled nursing) because this is a major life stressor common in later adulthood (Hawes, Phillips, Holan, Sherman, & Hutchison, 2005). This event has a clearly defined onset, unlike other life events (e.g., living with a disability that may have progressed over the course of years before the participant was enrolled in the study) or daily stressors (which may underlie chronic stressors, such as marital discord). Moreover, this stressor has been linked to negative psychosocial functioning, such as lower life satisfaction, depressive symptoms, and anxiety (Cummings, 2002; Watson et al., 2003). Yet there is also great heterogeneity in how people respond to this transition, which will allow us to explore individual differences that influence the course of CV changes.

Finally, we propose that CV changes may occur on multiple time scales. Many previous studies have focused on global, trait-like changes that unfold over several months or years. Yet psychological processes are known to show great intraindividual variability (within-person variability) and short-term changes (Fleeson & Jayawickreme, 2015; Smyth & Heron, 2014). Thus, it is possible that previous studies were inconclusive about whether CV changes are possible because they were not optimally designed to capture more short-term, dynamic changes in CV-relevant behaviors (e.g., Hofmann, Wisneski, Brandt, & Skitka, 2014). For example, it is possible that participants' self-perceptions of CV (e.g., trait gratitude) may show mean-level changes over longer time periods, but, in daily life, participants may exhibit greater changes in state CV, such as expressing and experiencing gratitude. We therefore assess CV at two levels: as global traits (what a person's CVs are like, on average across weeks or months) and as states (manifest as daily behaviors and mental states). Moreover, this research allows us to examine how intraindividual variability (e.g., short-term fluctuations in CV around one's own mean) may predict different types of changes in short- versus longer term CV. Recent work suggests that it is important to consider state–trait interactions and how short-term changes may predict longer term CV changes (Jayawickreme, Meindl, Helzer, Furr, & Fleeson, 2014; Noftle & Fleeson, 2015; Ram & Diehl, 2015)—possibilities that we test in the RELATE study.

RELATE Study Methodology

Participants

Data collection is ongoing and planned through the end of 2020. To date, a total of 201 participants have completed study procedures or are scheduled to complete the study procedures by the end of the study timeline. Participants are recruited from northern Colorado and the surrounding regions from our collaborations with senior housing facilities in the area, including independent living, assistant living, and skilled nursing care facilities. People who are on the waitlist to move to a senior housing facility or who express interest in moving into a senior housing facility (e.g., such as by taking a tour at a facility or paying a deposit) are given a study information flyer and encouraged to participate in our studies. Advertisements and study flyers are also used to recruit participants to our studies.

Overview of Study Procedures

The study uses a prospective longitudinal measurement burst design to examine CVs and personality prior to the major life event (move into senior housing) and at subsequent time points following the transition. The study consists of four "bursts" (i.e., study waves) of intensive data collection, including general questionnaires, health and cognitive assessments, and daily life surveys. Bursts will occur 2 weeks prior to the transition to senior housing, as well as 2 weeks, 1.5 months, and 3 months after the transition to senior housing (see Figure 7.1). During each burst, participants will complete global assessments via

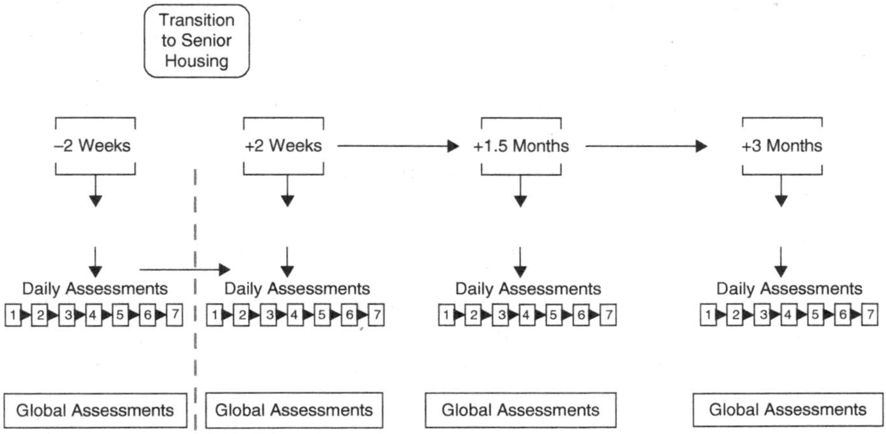

Figure 7.1 Overview of RELATE study procedures.

paper-and-pencil questionnaires and 7 days of ecological momentary assessments (EMA) surveys via mobile smartphones.

Study Procedures: Four Bursts of Global and Daily Life Assessments

After participants have been screened for eligibility criteria (free of dementia using the Mini Mental Status Exam [MMSE] tool, at least 55 years of age, and planning to move into a senior housing facility), they attend an information session to provide informed consent and receive detailed information on the study procedures.

Burst 1 Global Assessments. At the baseline information session (2 weeks before the transition to senior housing), participants are loaned mobile smartphones and instructed on how to use them to answer the EMA surveys regarding CV behaviors and mental states in daily life. In addition, participants are loaned a wrist-worn actigraph, which will passively and unobtrusively monitor and record their physical activity and sleep–wake cycles. During each burst, participants complete global (trait) assessments via paper-and-pencil questionnaires, followed by 7 days of EMA via mobile phones. The global questionnaires assess participants' demographic background, health and well-being, personality, stress and coping, and trait CVs using validated scales (i.e., altruism/prosociality, empathy, relatedness, open-mindedness, and gratitude).

Burst 1 EMA Surveys. EMA surveys are administered six times each day for 7 days during participants' reported waking hours. The surveys are programmed to occur no less than 30 minutes apart and no more than 3 hours apart to allow for appropriate experience sampling across the day. Participants, however, are not able to predict when the EMA surveys will occur, which allows us to randomly sample participants' daily experiences. The EMA surveys involve modified versions of the trait CV measures to assess the extent to which participants are engaging in these behaviors and mindsets at the time of the survey, such as performing a kind act for somebody (altruism) and how much gratitude, relatedness, and empathy they feel. They are also asked about other contextual information (e.g., whether a stressor had occurred, what activities they are currently doing) to better understand how context shapes CV behaviors in daily life. Following the 7-day EMA period, participants return the phones and equipment. Participants are scheduled for the next EMA burst and lab or in-home visit and provide updated contact information as needed (e.g., new mailing address, phone numbers). Participants receive regular appointment reminders to reduce attrition between bursts.

Bursts 2-4 Global and EMA Surveys. The same protocol is repeated for Bursts 2 through 4. To capture theoretically meaningful longitudinal changes that can be measured within the project timeframe, we chose to do follow-up assessments 2 weeks after the transition for immediate and short-term changes (Burst 2), 1.5 months (Burst 3), and 3 months (Burst 4) for assessments of relatively longer term changes. The same global and EMA assessments are administered at each time point, which allows us to test for changes in both daily CV behaviors and mindsets, as well as CV traits.

Debriefing and compensation. After the fourth burst of global and daily assessments, participants are debriefed and compensated. The compensation schedule is scaled such that each subsequent burst of assessments is worth more, and participants are given their compensation at the end of the study to increase study compliance and reduce attrition (e.g., Harari et al., 2017).

Leveraging Multiple Time Scales Data to Understand Processes of Change in Character Virtues

Myriad theories exist in the extant literature on underlying mechanisms of change associated with CVs and their implications for design and delivery of interventions. Several interpersonal theories (De Vries et al., 2017; Ryan, 2009) also underscore the importance of considering within-person changes within the context of social support, social networks, and interpersonal stressors. Integrating these longitudinal and interdisciplinary perspectives, a thorough understanding of life span–related changes in CV requires examination of (1) individuals as multilevel systems with several interrelated—intraindividual and interpersonal (e.g., partner, friend, family)—units of analysis; (2) the ways in which time- and person-specific factors may affect and interact with each other in multiple feedback loops to affect proximal outcomes; and (3) the reciprocal relations among the multiple momentary changes, proximal outcomes, and distal outcomes that unfold across multiple time scales to affect state- and trait-based differences in CVs.

To elucidate some of the distinctions between state- and trait-based differences, it is helpful to consider some of the concepts and methodologies rooted within a dynamical systems framework. A dynamical system is, broadly speaking, a system of variables that show some regularity in how they evolve over time (Chow, 2019; Scheinerman, 1996). Dynamical systems modeling tools are unique in that they place at the forefront the importance of examining the change mechanism that dictates *in what ways* the system has changed and any regularity and heterogeneity therein.

One possible mechanism for modeling the recurrence in a system's dynamics over time is through *differential equation* (DE) modeling. DE modeling has been widely employed as a modeling tool across multiple scientific disciplines before the advent of dynamical systems analytic approaches. As a class, DE models provide a framework for using derivatives (elaborated later) to describe *how* individuals are changing continuously over time. In practice, these models are particularly useful for the study of continuous processes that are observed at regular intervals (e.g., panel and observational studies), or intermittently.

Given repeated observations of a continuous process, $y_i(t)$, for unit (e.g., person) i ($i = 1, \ldots n$) at times $t = 0, \ldots T$, the first derivative (rate of change) of y at any arbitrary time point is the change in y that occurs within a (infinitely) small window of time, a. Formally,

$$\frac{dy_i(t)}{dt} = \lim_{a \to 0} \frac{y_i(t+a) - y_i(t)}{a}$$

The notation "(t)" is a continuous index of time that may take on any real value. A positive value of derivative $\frac{dy_i(t)}{dt}$ reflects an instantaneous increase or growth in the value of $y_i(t)$ at that particular moment; a negative value of $\frac{dy_i(t)}{dt}$ indicates an instantaneous decline. If $\frac{dy_i(t)}{dt} = 0$, then $y_i(t)$ is said to be "static" or manifest no change at that particular moment. Generally, fixed points for any dynamical system are values of the dependent variables for which the rates of change for all its constituent dependent variables, including derivative variables, are all equal to zero.

In a similar vein, the second derivative is the change in the rate of change of y:

$$\frac{d^2 y_i(t)}{dt^2} = \lim_{a \to 0} \frac{\left[\frac{y_i(t+a) - y_i(t)}{a}\right] - \left[\frac{y_i(t) - y_i(t-a)}{a}\right]}{a}$$
$$= \lim_{a \to 0} \frac{y_i(t+a) - 2y_i(t) + y_i(t-a)}{a^2}$$

where this change in instantaneous growth or decline may be conceptualized as the curvature in $y_i(t)$. Higher positive values of $\frac{d^2 y_i(t)}{dt^2}$ signify greater or more precipitous growth or decline in the level of $y_i(t)$, much like acceleration occurs when a car travels successively greater distances at close intervals; negative values of $\frac{d^2 y_i(t)}{dt^2}$ indicate reductions in growth or decline, much like deceleration in a car as travels decreasing distances. Other higher-order derivatives then capture further changes in these change qualities. All of the variables that determine the current values of a system, including level and derivative variables, constitute the *state space* of the dynamical system.

In the context of CVs, suppose an individual is expecting to move in 3 months out of a permanent home with a lifetime partner and into an assisted care facility. It is possible that the individual's anxiety level would increase (i.e., showing positive instantaneous rates of change), coupled with some decreases (negative instantaneous rates of change) in feelings of gratitude, empathy, and relatedness to the partner. Assuming that these changes are assessed on a weekly basis, the amounts of changes in anxiety and state CV values per week would constitute the first derivatives, or rates of change, in these constructs. Initially, there may be relatively sharp rises (acceleration) in anxiety that persist for months. However, as the actual move approaches, such rises in anxiety level may begin to level off (i.e., decelerating to an equilibrium). Following the move, the individual may eventually begin to show declines in anxiety level and renewed growth in their momentary CV feelings. Other patterns of weekly changes are possible. For instance, another individual moving into the assisted care facility may show relatively constant CV values over the 3-month span, characterized by only occasional spikes in anxiety during some isolated weeks. In some individuals, the changes in anxiety may drive the changes in CV values; in others, the dynamic relations between anxiety and CV may be bidirectional. These varying patterns of changes in anxiety and CV state values can assume rather distinct forms when evaluated at the daily, weekly, and monthly levels and thus may be triggered and/or moderated by disparate contextual (time-varying, e.g., one's physical health at the moment) and person-specific factors (e.g., other personality traits). A researcher who decides to assess these CV values only at one particular moment thus risks bypassing some of these rich intra- and interpersonal dynamics.

DE models are not the only possible model for representing these state- and trait-based differences. Another well-known class of models for representing possible connections among processes of change are time series methods such as autoregressive integrated moving average (ARIMA) models, ARMA model with exogenous input (ARMA-X), and their multivariate vector extensions (Box, Jenkins, & Reinsel, 1994; Chow, Haltigan, & Messinger, 2010; Lütkepohl, 2005; Shumway & Stoffer, 2006). Also prevalent in the behavioral sciences are extensions of these time series models involving the dynamics of latent variables (Browne & Nesselroade, 2005; Chow, Zu, Shifren, & Zhang, 2011; Molenaar, 1985; Song & Zhang, 2014). This model includes time-lagged effects of the same variables from previous time points on their current values (e.g., the influence of yesterday's CV on today's CV), as well as the cross-regression effects of other predictors from previous time points on current values of CV (e.g., the influence of yesterday's anxiety on today's CV).

Application of these models to multidimensional, vector autoregressive (VAR) contexts involving a large number of observed variables yields the so-called *dynamical network modeling* approaches, which have gained considerable traction in recent years as tools for investigating issues of directionality. Examples of these models include the unified structural equation model (uSEM), the group iterative multiple model estimation (GIMME) frameworks (Ka Gates et al., 2010; Gates & Molenaar, 2012), subgrouping within GIMME (Gates, Lane, Varangis, Giovanello, & Guiskewicz, 2017), and an alternative graphical VAR (gVAR) approach that uses the least absolute shrinkage and selection operator (Epskamp, Waldorp, Mõttus, & Borsboom, 2018)as a regularization method for simplifying network structures by retaining only the "important" coefficients in a model and shrinking the others to zero. Multilevel extensions of these models further allow for between-couple heterogeneity in these dynamic relations (Aspaoruhov, Hamaker, & Muthén, 2018).

Another alternative may be *regime-switching models* (S-M. Chow, Grimm, Guillaume, Dolan, & McArdle, 2013; S-M. Chow, Witkiewitz, Grasman, Hutton, & Maisto, 2014; S-M. Chow & Zhang, 2013; Yang & Chow, 2008), which provide a targeted way to model change as within-person progression through stages that may interact with a multitude of within-person processes and between-person differences to affect individuals' CV values. As distinct from other contemporary methods, regime-switching models allow for inter-individual differences in the timing and probability of transition through stages, as well as the possibility for regression to previous stages.

The RELATE project includes prospective longitudinal measurement burst data, which allows us to apply a number of these advanced modeling techniques to better understand processes of change and, in particular, to test theories about PTG in an older adult population. The project includes both objective and subjective assessments at multiple time scales to corroborate assessments and differentiate how different types of CVs may show varying trajectories of change. Currently, our data suggest that different CVs show distinct patterns of change and that there is great intra- (within-person) and interindividual (between-person) differences in these patterns. Although we have rich data to work with, it is important for researchers studying PTG to understand that collecting these types of data can be challenging because they are based on the context of community settings with older adults undergoing major life transitions that can be sometimes be unpredictable and challenging. Moreover, we have been collecting data before and during the outbreak of the novel coronavirus disease 2019 (COVID-19) in the United States around February 2020 (Pillemer, Subramanian, & Hubert, 2020). We next describe the challenges of collecting and using these types of data for research on PTG, particularly when a naturalistic adverse sociohistorical event—the COVID-19 outbreak—occurs during data collection.

Learning Lessons: Establishing Community-Academic Partnerships to Collect Data on Changes in Character Virtues in an Older Adult Sample

The RELATE project developed out of a collaboration between university researchers and community practitioners at a large local senior housing facility. Over many years, the relationship evolved from one devoted primarily to teaching and training to one that involved basic and applied research studies. The fundamental task of academic research is to ask insightful questions and conduct studies that generate new knowledge in service of answering those questions. In the social and life sciences, these kinds of questions might involve seeking a clearer understanding of basic and fundamental processes of life, studying how different individual and environmental factors increase or decrease the likelihood of disease or health, or investigating how to alter those basic processes in ways that enhance human health and well-being. To answer some of these questions, academics must engage community members as participants. Historically, academic researchers have conceptualized, developed, and carried out their research studies with little input from community stakeholders beyond having them supply data (Glasgow, Lichtenstein, & Marcus, 2003). This practice often generated a notable distance between researcher and community and a basic distrust of how and why data will be used (Begun, Berger, Otto-Salaj, & Rose, 2010). Findings and new knowledge from these studies were frequently disseminated by researchers to the "scientific community" of peers and colleagues rather than being shared with the community stakeholders. Given this, it is not surprising that community members are reluctant to participate in these processes.

Over the past several decades, new models of conducting research in communities have evolved, including community-based participatory research (CBPR), participatory action research (PAR), and community-partnered research. *Practice-driven research,* a model that blends the movement toward evidence-based practice with the expertise and experience of practitioners in service settings, has been applied to the care of aging and older adults (McDonald, 2019). The primary similarity across these models in that researchers and community collaborators engage in the research as equal partners. Similar to a "team science" approach, academic—community collaboration is built on the basic tenet of bringing together members with distinct sets of skills that improve the research process. Recently, Drahota and colleagues (2016) articulated a community—academic partnership (CAP) approach and defined this model as follows:

> Community-academic partnerships (CAP) are characterized by equitable control, a cause that is primarily relevant to the community of interest, and specific aims to achieve goal(s) and involves community members (representatives or agencies) that have knowledge of the cause, as well as academic researchers. (p. 192)

We use CAP to describe the collaboration between university faculty and community practitioners that helped guide the research processes of the RELATE project.

There are many benefits to CAPs. Such partnerships have often been used to reduce the *research-to-practice gap,* the time required to translate a clinical innovation to standard practice. That time frame has been estimated to be an average of 17 years (Balas & Boren, 2000). Embedding the research practice into a service organization potentially improves the acceptability of evidence-based practices for practitioners and service users (Palikas, He, Choy-Brown, & Hertel, 2017). Beyond the utility for prevention, intervention, and implementation research, CAPs have benefits for basic science studies as well; we highlight several that have been particularly useful for the RELATE project.

First, community stakeholders and practitioners have key experiences, first-hand knowledge, and unique insights with respect to the population and settings. This can help improve the quality of the research questions, study design, or both. When research questions and designs are co-created, they are more likely to be relevant to the community or setting needs (Baker, Homan, Schonhoff, & Kreuter, 1999) while also creating a balance of the needs across the partnership. Second, CAPs often embed the research procedures deeply in the context itself, which can generate more relevant, applicable, and translatable findings that are useful to the community partners (Palinkas et al., 2017). Depending on the study design and research questions, the benefits may be specific to the setting or may be generalizable to similar settings. Our CAP has worked together in a project associated with RELATE to infuse mindfulness and compassion training into some of the organization's settings. Results from the RELATE project can provide additional data regarding how the organizational practices and processes facilitate or hinder the adaptation of new residents. Third, local participation increases the likelihood that any relevant findings from an intervention or basic study will be incorporated into practices of the setting and sustain beyond the study period. Over the past few years our CAP has sustained mindfulness and compassion training and activities within this community partner setting, indicating that relevant findings from the RELATE project are also likely to be integrated into the organization's procedures. Fourth, CAPs can provide unique access to relevant populations. But beyond simple access to a pool of potential study participants, community partner knowledge and experience can provide access to the right people. That is, CAPs can help identify individuals with profiles that fit the study parameters. Community partners' experience can facilitate careful planning of efficient and effective recruitment strategies. Often, recruiting research participants can be one of the biggest challenges to a successful research study. The RELATE project benefitted from the CAP when recruitment waned, and problem-solving sessions elicited a variety of new strategies based on community partner knowledge and experience that broadened our recruitment strategies and increased our yield. In addition, when the COVID-19 pandemic broke out, researchers quickly discovered that older adults were a vulnerable population more likely to suffer more severe health complications or even death from the disease (Pillemer et al., 2020). Our ongoing CAP with local senior housing facilities allowed us access to our study population while upholding safety standards by moving the data collection procedures to an online format. Without the collaborations and relationships we had forged with the management of senior housing facilities, our continuing data collection would not be possible. Fifth, the timing of research procedures (e.g., recruitment, assessment, intervention participation, follow-up assessment) can enhance or hinder participation and completion of the project. Planning by the CAP can identify the most appropriate times to implement the research procedures in a way that is compatible with other procedures and practices of the organization. As depicted in Figure 7.1, the design of the RELATE project proposed to recruit participants *prior* to transitioning to senior housing so that an initial assessment could be done approximately 2 weeks ahead of this theoretically stressful event. Then, burst assessments would occur at theoretically meaningful times across the first 3 months of the transition. These procedures were set according to meaningful points in the processes of moving and acclimating to the new living facility. When challenges emerged to the timing of these assessments, adjustments were made in a way that fit the location but maintained design integrity.

Building a successful CAP takes time. Although the mechanisms and the various interpersonal and organizational processes of CAPs have not yet been empirically evaluated, systematic reviews highlight critical facilitating factors (Drahota et al., 2016) that occur over the duration of the partnership or at different phases (pre-research, during research, or post-research) of the research endeavor (Pellecchia et al., 2018). We highlight several of these and how these were done in RELATE. The most frequently cited characteristic of an effective CAP is a bidirectional partnership based on trust and mutual respect among partners (Drahota et al., 2016). The CAP from which the RELATE project emerged was built over time, developing out of nonresearch relationships and long conversations about different research ideas, the organization, and how the collaboration might work. Funding was obtained specifically to develop the partnership through relationship building, developing an operational structure, and evaluating various community needs and research ideas. Over this 1-year partnership development period, greater trust and respect was built in these relationships as members experienced that their ideas and beliefs were valued and were integrated into the research processes. Researchers saw how practitioners believed in the value of the research endeavor, and practitioners saw how the data might inform new practices. The partnership formed a leadership team comprised of members with knowledge, experience, and leadership skills. The leadership team met monthly to address progress, problem-solve, and plan for new phases of the partnership development and research processes. Another key facilitating factor identified in reviews is developing a shared mission, vision, or goals (Drahota et al., 2016). One of the first tasks of our CAP was to develop an operating agreement that included a mission statement, goals, and statements of roles and responsibilities that would guide all future CAP activities. We used several of our initial meetings to develop and discuss these documents. Having clearly differentiated roles of partners is also a facilitating factor of effective CAPs (Brookman-Frazee et al., 2016). While individuals fulfilling these roles and responsibilities changed over the course of the research projects, we worked to maintain the distinctions so that all could see their value to the CAP and projects.

While our CAP benefitted from the lessons learned by other groups and we were able to form a high-functioning partnership, we also identified some specific lessons that we continue to learn from and work through. One lesson is the critical nature of transitions. RELATE was designed to study adaptations to a challenging life transition, but, unlike some studies of traumatic life events, we had prior knowledge of *when* the transition would happen. Thus, we could address some research gaps by employing a longitudinal design to capture pre- and post-transition functioning. Even with this prior knowledge, the transition points of various people were fluid and required considerable adjustments by the research staff to accommodate recruitment and assessment. Working closely with practitioners to understand the organizational processes around this transition was critical to adapting the research procedures needed to capture the human processes we were investigating. A second lesson is organizational integration. The Tamarack Institute has described a spectrum of collaboration, with the highest level being "fully integrated programs, planning, and funding," which is often beyond the goals of a CAP. Academia and community service organizations have distinct career and organizational expectations and incentives that create challenges to full integration. We were fortunate that the academic department of CAP members is supportive of and values applied research in the community. Our CAP can work toward supporting integration of these processes, but full integration to normalize the research processes (e.g., design, recruitment, assessment, funding, etc.) into the operations of the community partner organization will require additional planning, infrastructure development, and revised processes. Yet that integration would facilitate the implementation of projects such as RELATE. A third lesson is fuller training in the purpose and methods of CAP for all CAP members. Several members of the leadership committee participated in training which was helpful for the development of the CAP, but providing additional training to members who joined the committee later would have facilitated their buy-in, learning, and participation while also increasing the likelihood of sustaining the CAP beyond a single research project. In addition, such buy-in has been helpful for continuing data collection even during the COVID-19 pandemic. Many of our collaborators at the senior housing facilities were deeply concerned about the safety of their older adult residents, but our CAP helped us to build the trust necessary to continue data collection. Although the COVID-19 pandemic has had a tragic toll, its timing during our study has also allowed us to address additional unique questions regarding how different naturally occurring major life events and sociohistorical situations may shape the course of PTG. Thus, while we continue to learn new lessons and are confronted with new challenges, our CAP has been instrumental to the success of the RELATE project.

CONCLUSION

In conclusion, the RELATE study builds on the literature and may serve as a model for other investigators interested in studying change processes, particularly for psychological variables that may unfold over different time scales, including fast-moving states and slower changing traits, such as with CVs or personality. The RELATE study capitalizes on a prospective measurement burst design to understand how older adults navigate the transition into senior housing and what changes, if any, are observed in their state and trait CVs. This project also includes potential mechanisms (mediators) and moderators of change that can be tested against current theoretical models. Moreover, the complexity of the multiple time scales data allows us to employ advanced modeling techniques that have greater granularity in the types of changes observed. These data were gathered by developing strong academic–community partnerships with senior housing facilities that provide mutual beneficial outcomes for researchers and community partners. Future studies will build on the methodological and conceptual contributions of the RELATE project.

ACKNOWLEDGMENTS

This research was supported by funding from the National Institute on Aging (K01AG056660 PI Gloria Luong) and grants from the Templeton Foundation/Pathways to Character Initiative and the Mind and Life Institute (PI Gloria Luong).

Correspondence concerning this article should be addressed to Gloria Luong, Department of Human Development and Family Studies, Colorado State

University, Campus Delivery 1570, Fort Collins, CO 80523-1570. E-mail: Gloria. Luong@colostate.edu.

REFERENCES

Aghababaei, N., Mohammadtabar, S., & Saffarinia, M. (2014). Dirty dozen vs. H factor: Comparison of the Dark Triad and honest-humility in prosociality, religiosity, and happiness. *Personality and Individual Differences, 67*, 6–10.

Baker, E. A., Homan, S., Schonhoff, S. R., & Kreuter, M. (1999). Principles of practice for academic/practice/community research partnerships. *American Journal of Preventive Medicine, 16*(3), 86–93.

Balas E. A., & Boren S. A. (2000). Managing clinical knowledge for health care improvement. In B. J. McCray (Ed.), *Yearbook of medical informatics 2000: Patient-centered systems* (pp. 65–70). Stuttgart, Germany: Schattauer.

Box, G. E. P., Jenkins, G. M., & Reinsel, G. C. (1994). *Time Series Analysis; Forecasting and Control, 3rd Edition*. Englewood Cliff, NJ: Prentice Hall.

Brookman-Frazee, L., Stahmer, A., Stadnick, N., Chlebowski, C., Herschell, A., & Garland, A. F. (2016). Characterizing the use of research-community partnerships in studies of evidence-based interventions in children's community services. *Administration and Policy in Mental Health and Mental Health Services Research, 43*(1), 93–104.

Browne, M. W., & Nesselroade, J. R. (2005). Representing psychological processes with dynamic factor models: Some promising uses and extensions of autoregressive moving average time series models. In A. Maydeu-Olivares & J. J. McArdle (Eds.), *Multivariate applications book series. Contemporary psychometrics: A festschrift for Roderick P. McDonald* (pp. 415–452). Lawrence Erlbaum Associates Publishers.

Chow, S.-M. (2019). Practical tools and guidelines for exploring and fitting linear and nonlinear dynamical systems models. *Multivariate Behavioral Research*. doi:10.1080/00273171.2019.1566050

Chow, S., Haltigan, J. D., & Messinger, D. S. (2010). Dynamic infant-parent affect coupling during the face-to-face/still-face. *Emotion, 10*, 101–114.

Chow, S. M., Zu, J., Shifren, K., & Zhang, G. (2011). Dynamic factor analysis models with time-varying parameters. *Multivariate Behavioral Research, 46*(2), 303–339.

Ciarrocchi, J. W., & Deneke, E. (2005). Happiness and the varieties of religious experience: Religious support, practices, and spirituality as predictors of well-being. *Research in the Social Scientific Study of Religion, 15*, 209–233.

Cohen, L. G., Hettler, T. R., & Pane, N. (1998). Assessment of posttraumatic growth. In R. G. Tedeschi, C. L. Park, & L. G. Calhoun (Eds.), *Posttraumatic Growth: Positive Changes in the Aftermath of Crisis* (pp. 23–42). Mahwah, NJ: Lawrence Erlbaum.

Cummings, S. M. (2002). Predictors of psychological well-being among assisted-living residents. *Health & Social Work, 27*, 293–302.

de Vries, B., LeBlanc, A. J., Frost, D. M., Alston-Stepnitz, E., Stephenson, R., & Woodyatt, C. R. (2017). The relationship timeline: A method for the study of shared lived experiences in relational contexts. *Advances in Life Course Research, 32*, 55–64.

Drahota, A. M. Y., Meza, R. D., Brikho, B., Naaf, M., Estabillo, J. A., Gomez, E. D., . . . Aarons, G. A. (2016). Community-academic partnerships: A systematic review of the state of the literature and recommendations for future research. *The Milbank Quarterly, 94*(1), 163–214.

Fleeson, W., & Jayawickreme, E. (2015). Whole trait theory. *Journal of Research in* Personality, *56*, 82–92.

Glasgow, R. E., Lichtenstein, E., & Marcus, A. C. (2003). Why don't we see more translation of health promotion research to practice? Rethinking the efficacy-to-effectiveness transition. *American Journal of Public Health, 93*(8), 1261–1267.

Hamby, S., Grych, J., & Banyard, V. (2018). Resilience portfolios and poly-strengths: Identifying protective factors associated with thriving after adversity. *Psychology of Violence, 8*, 172–183.

Harari, G. M., Müller, S. R., Aung, M. S., & Rentfrow, P. J. (2017). Smartphone sensing methods for studying behavior in everyday life. *Current Opinion in Behavioral Sciences, 18*, 83–90.

Hawes, C., Phillips, C. D., Holan, S., Sherman, M., & Hutchison, L. (2005). Assisted living in rural America: Results from a national survey. *Journal of Rural Health, 21*, 131–139.

Helm, J. L., Ram, N., Cole, P. M., & Chow, S.-M. (2016). Modeling self-regulation as a process using a multiple time-scale multiphase latent basis growth model. *Structural Equation Modeling, 23*, 635–648.

Hofmann, W., Wisneski, D. C., Brandt, M. J., & Skitka, L. J. (2014). Morality in everyday life. *Science, 345*, 1340–1343.

Infurna, F. J., Gerstorf, D., Ram, N., Schupp, J., & Wagner, G. G. (2011). Long-term antecedents and outcomes of perceived control. *Psychology and Aging, 26*, 559–575. http://dx.doi.org/10.1037/a0022890

Infurna, F. J., Gerstorf, D., & Zarit, S. H. (2013). Substantial changes in mastery perceptions of dementia caregivers with the placement of a care recipient. *Journals of Gerontology: Psychological Sciences, 68*, 202–214. doi:10.1093/geronb/gbs063

Jayawickreme, E., & Blackie, L. E. R. (2014). Post-traumatic growth as positive personality change: Evidence, controversies and future directions. *European Journal of Personality, 28*, 312–331.

Jayawickreme, E., Meindl, P., Helzer, E. G., Furr, R. M., & Fleeson, W. (2014). Virtuous states and virtuous traits: How the empirical evidence regarding the existence of broad traits saves virtue ethics from the situationist critique. *Theory and Research in Education, 12*, 283–308.

Kliegl, R., Smith, J., & Baltes, P. B. (1989). Testing-the-limits and the study of adult age differences in cognitive plasticity of a mnemonic skill. *Developmental Psychology, 25*, 247–256. http://dx.doi.org/10.1037/0012-1649.25.2.247

Luong, G., Arredondo, C. M., & Charles, S. T. (2020). Cultural differences in coping with interpersonal tensions lead to divergent shorter-and longer-term affective consequences. *Cognition and Emotion, 34*(7), 1499–1508.

Luong, G., Charles, S. T., & Fingerman, K. L. (2011). Better with age: Social relationships across adulthood. *Journal of Social and Personal Relationships, 28*, 9–23.

Luong, G., Charles, S. T., Rook, K. S., Reynolds, C. A., & Gatz, M. (2015). Age differences and longitudinal change in the effects of data collection mode on self-reports of psychosocial functioning. *Psychology and Aging, 30*, 106–119. http://dx.doi.org/10.1037/a0038502

Lütkepohl, H. (2005). *New introduction to multiple time series analysis*. Springer Science & Business Media.

McDonald, T. (2019). *Practice-driven research: A practical approach to aged care knowledge development.* Woodslane Press.

Molenaar, P. C. (1985). A dynamic factor model for the analysis of multivariate time series. *Psychometrika, 50*(2), 181–202.

Nisbett, R. E., & Wilson, T. D. (1977). Telling more than we can know: Verbal reports on mental processes. *Psychological Review, 84*, 231–259.

Noftle, E. E., & Fleeson, W. (2015). Intraindividual variability in adult personality development. In M. Diehl, K. Hooker, & M. J. Sliwinski (Eds.), *Handbook of Intraindividual Variability Across the Life Span* (pp. 176–197). New York: Routledge.

Palinkas, L. A., He, A. S., Choy-Brown, M., & Hertel, A. L. (2017). Operationalizing social work science through research–practice partnerships: Lessons from implementation science. *Research on Social Work Practice, 27*(2), 181–188.

Park, C. L., & Lechner, S. (2006). Measurement issues in assessing growth following stressful life experiences. In L. G. Calhoun & R. G. Tedeschi (Eds.). *Handbook of Posttraumatic Growth: Research and Practice* (pp. 47–67). Mahwah, NJ: Lawrence Erlbaum.

Pillemer, K., Subramanian, L., & Hubert, N. (2020). The importance of long-term care populations in models of COVID-19. Advanced online publication, June 5, 2020, *Journal of the American Medical Association.* doi:10.1001/jama.2020.9540

Post, S. G. (2005). Altruism, happiness, and health: It's good to be good. *International Journal of Behavioral Medicine, 12*, 66–77.

Pruchno, R. (2012). Not your mother's old age: Baby Boomers at age 65. *Gerontologist, 52*, 149–152.

Ptacek, J. T., Smith, R. E., Espe, K., & Raffety, B. (1994). Limited correspondence between daily coping reports and retrospective coping recall. *Psychological Assessment, 6*(1), 41–49. http://dx.doi.org/10.1037/1040-3590.6.1.41

Ram, N., & Diehl, M. (2015). Multiple-time-scale design and analysis: Pushing toward real-time modeling of complex developmental processes. In M. Diehl, K. Hooker, & M. J. Sliwinski (Eds.), *Handbook of Intraindividual Variability Across the Life Span* (pp. 308–323). New York: Routledge

Roisman, G. I., Masten, A. S., Coatsworth. J. D., & Tellegen, A. (2004). Salient and emerging developmental tasks in the transition to adulthood. *Child Development, 75*, 123–133.

Ryan, R. (2009). Self determination theory and well being. *Social Psychology, 84*(822), 848.

Scheinerman, E. R. (1996). *Invitation to Dynamical Systems*. Hoboken, NJ: Prentice Hall.

Shimai, S., Otake, K., Park, N., Peterson, C., & Seligman, M. E. P. (2006). Convergence of character strengths in American and Japanese young adults. *Journal of Happiness Studies, 7*, 311. https://doi.org/10.1007/s10902-005-3647-7

Shumway, R. H., & Stoffer, D. S. (2006). *Time series regression and exploratory data analysis*. Time Series Analysis and Its Applications: With R Examples. Springer Science & Business Media.

Smyth, J. M., & Heron, K. E. (2014). Ecological momentary assessment (EMA) in family research. In S. McHale, P. Amato, & A. Booth (Eds.), *Emerging Methods in Family Research, Vol. 4* (pp. 145–161). New York: Springer.

Song, H., & Zhang, Z. (2014). Analyzing multiple multivariate time series data using multilevel dynamic factor models. *Multivariate Behavioral Research*, *49*(1), 67–77.

Tedeschi, R. G., & Calhoun, L. G. (2004). Posttraumatic growth: Conceptual foundations and empirical evidence. *Psychological Inquiry*, *15*, 1–18.

Thomas, D. L., & Diener, E. (1990). Memory accuracy in the recall of emotions. *Journal of Personality and Social Psychology*, *59*, 291–297. http://dx.doi.org/10.1037/0022-3514.59.2.291

Walker, W. R., Skowronski, J. J., & Thompson, C. P. (2003). Life is pleasant—and memory helps to keep it that way! *Review of General Psychology*, *7*, 203–210.

Watson, L. C., Garrett, J. M., Sloane, P. D., Gruber-Baldini, A. L., & Zimmerman, S. (2003). Depression in assisted living: Results from a four-state study. *American Journal of Geriatric Psychiatry*, *11*, 534–542.

Yang, L., Krampe, R. T., & Baltes, P. B. (2006). Basic forms of cognitive plasticity extended into the oldest-old: Retest learning, age, and cognitive functioning. *Psychology and Aging*, *21*, 372–378. http://dx.doi.org/10.1037/0882-7974.21.2.372

8

Prospectively Examining the Effects of a Cancer Diagnosis on Patients, Spouses/Partners, and Their Relationship

ELAINE O. CHEUNG, FRANK J. PENEDO, JUDITH T. MOSKOWITZ, BETINA YANEZ, SHEETAL M. KIRCHER, SHILAJIT D. KUNDU, SARAH C. FLURY, AND PATRICIA I. MORENO ■

Receiving a diagnosis of cancer is a profound and often very stressful experience. A new diagnosis of cancer introduces uncertainty and distress as individuals navigate treatment decisions, experience disruptions to social/occupational roles and routines, and undergo arduous treatments such as surgery, radiation, and chemotherapy (Jacobsen & Andrykowski, 2015; Stanton, Rowland, & Ganz, 2015). Individuals who are newly diagnosed with cancer commonly experience decrements in quality of life and are at elevated risk for psychological and physical symptoms, including anxiety, depressed mood, fatigue, and pain (Jacobsen & Andrykowski, 2015; Jones et al., 2015; Mitchell et al., 2011). However, receiving a cancer diagnosis can also lead to opportunities for positive change as individuals engage in efforts to understand and find meaning in their experience (Algoe & Stanton, 2009; C. L. Park, Edmondson, Fenster, & Blank, 2008; Stanton, Bowers, & Low, 2006). Research over the past two decades has documented that individuals commonly report positive changes in response to traumatic or adverse events (e.g., greater appreciation of life and self-confidence, improved relationships), a phenomenon often referred to as *post-traumatic growth* (PTG; Helgeson, Reynolds, & Tomich, 2006; Jayawickreme & Blackie, 2014; Stanton & Low, 2004; Tedeschi & Calhoun, 2004). Given the significant impact of a cancer diagnosis on individuals and their loved ones, research examining PTG in cancer has flourished, making it the most widely studied disease context for PTG (Algoe & Stanton, 2009; Casellas-Grau, Ochoa, & Ruini, 2017; Jim & Jacobsen, 2008; Kolokotroni, Anagnostopoulos, & Tsikkinis, 2014; Koutrouli, Anagnostopoulos, & Potamianos, 2012; Moreno & Stanton, 2013; Rajandram, Jenewein, McGrath, & Zwahlen, 2011; Stanton et al., 2006; Sumalla, Ochoa, & Blanco, 2009).

BRIEF REVIEW OF RESEARCH ON POST-TRAUMATIC GROWTH IN CANCER

Most adult cancer survivors report experiencing some level of PTG in response to their experience (Jim & Jacobsen, 2008; Koutrouli et al., 2012; Stanton et al., 2006). Cognitive processing (Jim & Jacobsen, 2008; Kolokotroni et al., 2014; Rajandram et al., 2011) and approach-oriented coping strategies such as positive reappraisal, acceptance, active coping, and problem-focusing coping (Jim & Jacobsen, 2008; Kolokotroni et al., 2014; Koutrouli et al., 2012; Rajandram et al., 2011; Stanton et al., 2006) are associated with greater PTG among cancer survivors. This is consistent with central theories of PTG that posit cognitive processing and adaptive coping contribute to shifts in schema and, ultimately, PTG (Joseph & Linley, 2005; Tedeschi & Calhoun, 2004). Religious coping also is commonly associated with higher levels of PTG (Kolokotroni et al., 2014; Koutrouli et al., 2012; Rajandram et al., 2011). Social support from spouses, close others, and the healthcare team and less social constraint may facilitate PTG (Jim & Jacobsen, 2008; Rajandram et al., 2011); however, findings are mixed and include nonsignificant associations (Casellas-Grau et al., 2017; Kolokotroni et al., 2014; Koutrouli et al., 2012). More research is needed to better understand the processes by which social support received from close others, particularly spouses and partners, may contribute to PTG following a cancer diagnosis.

PTG among cancer survivors is generally associated with better psychological adjustment, including lower anxiety and depressive symptoms, as well as greater quality of life and positive well-being (e.g., meaning, optimism, hope, and positive affect) (Algoe & Stanton, 2009; Casellas-Grau et al., 2017; Rajandram et al., 2011; Stanton et al., 2006). Evidence of the relationship between PTG with intrusive thoughts and avoidance has documented both positive and negative associations (Jim & Jacobsen, 2008). According to the stress response theory proposed by Horowitz and colleagues (Horowitz, Wilner, & Alvarez, 1979; Zilberg, Weiss, & Horowitz, 1982), the presence of intrusive thoughts following a stressful event like cancer is indicative of incomplete cognitive processing of the stressor. Intrusive thoughts also can be perpetuated by avoidance, which paradoxically increases the frequency and intensity of intrusive thoughts and further impedes cognitive processing and eventual resolution of the stress response. Given that cognitive processing is strongly associated with PTG (both theoretically and empirically), the relationship between cognitive processing and PTG may partially drive observed positive associations between PTG with intrusive thoughts and avoidance.

Although findings are largely mixed regarding the association between medical and sociodemographic characteristics (e.g., education, socioeconomic status, cancer stage and treatment) and PTG (Jim & Jacobsen, 2008; Kolokotroni et al., 2014; Rajandram et al., 2011), evidence suggests that individuals who are more vulnerable to the impact of cancer may experience greater PTG. Younger age is most consistently associated with greater PTG (Jim & Jacobsen, 2008; Kolokotroni et al., 2014; Koutrouli et al., 2012), a finding that is supported by an extensive literature documenting the exceptional challenges young adult cancer survivors experience due to cancer-related disruption in social and occupational roles. Younger age is one of the most consistent predictors of worse quality of life and greater unmet needs among cancer survivors (Stanton, 2012). Consistent with well-documented quality of life disparities among racial and ethnic minority cancer survivors, there is also some evidence that racial and ethnic minorities report greater PTG than non-Hispanic/Latino white cancer survivors (Jim & Jacobsen, 2008; Koutrouli et al., 2012). Similarly, there is some evidence that greater perceived threat of cancer, such as concerns about recurrence and death and perceived stressfulness, are associated with greater PTG (Jim & Jacobsen, 2008; Kolokotroni et al., 2014; Stanton et al., 2006). Importantly, more time since diagnosis has also been associated with greater PTG (Kolokotroni et al., 2014; Koutrouli et al., 2012), suggesting that more time may be needed to process and cope with the experience of cancer before perceptions of growth can occur.

Advanced and Metastatic Cancer

In light of the unique challenges accompanying the experience of advanced cancer, the phenomenon of PTG may be distinct in patients with life-limiting disease as compared with more commonly studied samples of early-stage cancer survivors. Unlike patients diagnosed with early-stage or curable cancer, individuals with incurable, advanced cancer most likely will not have the opportunity to reflect on their experience and engage in meaning-making or positive changes after the disease has remitted. Instead, they are faced with the task of adapting to a life-limiting disease while actively enduring ongoing challenges during the remainder of their lives. Indeed, the commonly used term "*post*traumatic growth" is ill-fitted in this context, given that advanced cancer often has an uneven course, one not circumscribed to a definitive period of time with a beginning and end, as is more likely for natural disasters or curable illnesses. Similar to the broader literature on PTG in cancer survivors, a review of the literature found that many patients with advanced cancer both cite finding meaning at the end of life as important and perceive positive consequences as a result of their experience (Moreno & Stanton, 2013). In comparison to early-stage cancer or benign disease, advanced cancer may prompt greater perceptions of growth. However, findings are mixed and may indicate a complex, nonlinear relationship between cancer prognosis and perceptions of growth. Importantly, a co-occurrence of perceived growth with both distress and well-being in advanced cancer suggests that perceived growth in this unique context is characterized by perceived positive consequences in the face of considerable demands, which may be reflected by greater negative and positive markers of adjustment.

THEORETICAL DEBATES AND METHODOLOGICAL CONSIDERATIONS

An important consideration in the study of PTG that should guide interpretation of findings is that cancer survivors are typically are asked for their *perceptions* of positive changes in the cancer experience. Notably, these perceptions of growth may or may not reflect real, behaviorally evident positive changes (Jayawickreme & Blackie, 2014; C. L. Park, 2004; C. L. Park & Helgeson, 2006; Tennen & Affleck, 2009). Furthermore, the potential for bias in these perceptions has led some researchers to question whether the reported positive changes in response to cancer are real or illusory (Sumalla et al., 2009). Theoretical models positing that these positive changes are illusory (Maercker & Zoellner, 2004; Taylor, 1983; Widows, Jacobsen, Booth-Jones, & Fields, 2005) argue that the perception of positive changes reported by cancer survivors may reflect a defensive coping strategy and cognitive avoidance to protect the individual's sense of coherence, perceived control, and self-esteem against the threat of cancer. Thus, rather than reflecting actual change, these perceptions are thought to reduce emotional distress associated with the cancer diagnosis and treatment. Furthermore, there is some evidence suggesting that the perceptions of positive changes following a cancer diagnosis may be explained, in part, to cancer survivors perceiving their past attributes as lower or more negative than reality (McFarland & Alvaro, 2000; Widows et al., 2005).

In contrast, theoretical models that posit PTG to be real (Janoff-Bulman, 1992; Klauer, Ferring, & Kilipp, 1998; Maercker & Zoellner, 2004; Schaefer & Moos, 1998; Tedeschi & Calhoun, 1995; Widows et al., 2005) argue that an individual's struggle with trauma or adversity leads to the reconstruction of basic beliefs and world assumptions, and this reconstruction in turn forms the basis of real identity change. According to these models, a cancer diagnosis can challenge the individual's basic worldview about why things happen, which may lead the individual to review and revise their beliefs to make sense of the experience. The changes in the individual's cognitive schemas lead the individual to develop new structures of coherent beliefs about themselves, others, and the cancer diagnosis. In support of the assertion that PTG is real, there is some evidence that suggests that cancer survivors' perceptions of growth can be corroborated by informant reports from their close others (Weiss, 2002). The corroboration using information reports suggests that these positive changes are observable and may reflect real, objective changes. *It is important to note that regardless of whether these positive changes are real or illusory, the perception of growth and meaning are important in their own right during the process of reflection when individuals are making sense of their cancer experience.*

To date, these theoretical debates on whether these positive changes are real or illusory have been difficult to resolve due to several methodological limitations in the study of PTG. Most research examining positive changes in response to cancer and other adverse events has been limited by cross-sectional designs that use retrospective, self-report measures of perceived growth (Jayawickreme & Blackie, 2014; C. L. Park, 2004; C. L. Park & Helgeson, 2006; Tennen & Affleck, 2009). For instance, one systematic review on PTG in cancer (Casellas-Grau et al., 2017) found that 68% of studies used cross-sectional designs and 76% used the Posttraumatic Growth Inventory (PTGI; Tedeschi & Calhoun, 1996). The limitation of using retrospective self-report measures of PTG, such as the PTGI, is that they rely on the respondent's ability to recall and quantify the extent to which they have changed across various dimensions over time (e.g., relating to others, appreciation of life) and to be able to isolate and quantify the change that is attributable to the adverse event (e.g., the cancer diagnosis). As such, these measures require complex cognitive functions and are subject to bias (e.g., recall bias, social desirability bias) (Jayawickreme & Blackie, 2014; C. L. Park, 2004; C. L. Park & Helgeson, 2006; Tennen & Affleck, 2009). Furthermore, cross-sectional designs cannot capture discrete trajectories of change in respondents' positive traits as they unfold over time. For instance, individuals may show curvilinear or nonlinear trajectories of change over time that cannot be captured using cross-sectional approaches. Indeed, most cross-sectional studies on PTG have found null or mixed associations between PTG and psychological adjustment, whereas longitudinal studies have documented consistent, positive associations between PTG and subsequent psychological adjustment (Zoellner & Maercker, 2006). Thus, the current literature on PTG to date has been limited by cross-sectional designs and retrospective self-report measures of perceptions of growth that make it difficult to determine whether people show actual positive changes in response to cancer. To account for that assessment of individuals' perceptions of growth (whether true or illusory), we will typically use the term perceived growth: in place of PTG in this chapter to be inclusive and highlight the perceived nature of this change (Table 8.1).

To address these limitations, more recent studies have moved toward assessing whether actual changes in positive traits, termed *character strengths* (e.g., gratitude, empathy, and spirituality/meaning), occur in response to adversity. Character growth is defined as change in character strengths as measured through repeated assessments over time using a prospective design (Table 8.1). Although the vast majority of research in cancer survivors has examined perceived growth rather than character growth, a growing body of research suggests that individuals may exhibit positive changes in specific character strengths, including altruism (Muzzatti, Flaiban, Surbone, & Annunziata, 2015; Schreiber & Edward, 2015), empathy (Horgan, Holcombe, & Salmon, 2011; Mosher et al., 2017; Rosedale, 2009), gratitude (Ruini & Vescovelli, 2013), and spirituality/meaning (Ching, Martinson, & Wong, 2012; Connerty & Knott, 2013; C. L. Park et al., 2008; Totman, Pistrang, Smith, Hennessey, & Martin, 2015) following a cancer diagnosis.

Table 8.1 TERMINOLOGY

Term	Definition	Assessment
Perceived growth	An individual's perceptions of positive psychological changes he or she has experienced in response to an adverse or traumatic event like cancer. Also commonly referred to as post-traumatic growth, benefit finding, or personal growth.	Assessed by retrospective, self-report measures (e.g., Posttraumatic Growth Inventory, Benefit Finding Scale).
Character strengths	Positive psychological traits identified by Seligman and colleagues that reflect a strength of character, including gratitude, empathy, relatedness, spirituality/meaning, attachment, prosocial behavior, humility, relational humility, open-minded thinking, compassionate love, and identification with all humanity.	Assessed by self-report or peer-report measures (e.g., Gratitude Questionnaire Six-Item Form, Humility Inventory).
Character growth	Actual, measured change across time in character strengths in response to an adverse or traumatic event like cancer.	Assessed in a prospective, longitudinal design through repeated assessments of character strengths that demonstrate significant change over time following an identified event.
Relationship strengths	Positive facets of relationship functioning identified by Fletcher and colleagues including commitment, intimacy, trust, passion, love, and satisfaction.	Assessed by self- and partner-report measures (i.e., Perceived Relationship Quality Components Inventory).
Couple growth	Actual, measured change across time in relationship strengths in response to an adverse or traumatic event like cancer.	Assessed in a prospective, longitudinal design through repeated assessments of relationship strengths that demonstrate significant change over time following an identified event.

CANCER CAREGIVING AMONG SPOUSES AND PARTNERS

Romantic partners and spouses are by far the most common informal cancer caregivers, helping patients manage disease symptoms, treatment side effects, and emotional distress (Kent, Mollica, Buckenmaier, & Wilder Smith, 2019; Stenberg,

Ruland, & Miaskowski, 2010). Despite the significant burden of caregiving and its well-documented deleterious effects on psychological and physical health (Braun, Mikulincer, Rydall, Walsh, & Rodin, 2007; Hagedoorn, Buunk, Kuijer, Wobbes, & Sanderman, 2000; Kent & Dionne-Odom, 2018; Kim, Carver, Shaffer, Gansler, & Cannady, 2015; Nijboer et al., 1998; Northouse, Mood, Templin, Mellon, & George, 2000; Northouse, Williams, Given, & McCorkle, 2012; Ochoa, Lunsford, & Smith., 2020; Peh, Liu, & Mahendran, 2020; Pitceathly & Maguire, 2003; Shaffer, Kim, Carver, & Cannady, 2017; Stenberg et al., 2010; Tuinstra et al., 2004), markedly less attention has focused on whether providing care for cancer patients can also lead to positive changes in caregivers (Kang et al., 2013; Kim, Schulz, & Carver, 2007; Manne, Ostroff et al., 2004; Moore et al., 2011; Thornton & Perez, 2006; Wagner, Tanmoy Das, Bigatti, & Stomiolo, 2011; Weiss, 2004; Zwahlen, Hagenbuch, Carley, Jenewein, & Buchi, 2010). Furthermore, studies have almost exclusively measured perceived growth in cancer caregivers, with limited attention on character growth. Given that cancer patient and caregiver well-being are closely linked and reciprocally influence one another (Gesselman et al., 2016; Kim, Loscalzo, Wellisch, & Spillers, 2006; Kim, Kashy, Wellisch, Spillers, Kaw, & Smith, 2008; Lo, Hales, Braun, Rydall, Zimmermann, & Rodin, 2013; Lwi, Ford, Casey, Miller, & Levenson, 2017; Streck, Wardell, LoBiondo-Wood, & Beauchamp, 2020; Zhou et al., 2011), a comprehensive dyadic model of character growth in the cancer context is a crucial gap in the literature.

DEVELOPING A NEW DYADIC MODEL OF CHARACTER GROWTH

Central theories of perceived growth (Joseph & Linley, 2005; Tedeschi & Calhoun, 2004) posit that an adverse or traumatic event introduces significant challenges into one's life, which initially can result in distress and rumination (Figure 8.1A). These initial responses transform into cognitive processing and adaptive coping like meaning-making and ultimately contribute to shifts in schema and positive changes (Joseph & Linley, 2005; Tedeschi & Calhoun, 2004). Less attention has been given to the interpersonal processes hypothesized to underlie perceived growth: disclosure to empathic others and social support. Discussing a stressor and receiving support from an empathic close other are key mechanisms that feed back into cognitive processing, coping, and shifts in schema. In fact, perceived growth in cancer survivors is associated with greater disclosure to close others regarding the cancer experience and with both seeking and receiving social support (Cordova, Cunningham, Carlson, & Andrykowski, 2001; S. C. Danhauer et al., 2013; Manne, Sherman et al., 2004; McDonough, Sabiston, & Wrosch, 2014; Moreno & Stanton, 2013; Schroevers, Helgeson, Sanderman, & Ranchor, 2010; Schulz & Mohamed, 2004; Sears, Stanton, & Danoff-Burg, 2003; Shand, Cowlishaw, Brooker, Burney, & Ricciardelli, 2015; Thornton & Perez, 2006; Weiss, 2004). Research also demonstrates that several character strengths (i.e., spirituality/meaning, gratitude, empathy, attachment) are associated with disclosure,

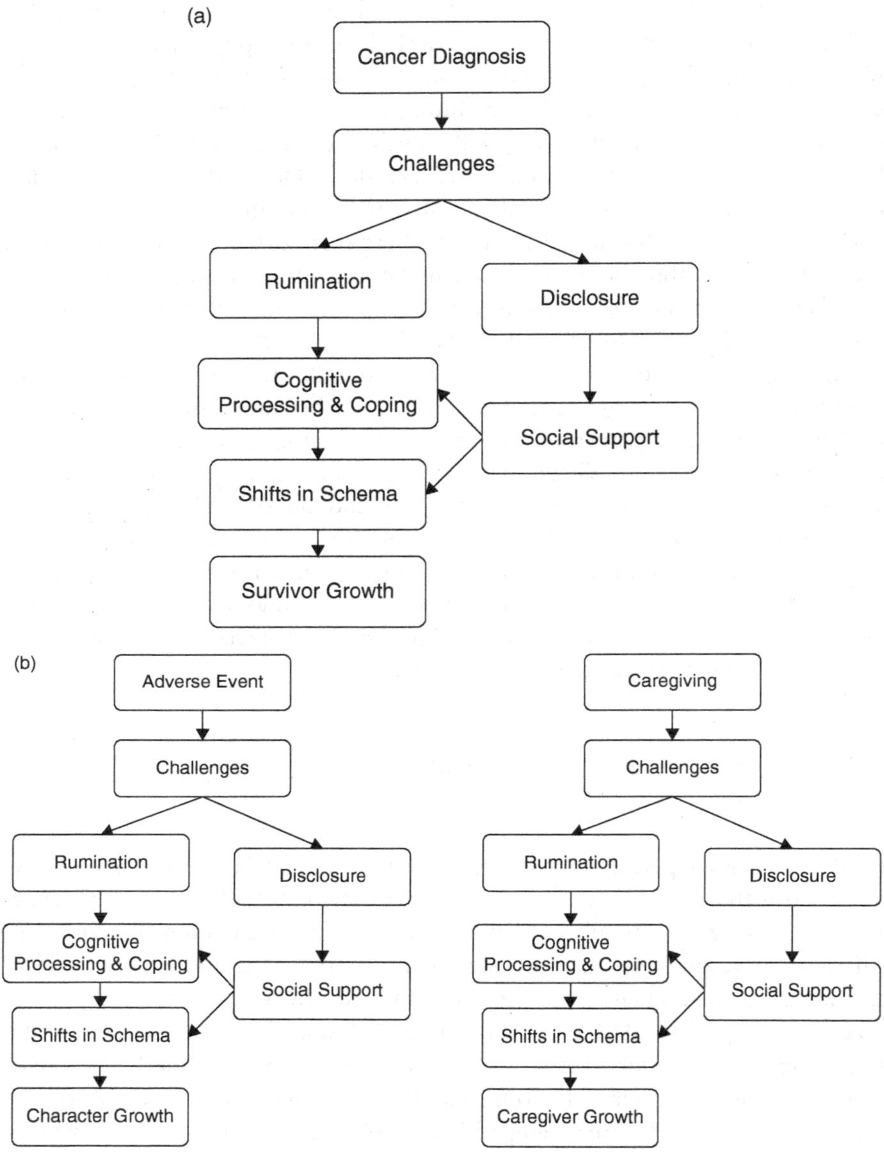

Figure 8.1 A. Conceptual model of character growth adapted from Tedeschi & Calhoun (2004). B. Parallel models of character growth in cancer patients and caregivers. C. Our expanded model illustrating both the intrapersonal and shared dyadic processes that we hypothesize drive character and couple growth in the patient–caregiver context.

social support, and partner empathy (Algoe & Stanton, 2012; Asendorpf & Wilpers, 2000; Devoldre, Davis, Verhofstadt, & Buysse, 2010; Lin & Yeh, 2014; Mikulincer & Shaver, 2009; Nicholls, Hulbert-Williams, & Bramwell, 2014; Péloquin, Lafontaine, & Brassard, 2011; Wood, Maltby, Gillett, Linley, & Joseph,

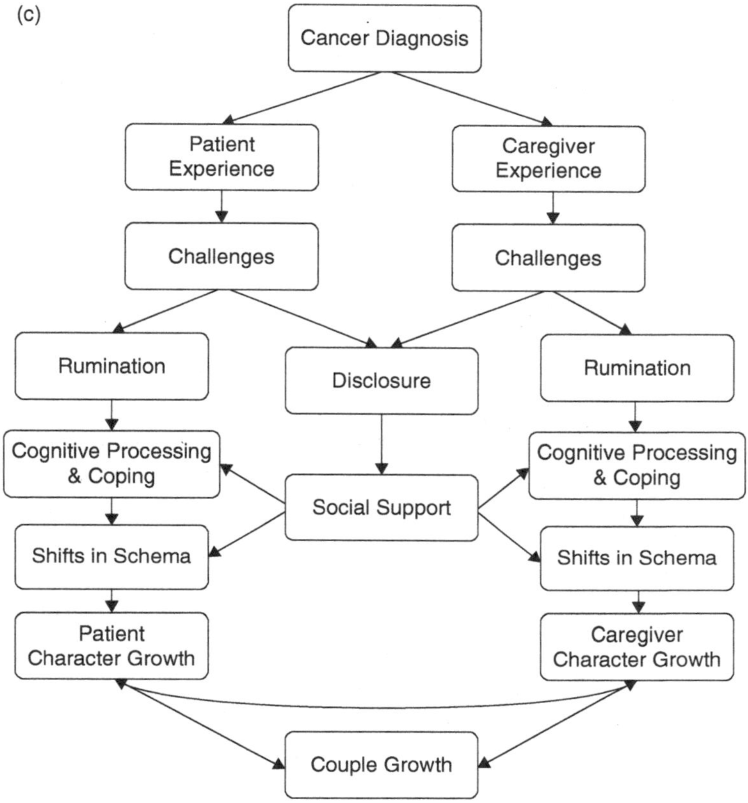

Figure 8.1 Continued.

2008). However, to date no studies have tested dyadic processes such as disclosure, support, empathy, and cognitive processing as mechanisms of character growth in patients or caregivers.

Previous studies have primarily examined positive changes in the cancer patient and caregiver as separate, parallel processes and have not considered the shared interpersonal context or whether a cancer diagnosis can lead to positive changes in the relationship (Figure 8.1B) (Hagedoorn et al., 2000; Kayser, Watson, & Andrad, 2007). The effects of cancer on a couple can vary considerably, with some relationships growing stronger (e.g., demonstrating greater closeness and intimacy) while others struggle and either experience greater strain or dissolution (Elliott (nee Murray), Scott, Monsour, & Nuwayhid, 2015; Northouse, Templin, Mood, & Oberst, 1998; Skerrett, 1998). Consistent with the conceptualization of assessing change over time in character strengths as a measure of character growth in each individual, we conceptualize change over time in relationship strengths (i.e., satisfaction, commitment, intimacy, trust, passion, love) (Fletcher, Simpson, & Thomas, 2000) as a measure of couple growth in the cancer patient–caregiver dyad (Table 8.1). We propose an expanded dyadic theoretical model adapted from Tedeschi and Calhoun (2004) that outlines the intrapersonal and shared dyadic processes that underlie positive changes over time in both individual and relationship outcomes: character and couple growth (Figure 8.1C).

RECOMMENDATIONS FOR FUTURE RESEARCH

Reviews examining the relationship of perceived growth with adjustment in cancer patients demonstrates mixed findings: although perceived growth is typically associated with greater positive psychological well-being, including quality of life and positive affect, results are mixed (and sometimes contradictory) with respect to markers of distress (Moreno & Stanton, 2013; Stanton et al., 2006). In contrast, both character and relationship strengths have well-documented associations with both increased positive psychological well-being and reduced distress (Brdar & Kashdan, 2010; Brosseau, McDonald, & Stephen, 2011; N. Park, Peterson, & Seligman, 2004; Peterson, Ruch, Beermann, Park, & Seligman, 2007; Proyer, Gander, Wellenzohn, & Ruch, 2013; Ruini & Vescovelli, 2013). Furthermore, previous research (Yanez, Stanton, Hoyt, Tennen, & Lechner, 2011; Frazier et al., 2009) demonstrates that perceived growth is unrelated to actual positive changes and that, compared to perceived growth, assessments of actual positive change (e.g., character growth) may show more consistent associations with both greater positive psychological well-being and reduced distress. Together, these findings suggest that, relative to perceived growth, character growth may offer unique predictive validity in its consequences for psychological adjustment. Consistent with evidence that individuals demonstrate discrete trajectories of perceived growth and psychological adjustment following a cancer diagnosis (S. Danhauer et al., 2015; Helgeson, Snyder, & Seltman, 2004; Wang, Chang, Chen, Chen, & Hsu, 2014), the study of character and couple growth following a cancer diagnosis may elucidate discrete profiles: stable strengths (no growth), increase in strengths (measured growth), decrease in strengths (measured loss). These profiles could ultimately help identify risk and protective factors that can inform intervention efforts (Antoni et al., 2001; Cruess et al., 2000; McGregor et al., 2004; Penedo et al., 2006) aimed at improving well-being in patients and their partners coping with cancer.

To address the limitations in the study of perceived growth (i.e., cross-sectional designs that rely on an individual's ability to retrospectively report positive changes; Jayawickreme & Blackie, 2014; C. L. Park, 2004; C. L. Park & Helgeson, 2006; Tennen & Affleck, 2009), we recommend that researchers use prospective designs with repeated assessments to examine whether actual changes in character strengths (e.g., gratitude, empathy, spirituality/meaning) occur in response to adversity. In addition, we recommend the use of observer reports (also known as informant reports or peer reports) in addition to self-report measures of character strengths in order to examine the observability of change in character strengths over time (i.e., character growth). Next, we provide an illustrative example from our study, funded by the John Templeton Foundation Pathways to Character Project, in which we employ a prospective, longitudinal repeated-measures design that examines patients and their partners in the year following a new cancer diagnosis.

An Example Study of Character Growth in the Cancer Context

The overarching aim of our study was to determine whether the challenges associated with a new cancer diagnosis engender character and couple growth in both the patient and caregiver, as defined by actual change in character and relationship strengths across time. Using a prospective design with quantitative approaches that model actor–partner effects, we are examining the predictors, mechanisms, and outcomes of character and couple growth in patients and caregivers and are testing the intrapersonal and shared dyadic processes that underlie character and couple growth in our expanded dyadic theoretical model. Furthermore, we are comparing trajectories of character and couple growth in cancer patient–caregiver couples with a comparison group of couples who undergo a cancer biopsy but receive a benign result (i.e., no cancer diagnosis). Importantly, we are using multimodal measurement, including daily-diary sampling to test dyadic processes as mechanisms of positive changes, traditional self-reports of perceived growth to differentiate perceived growth from actual measured changes in character strengths (i.e., character growth), and partner–informant reports of character strengths to examine the observability of character growth.

Trajectories of Character and Couple Growth

We are assessing prospective trajectories of character growth in cancer patients and caregivers as well as couple growth in their relationship in the year following a cancer diagnosis (prior to diagnosis, and 1, 6, and 9 months following a diagnostic biopsy). Specifically, we are assessing change across time in character strengths (e.g., gratitude, empathy, spirituality/meaning) as character growth in both individuals of the patient–caregiver dyad. In addition, we are also assessing change across time in relationship strengths (e.g., commitment, intimacy, trust) as couple growth in the patient–caregiver dyad. In addition, we are identifying whether there are discrete profiles of character and couple growth in cancer patients and caregivers following a diagnosis of cancer. We are comparing trajectories of character and couple growth in cancer patient–caregiver couples with a comparison group of couples who undergo a diagnostic biopsy and receive a benign result.

We hypothesize that a subset of cancer patients and caregivers will demonstrate character and couple growth as assessed by change over time in character and relationship strengths. Furthermore, we hypothesize that discrete trajectories of character and couple growth will emerge (e.g., stable strengths, increase in strengths, decrease in strengths). Given the role of mortality salience on perceived growth (Lykins, Segerstrom, Averill, Evans, & Kemeny, 2007), we hypothesize that a greater proportion of patient–caregiver couples will demonstrate character and couple growth than couples in our benign biopsy comparison group. However, couples who receive a benign biopsy result may also exhibit some character and couple growth as a result of the mortality salience related to a "cancer scare."

Addressing Methodological Limitations

We are also examining discriminant and convergent validity of character growth using multimodal measurement. We are examining correspondence between self and partner–informant reports in order to explore observability and validity of character growth. We are also comparing character growth with perceived growth in order to elucidate distinct functions and outcomes. Emerging evidence demonstrates that an individual's retrospective self-report of perceived growth following adversity (e.g., early stage and advanced cancer, life-threatening illness, loss of close other) is often corroborated by informant reports from partners and close others (Blackie, Jayawickreme, Helzer, Forgeard, & Roepke, 2015; Moore et al., 2011; C. L. Park, Cohen, & Murch, 1996; Weiss, 2002). Moreover, an individual's self-reported character strengths and Big Five personality traits also tend to be strongly corroborated by partner-informant reports (Busby & Gardner, 2008; Connolly, Kavanagh, & Viswesvaran, 2007; Costa & McCrae, 1988; Dijkstra, Barelds, Groothof, & van Bruggen, 2014; Kazmierczak, 2015; Piedmont, McCrae, Riemann, & Angleitner, 2000; Scharfe & Bartholomew, 1994). Furthermore, most studies exclusively assess relationship outcomes in a single member of the couple.

We hypothesize that character strengths will be observable (as indicated by corroboration between self and partner reports of character strengths), particularly in couples that are high in relationship strengths (i.e., intimacy, commitment, love, trust, passion, satisfaction). Based on previous research (Yanez et al., 2011), we hypothesize that perceived growth will be modestly related or unrelated with measured character growth and that perceived versus measured character growth may evidence differential associations with mechanisms and outcomes. Our assessment of relationship strengths in both patients and caregivers will uniquely allow us to examine both each member's perspective and correspondence between patients and caregivers in evaluations of relationship quality. Correspondence (or lack thereof) may provide a unique indicator of relationship dynamics, which may also predict the unfolding of character growth in patients and caregivers and couple growth.

Predictors, Mechanisms, and Outcomes of Character and Couple Growth

We are examining the predictors, mechanisms, and outcomes of character and couple growth in patients and caregivers. We aim to identify sociodemographic and medical characteristics that predict character and couple growth (e.g., age, socioeconomic status, gender, race/ethnicity, comorbidities, cancer stage, type and duration of cancer treatments). We will also test dyadic processes (disclosure, support, partner empathy, and cognitive processing) as mechanisms of character and couple growth in patient–caregiver couples through daily-diary sampling. We are examining the effect of character and couple growth on both positive psychological well-being and distress (e.g., depressive symptoms, life satisfaction, positive and negative affect, intrusive thoughts) and whether they demonstrate differential patterns of associations with perceived growth.

We hypothesize that the dyadic processes (i.e., disclosure, support, empathy, cognitive processing) in our expanded theoretical model will mediate change across time in character and relationship strengths. Based on a previous review examining the association of several sociodemographic and medical characteristics with perceived growth in cancer patients and survivors (Stanton et al., 2006), we hypothesize that younger age, female gender, ethnic/racial minority status, and greater disease severity (assessed by both cancer stage and medical comorbidities) may predict greater character and couple growth in the patient. For caregivers, we hypothesize that the caregivers' sociodemographic characteristics and the patient's disease severity will predict greater character and couple growth in the caregiver. Previous research examining the relationship between perceived growth and socioeconomic status and cancer treatment (type and duration) is inconclusive, therefore we do not have directional hypotheses for these relationships. In addition, we hypothesize that character and couple growth will predict both improved adjustment (i.e., greater positive psychological well-being and lower distress).

METHODS

Baseline and follow-up questionnaires will assess character strengths, relationship strengths, and psychological adjustment (Figure 8.2). All participants (approximately 225 couples) will complete the baseline assessment. All couples who receive a malignant biopsy result (i.e., cancer diagnosis) will complete follow-up assessments at 1, 6, and 9 months following the biopsy procedure. The first 50 couples who receive a benign biopsy result will complete follow-up assessments across the same timeframe. All other couples who receive a benign biopsy result will complete only the baseline assessment.

At each assessment, both members of the couple will complete measures of their partner's character strengths in addition to their own character strengths. Specifically, both members of the couple will complete measures of gratitude, empathy, relatedness, meaning, and attachment. In addition, both members of the couple will complete measures of the following relationship strengths: relationship satisfaction, commitment, intimacy, trust, passion, and love. In addition, both partners are completing measures of psychological adjustment, including depression, positive and negative affect, life satisfaction, stressful life events, financial toxicity, sexual functioning, and social constraints. For patients diagnosed with cancer, we will also assess measures of psychological adjustment to cancer, including their cancer-related quality of life, cancer-related intrusive thoughts and avoidance, and cancer supportive care needs. At the final assessment, all participants will complete the PTG inventory as a measure of perceived growth.

In addition to the baseline and follow-up assessments, participants will also complete daily-diary assessments once a day over a 1-week period at 3 months after their biopsy procedure. The daily-diary sampling will assess the dyadic

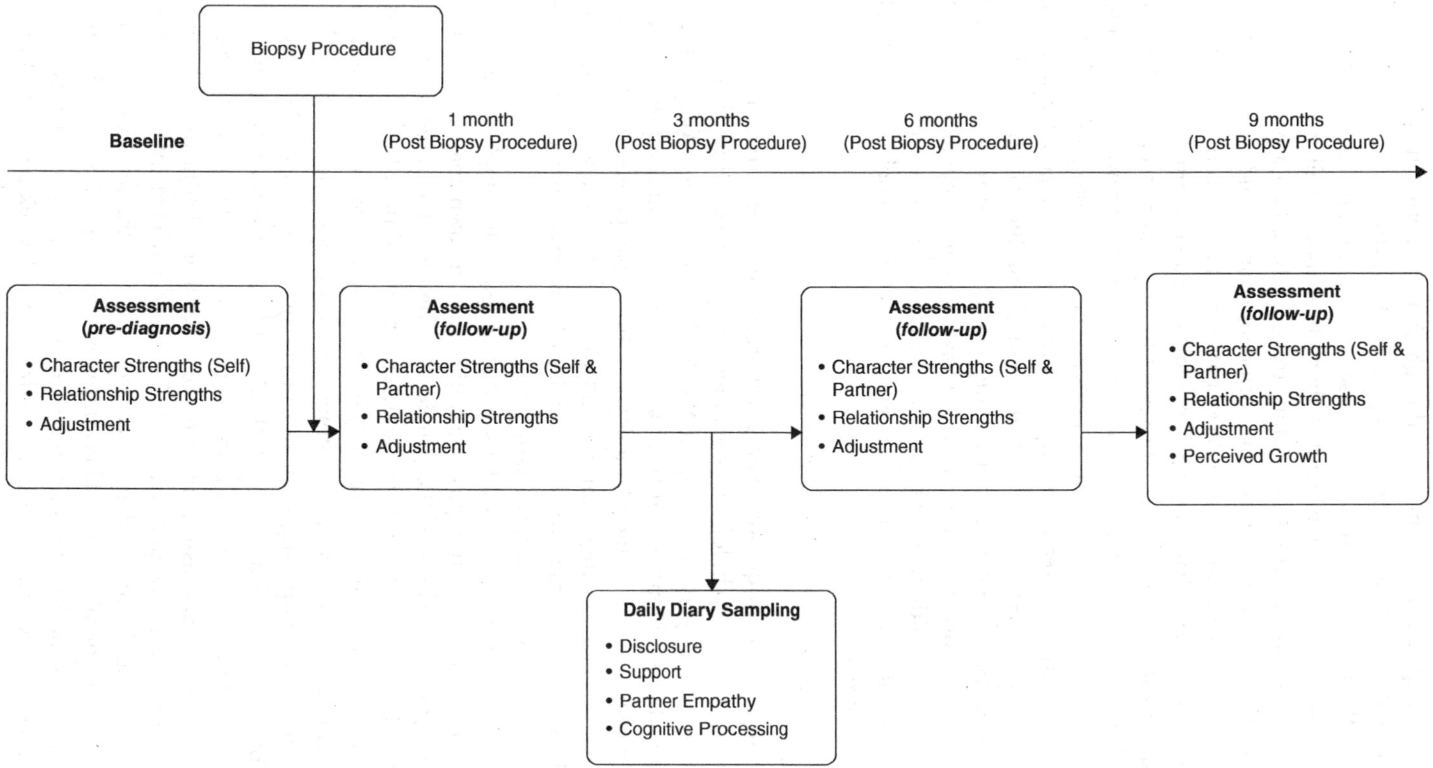

Figure 8.2 Study timeline.

mechanisms that we hypothesize underlie character growth: disclosure, support, empathy, and cognitive processing. Both partners will complete daily-diary measures drawn from previous literature that has assessed these constructs using daily-diary methodology and in the context of cancer–caregiver couples.

CONCLUSION

A cancer diagnosis is a profound and often very stressful experience for both patients and their partners. Spouses and partners are by far the most common informal cancer caregivers, helping patients manage disease symptoms, treatment side effects, and emotional distress. Despite these significant challenges, research over the past two decades demonstrates that cancer patients and caregivers commonly report positive changes, including greater appreciation of life and improved relationships with close others, following a diagnosis of cancer. However, most prior studies that have examined positive changes in cancer patients and their caregivers have solely relied on an individual's ability to retrospectively report whether or not he or she perceives these positive changes, which can be a biased method that does not capture true changes. More research is needed in order to study whether cancer patients and caregivers show actual changes in character strengths, such as gratitude, empathy, and humility, by measuring these characteristics both before and after a cancer diagnosis.

It is also important to consider the shared experience between the cancer patient and caregiver as well as identify how aspects of their relationship, including communication, empathy, and support, influence positive changes in both individuals and their relationship. Several theories posit that receiving empathy and support from close others helps individuals cope with adversity more adaptively and can promote positive changes in an individual by shifting schemas, or how the individual thinks about his or her experience. However, these mechanisms have not been tested. Furthermore, whether the experience of a cancer diagnosis leads to actual, positive changes in relationship strengths, including trust, commitment, and intimacy between a cancer patient and caregiver, has not been previously studied.

The example study described was developed to meet the goals of the Templeton Foundation Pathways to Character Project. The overarching aim of this project is to determine whether the challenges associated with a new cancer diagnosis engender character and couple growth in both the patient and caregiver, as defined by actual change in character and relationship strengths across time. We have also proposed a dyadic model that highlights the interpersonal processes that may underlie character and couple growth among cancer patients and caregivers. A prospective, multimodal, longitudinal design that includes repeated measurement of character and relationship strengths and daily-diary sampling of dyadic mechanisms is a crucial and needed next step to address current gaps in the literature and improve the conceptualization of positive psychological changes following adversity. We recommend that future researchers who are interested in interrogating adaptation to adversity among couples also consider including behavioral and neurobiological assessments in addition to self- and informant-report measures.

ACKNOWLEDGMENTS

Research was supported by a John Templeton Grant (Grant ID: 60699) awarded to Cheung and Moreno. Moreno was also supported by a National Institute of Minority Health and Health Disparities diversity supplement (R01MD010440).

REFERENCES

Algoe, S. B., & Stanton, A. L. (2009). Is benefit finding good for individuals with chronic disease? In C. L. Park, S. C. Lechner, M. H. Antoni, & A. L. Stanton (Eds.), *Medical Illness and Positive Life Change: Can Crisis Lead to Personal Transformation?* (pp. 173–193). Washington, DC: American Psychological Association. http://psycnet.apa.org/index.cfm?fa=search.displayrecord&uid=2008-12818-010

Algoe, S. B., & Stanton, A. L. (2012). Gratitude when it is needed most: Social functions of gratitude in women with metastatic breast cancer. *Emotion, 12*(1), 163–168. https://doi.org/10.1037/a0024024

Antoni, M. H., Lehman, J. M., Kilbourn, K. M., Boyers, A. E., Culver, J. L., Alferi, S. M., . . . Carver, C. S. (2001). Cognitive-behavioral stress management intervention decreases the prevalence of depression and enhances benefit finding among women under treatment for early-stage breast cancer. *Health Psychology, 20*(1), 20–32. https://doi.org/10.1037/0278-6133.20.1.20

Asendorpf, J. B., & Wilpers, S. (2000). Attachment security and available support: Closely linked relationship qualities. *Journal of Social and Personal Relationships, 17*(1), 115–138.

Blackie, L. E. R., Jayawickreme, E., Helzer, E. G., Forgeard, M. J. C., & Roepke, A. M. (2015). Investigating the veracity of self-perceived posttraumatic growth: A profile analysis approach to corroboration. *Social Psychological and Personality Science, 6*(7), 788–796. https://doi.org/10.1177/1948550615587986

Braun, M., Mikulincer, M., Rydall, A., Walsh, A., & Rodin, G. (2007). Hidden morbidity in cancer: Spouse caregivers. *Journal of Clinical Oncology, 25*(30), 4829–4834. https://doi.org/10.1200/JCO.2006.10.0909

Brdar, I., & Kashdan, T. B. (2010). Character strengths and well-being in Croatia: An empirical investigation of structure and correlates. *Journal of Research in Personality, 44*(1), 151–154. https://doi.org/10.1016/j.jrp.2009.12.001

Brosseau, D. C., McDonald, M. J., & Stephen, J. E. (2011). The moderating effect of relationship quality on partner secondary traumatic stress among couples coping with cancer. *Families, Systems, & Health, 29*(2), 114–126. https://doi.org/10.1037/a0024155

Busby, D., & Gardner, B. (2008). How do I analyze thee? Let me count the ways: considering empathy in couple relationships using self and partner ratings. *Family Process, 47*(2), 229–242.

Casellas-Grau, A., Ochoa, C., & Ruini, C. (2017). Psychological and clinical correlates of posttraumatic growth in cancer: A systematic and critical review. *Psycho-Oncology, 26*(12), 2007–2018. https://doi.org/10.1002/pon.4426

Ching, S. S. Y., Martinson, I. M., & Wong, T. K. S. (2012). Meaning making: Psychological adjustment to breast cancer by Chinese women. *Qualitative Health Research, 22*(2), 250–262.

Connerty, T. J., & Knott, V. (2013). Promoting positive change in the face of adversity: Experiences of cancer and post-traumatic growth. *European Journal of Cancer Care, 22*(3), 334–344. https://doi.org/10.1111/ecc.12036

Connolly, J. J., Kavanagh, E. J., & Viswesvaran, C. (2007). The convergent validity between self and observer ratings of personality: A meta-analytic review. *International Journal of Selection & Assessment, 15*(1), 110–117. https://doi.org/10.1111/j.1468-2389.2007.00371.x

Cordova, M. J., Cunningham, L. L. C., Carlson, C. R., & Andrykowski, M. A. (2001). Posttraumatic growth following breast cancer: A controlled comparison study. *Health Psychology, 20*(3), 176–185. http://dx.doi.org/10.1037/0278-6133.20.3.176

Costa, P. T., & McCrae, R. R. (1988). Personality in adulthood: A six-year longitudinal study of self-reports and spouse ratings on the NEO Personality Inventory. *Journal of Personality and Social Psychology, 54*(5), 853–863. https://doi.org/10.1037/0022-3514.54.5.853

Cruess, D. G., Antoni, M. H., McGregor, B. A., Kilbourn, K. M., Boyers, A. E., Alferi, S. M., . . . Kumar, M. (2000). Cognitive-behavioral stress management reduces serum cortisol by enhancing benefit finding among women being treated for early stage breast cancer. *Psychosomatic Medicine, 62*(3), 304–308.

Danhauer, S., Russell, G., Case, L., Sohl, S., Tedeschi, R., Addington, E., . . . Avis, N. (2015). Trajectories of posttraumatic growth and associated characteristics in women with breast cancer. *Annals of Behavioral Medicine, 49*(5), 650–659.

Danhauer, S. C., Case, L. D., Tedeschi, R., Russell, G., Vishnevsky, T., Triplett, K., . . . Avis, N. E. (2013). Predictors of posttraumatic growth in women with breast cancer. *Psycho-Oncology, 22*(12), 2676–2683. https://doi.org/10.1002/pon.3298

Devoldre, I., Davis, M. H., Verhofstadt, L. L., & Buysse, A. (2010). Empathy and social support provision in couples: Social support and the need to study the underlying processes. *Journal of Psychology: Interdisciplinary and Applied, 144*(3), 259–284. https://doi.org/10.1080/00223981003648294

Dijkstra, P., Barelds, D. P. H., Groothof, H. A. K., & van Bruggen, M. (2014). Empathy in intimate relationships: The role of positive illusions. *Scandinavian Journal of Psychology, 55*(5), 477–482. https://doi.org/10.1111/sjop.12142

Elliott (nee Murray), K.-E. J., Scott, J. L., Monsour, M., & Nuwayhid, F. (2015). Profiles of dyadic adjustment for advanced prostate cancer to inform couple-based intervention. *Psychology & Health, 30*(11), 1259–1273.

Fletcher, G. J. O., Simpson, J. A., & Thomas, G. (2000). The measurement of perceived relationship quality components: A confirmatory factor analytic approach. *Personality and Social Psychology Bulletin, 26*(3), 340–354. https://doi.org/10.1177/0146167200265007

Frazier, P., Tennen, H., Gavian, M., Park, C., Tomich, P., & Tashiro, T. (2009). Does self-reported posttraumatic growth reflect genuine positive change? *Psychological Science (0956-7976), 20*(7), 912–919. https://doi.org/10.1111/j.1467-9280.2009.02381.x

Gesselman, A. N., Bigatti, S. M., Garcia, J. R., Coe, K., Cella, D., & Champion, V. L. (2017). Spirituality, emotional distress, and post-traumatic growth in breast cancer survivors and their partners: an actor–partner interdependence modeling approach. *Psycho-oncology, 26*(10), 1691–1699.

Hagedoorn, M., Buunk, B. P., Kuijer, R. G., Wobbes, T., & Sanderman, R. (2000). Couples dealing with cancer: Role and gender differences regarding psychological distress and quality of life. *Psycho-Oncology, 9*(3), 232–242. https://doi.org/10.1002/1099-1611(200005/06)9:3<232::AID-PON458>3.0.CO;2-J

Helgeson, V. S., Reynolds, K. A., & Tomich, P. L. (2006). A meta-analytic review of benefit finding and growth. *Journal of Consulting and Clinical Psychology, 74*(5), 797–816. https://doi.org/10.1037/0022-006X.74.5.797

Helgeson, V. S., Snyder, P., & Seltman, H. (2004). Psychological and physical adjustment to breast cancer over 4 years: Identifying distinct trajectories of change. *Health Psychology, 23*(1), 3–15. https://doi.org/10.1037/0278-6133.23.1.3

Horgan, O., Holcombe, C., & Salmon, P. (2011). Experiencing positive change after a diagnosis of breast cancer: A grounded theory analysis. *Psycho-Oncology, 20*(10), 1116–1125.

Horowitz, M., Wilner, N., & Alvarez, W. (1979). Impact of Event Scale: A measure of subjective stress. *Psychosomatic Medicine, 41*(3), 209–218.

Jacobsen, P. B., & Andrykowski, M. A. (2015). Tertiary prevention in cancer care: Understanding and addressing the psychological dimensions of cancer during the active treatment period. *American Psychologist, 70*(2), 134–145. https://doi.org/10.1037/a0036513

Janoff-Bulman, R. (1992). *Shattered Assumptions: Towards a New Psychology of Trauma* (pp. xii, 256). New York: Free Press.

Jayawickreme, E., & Blackie, L. E. R. (2014). Post-traumatic growth as positive personality change: Evidence, controversies and future directions. *European Journal of Personality, 28*(4), 312–331. https://doi.org/10.1002/per.1963

Jim, H. S. L., & Jacobsen, P. B. (2008). Posttraumatic stress and posttraumatic growth in cancer survivorship: A review. *Cancer Journal, 14*(6), 414–419. https://doi.org/10.1097/PPO.0b013e31818d8963

Jones, S., LaCroix, A., Li, W., Zaslavsky, O., Wassertheil-Smoller, S., Weitlauf, J., . . . Danhauer, S. C. (2015). Depression and quality of life before and after breast cancer diagnosis in older women from the Women's Health Initiative. *Journal of Cancer Survivorship, 9*(4), 620–629. https://doi.org/10.1007/s11764-015-0438-y

Joseph, S., & Linley, P. A. (2005). Positive adjustment to threatening events: An organismic valuing theory of growth through adversity. *Review of General Psychology, 9*(3), 262–280. https://doi.org/10.1037/1089-2680.9.3.262

Kang, J., Shin, D. W., Choi, J. E., Sanjo, M., Yoon, S. J., Kim, H. K., . . . Yoon, W. H. (2013). Factors associated with positive consequences of serving as a family caregiver for a terminal cancer patient. *Psycho-Oncology, 22*(3), 564–571. https://doi.org/10.1002/pon.3033

Kayser, K., Watson, L. E., & Andrade, J. T. (2007). Cancer as a "we-disease": Examining the process of coping from a relational perspective. *Families, Systems, & Health, 25*(4), 404–418. https://doi.org/10.1037/1091-7527.25.4.404

Kazmierczak, M. (2015). Couple empathy: The mediator of attachment styles for partners adjusting to parenthood. *Journal of Reproductive & Infant Psychology, 33*(1), 15–27. https://doi.org/10.1080/02646838.2014.974148

Kent, E. E., & Dionne-Odom, J. N. (2018). Population-based profile of mental health and support service need among family caregivers of adults with cancer. *Journal of Oncology Practice, 15*(2), e122–e131. https://doi.org/10.1200/JOP.18.00522

Kent, E. E., Mollica, M. A., Buckenmaier, S., & Wilder Smith, A. (2019). The characteristics of informal cancer caregivers in the United States. *Seminars in Oncology Nursing, 35*(4), 328–332. https://doi.org/10.1016/j.soncn.2019.06.002

Kim, Y., Carver, C. S., Shaffer, K. M., Gansler, T., & Cannady, R. S. (2015). Cancer caregiving predicts physical impairments: Roles of earlier caregiving stress and being a spousal caregiver. *Cancer, 121*(2), 302–310. https://doi.org/10.1002/cncr.29040

Kim, Y., Kashy, D. A., Wellisch, D. K., Spillers, R. L., Kaw, C. K., & Smith, T. G. (2008). Quality of life of couples dealing with cancer: Dyadic and individual adjustment among breast and prostate cancer survivors and their spousal caregivers. *Annals of Behavioral Medicine, 35*(2), 230. https://doi.org/10.1007/s12160-008-9026-y

Kim, Y., Loscalzo, M. J., Wellisch, D. K., & Spillers, R. L. (2006). Gender differences in caregiving stress among caregivers of cancer survivors. *Psycho-Oncology, 15*(12), 1086–1092. https://doi.org/10.1002/pon.1049

Kim, Y., Schulz, R., & Carver, C. S. (2007). Benefit finding in the cancer caregiving experience. *Psychosomatic Medicine, 69*(3), 283–291. https://doi.org/10.1097/PSY.0b013e3180417cf4

Klauer, T., Ferring, D., & Filipp, S.-H. (1998). "Still stable after all this . . . ?": Temporal comparison in coping with severe and chronic disease. *International Journal of Behavioral Development, 22*(2), 339–355. https://doi.org/10.1080/016502598384405

Kolokotroni, P., Anagnostopoulos, F., & Tsikkinis, A. (2014). Psychosocial factors related to posttraumatic growth in breast cancer survivors: A review. *Women & Health, 54*(6), 569–592. https://doi.org/10.1080/03630242.2014.899543

Koutrouli, N., Anagnostopoulos, F., & Potamianos, G. (2012). Posttraumatic stress disorder and posttraumatic growth in breast cancer patients: A systematic review. *Women & Health, 52*(5), 503–516. https://doi.org/10.1080/03630242.2012.679337

Lin, C.-C., & Yeh, Y. (2014). How gratitude influences well-being: A structural equation modeling approach. *Social Indicators Research, 118*(1), 205–217. https://doi.org/10.1007/s11205-013-0424-6

Lo, C., Hales, S., Braun, M., Rydall, A. C., Zimmermann, C., & Rodin, G. (2013). Couples facing advanced cancer: Examination of an interdependent relational system. *Psycho-oncology, 22*(10), 2283–2290.

Lwi, S. J., Ford, B. Q., Casey, J. J., Miller, B. L., & Levenson, R. W. (2017). Poor caregiver mental health predicts mortality of patients with neurodegenerative disease. *Proceedings of the National Academy of Sciences, 114*(28), 7319–7324. https://doi.org/10.1073/pnas.1701597114

Lykins, E. L. B., Segerstrom, S. C., Averill, A. J., Evans, D. R., & Kemeny, M. E. (2007). Goal shifts following reminders of mortality: Reconciling posttraumatic growth and terror management theory. *Personality and Social Psychology Bulletin, 33*(8), 1088–1099. https://doi.org/10.1177/0146167207303015

Maercker, A., & Zoellner, T. (2004). The Janus face of self-perceived growth: Toward a two-component model of posttraumatic growth. *Psychological Inquiry, 15*(1), 41–48.

Manne, S., Ostroff, J., Winkel, G., Goldstein, L., Fox, K., & Grana, G. (2004). Posttraumatic growth after breast cancer: Patient, partner, and couple perspectives. *Psychosomatic Medicine, 66*(3), 442–454. https://doi.org/10.1097/01.psy.0000127689.38525.7d

Manne, S., Sherman, M., Ross, S., Ostroff, J., Heyman, R. E., & Fox, K. (2004). Couples' support-related communication, psychological distress, and relationship satisfaction among women with early stage breast cancer. *Journal of Consulting and Clinical Psychology, 72*(4), 660–670. https://doi.org/10.1037/0022-006X.72.4.660

McDonough, M. H., Sabiston, C. M., & Wrosch, C. (2014). Predicting changes in posttraumatic growth and subjective well-being among breast cancer survivors: The role of social support and stress. *Psycho-Oncology, 23*(1), 114–120. https://doi.org/10.1002/pon.3380

McFarland, C., & Alvaro, C. (2000). The impact of motivation on temporal comparisons: Coping with traumatic events by perceiving personal growth. *Journal of Personality and Social Psychology, 79*(3), 327–343. https://doi.org/10.1037/0022-3514.79.3.327

McGregor, B. A., Antoni, M. H., Boyers, A., Alferi, S. M., Blomberg, B. B., & Carver, C. S. (2004). Cognitive–behavioral stress management increases benefit finding and immune function among women with early-stage breast cancer. *Journal of Psychosomatic Research, 56*(1), 1–8. https://doi.org/10.1016/S0022-3999(03)00036-9

Mikulincer, M., & Shaver, P. R. (2009). An attachment and behavioral systems perspective on social support. *Journal of Social and Personal Relationships, 26*(1), 7–19. https://doi.org/10.1177/0265407509105518

Mitchell, A. J., Chan, M., Bhatti, H., Halton, M., Grassi, L., Johansen, C., & Meader, N. (2011). Prevalence of depression, anxiety, and adjustment disorder in oncological, haematological, and palliative-care settings: A meta-analysis of 94 interview-based studies. *Lancet Oncology, 12*(2), 160–174. https://doi.org/10.1016/S1470-2045(11)70002-X

Moore, A. M., Gamblin, T. C., Geller, D. A., Youssef, M. N., Hoffman, K. E., Gemmell, L., . . . Steel, J. L. (2011). A prospective study of posttraumatic growth as assessed by self-report and family caregiver in the context of advanced cancer. *Psycho-Oncology, 20*(5), 479–487. https://doi.org/10.1002/pon.1746

Moreno, P. I., & Stanton, A. L. (2013). Personal growth during the experience of advanced cancer: A systematic review. *Cancer Journal, 19*(5), 421–430. https://doi.org/10.1097/PPO.0b013e3182a5bbe7

Mosher, C. E., Adams, R. N., Helft, P. R., O'Neil, B. H., Shahda, S., Rattray, N. A., & Champion, V. L. (2017). Positive changes among patients with advanced colorectal cancer and their family caregivers: A qualitative analysis. *Psychology & Health, 32*(1), 94–109. https://doi.org/10.1080/08870446.2016.1247839

Muzzatti, B., Flaiban, C., Surbone, A., & Annunziata, M. A. (2015). Quality of life profile in Italian long-term cancer survivors. *Quality of Life Research, 24*(4), 959–967. https://doi.org/10.1007/s11136-014-0831-4

Nicholls, W., Hulbert-Williams, N., & Bramwell, R. (2014). The role of relationship attachment in psychological adjustment to cancer in patients and caregivers: A systematic review of the literature. *Psycho-Oncology, 23*(10), 1083–1095. https://doi.org/10.1002/pon.3664

Nijboer, C., Tempelaar, R., Sanderman, R., Triemstra, M., Spruijt, R. J., & Van Den Bos, G. A. M. (1998). Cancer and caregiving: The impact on the caregiver's health. *Psycho-Oncology, 7*(1), 3–13.

Northouse, L. L., Mood, D., Templin, T., Mellon, S., & George, T. (2000). Couples' patterns of adjustment to colon cancer. *Social Science & Medicine, 50*(2), 271–284. https://doi.org/10.1016/S0277-9536(99)00281-6

Northouse, L. L., Templin, T., Mood, D., & Oberst, M. (1998). Couples' adjustment to breast cancer and benign breast disease: A longitudinal analysis. *Psycho-Oncology, 7*(1), 37–48.

Northouse, L., Williams, A., Given, B., & McCorkle, R. (2012). Psychosocial care for family caregivers of patients with cancer. *Journal of Clinical Oncology, 30*(11), 1227–1234. https://doi.org/10.1200/JCO.2011.39.5798

Ochoa, C. Y., Lunsford, N. B., & Smith, J. L. (2020). Impact of informal cancer caregiving across the cancer experience: A systematic literature review of quality of life. *Palliative & Supportive Care, 18*(2), 220–240. https://doi.org/10.1017/S1478951519000622

Park, C. L. (2004). The notion of growth following stressful life experiences: Problems and prospects. *Psychological Inquiry, 15*(1), 69–76.

Park, C. L., Cohen, L. H., & Murch, R. L. (1996). Assessment and prediction of stress-related growth. *Journal of Personality, 64*(1), 71–105. https://doi.org/10.1111/1467-6494.ep9606210694

Park, C. L., Edmondson, D., Fenster, J. R., & Blank, T. O. (2008). Meaning making and psychological adjustment following cancer: The mediating roles of growth, life meaning, and restored just-world beliefs. *Journal of Consulting and Clinical Psychology, 76*(5), 863–875 https://doi.org/10.1037/a0013348

Park, C. L., & Helgeson, V. S. (2006). Introduction to the special section: Growth following highly stressful life events--Current status and future directions. *Journal of Consulting and Clinical Psychology, 74*(5), 791–796. https://doi.org/10.1037/0022-006X.74.5.791

Park, N., Peterson, C., & Seligman, M. E. P. (2004). Strengths of character and well-being. *Journal of Social and Clinical Psychology, 23*(5), 603–619. https://doi.org/10.1521/jscp.23.5.603.50748

Peh, C. X., Liu, J., & Mahendran, R. (2020). Quality of life and emotional distress among caregivers of patients newly diagnosed with cancer: Understanding trajectories across the first year post-diagnosis. *Journal of Psychosocial Oncology, 0*(0), 1–16. https://doi.org/10.1080/07347332.2020.1760994

Péloquin, K., Lafontaine, M.-F., & Brassard, A. (2011). A dyadic approach to the study of romantic attachment, dyadic empathy, and psychological partner aggression. *Journal of Social and Personal Relationships, 28*(7), 915–942. https://doi.org/10.1177/0265407510397988

Penedo, F. J., Molton, I., Dahn, J. R., Shen, B.-J., Kinsinger, D., Traeger, L., . . . Antoni, M. (2006). A randomized clinical trial of group-based cognitive-behavioral stress management in localized prostate cancer: Development of stress management skills improves quality of life and benefit finding. *Annals of Behavioral Medicine, 31*(3), 261–270.

Peterson, C., Ruch, W., Beermann, U., Park, N., & Seligman, M. E. (2007). Strengths of character, orientations to happiness, and life satisfaction. *Journal of Positive Psychology, 2*(3), 149–156.

Piedmont, R. L., McCrae, R. R., Riemann, R., & Angleitner, A. (2000). On the invalidity of validity scales: Evidence from self-reports and observer ratings in volunteer samples. *Journal of Personality and Social Psychology, 78*(3), 582–593. https://doi.org/10.1037/0022-3514.78.3.582

Pitceathly, C., & Maguire, P. (2003). The psychological impact of cancer on patients' partners and other key relatives: A review. *European Journal of Cancer, 39*(11), 1517–1524. https://doi.org/10.1016/S0959-8049(03)00309-5

Proyer, R. T., Gander, F., Wellenzohn, S., & Ruch, W. (2013). What good are character strengths beyond subjective well-being? The contribution of the good character on self-reported health-oriented behavior, physical fitness, and the subjective health status. *Journal of Positive Psychology, 8*(3), 222–232.

Rajandram, R. K., Jenewein, J., McGrath, C., & Zwahlen, R. A. (2011). Coping processes relevant to posttraumatic growth: An evidence-based review. *Supportive Care in Cancer, 19*(5), 583–589. https://doi.org/10.1007/s00520-011-1105-0

Rosedale, M. (2009). Survivor loneliness of women following breast cancer. *Oncology Nursing Forum, 36*(2), 175–183.

Ruini, C., & Vescovelli, F. (2013). The role of gratitude in breast cancer: Its relationships with post-traumatic growth, psychological well-being and distress. *Journal of Happiness Studies, 14*(1), 263–274.

Schaefer, J. A., & Moos, R. H. (1998). The context for posttraumatic growth: Life crises, individual and social resources, and coping. In *Posttraumatic Growth: Positive Changes in the Aftermath of Crisis* (pp. 99–125). Mahwah, NJ: Lawrence Erlbaum.

Scharfe, E., & Bartholomew, K. (1994). Reliability and stability of adult attachment patterns. *Personal Relationships, 1*(1), 23–43. https://doi.org/10.1111/j.1475-6811.1994.tb00053.x

Schreiber, J., & Edward, J. (2015). Image of God, religion, spirituality, and life changes in breast cancer Survivors: A qualitative approach. *Journal of Religion & Health, 54*(2), 612–622.

Schroevers, M. J., Helgeson, V. S., Sanderman, R., & Ranchor, A. V. (2010). Type of social support matters for prediction of posttraumatic growth among cancer survivors. *Psycho-Oncology, 19*(1), 46–53. https://doi.org/10.1002/pon.1501

Schulz, U., & Mohamed, N. E. (2004). Turning the tide: Benefit finding after cancer surgery. *Social Science & Medicine, 59*(3), 653–662.

Sears, S. R., Stanton, A. L., & Danoff-Burg, S. (2003). The yellow brick road and the emerald city: Benefit finding, positive reappraisal coping and posttraumatic growth in women with early-stage breast cancer. *Health Psychology, 22*(5), 487–497. http://dx.doi.org/10.1037/0278-6133.22.5.487

Shaffer, K. M., Kim, Y., Carver, C. S., & Cannady, R. S. (2017). Effects of caregiving status and changes in depressive symptoms on development of physical morbidity among long-term cancer caregivers. *Health Psychology, 36*(8), 770–778. https://doi.org/10.1037/hea0000528

Shand, L. K., Cowlishaw, S., Brooker, J. E., Burney, S., & Ricciardelli, L. A. (2015). Correlates of post-traumatic stress symptoms and growth in cancer patients: A systematic review and meta-analysis. *Psycho-Oncology, 24*(6), 624–634.

Skerrett, K. (1998). Couple adjustment to the experience of breast cancer. *Families, Systems, & Health, 16*(3), 281–298. https://doi.org/10.1037/h0089855

Stanton, A. L. (2012). What happens now? Psychosocial care for cancer survivors after medical treatment completion. *Journal of Clinical Oncology, 30*(11), 1215–1220. https://doi.org/10.1200/JCO.2011.39.7406

Stanton, A. L., Bower, J. E., & Low, C. A. (2006). Posttraumatic growth after cancer. In L. G. Calhoun & R. G. Tedeschi (Eds.), *Handbook of Posttraumatic Growth: Research & Practice* (pp. 138–175). Mahwah, NJ: Lawrence Erlbaum.

Stanton, A. L., & Low, C. A. (2004). Toward understanding posttraumatic growth: Commentary on Tedeschi and Calhoun. *Psychological Inquiry, 15*(1), 76–80. https://doi.org/10.2307/20447206

Stanton, A. L., Rowland, J. H., & Ganz, P. A. (2015). Life after diagnosis and treatment of cancer in adulthood: Contributions from psychosocial oncology research. *American Psychologist, 70*(2), 159–174. https://doi.org/10.1037/a0037875

Stenberg, U., Ruland, C. M., & Miaskowski, C. (2010). Review of the literature on the effects of caring for a patient with cancer. *Psycho-Oncology, 19*(10), 1013–1025.

Streck, B. P., Wardell, D. W., LoBiondo-Wood, G., & Beauchamp, J. E. S. (2020). Interdependence of physical and psychological morbidity among patients with cancer and family caregivers: Review of the literature. *Psycho-Oncology, 29*(6), 974–989. https://doi.org/10.1002/pon.5382

Sumalla, E. C., Ochoa, C., & Blanco, I. (2009). Posttraumatic growth in cancer: Reality or illusion? *Clinical Psychology Review, 29*(1), 24–33. https://doi.org/10.1016/j.cpr.2008.09.006

Taylor, S. E. (1983). Adjustment to threatening events: A theory of cognitive adaptation. *American Psychologist, 38*(11), 1161–1173. https://doi.org/10.1037/0003-066X.38.11.1161

Tedeschi, R. G., & Calhoun, L. G. (1995). *Trauma & Transformation: Growing in the Aftermath of Suffering* (pp. x, 163). Los Angeles: Sage. https://doi.org/10.4135/9781483326931

Tedeschi, R. G., & Calhoun, L. G. (1996). The Posttraumatic Growth Inventory: Measuring the positive legacy of trauma. *Journal of Traumatic Stress, 9*(3), 455–472. https://doi.org/10.1002/jts.2490090305

Tedeschi, R. G., & Calhoun, L. G. (2004). Posttraumatic growth: Conceptual foundations and empirical evidence. *Psychological Inquiry, 15*(1), 1–18. https://doi.org/10.1207/s15327965pli1501_01

Tennen, H., & Affleck, G. (2009). Assessing positive life change: In search of meticulous methods. In C. L. Park, S. C. Lechner, M. H. Antoni, & A. L. Stanton (Eds.), *Medical Illness and Positive Life Change: Can Crisis Lead to Personal Transformation?* (pp. 173–193). Washington, DC: American Psychological Association. http://psycnet.apa.org/index.cfm?fa=search.displayrecord&uid=2008-12818-010

Thornton, A. A., & Perez, M. A. (2006). Posttraumatic growth in prostate cancer survivors and their partners. *Psycho-Oncology, 15*(4), 285–296. https://doi.org/10.1002/pon.953

Totman, J., Pistrang, N., Smith, S., Hennessey, S., & Martin, J. (2015). "You only have one chance to get it right": A qualitative study of relatives' experiences of caring at home for a family member with terminal cancer. *Palliative Medicine, 29*(6), 496–507. https://doi.org/10.1177/0269216314566840

Tuinstra, J., Hagedoorn, M., Van Sonderen, E., Ranchor, A. V., Van den Bos, G. A. M., Nijboer, C., & Sanderman, R. (2004). Psychological distress in couples dealing with colorectal cancer: Gender and role differences and intracouple correspondence. *British Journal of Health Psychology, 9*(4), 465–478. https://doi.org/10.1348/1359107042304588

Wagner, C. D., Tanmoy Das, L., Bigatti, S. M., & Storniolo, A. M. (2011). Characterizing burden, caregiving benefits, and psychological distress of husbands of breast cancer patients during treatment and beyond. *Cancer Nursing, 34*(4), E21–E30. https://doi.org/10.1097/NCC.0b013e31820251f5

Wang, A. W.-T., Chang, C.-S., Chen, S.-T., Chen, D.-R., & Hsu, W.-Y. (2014). Identification of posttraumatic growth trajectories in the first year after breast cancer surgery. *Psycho-Oncology, 23*(12), 1399–1405. https://doi.org/10.1002/pon.3577

Weiss, T. (2002). Posttraumatic growth in women with breast cancer and their husbands: An intersubjective validation study. *Journal of Psychosocial Oncology, 20*(2), 65–80.

Weiss, T. (2004). Correlates of posttraumatic growth in husbands of breast cancer survivors. *Psycho-Oncology, 13*(4), 260–268.

Widows, M. R., Jacobsen, P. B., Booth-Jones, M., & Fields, K. K. (2005). Predictors of posttraumatic growth following bone marrow transplantation for cancer. *Health Psychology, 24*(3), 266–273. https://doi.org/10.1037/0278-6133.24.3.266

Wood, A. M., Maltby, J., Gillett, R., Linley, P. A., & Joseph, S. (2008). The role of gratitude in the development of social support, stress, and depression: Two longitudinal studies. *Journal of Research in Personality, 42*(4), 854–871. https://doi.org/10.1016/j.jrp.2007.11.003

Yanez, B. R., Stanton, A. L., Hoyt, M. A., Tennen, H., & Lechner, S. (2011). Understanding perceptions of benefit following adversity: How do distinct assessments of growth relate to coping and adjustment to stressful events? *Journal of Social and Clinical Psychology, 30*(7), 699–721. https://doi.org/10.1521/jscp.2011.30.7.699

Zhou, E. S., Kim, Y., Rasheed, M., Benedict, C., Bustillo, N. E., Soloway, M., . . . Penedo, F. J. (2011). Marital satisfaction of advanced prostate cancer survivors and their spousal caregivers: The dyadic effects of physical and mental health. *Psycho-Oncology, 20*(12), 1353–1357. https://doi.org/10.1002/pon.1855

Zilberg, N. J., Weiss, D. S., & Horowitz, M. J. (1982). Impact of Event Scale: A cross-validation study and some empirical evidence supporting a conceptual model of stress response syndromes. *Journal of Consulting and Clinical Psychology, 50*(3), 407–414. http://dx.doi.org/10.1037/0022-006X.50.3.407

Zoellner, T., & Maercker, A. (2006). Posttraumatic growth in clinical psychology: A critical review and introduction of a two component model. *Clinical Psychology Review, 26*(5), 626–653. https://doi.org/10.1016/j.cpr.2006.01.008

Zwahlen, D., Hagenbuch, N., Carley, M. I., Jenewein, J., & Buchi, S. (2010). Posttraumatic growth in cancer patients and partners: Effects of role, gender and the dyad on couples' posttraumatic growth experience. *Psycho-Oncology, 19*(1), 12–20. https://doi.org/10.1002/pon.1486

9

Using Culturally and Contextually Informed Theorizing in Research on Post-Traumatic Growth

REBECCA M. B. WHITE, GUSTAVO CARLO, GEORGE P. KNIGHT, JENN YUN-TEIN, NANCY A. GONZALES, AND ALEXANDRIA CURLEE

In the not-too-distant past, although there were exceptions (e.g., Super & Harkness, 1986; Whiting & Whiting, 1975), many psychological perspectives emphasized that the goal of socialization and growth was to produce individuals who could successfully fit into society at large; today, however, most psychologists recognize that growth takes place within a particular group and bounded community (Fuller & García Coll, 2010). The bounded group-community, by virtue of its demands and affordances, defines the very competencies that matter (White, Nair, & Bradley, 2018), including the character strengths, dispositions, and tendencies that are valued. This scholarly advance—from focusing on socialization and individual growth into *a society*, to recognizing the role of the *bounded group-community*—did not happen overnight. Rather, it reflected longer term trends in psychology that have ultimately produced more accurate knowledge about individuals broadly and about individuals among ethnic, racial, and cultural minority groups (hereafter referred to as minority groups) specifically. This shift, which is well established in other areas of psychological research (see, e.g., Causadias & Umaña-Taylor, 2018), however, has had limited influence on psychological understanding of character growth that occurs in response to exposure to adverse or traumatic circumstances.

Borrowing from multiple perspectives, we use the term "post-traumatic growth" (PTG) to refer to transformative psychological changes in growth-related domains that may occur following exposure to highly stressful or challenging adversities (Seery, Holman, & Silver, 2010; Tedeschi & Calhoun, 2004).

Adversities can include "schema-shattering" acute events (Tedeschi & Calhoun, 2004) as well as cumulative and chronic social and environmental stressors (e.g., poverty, unsafe neighborhoods; Seery et al., 2010). Several theories attempt to explain PTG as we have broadly defined it (Joseph & Linley, 2005; Pals & McAdams, 2004; Seery et al., 2010; Staub & Vollhardt, 2008; Tedeschi & Calhoun, 2004), commonly recognizing that adversity can be associated with adjustment-related difficulties, but also positing that growth and thriving are additional possibilities. Much of the extant research on PTG suffers design limitations (e.g., retrospective recall). More recently scholars have argued that addressing the big questions of PTG—namely, is character growth following adversity, challenge, or failure possible, and can psychologists accurately conceptualize and prospectively assess it (Infurna & Jayawickreme, 2019)—necessitate research designs that include direct, longitudinal assessment of individuals' current standings on growth-relevant domains before and after exposure to adversity (Jayawickreme & Blackie, 2014).

We argue that incorporating *culturally and contextually informed theorizing* into PTG research is similarly essential. That is, to advance a version of PTG research that can address the big questions, scholars will also need to integrate sophisticated theorizing about ethno-cultural diversity with sophisticated theorizing about contextual diversity into their research processes. To work toward the integration of ethno-cultural theorizing and contextual theorizing in PTG research, we provide an overview of culturally informed theorizing, which we argue can support sophisticated psychological research designs (Knight, Roosa, & Calderón-Tena, & Gonzales, 2009; Knight, Roosa, & Umaña-Taylor, 2009) and hypothesis testing (White, Knight, & Roosa, 2015) that reflects within- and between-group diversity. We also overview contextually informed theorizing, which we argue can help advance a more sophisticated view of contexts that support or undermine growth (White, Burleson, & Knight, 2016). We highlight the ways in which culturally and contextually informed theorizing should influence numerous steps of the PTG research process, from identification of the research questions, to methods, and interpretation of findings.

CULTURALLY AND CONTEXTUALLY INFORMED THEORIZING

Our approach to examining growth following adversity in context assumes that psychological notions about adversity, growth, and growing in response to adversity are best defined within a given *bounded group-community* (Fuller & García Coll, 2010; Super & Harkness, 1986; Whiting & Edwards, 1988). A bounded group-community is simultaneously characterized by group memberships (e.g., based on race, ethnicity, gender, sexuality, profession, roles, and others) and associated practices, beliefs, and attitudes, and by the shared settings or contexts to which members are exposed (Super & Harkness, 1986). These settings exist in both time and space. In terms of time, they exist ontogenetically and historically, but they also exist in terms of continuity or discontinuity, and periodicity

(Bronfenbrenner & Morris, 2006). In terms of contexts, they exist at the level of the microsystem on up to the macrosystem (Bronfenbrenner & Morris, 2006). Bounded group-communities, based on, for example shared racial, ethnic, and cultural backgrounds and shared sets of exposures (e.g., to racism in the United States, migration, cancer, violent victimization), define (explicitly or implicitly) the desired outcomes and the ways to achieve them (White et al., 2018). In this way, they work to define the areas of character growth that are valued and desired (e.g., spirituality, altruism, or relatedness) and how they can be achieved in the context of exposure to adversities, challenges, or failures.

Therefore, to guide high-quality research on PTG, scholars must engage in culturally and contextually informed theorizing that facilitates understanding of a target bounded group-community. This theorizing requires knowledge and understanding about correlates related to group membership and contexts. Culturally and contextually informed theorizing is the process of developing ideas about the ways in which these correlates might intersect with existing knowledge and/or theoretical models of PTG. There are numerous degrees of potential intersection. At one end of the continuum, a scholar may conclude that an existing theoretical model of PTG should explain growth among a target bounded group-community in a manner consistent with existing theoretical or empirical work on other bounded group-communities (often majority, mainstream, or unspecified group-communities). In such cases, no adjustments of the existing model are needed to accurately explain PTG in the target group-community. At the opposite end of this continuum, a scholar may conclude that an entirely new model is needed to explore PTG in a target group-community. Between these two extremes, and likely to be the more common case, a scholar may conclude that identified correlates related to membership in a given group-community have meaningful implications for an existing theory or model of PTG. In consequence, the existing theory may not explain growth in the target group as accurately as it has previously explained it in another group. Thus, modifications to existing theory are necessary. In sum, intersection involves the degree to which correlates related to the bounded group-community enhance, impact, or influence current PTG knowledge and theory.

The goal of culturally and contextually informed theorizing is to facilitate explanation and understanding of PTG in a bounded group-community by ensuring that variables somehow salient to membership in the group-community, or ones that represent significant sources of heterogeneity within it, are given appropriate consideration. The process is central to scholars' abilities to make accurate scientific inferences about causality and generalizability in PTG research because, in all but the most extreme cases (i.e., no intersection), a failure to consider these correlates will undermine both internal and external validity. Culturally and contextually informed theorizing has implications for the entire research process. It should be the basis for selecting a study's design via its impact on the development of research questions and hypotheses. It can be used to delineate sampling strategies most capable of achieving accurate representation of the target group-community. Finally, it is necessary to ensure accurate measurement of concepts of interest to the researcher (White, Zeiders, Knight, Roosa, & Tein, 2014).

Importantly, as the group-community are bound, so are culturally and contextually informed theorizing. In fact, it is often difficult to distinguish which correlates reflect group memberships (e.g., based on race, ethnicity, gender, sexuality, profession, roles, and others) and which reflect shared exposures to contexts. This is because, in many places around the world, characteristics of group membership (e.g., based on race, ethnicity, gender, sexuality, religion, immigrant status, and others) are used as social position variables to filter individuals into stratified contexts and settings (García Coll et al., 1996). We, however, in an attempt to offer a didactic resource to facilitate culturally and contextually informed scholarship on PTG, offer a set of tools to facilitate culturally informed theorizing and a separate set of tools to facilitate contextually informed theorizing. In some cases, the strategies may lead to completely overlapping considerations, as when group membership is very tightly bound to contextual exposures. In other cases, especially when there is within-group variability in contextual exposures, these strategies will produce a range of considerations with potentially less overlap.

Culturally Informed Theorizing

Broadly, culturally informed theorizing is the process of developing ideas about the ways in which variables related to group-community membership might intersect with existing psychological knowledge and/or theory related to PTG. Although these variables can describe differences between two group-communities, they can also be descriptive of the cultural differences among individuals within a given group-community because of substantial within-group heterogeneity. To engage in the process of culturally informed theorizing about PTG, scholars must acquire knowledge and understanding about the correlates that describe differences between one group-community and another, or among individuals within a single group-community. Scholars then must consider the implications of those group correlates for the existing body of empirical knowledge and theory related to PTG.

We present three domains of group-community correlates: demographic, cultural, and minority status. Demographic variables reflect the general population characteristics (e.g., socioeconomic distributions, age distributions, family structures, and immigration) of a target group-community. Cultural variables reflect a groups' shared language, belief systems, values, and customs. Minority status variables reflect experiences, challenges, and threats to which members of groups that experience marginalization are exposed. We offer these categorizations as a heuristic to guide culturally informed theorizing, recognizing that the three domains are not orthogonal. Indeed, many group correlates have demographic markers that have been employed as proxies of culture or minority status in research. Furthermore, several demographic variables may, at least in part, reflect culture (e.g., the prevalence of two-parent households may reflect strong family orientation), minority status (e.g., socioeconomic status (SES) may be a function of racism or xenophobia), or both. In this discussion, we simply aim to provide a tool to assist PTG researchers as they engage in culturally informed theorizing.

Demographic variables can include, among others, nativity, generational status, migration, SES, educational attainment, family structure and size, birth and death rates, gender, and racial-ethnic background. These demographic variables may have meaningful implications for existing PTG theory and may undermine scholars' ability to make inferences about one group from post-traumatic research based on demographically distinct groups. For example, in PTG research focusing on a demographic group that displays substantial within- or between-group diversity on nativity status, assessments of trauma or adversity that did not capture events more likely to occur in the context of migration would likely underestimate adversity exposure in the foreign-born group. Depending on both sending and receiving contexts, migrants can be exposed to a variety of stressful or traumatic experiences, including detainment, deportation, family separation, and numerous aspects of victimization. Similarly, differences in family structures and sizes can influence the availability of and access to emotional support resources. Given that support and coping are hypothetical mechanisms via which PTG can be achieved (Jayawickreme & Blackie, 2014; Sandler, Tein, & West, 1994), it would be important for scholars to theorize likely or appropriate PTG mechanisms that can trigger PTG within the context of this demographic knowledge. Consequently, PTG researchers' operationalizations of adversity exposure and identification of theoretical mechanisms in these cases will benefit from careful consideration of within- and between-group demographic diversity.

Cultural variables are group correlates that must be treated as central components of culturally informed theorizing in PTG research. Cultural variables include two overarching concepts: cultural orientations and cultural adaptations. First, *cultural orientation* refers to an individual's standing on numerous dimensions of culture, including their cultural beliefs, values, practices, language(s), and affiliations. Cultural orientations produce substantial variability between one group and another and among individuals within a given group. *Cultural adaptations* involve individual changes in cultural orientations as a results of intergroup contact (Gonzales, Fabrett, & Knight, 2009). This intergroup contact can occur in the context of migration and/or globalization (Ferguson & Bornstein, 2012). *Acculturation* (adaptation to a second culture) and *enculturation* (adaptation to the heritage culture) processes take place over time and within individuals. These distinct processes impact individuals on numerous dimensions, including their cultural beliefs, values, competencies, behaviors, language, sense of belonging to both cultures, and affiliations. Notably, in some cases it is also possible that these processes can result in acute or cumulative psychological and physiological demands and stressors on individuals experiencing them.

Cultural variables represent significant sources of heterogeneity within and between bounded group-communities, which may intersect with existing PTG theory and empiricism. For example, some PTG frameworks emphasize growth in specific domains, including relatedness, new life possibilities, self-perceived strengths, spirituality, or life appreciation (Tedeschi & Calhoun, 2004). Some of these domains can be more and less salient to different cultural groups. That is, groups with diverse cultural beliefs and values may have similarly diverse notions of what constitutes desirable and undesirable dispositions when it comes to relatedness, new life possibilities, self-perceived strengths, spirituality, and life appreciation. Research with Mexican populations in the United States, for example, demonstrates that those with stronger orientations toward their heritage culture are sanctioning certain prosocial behaviors more so than others and, furthermore, that the sanctioned prosocial behaviors are those that are more consistent with heritage cultural scripts and values (Knight & Carlo, 2012). In this way, any study of PTG would benefit from careful theorizing about how cultural orientations and cultural change (i.e., acculturation and enculturation) can shape a bounded-group community's sanctioned dispositions.

Minority status variables are those related to experiencing minoritized social positions within societies that are stratified by, for example, race, ethnicity, immigrant status, citizenship, sexuality, gender, religion, and SES. Minority status variables demonstrate how members of certain groups are received and treated by members of dominant groups. Minority status variables can include, among others, experiences of stereotyping, discrimination, prejudice, oppression, segregation, profiling, and fear of deportation. Many of these constructs are employed in theoretical models designed to describe experiences of minority groups in the United States generally (e.g., García Coll et al., 1996). Most of these are not, however, incorporated into models that were based on dominant groups in psychological research generally, or in research on PTG specifically. Consequently, psychologists are responsible for considering how these experiences might intersect with models of PTG. Continuing from prior examples, any operationalization of trauma or adversity that does not incorporate, for example, racial trauma, racism, and racial discrimination, is likely to underestimate trauma in groups that are at risk for such exposures (e.g., African Americans in the United States). Similarly, any operationalization of trauma or adversity that does not incorporate the threat of deportation or family separation is likely to underestimate levels of adversity and trauma in groups that are at high risk for these exposures (e.g., Mexicans in the United States).

Contextually Informed Theorizing

Contextually informed theorizing is the process of developing ideas about the ways in which variables that describe within- and between-setting diversity might intersect with existing psychological knowledge and/or theory related to PTG. Although these variables will certainly describe differences *between* two settings, they can also describe differences in exposure within a given setting. To engage in the process of contextually informed theorizing about PTG, scholars mush acquire knowledge and understanding about correlates that describe differences between and among diverse contexts to which a target bounded group-community is exposed. Scholars must then consider the implications of these contextual correlates for the existing body of empirical knowledge and theory related to

PTG. That is, accurate PTG prediction and explanation likely necessitates attention to within- or between-setting diversity in contextual correlates.

We propose two domains to consider when thinking about contextual correlates in PTG research: structural variable and process variables. *Structural variables* reflect the diversity of demographic, environmental, and institutional resources within and across settings. *Process variables* represent heterogeneity in the nature, quality, and quantity of social interactions taking place within and across settings. We offer these categorizations as tools to guide contextually informed theorizing while recognizing that the domains are not orthogonal. We do this in the spirit of offering tools to assist scholars as they engage in contextually informed theorizing in PTG research.

Structural variables are central components of contextually informed theorizing. Contexts vary on key structural characteristics (Tseng & Seidman, 2007), including their distributions of demographic, environmental, and institutional resources. Such distributions represent significant sources of heterogeneity both between and within contexts. Addressing variability in demographic resources requires attention to the collective characteristics of individuals inhabiting or participating in a given context. In this way, basic demographic distributions, including, for example, SES; age; ethnic, racial, and immigrant concentrations; and changes in these population characteristics over time, represent important structural variables that may be salient to characterizing the bounded group-community. Additionally, the resources of a context can represent important structural variables for describing heterogeneity within and between contexts. These can include, for example, the availability of institutional resources, like the prevalence of community organizations, social service organizations, cancer treatment centers, and religious and cultural institutions. Access to such resources will likely prove important to theorizing the diverse structures of contexts to which bounded group-communities are exposed. Notably, and reflecting an important distinction between structural and process variables, the presence of institutional resources does not necessarily determine that individuals inhabiting or participating in the context are interacting with or accessing them.

Process variables are also central components of contextually informed theorizing. Contexts can vary on the quality and quantity of social processes taking place within and between settings. The processes can occur at the level of the organism interacting with "persons, objects, and symbols in its immediate external environment" (Bronfenbrenner & Morris, 2006, p. 797; e.g., an interaction between a Latina cancer patient and her physician). However, we, like Tseng and Seidman (2007), argue that processes and interactions relevant to psychological research can also occur at higher levels of the nested ecological system. For example, they can include group-level interactions, such as between cancer survivorship coalitions and policy-makers. They can include institutional-level interactions, such as the business relationships between medical language interpreters and cancer clinics. Whereas a consideration of structural variables that may intersect with PTG among Latina cancer patients may emphasize the need to consider cancer physician density in a given city, consideration of setting process variables might emphasize the need to consider whether cancer treatment center physicians, nurses, and staff (a) speak Spanish, (b) are inclusive toward Latinx populations, or (c) offer treatment and support informational resources in the appropriate languages. All of these factors are likely to intersect with research questions related to PTG.

USING CULTURALLY AND CONTEXTUALLY INFORMED THEORIZING TO INFORM POST-TRAUMATIC GROWTH RESEARCH DESIGN

Research with specific bounded group-communities contributes to an understanding of the potential for growth following adversity by, as our examples have shown, advancing specificity relative to the range and types of adversity exposures, the domains of growth (e.g., spirituality, altruism, relatedness), and the specific mechanisms that might facilitate growth following adversity. Thus, culturally and contextually informed theorizing should be the basis for selecting a study's design via its impact on the development of research questions and hypotheses. In our work with US Mexicans, for example, we use culturally and contextually informed theorizing to identify (a) the relevant mechanisms for growth, (b) the types of adversities we should assess, and (c) the possible domains of growth to consider. In terms of mechanisms, PTG may require higher degrees of cognitive complexity and flexibility (Kashdan & Rottenberg, 2010; Tennen & Affleck, 1998). Individuals high in social supports may also be more likely to experience PTG (Jayawickreme & Blackie, 2014). These mechanisms may be especially salient in the context of the US Mexican bounded group community. For example, key aspects of adapting to life in the United States (Umaña-Taylor et al., 2014) are associated with increased cognitive complexity (Benet-Martínez, Lee, & Leu, 2006; Costa, Hernández, & Sebastián-Gallés, 2008). Thus, a focus on a major immigrant group may facilitate observation of PTG. Additionally, US Mexicans vary on their endorsements of familism beliefs (Knight et al., 2010), which characterize the feeling that the family is always there for you, and familism beliefs may provide individuals with the psychosocial buffer needed to be resilient to adversities (White, Liu, Nair, & Tein, 2015; White & Roosa, 2012; White, Roosa, & Zeiders, 2012) and experience PTG.

We used culturally informed theorizing to identify domains of growth and adversity exposures that may be particularly salient to US Mexicans. Extant theories of PTG emphasize growth in relatedness, new life possibilities, self-perceived strengths, spirituality, and life appreciation (Tedeschi & Calhoun, 2004). Relatedness, the degree of positive connection to others (Allen, Hauser, Bell, & O'Connor, 1994; Zhang & Slesnick, 2017), may be particularly valued in a US Mexican bounded group-community because it is consistent with cultural scripts emphasizing collectivism and cohesion (Schwartz et al., 2016; Knight et al., 2010). Likewise, relative to spirituality, defined as a transcendent closeness to a higher power and the universe (Myers, 2005; Paloutzian & Ellison, 1982), existing evidence suggests that religious (vs. secular) spirituality is more salient to Latinx populations (Cavazos, Johnson, & Sparrow, 2010), probably because it is consistent with cultural scripts emphasizing religiosity (Knight et al., 2010). Consequently, we focused on these domains when advancing research questions relative to the potential for PTG within this bounded group-community. Because of structural racism, US Mexicans, or Latinx populations more broadly, demonstrate disproportionately high rates of exposure to chronic adverse stressors, including poverty, low-quality social institutions, dangerous neighborhoods (Macartney, Bishaw, & Fontenot, 2013; Massey, 2016; Reardon & Robinson, 2007), language hassles (Nair, White, Zeiders, & Roosa, 2013), ethnic-based discriminatory experiences (Schmitt, Branscombe, Postmes, & Garcia, 2014; Unger, Soto, & Baezconde-Garbanati, 2016), and deportation fears (Suárez-Oroco et al., 2015). Similarly, in terms of acute events, US Mexicans and Latinx immigrants experience disproportionate exposure to family separation, deportation, and racialized violence (Golash-Boza & Hondagneu-Sotelo, 2013; Yoshikawa, Suárez-Orozco, & Gonzles, 2017). Consequently, to conduct high-quality research related to PTG in this bounded group-community, our assessments of adversity exposure needed to incorporate these considerations. Once culturally and contextually informed theorizing has been used to support the development of research questions and hypotheses, it can influence other design considerations, including sampling and measurement.

Sampling the Bounded Group-Community

Second, culturally and contextually informed theorizing can be used to delineate appropriate sampling frames and samples derived from a target bounded group-community (Knight, Roosa, & Calderón-Tena, & Gonzales, 2009; Knight, Roosa, & Umaña-Taylor, 2009). Due to challenges outlined elsewhere (Jayawickreme & Blackie, 2014), the feasibility of probability-based sampling in research on PTG remains low. Continued reliance on convenience samples in research on PTG, therefore, is highly likely. Indeed, many samples used in psychology research are convenience or other types of nonprobability samples. Samples derived from nonprobability sampling strategies, when compared to samples derived from well-executed probability-based sampling strategies, demonstrate unclear generalizability. Under circumstances of unclear sample generalizability, estimates describing the associations between variables (e.g., trauma and altruism), can be biased. In light of such circumstances, it is critical to identify ways to augment the advantages and minimize the disadvantages of nonprobability convenience samples (Jager, Putnick, & Bornstein, 2017) in research on PTG.

To this end, homogenous convenience samples—samples drawn from sampling frames intentionally constrained to specific bounded group-communities (e.g., US Mexicans, or young adults of Syrian origin who seek or have refugee status in the Netherlands), "should, on average, provide more accurate population estimates, albeit of a more circumscribed population" than more conventional convenience samples derived from sociodemographically broader sampling frames (Jager et al., 2017; p. 23). We argue that culturally and contextually informed theorizing should serve as the basis for identifying the characteristics on which to homogenize a sample. For example, our processes of culturally and contextually informed theorizing relative to the US Latinx population indicated that there was considerable within-group heterogeneity on numerous demographic, cultural, and minority status variables as well as on settings structures and processes (Portes & Rumbaut, 2001). Thus, one way we sought to homogenize our sample was to focus on US Mexicans, which excluded all other Latinx backgrounds (Roosa et al., 2008). This sample could be further homogenized, depending on the research question, to focus only on first-generation immigrants, Spanish speakers, or US Mexicans in a border region, for example.

Measurement in the Bounded Group-Community

Culturally and contextually informed theorizing is necessary to ensure accurate measurement of concepts of interest to PTG researchers, including measures of exposure, domains of growth, and mechanisms. Measurement involves the process of operationalizing a concept of interest to researchers. Measurement equivalence involves the degree to which a measure is similarly reliable and valid across diverse bounded group-communities, or the degree to which the measure assesses the same psychological construct in the same way and to the same degree of accuracy between and within bounded group-communities. Language is one particularly noteworthy correlate that can affect measurement. Language availability involves either the simultaneous development of a measure in multiple languages or the translation of an existing measure into another language. Many measures used by PTG researchers have been developed with predominately European American and middle-class samples. Too often, the adoption of measures for use with other groups has occurred without the benefit of culturally and contextually informed theorizing.

Culturally and contextually informed theorizing should be used to identify a concept needing to be measured, theoretically define it, identify items that represent it, and specify expected relations between the measured concept and other concepts. A concept's theoretical definition specifies indicators of a measured construct by defining the basic nature of a concept (among a bounded group-community). It provides the basis for identifying the items or observations that reflect the concept (among a bounded group-community) as well as the relations the measured construct has to other concepts (among a bounded group-community). Consequently, the theoretical definition of a PTG concept can be used to both identify items that can be used as indicators of the measured construct (for a bounded group-community) and to examine the degree to which those items, together, adequately represent the concept (as it manifests among a bounded group-community). We do not suggest that all concepts have culturally distinct theoretical definitions. Parallel to our suggestion that culturally and contextually informed theorizing is necessary to establish the degree of intersection between group and contextual correlates and existing PTG knowledge or theory, we suggest here that culturally and contextually informed theorizing is necessary to determine the degree that these correlates intersect with a concept's theoretical definition, indicators, or relation to other concepts.

Language Availability and Translation

Addressing the need to have multiple language versions can involve two unique processes: the translation of existing measures from English to another language or languages, or the simultaneous construction of measures in multiple languages. Both processes should rely on culturally and contextually informed theorizing. Here, we focus on how culturally and contextually informed theorizing should influence translation processes from English to another language, including translation approaches and procedures. The *literal translation approach* involves substitution of English words or phrases with non-English words and phrases. The *conceptual translation approach* involves the substitution of concepts and ideas expressed in a second language for comparable concepts and ideas expressed in English. Each of these approaches may be produced via one-way translation, back translation, or committee translation procedures. *One-way translation* involves one bilingual individual translating an instrument from one language (e.g., English) into a target language (e.g., Spanish). *Back translation* first involves a bilingual individual translating the instrument from the source language (e.g., English) to a target language (e.g., Spanish). Then, another, independent, bilingual person translates the target-language version (e.g., Spanish) back into the source language (e.g., English). If the two source-language versions are reasonably comparable, the procedure is complete. Otherwise, the procedure is repeated until comparable source-language versions are obtained. This process can also involve a decentering of the source language version by adjusting the source language version to resolve detected discrepancies. *Committee translation* involves a group of bilingual people who translate a measure and meet to review the translations.

Culturally and contextually informed theorizing can, to some degree, inform the selection of a translation approach. On one end of the continuum there may be little to no intersection between correlates and the target concept. This scenario is most likely to occur for very simple psychological concepts that are expressed with ideas and words that have exact counterparts and grammatical structures in both languages (Knight, Roosa, Calderón-Tena, & Gonzales, 2009, Knight, Roosa, & Umaña-Taylor, 2009). At this end of the continuum, literal approaches may meet the researcher's needs. Moving beyond simple psychological concepts, however, there is likely to be considerable intersection between group and contextual correlates and target concepts. Consequently, conceptual approaches are more likely to achieve a valid and reliable second-language version of the target measure or measures. The substitutions made in the process of conceptual translation will inherently involve culturally and contextually informed theorizing about the cultural (including sociolinguistic), ethnic minority, and demographic context of the bounded group-community (Martinez, Marín, & Schoua-Glusberg, 2006).

Culturally and contextually informed theorizing should also inform the translation procedure. Ultimately, a mix of back-translation, decentering, and committee procedures is likely to be most effective in producing valid and reliable measures in the target language (Bracken & Barona, 1991). Still, these procedures rely on bilingual individuals. An examination of group and contextual correlates may reveal that a substantial proportion of a targeted bounded group-community are not bilingual. Furthermore, there are numerous potential differences in the distribution of correlates between bilingual and monolingual individuals. Bilingual individuals may be, on average, more educated, more bicultural, more cognitively flexible, and less familiar with local sociolinguistic nuances than the target population. Consequently, to the extent that the makeup of the committee does not accurately reflect the cultural, ethnic minority, and demographic makeup of the target population, traditional committee procedures may pose significant threats to the validity and reliability of the target-language version and—to the extent decentering was used—of the source language version. Careful theorizing about the different distribution of correlates across these two groups results in uncertainty about whether translations conducted by a team of bilingual individuals will generalize to the full range of a target group-community. To combat some of this uncertainty and produce translations that are a better match to the target population, Erkut and colleagues (1999) recommend the inclusion of monolingual English and monolingual non–English speakers on translation committees.

Measurement Equivalence

Measurement equivalence is a question of the similarity of reliability and construct validity coefficients of a measure across two or more groups. Unless a construct is measured similarly across two subsamples, findings from (a) data pooled across subsamples or (b) subsample comparisons may be misleading. Hui and Triandis (1985) defined several types of equivalence: conceptual, item, functional, and scalar. *Conceptual equivalence* involves assessment of whether the concept is relevant to all the subsamples involved and should rely heavily on culturally and contextually informed theorizing (White et al., 2015). *Item equivalence* involves assessments of whether individual scale items relate to the theoretical concept similarly across subsamples. *Functional equivalence* of a measure involves assessments of whether the degree to which the goals of the behaviors being measured are similar in all subsamples. *Scalar equivalence* involves assessments of whether scale scores refer to the same degree, intensity, and magnitude of the construct in the subsamples being studied.

Item, Functional, and Scalar Equivalence

The processes used to establish item, functional, and scalar equivalence rely on a combination of analytical techniques and culturally and contextually informed theorizing. The analytical techniques establish the degree of similarity in the internal structure of a measure across groups (measurement invariance or factorial invariance) and the degree of similarity in the construct validity associations of that measure across groups (construct validity equivalence). These are described in great detail elsewhere (e.g., Knight, Roosa, & Umaña-Taylor, 2009). Culturally and contextually informed theorizing are used to define what pattern of reliability and validity associations is to be considered consistent with equivalence. That is, they establish what pattern of internal structural relations and construct validity associations is consistent with factorial invariance and construct validity equivalence, respectively. When the theorizing converges on a conclusion that group or contextual correlates do not intersect appreciably with the measurement of a concept, a scholar would expect that both the internal structure and construct validity associations should be identical across subgroups. If, however, the theorizing suggests that correlates do intersect notably with a concept's theoretical definition, indicators, or relation to other concepts, then the scholar should define a set of patterns regarding internal structure and/or construct validity relations that would be consistent with measurement equivalence under that intersection. For example, if theorizing indicates that the concept is differentially related to some other concept across two groups of US Mexicans or that some subtle differences in the item functioning and factor structures across these groups exists, then measurement equivalence would be indicated by somewhat different but theoretically consistent interrelationships with other concepts or among items.

Example in Research on Character Growth

Consider, for example, the Prosocial Tendencies Measure (PTM) used to assess six distinct forms of prosocial behaviors (Carlo & Randall, 2002). The PTM was originally conceived as a measure to address the substantive evidence that there are multiple types of prosocial behaviors, that there are unique correlates and developmental trajectories of each form of prosocial behavior, and to account for individual and culture group differences in prosocial behaviors (Carlo & Randall, 2001). Based on these conceptual grounds and a thorough review of existing measures of prosocial behaviors, the PTM was developed and piloted. Items were created for each of the six types of prosocial behaviors: altruistic (i.e., helping others without expectation for self-rewards), public (i.e., helping in front of an audience), emotional (i.e., assisting others who are clearly emotionally distraught), dire (i.e., helping in emergency situations), anonymous (i.e., helping indirectly and without the helpee's knowledge), and compliant (i.e., helping when asked to do so). Of particular relevance and importance is the ability of the PTM to assess altruistic prosocial behaviors because such actions are directly relevant to examining post-traumatic moral growth.

The initial form of the PTM was developed for use with late adolescents and young adults; for use with predominantly White, European American samples; and consisted of 25 total items. Once initial evidence for the reliability and validity of the PTM was provided, a shorter, modified (age-appropriate items were retained and wording was simplified) version (the PTM-Revised) was created to use with young adolescents. Evidence of the PTM-R was also published (Carlo, Hausmann, Christiansen, & Randall, 2003). In general, the PTM and PTM-R, however, were not originally designed to use with US Latinx populations.

Based on subsequent funding from a grant from the National Science Foundation, the PTM-R was refined to use with a sample of US Mexicans using processes of culturally and contextually informed theorizing. The validity of the original PTM-R was also examined in this study with a comparison sample of European American young adolescents. To accomplish the PTM-R refinement and validation, several focus groups of European American and US Mexican (both Spanish-speaking and English-speaking) mothers were conducted, and the mothers were asked to spontaneously identify common prosocial behaviors observed in their adolescent children and, later, to validate the items of the PTM-R. For Spanish-speaking mothers, the PTM-R was translated and back-translated to develop a Spanish-language version to review. Findings from the focus groups confirmed that the scales/items of the PTM-R captured commonly observed forms of prosocial behaviors, and the evaluation of the PTM-R by the mothers also validated the PTM-R to use with both US Mexican and European American adolescents. Several published studies have provided substantive supportive psychometric evidence that the PTM-R is acceptable to use with US Mexican and US Latinx youth (see Carlo, 2014; Knight & Carlo, 2012).

Using an independent sample of US Mexican and European American adolescents, Carlo and his colleagues (2010) presented evidence that the hypothesized six-factor solution was the best-fitting model (as compared to alternative factor solutions) and that there was evidence of weak and strong configural factor equivalence, scalar equivalence, and item equivalence. The PTM and PTM-R have also demonstrated conceptual and functional equivalence across adolescents and young adults from other Latin American countries (e.g., Argentina, Columbia, Costa Rica), non–Latin American countries (e.g., Turkey, Spain, Greece, Taiwan), and various subgroups (e.g., gender, SES, nativity) within nationalities (see Carlo & Maiya, 2019; McGinley et al., 2009; Xiao, Hashi, Korous, & Eisenberg, 2019, for reviews). For example, in a recent meta-analytic review, Xiao et al. (2019) showed that the six-factor solution is the best-fitting solution across many studies and that gender differences in the subscales of the PTM and PTM-R are generally consistent with theory. In addition, there is growing evidence that the PTM and PTM-R are significantly linked to behavioral task measures of prosocial behaviors (e.g., Rodrigues, Ulrich, Mussel, Carlo, & Hewig, 2017; Su, Tian, & Huebner, 2019) and sensitive to intervention programs (e.g., Garbanzo-Rodriguez, Rivera-Villareal, Smith-Castro, & Perez-Sanchez, 2017; Sukys, Majauskiene, & Dumciene, 2017).

CONCLUSION

Research with specific bounded group-communities contributes to an understanding of the potential for growth following adversity by advancing specificity relative to the range and types of adversity exposures, the domains of growth, and the specific mechanisms that might facilitate growth following adversity. That is, high-quality culturally and contextually informed theorizing supports identification of relevant adversity exposures, growth domains, and mechanisms for every bounded group-community. Likewise, as we have shown, culturally and contextually informed theorizing is critical for determining PTG research designs, including critical sampling and measurement choices (and associated translation procedures, if necessary). For these reasons, in building on Jayawickreme and Blackie's (2014) recommendations that PTG research designs include direct, longitudinal assessment of individuals' current standings on growth-relevant domains before and after exposure to adversity (Jayawickreme & Blackie, 2014), we strongly advocate that PTG researchers rely on culturally and contextually informed theorizing during all stages of the research process.

REFERENCES

Allen, J. P., Hauser, S. T., Bell, K. L., & O'Connor, T. G. (1994). Longitudinal assessment of autonomy and relatedness in adolescent–family interactions as predictors of adolescent ego development and self-esteem. *Child Development, 65*(1), 179–194. doi:10.2307/1131374

Benet-Martínez, V., Lee, F., & Leu, J. (2006). Biculturalism and cognitive complexity: Expertise in cultural representations. *Journal of Cross-Cultural Psychology, 37*(4), 386–407. doi:10.1177/0022022106288476

Bronfenbrenner, U., & Morris, P. A. (2006). The bioecological model of human development. In R. M. Lerner (Ed.), *Handbook of Child Psychology: Vol. 1. Theoretical Models of Human Development* (6th ed., pp. 993–1028). New York: Wiley. doi:10.1002/9780470147658.chpsy0114

Bracken, B. A., & Barona, A. (1991). State of the art procedures for translating, validating and using psychoeducational tests in cross-cultural assessment. *School Psychology International, 12*, 119–132. doi:10.1177/0143034391121010

Carlo, G. (2014). The development and correlates of prosocial moral behaviors. In M. Killen & J. G. Smetana (Eds.), *The Development and Correlates of Prosocial Moral Behaviors* (2nd ed., pp. 208–234). New York: Psychology Press.

Carlo, G., Hausmann, A., Christiansen, S., & Randall, B. A. (2003). Sociocognitive and behavioral correlates of a measure of prosocial tendencies for adolescents. *Journal of Early Adolescence, 23*(1), 107–134. doi:10.1177/0272431602239132

Carlo, G., Knight, G. P., McGinley, M., Zamboanga, B. L., & Jarvis, L. H. (2010). The multidimensionality of prosocial behaviors and evidence of measurement equivalence in Mexican-origin and European American early adolescents. *Journal of Research on Adolescence, 20*, 334–358. doi:10.1111/j.1532-7795.2010.00637.x

Carlo, G., & Maiya, S. (2019). Methodological issues in cross-cultural research on prosocial and moral development. In N. A. Jones, M. Platt, K. D. Mize, & J. Hardin (Eds.), *Conducting Research in Developmental Psychology: A Topical Guide for Research Methods Utilized Across the Lifespan* (pp. 171–199). New York: Routledge.

Carlo, G., & Randall, B. A. (2001). Are all prosocial behaviors equal? A socioecological developmental conception of prosocial behavior. In F. Columbus (Ed.), *Advances in Psychology Research, Vol. III* (pp. 151–170) Hauppauge, NY: Nova Science.

Carlo, G., & Randall, B. A. (2002). The development of a measure of prosocial behaviors for late adolescents. *Journal of Youth and Adolescence, 31*(1), 31–44. doi:10.1023/A:1014033032440

Causadias, J. M., & Umaña-Taylor, A. J. (2018). Reframing marginalization and youth development: Introduction to the special issue. *American Psychologist, 73*(6), 707–712. https://dx.doi.org/10.1037/amp0000336

Cavazos, J., Jr., Johnson, M. B., & Sparrow, G. S. (2010). Overcoming personal and academic challenges: Perspectives from Latina/o college students. *Journal of Hispanic Higher Education, 9*(4), 304–316. doi:10.1177/1538192710380744

Costa, A., Hernández, M., & Sebastián-Gallés, N. (2008). Bilingualism aids conflict resolution: Evidence from the ANT task. *Cognition, 106*(1), 59–86. doi:10.1016/j.cognition.2006.12.013

Erkut, S., Alarcón, O., Coll, C. G., Tropp, L., & García, H. V. (1999). The dual-focus approach to creating bilingual measures. *Journal of Cross-Cultural Psychology, 30*, 206–218.

Ferguson, G. M., & Bornstein, M. H. (2012). Remote acculturation: The "Americanization" of Jamaican Islanders. *International Journal of Behavioral Development, 36*(3), 167–177. https://doi.org/10.1177/0165025412437066

Fuller, B., & García Coll, C. (2010). Learning from Latinos: Contexts, families, and child development in motion. *Developmental Psychology, 46*(3), 559–565. doi:10.1037/a0019412

Garbanzo-Rodríguez, G., Rivera-Villareal, C., Smith-Castro, V., & Pérez-Sánchez, R. (2017). Effects of a simulation videogame on altruistic tendencies in an open education context. *Revista Colombiana de Educación, 73*, 41–57. https://dx.doi.org/10.17227/01203916.73rce39.56

García Coll, C., Crnic, K., Lamberty, G., Wasik, B. H., Jenkins, R., Garcia, H. V., & McAdoo, H. P. (1996). An integrative model for the study of developmental competencies in minority children. *Child Development, 67*(5), 1891–1914. doi:10.1111/j.1467-8624.1996.tb01834.x

Golash-Boza, T., & Hondagneu-Sotelo, P. (2013). Latino immigrant men and the deportation crisis: A gendered racial removal program. *Latino Studies, 11*(3), 271–292.

Gonzales, N. A., Fabrett, F., & Knight, G. P. (2009). Acculturation, enculturation, and the psychosocial adaptation of latino youth. In F. A. Villarruel, G. Carlo, J. M. Grau, M. Azmitia, N. J. Cabrera & T. J. Chahin (Eds.), *Handbook of US Latino Psychology* (pp. 115–134). Thousand Oaks, CA: Sage.

Hui, C. H., & Triandis, H. C. (1985). Measurement in cross-cultural psychology: A review and comparison of strategies. *Journal of Cross-Cultural Psychology, 16*(2), 131–152. doi:10.1177/0022002185016002001

Infurna, F. J., & Jayawickreme, E. (2019). Fixing the growth illusion: New directions for research in resilience and posttraumatic growth. *Current Directions in Psychological Science, 28*(2), 152–158. https://doi.org/10.1177/0963721419827017

Jayawickreme, E., & Blackie, L. E. (2014). Post-traumatic growth as positive personality change: Evidence, controversies and future directions. *European Journal of Personality, 28*(4), 312–331. doi:10.1002/per.1963

Jager, J., Putnick, D. L., & Bornstein, M. H. (2017). More than just convenient: The scientific merits of homogeneous convenience samples. *Monographs of the Society for Research in Child Development, 82*(2), 13–30. doi:10.1111/mono.12296

Joseph, S., & Linley, P. A. (2005). Positive adjustment to threatening events: An organismic valuing theory of growth through adversity. *Review of General Psychology, 9*(3), 262–280. doi:10.1037/1089-2680.9.3.262

Kashdan, T. B., & Rottenberg, J. (2010). Psychological flexibility as a fundamental aspect of health. *Clinical Psychology Review, 30*(7), 865–878. doi:10.1016/j.cpr.2010.03.001

Knight, G. P., & Carlo, G. (2012). Prosocial development among Mexican American youth. *Child Development Perspectives, 6*(3), 258–263. doi:10.1111/j.1750-8606.2012.00233.x

Knight, G. P., Gonzales, N. A., Saenz, D. S., Bonds, D. D., Germán, M., Deardorff, J., . . . Updegraff, K. A. (2010). The Mexican American cultural values scale for adolescents and adults. *Journal of Early Adolescence, 30*(3), 444–481. doi:10.1177/0272431609338178

Knight, G. P., Roosa, M. W., Calderón-Tena, C. O., & Gonzales, N. A. (2009). Methodological issues in research on Latino populations. In F. A. Villarruel, G. Carlo, J. M. Grau, M. Azmitia, N. J. Cabrera, & T. J. Chahin (Eds.), *Handbook of US Latino Psychology: Developmental and Community-Based Perspectives* (pp. 45–62). Thousand Oaks, CA: Sage.

Knight, G. P., Roosa, M. W., & Umaña-Taylor, A. J. (2009). *Studying Ethnic Minority and Economically Disadvantaged Populations: Methodological Challenges and Best Practices*. Washington, DC: American Psychological Association.

Macartney, S. E., Bishaw, A., & Fontenot, K. (2013). Poverty rates for selected detailed race and Hispanic groups by state and place: 2007-2011. ACSBR/11-17. https://www.census.gov/library/publications/2013/acs/acsbr11-17.html

Martinez, G., Marín, B. V., & Schoua-Glusberg, A. (2006). Translating from English to Spanish: The 2002 national survey of family growth. *Hispanic Journal of Behavioral Sciences, 28*(4), 531–545. doi:10.1177/0739986306292293

Massey, D. S. (2016). Residential segregation is the linchpin of racial stratification. *City & Community, 15*(1), 4–7. doi:10.1111/cico.12145

McGinley, M., Carlo, G., Crockett, L. J., Raffaelli, M., Stone, R. A. T., & Iturbide, M. I. (2009). Stressed and helping: The relations among acculturative stress, gender, and prosocial tendencies in Mexican Americans. *Journal of Social Psychology, 150*(1), 34–56. doi:10.1080/00224540903365323

Myers, D. G. (2005). Psychological science and spiritual pursuits. In C. L. Harper, Jr. (Ed.), *Spiritual information: 100 perspectives on science and religion* (pp. 433–439). Radnor, PA: Templeton Foundation Press.

Nair, R. L., White, R. M. B., Zeiders, K. H., & Roosa, M. W. (2013). Cultural stressors and mental health symptomatology among Mexican Americans: Examining the impact of family and neighborhood contexts. *Journal of Youth and Adolescence, 42*, 1611–1623. doi:10.1007/s10964-012-9834-z

Paloutzian, R. F., & Ellison, C. W. (1982). Loneliness, Spiritual Well-Being and the Quality of Life. In L. A. Peplau & D. Perlman (Eds.), *Loneliness: A Sourcebook of Current Theory, Research and Therapy* (pp. 224–236). New York: John Wiley & Sons.

Pals, J. L., & McAdams, D. P. (2004). The transformed self: A narrative understanding of posttraumatic growth. *Psychological Inquiry*, 65–69.

Portes, A., & Rumbaut, R. (2001). *Legacies: The Story of the Immigrant Second Generation*. Berkeley: University of California Press.

Reardon, S. F., & Robinson, J. P. (2007). Patterns and trends in racial/ethnic and socioeconomic academic achievement gaps. In H. F. Ladd & E. B. Fiske (Eds.), *Handbook of Research in Education Finance and Policy* (pp. 499–518). Mahwah, NJ: Erlbaum.

Rodrigues, J., Ulrich, N., Mussel, P., Carlo, G., & Hewig, J. (2017). Measuring prosocial tendencies in Germany: Sources of validity and reliability of the revised prosocial tendency measure. *Frontiers in Psychology, 8*, 2119. doi:10.3389/fpsyg.2017.02119

Roosa, M. W., Liu, F. F., Torres, M., Gonzales, N. A., Knight, G. P., & Saenz, D. (2008). Sampling and recruitment in studies of cultural influences on adjustment: A case study with Mexican Americans. *Journal of Family Psychology, 22*(2), 293–302. doi:10.1037/0893-3200.22.2.293

Sandler, I. N., Tein, J. Y., & West, S. G. (1994). Coping, stress, and the psychological symptoms of children of divorce: A cross-sectional and longitudinal study. *Child Development, 65*(6), 1744–1763.

Schmitt, M. T., Branscombe, N. R., Postmes, T., & Garcia, A. (2014). The consequences of perceived discrimination for psychological well-being: A meta-analytic review. *Psychological Bulletin, 140*(4), 921–948. doi:10.1037/a0035754

Schwartz, S. J., Unger, J. B., Baezconde-Garbanati, L., Zamboanga, B. L., Córdova, D., Lorenzo-Blanco, E. I., . . . Szapocznik, J. (2016). Testing the parent–adolescent acculturation discrepancy hypothesis: A five-wave longitudinal study. *Journal of Research on Adolescence, 26*(3), 567–586. doi:10.1111/jora.12214

Seery, M. D., Holman, E. A., & Silver, R. C. (2010). Whatever does not kill us: Cumulative lifetime adversity, vulnerability, and resilience. *Journal of Personality and Social Psychology, 99*(6), 1025. doi:10.1037/a0021344

Staub, E., & Vollhardt, J. (2008). Altruism born of suffering: The roots of caring and helping after victimization and other trauma. *American Journal of Orthopsychiatry, 78*(3), 267–280.

Su, T., Tian, L., & Huebner, E. S. (2019). The reciprocal relations among prosocial behavior, satisfaction of relatedness needs at school, and subjective well-being in school: A three-wave cross-lagged study among Chinese elementary school students. *Current Psychology*. doi:10.1007/s12144-019-00323-9

Suárez-Oroco, C., Katsiaficas, D., Birchall, O., Alcantar, C., Hernandez, E., Garcia, Y., . . . Teranishi, R. T. (2015). Undocumented undergraduates on college campuses: Understanding their challenges and assets and what it takes to make an undocufriendly campus. *Harvard Educational Review, 85*(3), 427–463. doi:10.17763/0017-8055.85.3.427

Sukys, S., Majauskiene, D., & Dumciene, A. (2017). The effects of a three-year integrated Olympic education programme on adolescents' prosocial behaviours. *European Journal of Sport Science, 17*(3), 335–342. doi:10.1080/17461391.2016.1254280

Super, C. M., & Harkness, S. (1986). The developmental niche: A conceptualization at the interface of child and culture. *International Journal of Behavioral Development, 9*(4), 545–569. doi:10.1177/016502548600900409

Tedeschi, R. G., & Calhoun, L. G. (2004). Posttraumatic growth: Conceptual foundations and empirical evidence. *Psychological Inquiry, 15*(1), 1–18. doi:10.1207/s15327965pli1501_01

Tennen, H., & Affleck, G. (1998). Personality and transformation in the face of adversity. In R. G. Tedeschi, C. L. Park, & L. G. Calhoun (Eds.), *Posttraumatic Growth: Positive Changes in the Aftermath of Crisis* (pp. 65–98). Mahwah, NJ: Routledge.

Tseng, V., & Seidman, E. (2007). A systems framework for understanding social settings. *American Journal of Community Psychology, 39*(3–4), 217–228. doi:10.1007/s10464-007-9101-8

Umaña-Taylor, A. J., Quintana, S. M., Lee, R. M., Cross, W. E., Rivas-Drake, D., Schwartz, S. J., . . . Seaton, E. (2014). Ethnic and racial identity during adolescence and into young adulthood: An integrated conceptualization. *Child Development, 85*(1), 21–39. doi:10.1111/cdev.12196

Unger, J. B., Soto, D. W., & Baezconde-Garbanati, L. (2016). Trajectories of perceived discrimination from adolescence to emerging adulthood and substance use among Hispanic youth in Los Angeles. *Addictive Behaviors, 53*, 108–112. doi:10.1016/j.addbeh.2015.10.009

White, R. M. B., Burleson, E., & Knight, G. P. (2016). Future prospects for studying ethnic and racial minority youths and families in diverse rural and nonrural contexts. In L. J. Crockett, & G. Carlo (Eds.), *Rural Ethnic Minority Youth and Families in the United States: Theory, Research, and Applications* (pp. 267–286). New York: Springer.

White, R. M. B., Knight, G. P., & Roosa, M. W. (2015). Using culturally informed theory to study Mexican American children and families. In Y. M. Caldera & E. W. Lindsey (Eds.), *Mexican American Children and Families: Multidisciplinary Perspectives* (pp. 27–43). New York: Routledge.

White, R. M. B., Liu, Y., Nair, R. L., & Tein, J. (2015). Longitudinal and integrative tests of family stress model effects on Mexican origin adolescents. *Developmental Psychology, 51*(5), 649–662. doi:10.1037/a0038993

White, R. M. B., Nair, R. L., & Bradley, R. H. (2018). Theorizing the benefits and costs of adaptive cultures for development. *American Psychologist, 73*(6), 727–739. doi:10.1037/amp0000237

White, R. M. B., & Roosa, M. W. (2012). Neighborhood contexts, fathers, and Mexican American young adolescents' internalizing symptoms. *Journal of Marriage and Family, 74*(1), 152–166. doi:10.1111/j.1741-3737.2011.00878.x

White, R. M. B., Roosa, M. W., & Zeiders, K. H. (2012). Neighborhood and family intersections: Prospective implications for Mexican American adolescents' mental health. *Journal of Family Psychology, 26*(5), 793–804. doi:10.1037/a0029426

White, R. M. B., Zeiders, K. H., Knight, G. P., Roosa, M. W., & Tein, J. (2014). Mexican origin youths' trajectories of perceived peer discrimination from middle childhood to adolescence: Variation by neighborhood ethnic concentration. *Journal of Youth and Adolescence, 43*(10), 1700–1714. doi:10.1007/s10964-014-0098-7

Whiting, B. B., & Edwards, C. P. (1988). *Children of Different Worlds: The Formation of Social Behavior*. Cambridge, MA: Harvard University Press.

Whiting, B. B., & Whiting, J. W. M. (1975). *Children of Six Cultures: A Psycho-Cultural Analysis*. Cambridge, MA: Harvard University Press.

Xiao, S. X., Hashi, E. C., Korous, K. M., & Eisenberg, N. (2019). Gender differences across multiple types of prosocial behavior in adolescence: A meta-analysis of the prosocial tendency measure-revised (PTM-R). *Journal of Adolescence, 77*, 41–58. https://doi.org/10.1016/j.adolescence.2019.09.003

Yoshikawa, H., Suárez-Orozco, C., & Gonzales, R. G. (2017). Unauthorized status and youth development in the United States: Consensus statement of the society for research on adolescence. *Journal of Research on Adolescence, 27*(1), 4–19.

Zhang, J., & Slesnick, N. (2017). Discrepancies in autonomy and relatedness promoting behaviors of substance using mothers and their children: The effects of a family systems intervention. *Journal of Youth and Adolescence, 46*(3), 668–681. doi:10.1007/s10964-016-0549-4

10

Modeling Growth and Resilience Among Military Personnel

How Using Different Models Yields Different Answers

WILLIAM J. CHOPIK ■

The prospect that people can be resilient to—or even grow from—a stressful experience is an alluring possibility. This is especially true of soldiers and veterans. Some have proposed that deploying and military experiences provide soldiers with enduring mental resources and toughness that are protective for the rest of their lives (Gallaway, Millikan, & Bell, 2011; Tedeschi & McNally, 2011). To date, however, consistent evidence for the possibility of growth and resilience among soldiers and veterans has proved elusive, at least with respect to how it is currently operationalized (Habib, Stevelink, Greenberg, & Williamson, 2018; Jayawickreme & Blackie, 2014; Jayawickreme et al., 2020; Mark, Stevelink, Choi, & Fear, 2018). There are many reasons for our uncertainty about how common resilience and growth are among military personnel and people facing adversity more generally, both conceptually and methodologically (Mark et al., 2018; Tedeschi & McNally, 2011). Most relevant to this chapter are the reasons most closely aligned with study design and data analysis. Specifically, these considerations include the lack of prospective, longitudinal data on soldiers and veterans and the ways researchers have historically modeled, analyzed, and conceptualized growth and resilience (Infurna, Gerstorf, Ram, & Heckhausen, 2016; Infurna & Jayawickreme, 2019; Infurna & Luthar, 2016c; Jayawickreme & Blackie, 2014; Jayawickreme et al., 2020; Tennen & Affleck, 2009). In this chapter, I provide a conceptual and methodological overview of how growth and resilience have been traditionally studied among soldiers and veterans, including two empirical examples showcasing how methodological flexibility can yield different inferences in how military personnel adapt to stressful circumstances.

POST-TRAUMATIC GROWTH AND RESILIENCE

The idea that individuals can grow from adversity has a long history in psychology. However, a great deal of research has focused on *resilience* to adversity and found that individuals do not change considerably following adverse events. Some of the first evidence suggesting resilience in children appeared nearly 60 years ago (Luthar, 2006). The path to growth and resilience, particularly among military personnel, has been hypothesized to contain specific elements that involve distinct emotion regulatory achievements and reframing of the experience. For example, Tedeschi and McNally (2011) suggest that soldiers must at least acknowledge the potential of trauma as a precursor to growth, enhance emotion regulation (e.g., the reduction of anxiety and controlling intrusive thoughts), self-disclose to solicit social support, develop a trauma narrative that cultivates and encourages growth and resilience, and develop principles that will presumably serve them well when they encounter future challenges. Although this stage-based model has not been explicitly tested, this final point—that resources built during this process serve soldiers well in the future—is a critical element. In other words, through trauma, people become stronger people for life (Calhoun & Tedeschi, 1999, 2006). The tools that helped individuals weather an initial trauma serve them well with adversity later in life.

Before establishing the exact process through which growth and resilience occur, researchers have rightly devoted their attention to documenting if and how adults adapt to adverse circumstances (Bonanno, 2004). From these efforts, the field to date is left with the perception that resilience is a common consequence of adversity, with some estimates of resilience approaching 70–80% (Bonanno et al., 2012; Infurna & Luthar, 2016b). High levels of resilience have also been found across a wide variety of traumatic experiences (Bonanno, 2005; Bonanno & Diminich, 2013; Bonanno, Galea, Bucciarelli, & Vlahov, 2006, 2007; Bonanno & Kaltman, 2001; Bonanno et al., 2002). Few studies have successfully documented *growth* following adversity in a prospective way. In the aforementioned studies, the percentages of individuals reporting improvements in well-being after adversity are low and not found in every study (e.g., often in the 4.8–8% range when it is found; Bonanno et al., 2012; Porter, Bonanno, Frasco, Dursa, & Boyko, 2017). Nevertheless, the collective results from these studies paint an optimistic picture of how individuals adapt to adversity: they are largely resilient.

Although there is cause for optimism about the rates of resilience observed for individuals experiencing adversity, there is also cause for skepticism. Specifically, there are several methodological considerations and decisions that researchers make that might result in the overestimation of growth and resilience. These factors range from how the data are collected to how the data are analyzed and reported.

DESIGN CONSIDERATIONS IN THE STUDY OF GROWTH AND RESILIENCE

In conceptualizing growth and resilience following adversity, there are a few characteristics that should ostensibly be present in every study. Ideally, there would be information on individuals both before and after the adversity occurs, measured prospectively.

Many of the studies that purport to find high rates of post-traumatic growth (PTG) and resilience rely on cross-sectional samples, small sample sizes, and retrospective measures. The problems of cross-sectional samples and small sample sizes have been extensively documented (Caruana, Roman, Hernández-Sánchez, & Solli, 2015; Simmons, Nelson, & Simonsohn, 2011). In addition to the interpretational difficulties that accompany cross-sectional designs, cross-sectional data also limit researchers' abilities to model the mechanisms that give rise to character development across adverse experiences over time (Maxwell & Cole, 2007). Furthermore, a typical way of assessing PTG is through retrospective measures in which participants are advised to reflect on how an experience might have changed them (Barakat, Alderfer, & Kazak, 2006; Tedeschi & Calhoun, 1996). The use of retrospective measures requires a great deal of mental effort to be exerted—effort that may not always result in accurate responses. When applying retrospective measures to the study of adversity, participants must discern their current standing on some dimension (e.g., well-being), previous standing on that same dimension before an event occurred, compare these standings and calculate the amount of change that occurred, and evaluate how much of this change can be attributed to an adverse event (Frazier et al., 2009; Jayawickreme & Blackie, 2014; Tennen & Affleck, 1998, 2009). Such an effort is a tall order for quantifying how people change in response to adverse life events. As a result, a rigorous standard is to have prospective assessments of a construct before and multiple times after an event occurs.

Regarding conceptual considerations, there is generally a hierarchy of personal characteristics that are expected to be malleable to adverse life events (McAdams & Pals, 2006). For example, well-being and broader measures of adjustment (e.g., post-traumatic stress, depressive symptoms) have reliably been shown to change in response to life events (Bonanno et al., 2012; Lucas, 2005, 2007a; Luhmann & Eid, 2009). The same is true for more intensely measured phenomena, like individuals' affect or even behavior measured repeatedly over shorter intervals (Almeida, 2005; Prentice, Jayawickreme, & Fleeson, 2020). There are also more stable, enduring characteristics (e.g., personality, character) that might not change as dramatically in response to adverse life events. This may be one explanation for why the existing literature has yet to find consistent evidence for systematic personality changes before and after life events (Bleidorn, Hopwood, & Lucas, 2018). The same can also be said about narratives that people construct about who they are, which also change over time and in response to life events (e.g., McAdams,

1995; Newton, Herr, Pollack, & McAdams, 2014). Specifying the expectations for how individuals change in response to adversity also necessarily requires a discussion about the specific ways in which they change. Do they become happier? Do they have more or fewer depressive symptoms? Do their personalities change? Do their reflections about an event change over time, and are these changes related to well-being? Each of these individual characteristics might be accompanied by different expectations about the magnitude and direction of changes. However, the magnitude of growth and occurrence of resilience are rarely contextualized in this layered framework (Jayawickreme et al., 2020).

ANALYTIC FLEXIBILITY

In addition to the study of growth and resilience being dependent on how growth and resilience are measured and conceptualized, the particular analytic model can have large implications for the conclusions one can draw. These analytic models vary in both how the types of inferences they are meant to make (e.g., between vs. within-subjects differences) and the types of assumptions they make (e.g., whether individuals vary in where they start and how they change over time). Of course, many different designs can prospectively test growth and resilience processes, including multiphasic growth curve models, more short-term longitudinal studies, and studies that incorporate measurement-burst designs in the context of macro-longitudinal studies (Infurna et al., 2016; Zachry, Phan, Blackie, & Jayawickreme, 2018). In the examples given here, I focus more on traditional, longer term change among individuals assessed over multiple years. A thorough treatment of the differences between these approaches can be found elsewhere (Infurna et al., 2016); the following sections are just illustrations of a few of these models applied to a specific question to give you a sense of what is possible.

A Story of Three Types of Resilience Studies

To illustrate how resilience and growth can be modeled with varying degrees of analytic flexibility, I draw on three different but related models that seek to answer approximately the same question: How does the onset of disability change veterans' depressive symptoms? Whether and how disability impacts well-being has been studied in the past, concerning normative impacts of disability as well as potential moderating factors of the impact of disability on well-being (Harder, Kelly, & Chopik, 2019; Lucas, 2007a, 2007b; Lucas & Chopik, 2020). In short, the onset of a disability leads to immediate and often long-lasting negative changes in well-being. However, it could be the case that there are subgroups of veterans who might be resilient to the onset of a disability. For example, disabled veterans might have developed the mental resources and capacity to withstand such a significant life stressor, as some frameworks of growth and resilience might suggest (Calhoun & Tedeschi, 2006; Tedeschi & McNally, 2011). Likewise, experiencing an adverse life event might change veterans' perspectives, making them feel more grateful about other areas in their lives. Although these possibilities might seem preposterous if one is not steeped in the literature on growth and resilience, the idea that there might be individual differences in changes in depressive symptoms (i.e., some people increase, decrease, or stay the same) following a life event is a reasonable one that has been tested in other, adjacent questions (Luchetti et al., 2020).

I revisit this question using data on the veteran sample from the Health and Retirement Study (HRS; Sonnega et al., 2014). Specifically, I examined a sample of 266 veterans without a disability at study entry who experienced some form of permanent disability over the 26-year history of HRS (M_{age} = 61.62 at baseline, standard deviation [*SD*] = 8.28; $M_{YearsOfEducation}$ = 12.97; 16.2% female; 83.8% white/Caucasian). The measure of interest is depressive symptoms, which is a count variable. The measure of disability was whether veterans experienced a new functional limitation from which they never recovered. Although this admittedly superficial distinction of disability has its limitations—it is agnostic to severity and official distinctions of what constitutes a disability—I viewed it as sufficient for at least some illustrative demonstrations of a life event that might spur psychological change. Other studies have used different definitions of disability and provide deeper considerations of how disability status can be measured (Infurna & Wiest, 2016; Lucas, 2007b; see Palmer & Harley, 2012, for an in-depth discussion about how disability is conceptualized and measured in survey research). Using a dataset with so many assessment waves allowed me to model changes from before to after the onset of the disability.

Between-Subjects Changes and Modeling

In one common approach to modeling changes in growth and resilience over time, researchers will employ a growth curve modeling approach (Little, Bovaird, & Slegers, 2006; Singer & Willett, 2003). Essentially, multiple assessments of individuals followed over time allow for the estimation of an intercept and slope in a given construct. If studying a specific population (e.g., veterans), these designs could also include matched controls (e.g., non-veterans) to further isolate the effects of disability on well-being (Austin, 2011; Schwaba & Bleidorn, 2019). From this basic framework, researchers have been flexible in how they have applied growth curve modeling to the study of resilience and growth. For instance, there are examples in which a researcher might conduct a sample-level growth curve model in which an overall intercept and slope for the entire sample are estimated. From there, they might predict variation in the intercepts and slopes based on a life event (i.e., does the slope vary depending on whether someone experienced a disability or not?), group membership (i.e., does the slope vary depending on being a veteran or not?), or both (i.e., do veterans who experience a disability change differently than other groups?)(see Chopik, Oh, et al., 2021; Jackson & Allemand, 2014). There are also more formalized models in which multigroup comparisons can be run, specifically comparing measurement properties and the structure and nature of changes between veterans and non-veterans (i.e., do depressive symptoms change in a curvilinear way among veterans but a linear way among everyone else? Is the underlying factor structure of the measure similar between veterans and everyone else, and over time?).

Using this approach, researchers can model how people with and without disabilities change in depressive symptoms over the study window, which can yield useful insights. As seen in Figure 10.1A, veterans who would eventually develop a disability over the study window were initially higher in depressive symptoms and increased in depressive symptoms over time. Those who did not develop a permanent disability (a control group of 14,754 participants that includes veterans and non-veterans) were relatively stable in their depressive symptoms over time. Aligned with the aforementioned process, veteran status significantly predicted the intercept (i.e., veterans had higher depressive symptoms on average) and the quadratic slope of depressive symptoms (i.e., veterans increased in depressive symptoms over time). From this approach, on average, the onset of a disability is associated with an increase in depressive symptoms.

Within-Subjects Changes and Modeling

Another approach is to examine how one group of people (i.e., veterans who experience a disability) change from before to after an event, like the onset of a disability. This within-subject approach is a departure from the between-subjects approach mentioned earlier. Rather than comparing two disparate groups of people, the "within" approach I am operationalizing and highlighting here instead focuses on pre to post-disability changes in depressive symptoms among veterans who experience a disability *only* (see Lucas, 2005; Lucas, 2007a; 2007b for examples). One major benefit of this approach is to more clearly isolate the effect that an event has on changes in an outcome. With the traditional approach described earlier, the year-to-year changes in depressive symptoms were obscured without the additional modeling of something akin to piecewise or multiphase changes (Infurna et al., 2016; Ning & Luo, 2017). Because many participants in a sample experience the onset of a disability at different waves, this approach centers the onset of the event for every participant who experiences it. This centering allows for an examination of changes that occur before and after an event to be examined rather than overall changes both among those who experience an event or don't (i.e., a between-subjects question). Worth noting, psychological characteristics occasionally change immediately before the onset of an event. For example, some declines in well-being occur in the year *before* a divorce, which likely reflects the relationship dynamics of a couple or the contentious nature of a divorce rather than the actual divorce being finalized (Lucas, 2005). In this way—across all of these models—special adaptation characteristics (like whether adaptation occurs in the year immediately prior to or immediately after an event) can be estimated as well. Between-subject considerations can also be integrated into the model. For example, within-subject adaptions might vary according to some between-subjects characteristic like gender, age, or another psychological characteristic.

Using this approach and honing in on just the individuals who experience a life event (i.e., veterans who experience a disability), researchers can model

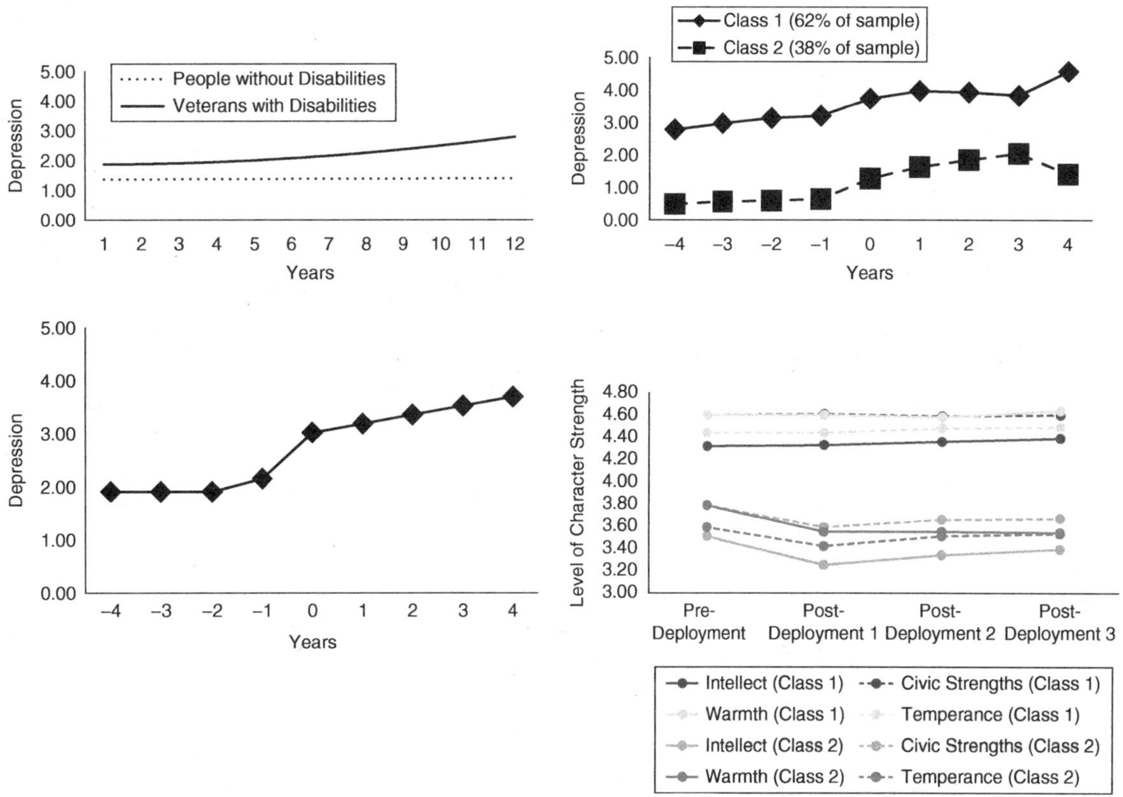

Figure 10.1 A. Between-subject changes. B. Within-subject changes. C. Growth mixture modeling. D. Growth mixture modeling of character strengths.

anticipatory, event-based, and adaptation processes among those who experienced a life event. As seen in Figure 10.1B, veterans experienced a dramatic increase in depressive symptoms upon experiencing a disability. Furthermore, there was no evidence of adaptation: depressive symptoms continued to increase over time after the onset of a disability. There was also some evidence for anticipatory increases in depressive symptoms in the year immediately before the onset of a disability. From this approach, on average, the onset of a disability is associated with an average increase in depressive symptoms. However, the within-subjects approach allowed me to better track whether the changes in depressive symptoms could be attributable to the event in question. Worth noting, there were significant differences in veterans' starting levels of depression (i.e., intercepts) and how they changed following the disability (i.e., slopes) but not in the average increase as a result of the disability onset. These individual differences in intercepts and slopes can be further explored in expanded models that examine predictors of intercepts and moderators of change over time.

Growth Mixture Modeling

Yet another approach that merges many of the considerations made so far is growth mixture modeling (Grimm & Ram, 2009; Ram & Grimm, 2009). Growth mixture modeling is an amalgamation of latent growth curve and mixture modeling that enables researchers to (a) examine trajectories of growth and resilience and (b) identify different latent classes that show specific trajectories. In other words, it allows for the possibility that one group of individuals may begin high on depressive symptoms, decline across a life event, and then rebound to a moderate level. Likewise, another group may start low and increase across the onset of an event (as seen with the previous approaches). Permitting multiple growth trajectories is an advantage over other models that have been traditionally used to model longitudinal data (e.g., growth curve modeling) and that assume the population under study develops in one way over time and that individuals vary with where they start (an intercept) and change over time (slope).

In this field, the use of growth mixture modeling has been historically used to characterize growth, resilience, and adaptation following adverse life events, often yielding high rates of resilience or growth. However, recent considerations have been made concerning the appropriate use and specification of mixture modeling for these purposes. One of the decision points at which analytic flexibility can affect the results is whether researchers allow subgroups and individuals within a particular subgroup to vary in where they start and how they change over time. Traditionally, most of these parameters are constrained to zero or to be equal across groups (Bonanno et al., 2012; Bonanno et al., 2002; Galatzer-Levy, Huang, & Bonanno, 2018). Estimating parameters in such a way assumes no variability in intercepts and slopes and can potentially alter a researcher's conceptual model (e.g., people vary just as much from the typical slope in one group as they do in a different group). Importantly, allowing these parameters to be freely estimated dramatically changes (a) the number of distinct trajectories the analysis yields and (b) the distribution of individuals within each trajectory. Following an initial demonstration by Infurna and Luthar, there have now been several examples of how selectively varying a few assumptions in growth mixture modeling can lead to wildly different interpretations for how individuals adapt to challenging circumstances compared to traditional forms of the analysis (Chambers et al., 2017; Infurna & Grimm, 2017; Infurna & Luthar, 2016a, 2016c, 2017b; Infurna et al., 2017). Again, like the other approaches, the model is flexible and can be customized to answer specific questions and model discontinuous growth.

Using this approach, researchers can identify subgroups in the sample that might vary in their adaptation to an adverse event. This is particularly important for studying growth and resilience processes: growth mixture modeling can identify if there is a detectable group of individuals who are showing growth or resilience as a departure from the sample-wide pattern seen in other approaches. As seen in Figure 10.1C, after allowing the aforementioned parameters to be freely estimated, two separate patterns of change were identified. This suggests that a growth mixture modeling approach was worthwhile for demonstrating that there might be subgroups of veterans experiencing the onset of disability differently. Specifically, the changes in depressive symptoms for Class 1 (62% of the sample) resembled what we saw earlier: an increase in depressive symptoms upon disability onset followed by increases in depressive symptoms. A second class (38% of the sample) also emerged which was initially lower on depressive symptoms, experienced an increase in depressive symptoms upon obtaining a disability, and experiencing some adaptation, albeit not until a few years later. From this approach, the onset of disability is again shown to increase depressive symptoms. However, some of the sample (the 38% in Class 2) were lower on depressive symptoms initially and experienced some adaptation, albeit they never fully returned to their pre-disability levels of depressive symptoms.

AN EXAMPLE OF SOLDIERS' CHARACTER DEVELOPMENT ACROSS THE DEPLOYMENT TRANSITION

Analytic flexibility and model selection can dramatically alter the conclusions that one can make regarding growth and resilience. In the three examples just presented, veterans with disabilities were shown to have increased in depressive symptoms over time (Figure 10.1A), increase immediately before and pre- to post-disability (Figure 10.1B), and demonstrate some adaptation after the onset of disability (Figure 10.1C). Next, I present an example that extends the previous models to include more stable, trait-like characteristics (e.g., character strengths) and predictors of change.

Is a potentially stressful transition like a military deployment cycle sufficient to spur character change? Are any character changes permanent, or do individuals return to their preexisting character levels before the deployment (Lucas, 2007a)? What we do know about *growth* of positive characteristics in soldiers often comes from research in which soldiers are asked about their responses and experiences *after the fact* (e.g., Feder et al., 2008) or from studies that have focused more on well-being and post-traumatic stress symptoms (Bonanno et al., 2012; Porter et al., 2017). Although the literature on growth and resilience explicitly discusses positive characteristics, these characteristics are rarely the focus of longitudinal studies involving stressful events. Rather, researchers have traditionally focused on evaluations of well-being (as we did earlier) rather than on more trait-like, individual difference constructs. In Jayawickreme and Blackie (2014)'s conceptualization of PTG as positive personality change, they leveraged the PTG literature in the context of personality change processes. Specifically, growth and resilience are often framed in terms of how individuals' traits change in response to non-normative life events (Tennen & Affleck, 1998, 2009).

One important taxonomy of positive characteristics is Peterson and Seligman's (2004) conceptualization of strengths and virtues within the Values in Action Inventory of Strengths. The inventory of strengths includes 24 positive characteristics on which individuals can vary (e.g., creativity, kindness, hope, gratitude, leadership). These character strengths are considered to be enduring individual characteristics with a moderate degree of stability over time and across the life span (Disabato, Kashdan, Short, & Jarden, 2017). Although longitudinal data on character strengths are relatively rare, there is an implicit assumption in the field that character strengths are at least somewhat malleable and changeable. Studies of cross-sectional age differences suggest that normative changes may be possible, although it is unclear from where these changes might originate (Chopik et al., 2018; Martínez-Martí & Ruch, 2014). There is also some evidence that character strengths vary considerably across different cultures, subpopulations, and settings, suggesting that there may be at least some contextual influences on the development of character strengths (McGrath, 2015). Worth noting, despite the initial introduction of the character strengths taxonomy being primarily conceptual (Peterson & Seligman, 2004), more recent efforts have focused on developing a more empirical taxonomy of character strengths (Vanhove, Harms, & DeSimone, 2016; Vie, Scheier, Lester, & Seligman, 2016). These efforts have resulted in more succinct organizations of character strengths into four broader character strengths—intellect, warmth, civic strengths, and temperance. We used this particular taxonomy in the study I describe next because it was specifically developed on a sample of military personnel.

My colleagues and I took this charge seriously by examining changes in character strengths among 212,386 American Army soldiers deploying for the first time (Chopik, Kelley, Vie, Oh, et al., 2021). Adopting the approach of Infurna and Luther (2016c) to allow the variability of the intercepts and slopes to vary within and between classes, we found evidence for two classes of character change (see Figure 10.1D). The first class (which represented anywhere between 52% and 63% of the sample, depending on which character strength being examined) were resilient—the soldiers in this group were higher on character strengths to begin with and stayed high across the deployment cycle. The second class (representing 37–48% of the sample) experienced pre- to post-deployment declines in character strengths from which they never rebounded. In this example, soldiers were largely resilient—they had relatively stable levels of character strengths. However, there was still the common maladjustment that we saw in the previous examples—a portion of the soldiers experienced declines in their character strengths which did not increase again in the years immediately after the deployment. When examining more trait-like constructs like character strengths, most of the sample showed stable levels of each strength domain, which is a departure from other studies examining adjustment-related outcomes like depressive symptoms, post-traumatic stress, and well-being (Bonanno et al., 2012; Porter et al., 2017). As previously discussed, these differences demonstrate the hierarchy of personal characteristics that are susceptible to changes in response to life events: traits may be less malleable compared to global evaluations of well-being or adjustment. Nevertheless, as in our previous example, we did not observe a group of soldiers who fared *better* following adversity.

Predictors of Change

After identifying patterns of change, a natural next step involved examining the antecedents of those changes. In other words, were there personal or experiential characteristics that made someone more likely to be resilient? As an illustration, I will detail how a researcher might go about predicting resilience and growth in the framework of growth mixture modeling. In a follow-up study, we looked at a wide variety of predictors of resilience: demographic characteristics (e.g., age, race/ethnicity), military characteristics (e.g., rank, time in service), health characteristics (e.g., both mental and physical health), and deployment characteristics (e.g., combat stress, combat injury). Using a logistic regression, we predicted group membership into the resilience trajectory group mentioned earlier (Chopik, Kelley, Vie, Lester, et al., 2021).

Higher age predicted resilience, with each additional decade corresponding to a 32% increased odds of being in the overall character resilient group (odds ratio [OR] = 1.32, 95% confidence interval [CI] 1.27–1.37). Being male (OR = 1.20, CI 1.15–1.25), having more than a high school education (OR = 1.16, 95% CI 1.11–1.22), and identifying as non-Hispanic white were each associated with being classified in the high resilience trajectory. Regarding military characteristics, officers had a greater odds of being in the resilient class in the overall character analysis (OR = 1.26, CI 1.17–1.35). Reserve and National Guard soldiers were each more likely to be in the overall character resilient group than were active duty soldiers (OR = 1.45, CI 1.37–1.54 and OR = 1.34, CI 1.28–1.40, respectively). However, time in service was largely unrelated to character strength development. Finally, both mental and physical health measured before the deployment were associated with character development after the deployment. Each unit increase in self-rated health was associated with a 64% greater odds of being in the resilient group in the overall character analysis (OR = 1.64, CI 1.61–1.67). Psychiatric treatment in the year prior to deployment, on the other hand, was again associated with a lower odds of being in the resilient class in the overall character analysis (OR = 0.67, CI 0.62–0.72).

Importantly, experiences during deployment affected soldiers' odds of being resilient. Injury during deployment, combat stress, and longer deployments were each associated with lower odds of being in the resilient class. Soldiers injured while deployed had a 14% lower odds of being in the resilient group (OR = 0.86, CI 0.83–0.90). Combat stress was also negatively related to resilience in all analyses, with 4–8% decreased odds of belonging to the resilient class with each successive combat stressor. Longer deployment lengths also showed a negative association with resilience, such that every additional month of deployment was associated with 3% lower odds of being in the overall character resilient class (OR = 0.97, CI 0.97–0.98).

Altogether, many characteristics that are associated with the development of psychological traits outside of adverse experiences (e.g., health) also predicted resilience and change in character across the deployment cycle. Physical and mental health were the largest predictors of trajectory group membership. But individual and deployment characteristics played a role as well—age, branch of the military, and the severity of the combat experience (e.g., stress, injury, length)—also predicted how soldiers changed over time.

FUTURE DIRECTIONS

One of the main purposes of this chapter was to provide some illustrations for how to model resilience and growth using veterans and soldiers as exemplars. In both examples, there was little evidence of growth—that individuals thrive following adversity. This can be attributable to a common if uncontroversial conclusion about adversity: it introduces stress and difficulty into people's lives, and people likely rarely benefit from it. Adversity likely changes health and well-being (as we saw in the veteran examples), but it might not be sufficient to fundamentally change character in a dramatic way (as we saw from the stability and small changes among deploying soldiers). The two forms of adversity are fundamentally different, introduce different challenges, and are not comparable in most ways. However, they do highlight some of the many ways to go about answering questions related to growth and resilience.

Methodological and analytic discussions about how to appropriately model growth and resilience have brought to light a dire and uncomfortable realization for researchers—that growth and resilience (particularly in well-being) might not be as common as cultural narratives and previous research might have us believe. Furthermore, it is also unclear what the functions of growth would be for individuals, including military personnel. It is likely that people might feel better or be more well-adjusted if they improved in most character strengths, and that could be a goal in and of itself. However, does growth in character make for better people, better interpersonal relationships, more effective military personnel, or help people live longer? Such *consequences* of growth are rarely examined. Of course, there are many unanswered questions about the study of growth and resilience. Here, I highlight just a few future directions that can increase our understanding of growth and resilience. They range from conceptual to methodological directions that researchers can consider.

For one, the lack of prospective data and detailed information about adversity is one of the main limitations that has affected our inferences about growth and resilience. Even the typical approaches I outlined with respect to veterans experiencing a disability run afoul of this limitation. This is also a broader point about how life events affect psychosocial characteristics more broadly. When researchers examine pre to post changes in a construct, they often strip that event of its context and merely look at whether an event occurred or not (Bleidorn et al., 2018). I've done this myself, and even the predictors of resilience highlighted here are also measured in short, relatively crude ways (Chopik, 2018; Chopik, Oh, et al., 2021). Life events vary on several dimensions, and few taxonomies exist that characterize which life events are most likely to lead to changes in psychological characteristics (Chopik et al., 2019). In one of the few exceptions, Luhmann, Fassbender, Alcock, and Haehner (2020) have provided an initial framework for describing how and why some events, like deployment, might lead to lasting changes in psychological characteristics. This framework includes a description of the many different dimensions on which life events can vary, including the appraisal and controllability of the events. Such features of a deployment experience might explain why character strengths change for some soldiers and not others (and how some life events spur change and others do not, in general). The same can be said about the context in which resilience and growth are hypothesized to happen—the long period after a life event occurs. These post-event contexts might alter one's interpretation of the event and ultimately the downstream consequences of not only that event but also any psychological changes that result from it (Tedeschi & McNally, 2011). Moving forward, it is crucial that studies are designed so that accurate portrayals of what life is like before and well-after an event occur. Guidelines for considerations about new primary forms of data collection, how to best utilize existing data sources, and data analyses can be found elsewhere (Jayawickreme et al., 2020). But, in summary, greater attention to measurement and specificity and long-term longitudinal data are needed in the study of growth and resilience.

Second, the two projects here also highlight the need to broaden our definition of what is considered successful growth and resilience. For example, in the veterans' analysis, there was little evidence for resilience in depressive symptoms following the onset of a disability. In the soldiers' analysis, there was a high degree of resilience in character strengths. The differences between the two are attributable to many things: that deployments and disabilities are different things, the heterogeneous experiences of both, the composition of the samples, and the outcome variables under investigation. However, because of the few datasets that contain a suite of possible growth and resilience indicators (e.g., studies that have measures of depressive symptoms and traits), there is a current ignorance about how much change to expect and in which characteristics. It is very uncommon to see comprehensive studies of growth and resilience that can draw firm and specific conclusions about how adversity can change some indicators (e.g., well-being) and not others (e.g., personality). It is more often the case that a study focuses on just a single indicator of adjustment. The few exceptions have been very useful: even in studies that examine relatively similar constructs (e.g., life satisfaction, positive/negative affect), there is evidence that growth and resilience are heterogeneous experiences (Infurna & Luthar, 2017a). For example, people might still report that their lives are relatively happy overall (i.e., life satisfaction) or be just as agreeable but nevertheless report worse mood or health following an adverse event. Would such a person be considered resilient? Or does only happiness and health matter, and personality is less relevant? The exact criteria for what is considered a growing or resilient person is controversial (Infurna & Jayawickreme, 2019). To maximize the utility of the approaches outlined in this chapter, we first need an understanding of what domains are most important to look at and, just as important, actual data that measures a diversity of outcomes so that we can achieve this goal.

CONCLUSION

This chapter began with the observation that, although it might be natural for people to want to believe in growth and resilience, finding definitive evidence for whether and why it exists is a much harder task. I reviewed a few different examples that provide illustrations of how one might go about asking these types of questions. Do people who experience adversity differ from those who don't, on average? How do people change before to after adversity? Are there subgroups of people who respond differently to adversity? Are there be reliable predictors of these individual differences in change? Each of these questions involves a different analytic approach that can have large implications for the inferences that can be made. Even if growth and widespread resilience do not exist or are not common, evaluating the time course of adjustment and predictors of individual differences in adjustment among military personnel is a worthwhile endeavor. But doing so involves careful consideration of methodological and analytic flexibility—historically, a lack of consideration has led to the impression that growth and resilience are commonplace. The hope is that new studies and methods will be able to accurately capture processes of adaptation moving forward.

REFERENCES

Almeida, D. M. (2005). Resilience and vulnerability to daily stressors assessed via diary methods. *Current Directions in Psychological Science, 14*(2), 64–68.

Austin, P. C. (2011). An introduction to propensity score methods for reducing the effects of confounding in observational studies. *Multivariate Behavioral Research, 46*(3), 399–424.

Barakat, L. P., Alderfer, M. A., & Kazak, A. E. (2006). Posttraumatic growth in adolescent survivors of cancer and their mothers and fathers. *Journal of Pediatric Psychology, 31*(4), 413–419.

Bleidorn, W., Hopwood, C. J., & Lucas, R. E. (2018). Life events and personality trait change. *Journal of Personality, 86*(1), 83–96.

Bonanno, G. A. (2004). Loss, trauma, and human resilience: Have we underestimated the human capacity to thrive after extremely aversive events? *American Psychologist, 59*(1), 20.

Bonanno, G. A. (2005). Resilience in the face of potential trauma. *Current Directions in Psychological Science, 14*(3), 135–138.

Bonanno, G. A., & Diminich, E. D. (2013). Positive adjustment to adversity: Trajectories of minimal-impact resilience and emergent resilience. *Journal of Child Psychology and Psychiatry, 54*(4), 378–401.

Bonanno, G. A., Galea, S., Bucciarelli, A., & Vlahov, D. (2006). Psychological resilience after disaster: New York City in the aftermath of the September 11th terrorist attack. *Psychological Science, 17*(3), 181–186.

Bonanno, G. A., Galea, S., Bucciarelli, A., & Vlahov, D. (2007). What predicts psychological resilience after disaster? The role of demographics, resources, and life stress. *Journal of Consulting and Clinical Psychology, 75*(5), 671–682. https://doi.org/10.1037/0022-006X.75.5.671

Bonanno, G. A., & Kaltman, S. (2001). The varieties of grief experience. *Clinical Psychology Review, 21*(5), 705–734.

Bonanno, G. A., Mancini, A. D., Horton, J. L., Powell, T. M., LeardMann, C. A., Boyko, E. J., . . . Smith, T. C. (2012). Trajectories of trauma symptoms and resilience in deployed US military service members: Prospective cohort study. *British Journal of Psychiatry, 200*(4), 317–323.

Bonanno, G. A., Wortman, C. B., Lehman, D. R., Tweed, R. G., Haring, M., Sonnega, J., . . . Nesse, R. M. (2002). Resilience to loss and chronic grief: A prospective study from preloss to 18-months postloss. *Journal of Personality and Social Psychology, 83*(5), 1150.

Calhoun, L. G., & Tedeschi, R. G. (1999). *Facilitating Posttraumatic Growth: A Clinician's Guide*. Mahwah, NJ: Erlbaum.

Calhoun, L. G., & Tedeschi, R. G. (2006). The foundations of posttraumatic growth: An expanded framework. In L. G. Calhoun & R. G. Tedeschi (Eds.), *Handbook of Posttraumatic Growth: Research and Practice* (pp. 3–23). Mahwah, NJ: Erlbaum.

Caruana, E. J., Roman, M., Hernández-Sánchez, J., & Solli, P. (2015). Longitudinal studies. *Journal of Thoracic Disease, 7*(11), E537–E540.

Chambers, S. K., Ng, S. K., Baade, P., Aitken, J. F., Hyde, M. K., Wittert, G., Frydenberg, M., & Dunn, J. (2017). Trajectories of quality of life, life satisfaction, and psychological adjustment after prostate cancer. *Psycho-Oncology, 26*(10), 1576–1585. https://doi.org/10.1002/pon.4342

Chopik, W. J. (2018). Does personality change following spousal bereavement? *Journal of Research in Personality, 72*, 10–21.

Chopik, W. J., Jayawickreme, E., Renz, U., & Yang, E. (2019). Conceptual and methodological considerations for the study of wisdom arising from adversity. *Journal of Value Inquiry, 53*(3), 393–396.

Chopik, W. J., Kelley, W. L., Vie, L. L., Lester, P. B., Bonett, D. G., Lucas, R. E., & Seligman, M. E. (2021). Individual and experiential predictors of character development across the deployment cycle. *European Journal of Personality*. doi:08902070211012931.

Chopik, W. J., Kelley, W. L., Vie, L. L., Oh, J., Bonett, D. G., Lucas, R. E., & Seligman, M. E. (2021). Development of character strengths across the deployment cycle among US Army soldiers. *Journal of Personality, 89*(1), 23–34.

Chopik, W. J., Newton, N. J., Ryan, L. H., Kashdan, T. B., & Jarden, A. J. (2019). Gratitude across the life span: Age differences and links to subjective well-being. *Journal of Positive Psychology, 14*(3), 292–302.

Chopik, W. J., Oh, J., Kim, E. S., Schwaba, T., Krämer, M. D., Richter, D., & Smith, J. (2020). Changes in optimism and pessimism in response to life events: Evidence from three large panel studies. *Journal of Research in Personality, 88*, 103985.

Disabato, D. J., Kashdan, T. B., Short, J. L., & Jarden, A. (2017). What predicts positive life events that influence the course of depression? A longitudinal examination of gratitude and meaning in life. *Cognitive Therapy and Research, 41*(3), 444–458.

Feder, A., Southwick, S. M., Goetz, R. R., Wang, Y., Alonso, A., Smith, B. W., . . . Vythilingam, M. (2008). Posttraumatic growth in former Vietnam prisoners of war. *Psychiatry, 71*(4), 359–370.

Frazier, P., Tennen, H., Gavian, M., Park, C., Tomich, P., & Tashiro, T. (2009). Does self-reported posttraumatic growth reflect genuine positive change? *Psychological Science, 20*(7), 912–919.

Galatzer-Levy, I. R., Huang, S. H., & Bonanno, G. A. (2018). Trajectories of resilience and dysfunction following potential trauma: A review and statistical evaluation. *Clinical Psychology Review, 63*, 41–55.

Gallaway, M. S., Millikan, A. M., & Bell, M. R. (2011). The association between deployment-related posttraumatic growth among U.S. army soldiers and negative behavioral health conditions. *Journal of Clinical Psychology, 67*(12), 1151–1160.

Grimm, K. J., & Ram, N. (2009). A second-order growth mixture model for developmental research. *Research in Human Development, 6*(2–3), 121–143.

Habib, A., Stevelink, S. A. M., Greenberg, N., & Williamson, V. (2018). Post-traumatic growth in (ex-) military personnel: Review and qualitative synthesis. *Occupational Medicine, 68*(9), 617–625.

Harder, J. A., Keller, V. N., & Chopik, W. J. (2019). Demographic, experiential, and temporal variation in ableism. *Journal of Social Issues, 75*(3), 683–706.

Infurna, F. J., Gerstorf, D., Ram, N., & Heckhausen, J. (2016). Analytic strategies for the study of adaptation to major life events: Making the most of large-scale longitudinal surveys. In H.-P. Blossfeld, J. von Maurice, M. Bayer, & J. Snopek (Eds.), *Methodological Issues of Longitudinal Surveys: The Example of the National Educational Panel Study* (pp. 19–35). New York: Springer VS.

Infurna, F. J., & Grimm, K. J. (2018). The use of growth mixture modeling for studying resilience to major life stressors in adulthood and old age: Lessons for class size and identification and model selection. *Journals of Gerontology: Series B, 73*(1), 148–159.

Infurna, F. J., & Jayawickreme, E. (2019). Fixing the growth illusion: New directions for research in resilience and posttraumatic growth. *Current Directions in Psychological Science, 28*(2), 152–158.

Infurna, F. J., & Luthar, S. S. (2016a). Parents reactions to the loss of their child: Resilience is by no means typical. *International Journal of Psychology, 51*, 374.

Infurna, F. J., & Luthar, S. S. (2016b). Resilience has been and will always be, but rates declared are inevitably suspect: Reply to Galatzer-Levy and Bonanno. *Perspectives on Psychological Science, 11*(2), 199–201.

Infurna, F. J., & Luthar, S. S. (2016c). Resilience to major life stressors is not as common as thought. *Perspectives on Psychological Science, 11*(2), 175–194.

Infurna, F. J., & Luthar, S. S. (2017a). The multidimensional nature of resilience to spousal loss. *Journal of Personality and Social Psychology, 112*(6), 926–947.

Infurna, F. J., & Luthar, S. S. (2017b). Parents' adjustment following the death of their child: Resilience is multidimensional and differs across outcomes examined. *Journal of Research in Personality, 68*, 38–53.

Infurna, F. J., & Wiest, M. (2016). The effect of disability onset across the adult life span. *Journals of Gerontology: Series B, 73*(5), 755–766.

Infurna, F. J., Wiest, M., Gerstorf, D., Ram, N., Schupp, J., Wagner, G. G., & Heckhausen, J. (2017). Changes in life satisfaction when losing one's spouse: Individual differences in anticipation, reaction, adaptation and longevity in the German Socio-economic Panel Study (SOEP). *Ageing & Society, 37*(5), 899–934.

Jackson, J. J., & Allemand, M. (2014). Moving personality development research forward: Applications using structural equation models. *European Journal of Personality, 28*(3), 300–310.

Jayawickreme, E., & Blackie, L. E. R. (2014). Post-traumatic growth as positive personality change: Evidence, controversies and future directions. *European Journal of Personality, 28*(4), 312–331.

Jayawickreme, E., Infurna, F. J., Alajak, K., Blackie, L. E., Chopik, W. J., Chung, J. M., . . . Zonneveld, R. (2021). Post-traumatic growth as positive personality change: Challenges, opportunities, and recommendations. *Journal of Personality, 89*(1), 145–165.

Little, T. D., Bovaird, J. A., & Slegers, D. W. (2006). Methods for the analysis of change. In D. K. Mroczek & T. D. Little (Eds.), *Handbook of Personality Development* (pp. 181–211). Mahwah, NJ: Lawrence Erlbaum.

Lucas, R. E. (2005). Time does not heal all wounds: A longitudinal study of reaction and adaptation to divorce. *Psychological Science, 16*(12), 945–950.

Lucas, R. E. (2007a). Adaptation and the set-point model of subjective well-being: Does happiness change after major life events? *Current Directions in Psychological Science, 16*(2), 75–79.

Lucas, R. E. (2007b). Long-term disability is associated with lasting changes in subjective well-being: Evidence from two nationally representative longitudinal studies. *Journal of Personality and Social Psychology, 92*(4), 717.

Lucas, R. E., & Chopik, W. J. (2020). Testing the buffering effect of social relationships in a prospective study of disability onset. *Social Psychological and Personality Science*. doi:1948550620979200.

Luchetti, M., Lee, J. H., Aschwanden, D., Sesker, A., Strickhouser, J. E., Terracciano, A., & Sutin, A. R. (2020). The trajectory of loneliness in response to COVID-19. *American Psychologist, 75*(7), 897–908. https://doi.org/10.1037/amp0000690

Luhmann, M., & Eid, M. (2009). Does it really feel the same? Changes in life satisfaction following repeated life events. *Journal of Personality and Social Psychology, 97*(2), 363–381.

Luhmann, M., Fassbender, I., Alcock, M., & Haehner, P. (2020). A dimensional taxonomy of perceived characteristics of major life events. *Journal of Personality and Social Psychology*. Advance online publication. https://doi.org/10.1037/pspp0000291

Luthar, S. S. (2006). Resilience in development: A synthesis of research across five decades. In D. Cicchetti & D. J. Cohen (Eds.), *Developmental Psychopathology* (2nd ed., pp. 739–795). New York: Wiley.

Mark, K. M., Stevelink, S. A. M., Choi, J., & Fear, N. T. (2018). Post-traumatic growth in the military: A systematic review. *Occupational and Environmental Medicine, 75*(12), 904–915.

Martínez-Martí, M. L., & Ruch, W. (2014). Character strengths and well-being across the life span: Data from a representative sample of German-speaking adults living in Switzerland. *Frontiers in Psychology, 5*(1253).

Maxwell, S. E., & Cole, D. A. (2007). Bias in cross-sectional analyses of longitudinal mediation. *Psychological Methods, 12*(1), 23.

McAdams, D. P. (1995). What do we know when we know a person? *Journal of Personality, 63*(3), 365–396.

McAdams, D. P., & Pals, J. L. (2006). A new Big Five: Fundamental principles for an integrative science of personality. *American Psychologist, 61*(3), 204–217.

McGrath, R. E. (2015). Character strengths in 75 nations: An update. *Journal of Positive Psychology, 10*(1), 41–52.

Newton, N. J., Herr, J. M., Pollack, J. I., & McAdams, D. P. (2014). Selfless or selfish? Generativity and narcissism as components of legacy. *Journal of Adult Development, 21*(1), 59–68.

Ning, L., & Luo, W. (2017). Specifying turning point in piecewise growth curve models: challenges and solutions. *Frontiers in Applied Mathematics and Statistics, 3*(1), 1–19. https://doi.org/10.3389/fams.2017.00019

Palmer, M., & Harley, D. (2012). Models and measurement in disability: An international review. *Health Policy Plan, 27*(5), 357–364.

Peterson, C., & Seligman, M. E. P. (2004). *Character Strengths and Virtues: A Handbook and Classification*. New York: Oxford University Press.

Porter, B., Bonanno, G. A., Frasco, M. A., Dursa, E. K., & Boyko, E. J. (2017). Prospective post-traumatic stress disorder symptom trajectories in active duty and separated military personnel. *Journal of Psychiatric Research, 89*, 55–64.

Prentice, M., Jayawickreme, E., & Fleeson, W. (2020). An experience sampling study of the momentary dynamics of moral, autonomous, competent, and related need satisfactions, moral enactments, and psychological thriving. *Motivation and Emotion, 44*(2), 244–256.

Ram, N., & Grimm, K. J. (2009). Growth mixture modeling: A method for identifying differences in longitudinal change among unobserved groups. *International Journal of Behavioral Development, 33*(6), 565–576.

Schwaba, T., & Bleidorn, W. (2019). Personality trait development across the transition to retirement. *Journal of Personality and Social Psychology, 116*(4), 651–665.

Simmons, J. P., Nelson, L. D., & Simonsohn, U. (2011). False-positive psychology: Undisclosed flexibility in data collection and analysis allows presenting anything as significant. *Psychological Science, 22*(11), 1359–1366.

Singer, J. D., & Willett, J. B. (2003). *Applied Longitudinal Data Analysis: Modeling Change and Event Occurrence*. New York: Oxford University Press.

Sonnega, A., Faul, J. D., Ofstedal, M. B., Langa, K. M., Phillips, J. W. R., & Weir, D. R. (2014). Cohort profile: The Health and Retirement Study (HRS). *International Journal of Epidemiology, 43*(2), 576–585.

Tedeschi, R. G., & Calhoun, L. G. (1996). The posttraumatic growth inventory: Measuring the positive legacy of trauma. *Journal of Traumatic Stress, 9*(3), 455–471.

Tedeschi, R. G., & McNally, R. J. (2011). Can we facilitate posttraumatic growth in combat veterans? *American Psychologist, 66*(1), 19–24.

Tennen, H., & Affleck, G. (1998). Personality and transformation in the face of adversity. In R. G. Tedeschi, C. Park, & L. G. Calhoun (Eds.), *Posttraumatic Growth: Positive Changes in the Aftermath of Crisis* (pp. 65–98). Mahwah, NJ: Lawrence Erlbaum.

Tennen, H., & Affleck, G. (2009). Assessing positive life change: In search of meticulous methods. In C. R. Snyder & S. J. Lopez (Eds.), *Handbook of Positive Psychology* (pp. 584–597). New York: Oxford University Press.

Vanhove, A. J., Harms, P. D., & DeSimone, J. A. (2016). The Abbreviated Character Strengths Test (ACST): A preliminary assessment of test validity. *Journal of Personality Assessment, 98*(5), 536–544.

Vie, L. L., Scheier, L. M., Lester, P. B., & Seligman, M. E. P. (2016). Initial validation of the U.S. Army Global Assessment Tool. *Military Psychology, 28*(6), 468–487.

Zachry, C. E., Phan, L. V., Blackie, L. E. R., & Jayawickreme, E. (2018). Situation-based contingencies underlying wisdom-content manifestations: Examining intellectual humility in daily life. *Journals of Gerontology: Series B, 73*(8), 1404–1415.

11

Studying Post-Traumatic Growth Across the Adult Life Span

Conceptual and Methodological Considerations

OMAR E. STABEN, MOLLY J. GARDNER, FRANK J. INFURNA, SUNIYA S. LUTHAR, AND KEVIN J. GRIMM ■

Character strengths are psychological traits that represent positive aspects of personality and aid individuals in establishing a genuine connection with others and more broadly, humanity (Fleeson, Furr, Jayawickreme, Meindl, & Helzer, 2014; Fleeson et al., 2014; Peterson & Seligman, 2004). Much of the literature regarding character strengths has predominantly utilized cross-sectional research designs that involve one-time assessments and assume character strengths to be relatively stable over time. However, the concept of malleability within character strengths is explicitly embedded in its definition. A main issue that we seek to evaluate in this chapter is whether and what qualities from "within" a person or aspects of an individual's character strength change across the adult life span and, in particular, in relation to adversity or trauma. Are character strengths stable or malleable across adulthood and into old age, and to what extent are there interindividual differences when individuals are confronted with adversity or trauma? And what, if any, age-related changes across the life span bring forth the qualities from "within" a person? This could translate into the possibility for character strengths to be cultivated, trained, or even acknowledged by interventions that may lead to changes in character. Recent research on character strengths has primarily been done in the context of post-traumatic growth (PTG) by studying the extent to which individuals exhibit transformational improvements following an adversity or trauma (Jayawickreme & Blackie, 2014). Although this research can provide a glimmer of hope in better understanding character growth following adversity, limitations such as the use of retrospective self-perceived measures and cross-sectional designs, have long been discussed in the literature (Infurna & Jayawickreme, 2019).

In this chapter, our goal is to discuss character strengths in the context of their potential to change across the adult life span and grow or show transformational changes following adversity or trauma. We hope to bring to light the potential for character strengths to change across the adult life span (young adulthood, midlife, and into old age) and discuss how the meaning and measurement of character strengths could differ based on one's position in the life span. The sections that follow focus on (a) character strengths research in the context of PTG; (b) theoretical and empirical research on developmental age-related changes in character strengths; (c) key measurement considerations, such as measurement invariance when conducting research involving samples from across the adult life span; and (d) examples of constructs that have and have not been rigorously tested in the context of measurement invariance. We conclude by discussing directions for future research.

CONCEPTUAL CONSIDERATIONS

This section discusses conceptual considerations in the study of character strengths across the adult life span. As a first step, we discuss the nature of character strengths and virtues in the context of PTG as well as seminal work that has paved the way in this arena. Second, we discuss the theoretical and empirical age-related trends in these character strengths. We do this by highlighting key areas of research, namely, longitudinal examination of character strengths and the stability of these strengths as a point of focus. Last, we provide potential avenues for future inquiry when considering character strengths and virtues as a catalyst for growth.

Character Strengths and Post-Traumatic Growth

Character strengths and virtues have been of interest to psychologists for nearly a century (Hartshorne & May, 1928; McCullough & Snyder, 2000). However, prior to arriving to the study of character strengths, the work by Harthorne and May (1928) led the way in first demonstrating the reality of personality traits. They set out to evaluate the moral conduct of school children in a study aiming to understand whether children had general traits of honesty or dishonesty and found that, in many cases, depending on the situation, children would lie or cheat. Ultimately, these findings implied that moral conduct was not consistent given the weak positive correlations, but it signified a step in the right direction in understanding personality traits.

Hartshorne and May's (1928) work led many researchers to question the assumptions of consistency with respect to any personality trait. Most notably, Mischel (1968) questioned this assumption of validity for any personality trait and suggested that personality theories were generally wrong; he replaced them with a theoretical framework that placed "personality" in certain situations. Arguably, it was this dismissal of personality theory that prompted research in personality to shift in its theoretical perspective toward more objective components of personality rather than psychological components of character (Peterson, 1992).

Given all this, the study of these strengths did not gain traction for some years to come as psychological research favoring personality-based research over that of personal values became the norm. Allport (1921) was one of the early proponents of personality psychology and argued that character strengths belonged not in psychology, but instead in the field of social ethics. Moreover, Allport's (1921) rigid perspective on positivism reflected the urgency for psychology to differentiate between fact and value. This meant that fact lay in the realm of science, and anything relating to character strengths and values remained in philosophy. It was not until the emergence of positive psychology in the 1980s and 1990s that the study of character strengths was brought to the forefront in psychology and regained attention as a legitimate research topic. Since then, the study of character strengths has become an up-and-coming substantive area of study given the influx of interest in the way that these strengths can be relevant indicators of overall individual health and well-being. However, many current issues surrounding the study of character strengths lie in whether and to what extent character strengths and virtues can change—or not—as a function of age and their measurement properties to assess this meaningful change.

Theoretical Considerations on Character Strengths

In 2004, Peterson and Seligman published the seminal book *Character Strengths and Virtues: A Handbook and Classification*, in which their work combined cultural and philosophical traditions concerning the "good life" with psychological inquiries developed in the Values in Action (VIA) Classification of Strengths and Virtues. The VIA Classification primarily identified 24 strengths making up the good life not only for the self, but also others. These character strengths represented traits that were inherently positively valued and represent the different paths to virtues. For any character strength to be considered, it had to fulfill a minimum criterion that includes being morally valued; being trait-like; and manifested in one's thoughts, feelings and behaviors, as well as being fundamentally distinct from other strengths (Peterson & Seligman, 2004). However, Peterson and Seligman (2004) also theorized that there may be some degree of malleability in character strengths by definition. Despite this, there is very little empirical evidence about to what degree character strengths (and the subsequent assessments) fulfill the definition of malleability and stability over time.

The groundwork laid out by Peterson and Seligman brought the study of character strengths and virtues to be a legitimate topic within psychology, in comparison to the more value-neutral personality traits that have been front and center in personality psychology for some time (see Allport, 1921). With the interest in psychology from studying negative outcomes to more positive outcomes becoming much more a reality, in particular with health and well-being, character strengths and virtues can be expected to play a much more significant role than personality traits by which to study these aspects.

Several empirical studies have provided evidence linking character strengths to multiple indicators of well-being (Gillham et al., 2011; Martínez-Martí & Ruch, 2014; Ruch et al., 2010) and physical health (Proyer, Ruch, & Buschor, 2013). For example, reporting higher levels of character strengths such as gratitude, curiosity, love, zest, and hope are positively correlated with life satisfaction (see Park et al. 2004; Ruch et al., 2010; Ruch, Weber, Park, & Peterson, 2013). Studies have shown a positive correlation between character strengths and positive affect (e.g., Güsewell & Ruch, 2012; Littman-Ovadia and Lavy, 2012; Azañedo, Fernández-Abascal, & Barraca, 2014). Littman-Ovadia and Lavy (2012) found that the character strengths that were most highly correlated with positive affect were curiosity, love of learning, hope, and perspective. Similar findings were found by Azanedo et al. (2014) in that the strengths that most highly correlated with positive affect were hope, curiosity, creativity, and perspective. Conversely, Azanedo et al. (2014) found that the character strengths with highest negative correlations with negative affect were hope, self-regulation, persistence, gratitude, and forgiveness. Littman-Ovadia and Lavy (2012) found the character strengths with highest negative correlations were hope, curiosity, love, and self-regulation. Cumulatively, correlations were larger in size with positive affect than with negative affect in the studies mentioned. While this may point toward the benefit that these character strengths may have in promoting positive behaviors and outcomes as opposed to attempting to mitigate negative ones, there are limitations with the way the Values in Action Inventory of Strengths (VIA-IS) survey measures character strengths. These limitations will be further discussed in the section on "Methodological Considerations." We now turn our attention toward theoretical considerations in PTG research.

Theoretical Considerations on Post-Traumatic Growth

A growing body of behavioral research has incorporated the study of character strengths in the context of whether they could potentially change or grow following adversity or trauma (Tedeschi & Calhoun, 1996; Park & Helgeson, 2006; Park, Cohen, & Murch 1996). In the mid-1990s, Tedeschi and Calhoun (1996, 2004) coined the term "post-traumatic growth" to capture the positive changes that their clients reported in the aftermath of adversity and traumatic experiences. The measurement instrument that has been used for studies of this nature is the Post-Traumatic Growth Inventory (PTGI). This construct has gained much interest in the scientific community due to its potential for observing supposed psychological benefits following the experience of an adversity or trauma. As of today, the PTGI remains the most commonly used inventory to measure these potential psychological benefits to trauma despite the large amount of research documenting its limitations, such as its retrospective assessment and use in cross-sectional designs (for discussion, see Jayawickreme & Blackie, 2016; Tennen & Affleck, 2009).

In the time since its inception, many theoretical approaches regarding PTG have emerged (Jayawickreme & Blackie, 2014; Joseph & Linley, 2004; 2006; Park & Helgeson, 1996; Park & Helgeson, 2006; Tedeschi & Calhoun, 1996). One of these approaches is the *dynamic systems framework*. This perspective theorizes that people's self-perceptions of growth are, in fact, reflected in multiple sources and/or systems that happen at the psychological and social levels (Cicchetti & Toth, 2009; Masten 2004; Tennen & Affleck, 2009). This suggests that PTG has the potential to reflect personality change and lead to different perceptions of reality, appraisals, ways of discussing emotions, and beliefs of their past selves being worse than their present selves (Tennen & Affleck, 2009).

From a measurement perspective, the PTGI assumes that individuals are able to recall the multiple degrees of certain events accurately. Previous research has also elucidated that this may not necessarily be the case since one's perceptions of change are not strongly associated with subsequent change (Robins et al., 2005; Herbst et al., 2000). Jayawickreme and Zachry (2018) found that individuals are likely to not have an ability to recall the extent to which certain events trigger personality change, nor identify the characteristics that led to growth from these adversities. Furthermore, individuals may also have particular difficulty recalling or even accepting what state they were in prior to the adverse event happening (McFarland & Alvaro, 2000). Many times, individuals have a hard time with certain events and may sometimes confuse growth with actual coping mechanisms, which are not the same. Much work over the past 20 years has tried to differentiate both PTG and the coping or "recovery" phase after an event (Jayawickreme & Blackie, 2016). While the concept of PTG has long suggested that the positive change that individuals experience occurs in specific areas (specific domains), this approach may be oversimplifying the construct of growth that stems from character strengths. Results from a meta-analysis by Mangelsdorf et al. (2019) suggested that prevalence rates of PTG may be in fact lower than that assumed in the literature.

Developmental Trends in Character Strengths Across Adulthood and Old Age

While the relationship between character strengths and well-being has been documented, a question that still remains largely unexplored is the degree to which this relationship may differ for individuals across periods of the life course. Drawing from Erikson's (1959) account of stages of psychosocial development, it is possible to believe that strengths may help individuals adapt differentially to the several stages of life. Erikson described eight stages of psychosocial development, three of which are in adulthood: young adulthood (intimacy vs. isolation), adulthood (generativity vs. stagnation), and old age (integrity vs. despair). According to Erikson, all these stages are fundamentally shaped via developmental qualities that can come to relative dominance but also lead to a meaningful crisis. However, it is important to note that all functions specific to a life stage, according to Erikson, do not disappear in the next stage but instead assume new values. Erikson (1959) states that the adulthood stage is characterized by a set of psychosocial crises between generativity and stagnation. According to Erikson, the spirit of adulthood relies on the notion of maintenance of the world or the commitment to take care of the persons, products, and ideas one has learned to care for. In old age, these crises shift, and the person faces dealing with having a sense of integrity, coherence, and wholeness versus a sense of despair. When considering Erikson's (1959) theory, character strengths that may help fulfill the specific functions of a stage of life should theoretically have a larger relationship with well-being in comparison to other strengths and in other life stages.

While the nature of psychosocial development across the life span is important, focusing on adult development has been an area of increased research interest in the past few decades. Stage theories of development, as well as those that frame development in terms of life events and key transitions, are among the most enduring and influential in the adult literature. Levinson's theory of adult development (1986) depicts the different stages of the life course, structure, and adult development of life structure starting from early and middle adulthood. For Levinson (1986), development consists of periods of relative stability interwoven with periods of transitions; this all happens in the context of one's life structure, which is the pattern or design of a person's life at any given time and serves as the main component of his conception of adult development. Levinson's theoretical framework organizes the alternating periods of stability and transition throughout life into four eras, each with its own biopsychosocial character and with three of the four eras taking place during adulthood.

The first—early adulthood—lasts from approximately age 17 to 45 and is characterized as the era of "greatest energy and abundance and of greatest contradiction and stress . . . we are most buffeted by our passions and ambitions from within and by the demands of family, community, and society from without" (p. 5). It is right after early adulthood that individuals enter the midlife transition, which spans the ages of 40 to 45. A key developmental task of this transition marks the step into individuation. Levinson (1986) highlights that individuals can become more compassionate, more reflective, and more judicious; less tyrannized by inner conflicts and demands; and more loving of themselves and others. The second era—middle adulthood—lasts from roughly ages 40 to 65. The biological capacities of adults during this era, although diminished when compared with those in early adulthood, are "normally still sufficient for an energetic, personally satisfying and socially valuable life" (p. 6). It is during this time that most adults become "senior members" in their own worlds, responsible not only for their own work and "perhaps the work of others, but also for the development of the current generation of young adults who will soon enter the dominant generation" (p. 6). The era of late adulthood—the last era of the adult years—begins at approximately age 60. During this time, an individual confronts the self and makes peace with the world. Although his initial research was limited to middle-class American men, Levinson maintains that his theory also applies to women, different social classes, diverse cultures, and other periods of history (Levinson & Levinson, 1996).

Levinson (1986) further proposes an issue that by far and away questions our understanding of adult development, which is whether and to what extent there are age-related developmental periods in adulthood. He notes that the available evidence goes against hypotheses of age-linked stages in adult personality development. Careful attention should be particularly given to considering adulthood as a series of major life events, such as marriage, unemployment, and retirement, that may bring about changes in individual adaptation or personality. Because these happen at varying ages, they put into question any temporal order of changes in adulthood.

Empirical Evidence

Despite the early theoretical and empirical work on life stages in adult development, there has been a dearth of research on the examination of age-related changes in character strengths through the use of longitudinal data. Most work in this area has largely focused on cross-sectional research designs and/or examined these strengths across different age groups at one single point in time. One study appears to show limited evidence exploring longitudinal change in empathy over the adult life span across six different samples (Oh, Chopik, Konrath, & Grimm, 2019); empathy increased across the life span, particularly after age 40, with more recent cohorts being more likely to report higher levels in empathy. On the other hand, an earlier study examined changes in empathy in a four-wave longitudinal study across 12 years in a sample ranging in age from 10 to 87 at baseline (Grühn, Rebucal, Diehl, Lumley, & Labouvie-Vief, 2008). These researchers found cross-sectional and longitudinal associations, where cross-sectional analyses suggested that older adults had lower empathy scores than younger adults. Longitudinal analyses revealed there were no age-related declines in empathy. While there appears to be some evidence of age-related changes in empathy across adulthood, there are still some questions as to whether and to what extent this is the case. All in all, future research focusing on age-related change is needed across the different character strengths and populations throughout the adult life span.

Considering the available information on current assessment instruments, there are significant gaps in existing research that concern the stability and malleability of character strengths. First, there is seemingly only a few sources that use the VIA-IS inventory to compare the high stability of character strengths found. One potential source of comparison lies in the assessment of the PTGI (Tedeschi & Calhoun, 1996) in which participants are asked to recall retrospectively how they were before they experienced an adverse event, estimate how much they have changed since the event, and ultimately assess the extent to which change can be attributed to the adverse event (Ford, Tennen, & Albert, 2008). One study focused on measuring both trait and state measures of PTG in an experience sampling procedure and found significant variability in individuals' PTG on a moment-to moment basis; individuals' trait PTG was unrelated to state PTG (Blackie et al.,

2017). Therefore, it is unclear whether these stabilities are a mere characteristic of the instrument used (e.g., VIA-IS, PTGI) or an underlying construct (the strengths themselves).

Second, there appears to be little research that considers different aspects of stability, such as examining mean-level stability. Up to this point, research studies that have primarily used the standard 240-item instrument for the assessment of character strengths (the VIA-IS; Peterson, Park, & Seligman, 2005) showed rank-order stabilities ranging from $r = .62$ (authenticity) to $r = .85$ (spirituality) over a period of 9 months (Ruch et al., 2010). Hausler and colleagues (2017) reported stabilities in a similar range for a longer period of time (12 months) using a short version of the questionnaire that ranged from $r = .56$ (authenticity) to $r = .86$ (spirituality). Although it is not clear that the VIA-IS assesses character strengths in a valid way, it is still a widely used instrument. Mean-level stability is theoretically distinct from the typical rank-order stability found in studies that examine character strengths. Rank-order stability describes whether the position of individuals on a given trait is consistent over time. On the other hand, subgroups of individuals may show substantial changes (mean-levels) in a trait while rank-order is maintained. For example, one study found that age had complex curvilinear influences on levels of personality and that the rank-order stabilities of emotional stability, agreeableness, openness, and extraversion showed an inverse U-shaped function peaking at age 40–60 and decreasing afterward (Specht, Egloff, & Schmukle, 2011). Conversely, they found conscientiousness to increase in rank-order stability across adulthood. This example shows that, if looked at from an interventional perspective, examining whether mean-level changes are possible is of prime concern. Understanding whether it is possible for an individual to increase their expression on a trait—regardless of their position in the population—is important to consider.

Analyzing character strength mean-level changes can contribute significant understanding of developmental processes. For example, the mean-level change in a given trait in a population can be examined and compared with changes in another trait. However, there is a possibility that the amount of mean-level change is confounded by measurement error due to the limited reliability of measurement instruments. Therefore, it is of utmost importance to consider the reliability of a measure by analyzing the frequency of those changes to rule out chance (e.g., Reliable Change Index Computed; Christensen & Mendoza, 1986). Analyzing mean-level changes would open possibilities for comparing stability versus malleability among character strengths and provide evidence of whether and which strengths may be more easily modifiable over time. Changes in character have been examined in a limited fashion thus far. Frazier et al. (2009) found limited evidence to suggest reliable increases across outcomes that map onto the PTGI in a sample of undergraduate students who experienced a traumatic event across two waves of assessment.

A main reason why it has been difficult to examine changes in character strengths may be due to lack of longitudinal examinations of these strengths over extended periods of time. This is despite examining the stability and changes in constructs having a long-standing practice of longitudinal research. Kenny and Zautra (1995, 2001) were early proponents of investigating early trait models to determine the extent to which constructs should be deemed trait-like or more state-like. They proposed the Stable Trait, Autoregressive Trait, and State (STARTS) model, which allows for the individual differences measured across time to be decomposed into three sources of variation: a time-invariant stable component; a time-varying, partly stable autoregressive component; and an occasion-specific state component.

A STARTS model analysis may show that a certain percentage of interindividual differences in a given trait can be explained by a stable trait factor and the effects of factors that are completely stable over time (e.g., child environment; Anusic & Schimmack, 2016). Another percentage of the variation in a given trait can be attributed to the autoregressive trait factor and reflects the effects of changing factors that may be partly stable and enduring across time (e.g., social engagements/relationships). For example, research on the Big Five personality measures has found that the five personality factors range from 84% to 94% for stable traits, 91% to 96% for autoregressive traits, and 6% to 16% for state (Anusic, Lucas, & Donnellan, 2012). Research on life satisfaction has observed that life satisfaction is 34–38% stable trait, 29–34% autoregressive trait, and 33% state (Lucas & Donnellan, 2007). It is important to note that for life satisfaction the interpretation of the estimates provided by the STARTS models depend on the test-retest interval and duration of the study; this is the reason that differences are noted across the studies mentioned (yearly vs. monthly assessments). Therefore, understanding the extent of the stable and more malleable components of a given construct is imperative not only to inform current and future theory but also because it has the potential to play a role in interventions aiming to change characteristics (Cole & Martin, 2005).

METHODOLOGICAL CONSIDERATIONS

In this section, we discuss methodological considerations pertaining to studying character strengths in the context of adversity, with a focus on measurement. We first address the use of convenience sampling in scale development and describe why this may be potentially problematic when studying PTG across the adult life span. Next, we discuss measurement invariance and why it is important to take this into consideration, especially when studying character strengths and PTG. We do this by briefly describing four commonly used hierarchical models of measurement invariance that are housed within the multigroup, confirmatory factor analytic framework. Then, we provide examples of measures that were tested for measurement invariance. Finally, we discuss other measurement methods that may shed light on future directions for PTG researchers.

The Use of Convenience Sampling in Scale Development

Scale development in the social and behavioral sciences often relies on convenience sampling, namely undergraduate psychology students. The age range for this sample is typically from 18 to 25 years. While this may be cost effective and overall highly feasible, it can potentially impose limitations on the scale's generalizability to other population segments. The problem is that easy-to-reach college students may not be representative of other populations that are older, younger, less educated, or vary by some other primary characteristic. This is problematic if there is reason to believe that there is a fundamental difference in how different segments of the population experience the construct and interpret the items.

Many measures pertaining to character strengths, such as gratitude (the Gratitude Questionnaire; McCullough, Emmons, & Tsang, 2002), empathy (the Empathy Assessment Index; Lietz et al., 2011), compassion toward self and others (the Self-Compassion Scale; Neff, 2003; the Compassionate Love Scale; Sprecher & Fehr, 2016), humility (the Humility Inventory; Brown, Chopra, & Schiraldi, 2013), meaning-making (Meaning in Life Questionnaire; Steger, Frazier, Oishi, & Kaler, 2006), and optimism (the revised Life Orientation Test; Scheier, Carver, & Bridges, 1994), among others, were developed on convenient samples of undergraduate students. As one could imagine, this can potentially introduce issues if the construct of interest constitutes something different for middle-aged adults as opposed to young adults (i.e., the sample the measure was created on). The common assumption is that the items measure the same construct in the same scale across different groups (or over time for a group of people), yet this is rarely tested. Next, we formalize a definition of measurement invariance and explore its significance in more depth.

Measurement Invariance

A key issue when examining character strengths is the measurement properties of the scales being used. *Measurement invariance* (also referred to as factorial invariance) is one of these properties and refers to measuring the same construct in the same scale across time or across different groups of people. The role of measurement invariance in the social and behavioral sciences is widely applicable and important, yet it is often overlooked or assumed. The implications of failing to meet this assumption call into question the validity of the scientific inferences one makes (Horn & McArdle, 1992).

There are a variety of contexts in which it is of great importance to examine measurement invariance. For example, if comparative research is being conducted and one wishes to investigate group differences (e.g., men vs. women, young adults vs. older adults, or those who did not vs. did experience trauma), then it is imperative to establish that the measuring device (i.e., scale, questionnaire, survey, test, instrument) is measuring the same construct, in the same scale, across all groups. Establishing measurement invariance is also important when an investigator is *not* comparing groups, but rather is using the measurement device on a sample that is nonrepresentative of the original sample in some fundamental way (e.g., age, race, gender).

It is often the case that researchers will use a previously validated scale on a population that is quite different from the population that the scale was validated on. An example of this would be using a scale that was developed on a sample consisting of undergraduate students aged 18–22, on older adults aged 65 and older. "Instruments that have been evaluated thoroughly in one or more population groups may eventually be administered in additional groups for which there is no supporting psychometric assessment" (Gregorich, 2006, p. 88). If an investigator wishes to examine PTG in older adults and uses a scale that was developed on a sample of undergraduate psychology students, then it is possible that the construct indicators (i.e., items) may not carry the same meaning and scale across groups. A lack of measurement invariance in this context is problematic if there is reason to believe that there is a fundamental difference in how each group experiences the construct (i.e., interprets the items). Unfortunately, research on this latter type of measurement invariance is severely lacking, specifically in the context of character strengths and PTG across the adult life span and across cultures.

A common approach to examining measurement invariance across groups is *multigroup confirmatory factor analysis*. The primary forms of measurement invariance that can be examined using this approach are configural, metric, scalar, and strict. These tests are sequential and form a nested hierarchy of increasingly restrictive hypotheses by placing additional cross-group equality constraints on factor loading, item intercept, and residual variance parameters in order to achieve stronger forms of invariance. We next describe the common forms of measurement invariance in turn, in the context of a hypothetical sample comprised of adults between the ages of 18 and 90, using the Gratitude Questionnaire (GQ-6; McCullough et al., 2002) as the scale in question/running example.

Configural Invariance

Configural invariance (Horn & McArdle, 1980, 1992) refers to the invariance of the *pattern* of factor loadings. Configural invariance requires that the configuration of fixed and free factor loadings is equivalent across groups. For example, the GQ-6 (McCullough et al., 2002) is considered a unidimensional assessment because all six items share (i.e., load onto) only one common factor (dispositional gratitude). In our hypothetical sample, configural invariance would require that these six items comprise only one common factor across all age groups in our sample. This level of invariance only requires that the *configuration* (i.e., pattern) of loadings be equivalent across groups, and therefore it is the least constrained model of measurement invariance. The next level, *metric* invariance, assumes that configural invariance has been established.

Metric Invariance

Assuming configural invariance, metric invariance (Horn & McArdle, 1980, 1992) requires the factor loadings to be equal across groups. Factor loadings indicate the strength of the relationship between the indicator variable (i.e., observed variable, item response) and the common factor, and, in this way, they define the common factor. Therefore, if metric invariance (also referred to as *weak invariance*) is established, it indicates that the same construct is being measured across groups. In our hypothetical sample of participants and continuing to use the GQ-6 (McCullough et al., 2002) as an example, we would constrain the factor loadings pertaining to the six items of the GQ-6 to be the same for each age group in our sample (e.g., young adults, middle-aged adults, and older adults). If this additional set of constraints does not result in poorer model fit compared to the configural model fit, then it serves as sufficient evidence that the investigator is measuring the same construct (in this case, dispositional gratitude) across age groups. However, if one wants to conduct comparative research—that is, compare group means and attribute the differences in observed means to actual differences in the latent variable—then one needs to test for *scalar* invariance.

Scalar Invariance

Scalar invariance (also referred to as *strong invariance*) builds on metric invariance by additionally requiring the item intercepts to be equivalent across groups (Meredith, 1993). To justify comparison of group means, it is imperative to establish scalar invariance. If scalar invariance is not obtained, then observed mean differences do not necessarily reflect differences in the factor level; instead, they reflect differences in the measurement of the construct. That is to say, there is measurement bias. Continuing with our hypothetical sample of participants and using the GQ-6 (McCullough et al., 2002) as an example, we would constrain the six intercepts corresponding to the six items of the GQ-6 to be equivalent across all age groups in our sample. If this does not result in significantly poorer model fit compared to the metric model fit, then it serves as sufficient evidence that any observed group differences are reflections of true differences in the underlying psychological processes that comprise dispositional gratitude.

Strict invariance is the most restrictive model because cross-group equality constraints are imposed on corresponding factor loadings, item intercepts, and item residual (unique) variances. Obtaining strict invariance allows the researcher to attribute observed differences in the variances, covariances, and means of the observed variables to differences in the common factors. Because this is the most restrictive model, it can be difficult to obtain in practice, and therefore behavioral researchers often strive for scalar invariance. We next provide an in-depth examination of measurement invariance in the context of some of the most widely used scales measuring character strengths, including the VIA-IS, the GQ-6, and the Meaning in Life Questionnaire.

MEASUREMENT VARIANCE IN THE CONTEXT OF WIDELY USED MEASURES ASSESSING VARIOUS CHARACTER STRENGTHS

Values in Action Inventory of Strengths

As mentioned previously, the VIA Classification of Character Strengths and Virtues provided the basis for the 240-item VIA-IS (Peterson & Seligman, 2004).

In addition to the 24 strengths identified in the VIA Classification, there are six virtues: Wisdom & Knowledge, Courage, Humanity, Justice, Temperance, and Transcendence. Conceptually, the character strengths are thought of as the "psychological ingredients" that define the virtues (Peterson & Seligman, 2004). That is, each virtue consists of a cluster of strengths that most closely resemble that virtue (McGrath & Wallace, 2021). Although the VIA-IS is widely used, it does not come without issues, which is where we turn our attention to next.

One of the prominent criticisms of the VIA-IS is that it does not include scales that directly measure virtues, only character strengths. This has led to a consistent failure to replicate the hypothesized six-factor structure. Many researchers have used exploratory factor analysis to evaluate the factor structure of the VIA-IS and have found a three-, four-, or five-factor solution to be more amenable to the data (as cited in McGrath & Wallace, 2021). The most replicable model has consisted of three global factors that have been labeled Caring, Inquisitiveness, and Self-Control (McGrath, 2015a). Given that the conceptual model includes two levels of positive functioning (i.e., strengths *and* virtues), the absence of virtue scales in the VIA-IS leads to an incomplete representation of the VIA Classification (McGrath & Wallace, 2021).

Other criticisms of the VIA-IS are that all items are keyed in the same direction, such that "very much unlike me" is always associated with less of the character strength, which may promote socially desirable responses and/or response bias. Moreover, this potential response bias could lead to inflated correlations between strengths (McGrath, 2014; McGrath & Wallace, 2021). Additionally, the VIA-IS has been criticized for being too long; 240 items may be too cognitively taxing to complete in one sitting and therefore may lead to participant fatigue and/or response biases. Extensive work has been done to address these issues, one of which is examining measurement invariance of the VIA-IS, which is discussed next.

The VIA Classification was designed to include strengths that are universally recognized as valuable traits (McGrath, 2015b). That is, the strengths are believed to be generalizable across cultures. Due to this assumption, many researchers have translated the VIA-IS and used it for data collection. This has allowed for the examination of measurement invariance across cultures. McGrath (2015b) conducted multigroup confirmatory factor analysis to test whether the strengths are equivalent and have the same meaning across cultures. He used data that had been collected online between 2010 and 2012; 15 nations were included in the study for a total $N = 15{,}540$. The mean age for the sample was 33.61 years (SD = 11.97 years), 56.67% female, 43.33% male. Three levels of invariance were tested: configural, metric, and scalar. The results showed that a configural invariance model fit the data best, but the metric invariance model showed relatively little change in fit from that of the configural model. Thus, support was provided for the presence of configural and metric equivalence across nations and translations. This suggests that, in general, responses across translations have a common underlying structural model. Fortunately, these findings are consistent with the assumption of cross-cultural generalizability of character strengths (McGrath, 2015b). Next, we highlight other recent initiatives taken to improve the validity and reliability of the VIA-IS.

In 2014, the VIA Institute launched an endeavor to revise the VIA-IS in light of criticisms. A complete technical report describing the entire revision process and its outcomes is provided in McGrath (2019). Some of the key objectives included the development of inventories for the direct measurement of virtues and the development and validation of a short-form that included reversed-key items. Furthermore, McGrath and Wallace (2021) conducted a cross-validation study examining the psychometric properties of the revised VIS-IS and its short forms. Results suggested that the new versions demonstrated acceptable levels of reliability and validity and offered several advantages over the original version. Even though the newer versions are an improvement over the original VIA-IS, the authors suggest exercising caution when using these scales due to the ambiguity in how to measure character strengths (McGrath & Wallace, 2021). While the VIA-IS provides a starting point for examining character strengths, more emphasis needs to be placed on the measurement model when conducting this line of research.

Gratitude

The GQ-6 was developed by McCullough and colleagues (2002), and its aim was to measure dispositional gratitude, which they defined as the "generalized tendency to recognize and respond with grateful emotion to the roles of other people's benevolence in the positive experiences and outcomes that one obtains" (p. 112). The GQ-6 consists of six items that were developed on a sample of 238 undergraduate psychology students, of whom 73% were female. The mean age for this sample was 21 years (range, 19–44). Exploratory factor analysis and subsequent structural equation modeling indicated that a one-factor model provided an adequate fit to the data. The single-factor measurement model was then cross-validated on a sample of 1,228 non-student volunteers. The mean age for this sample was 44 years (SD = 12.0; range, 18–75); it should be noted that 80% of the sample was female. This raises the concern of gender distribution in scale development and validation. Such unequal gender distribution in the original studies may obscure subsequent validation efforts in more (or less) representative samples. Numerous studies have since examined measurement invariance of the GQ-6 (McCullough et al., 2002) with respect to gender and language, and the results are inconsistent. For example, in a sample of 471 Brazilian undergraduate students (M_{age} = 22.8, 59.2% female), Gouveia and colleagues (2019) were only able to establish configural invariance across gender and unable to obtain partial metric invariance, suggesting that the items of the GQ-6 are understood differently across Brazilian men and women. Yet, in a sample of 1,151 Chinese adults (M_{age} = 26.92, SD = 5.59, 54.6% female), Kong, You, and Zhao (2017) established scalar invariance across gender, suggesting not only that the items are understood the same way but also that a direct comparison of scores across men and women is appropriate.

The previous examples used the six-item version of the GQ-6, several studies have shown a five-item Spanish and five-item Chinese version to be invariant across gender (e.g., Valdez, Yang, & Datu, 2017; Cabrera et al., 2019; Magallares, Recio, & Sanjuan, 2018; Chen & Kee, 2008). The sixth item ("Long amounts of time can go by before I feel grateful to something or someone") is often excluded due to translation difficulties. Interestingly, though, Langer, Ulloa, Aguilar-Parra, Araya-Veliz, and Brito (2016) found that a five-item Spanish version was invariant across gender for a younger sample, but not an older sample of Chilean adults. However, the six-item version was invariant across gender for the older sample. This suggests that the sixth item is interpreted differently depending on age. While there is an abundance of literature examining the measurement invariance of the GQ-6 across gender and ethnicity, there is very little research on how the GQ-6 performs across adult age groups (see Froh et al., 2011) and over time (temporal stability).

There is also the interesting question of whether the GQ-6 actually measures gratitude or something closer to life satisfaction. This points to a broader issue: the extent to which measures of character strengths capture the core content of the strength in a valid way. It is important to be clear about how the construct is conceptualized because there is often conceptual variability. For example, Diener and colleagues (1985) defined life satisfaction as "a cognitive-judgmental process" (p. 71). They emphasize that life satisfaction is based on an internal judgment of oneself and one's life. In contrast, dispositional gratitude, as defined by McCullough and colleagues (2002) focuses on things that are externally imposed, such as other people's benevolence.

Furthermore, McCullough and colleagues (2002) distinguished dispositional gratitude from life satisfaction by comparing the fit of a one-factor versus two-factor model. Both models consisted of all items from the GQ-6 and the Satisfaction with Life Scale (SWLS; Diener et al., 1985). The idea was that if the addition of a second factor improved model fit (by accounting for more covariance among the items than the one-factor model), then it was sufficient to conclude that dispositional gratitude and life satisfaction are reasonably distinct from one another. The results indicated that the two-factor solution was superior to the one-factor solution, (McCullough et al., 2002). However, it is not unreasonable to see how the constructs of gratitude and life satisfaction could overlap in their conceptualization. In fact, in this sample, the latent factors of gratitude and life satisfaction were significantly correlated, (McCullough et al., 2002). While this suggests that there is some content overlap in the measures, a closer examination of the items reveals that they are tapping distinct constructs.

Meaning in Life

Meaning in life is another construct of interest to PTG researchers because it has been examined as an outcome of change following adversity as well as a resource for promoting well-being by buffering against the negative effects of adversity (Frazier et al., 2009). The Meaning in Life Questionnaire (MLQ; Steger et al., 2006) was developed on a sample of 151 undergraduate introductory psychology students (M_{age} = 19.8, 64% female) and serves as another example where measurement invariance was not addressed initially, but efforts have been made subsequently. Recognizing the need to establish the structural and factorial invariance of the MLQ across age groups, Steger, Oishi, and Kashdan (2009) conducted a post hoc examination of the dimensions of meaning in life across the adult life span. The study's sample consisted of 8,756 individuals who were sorted into four age groups: emerging adults (18–24 years), young adults (25–44 years), middle-aged adults (45–64 years), and older adults (older than 65). Steger and colleagues (2009) provided clear descriptions of their analyses, and the results revealed that scalar measurement invariance was obtained across age groups. This implies that "any mean differences observed using this scale are due to differences in levels of the presence of and search for meaning in life of participants at different life stages" (p. 47). Overall, there were significant differences across age groups for both the presence and search components. Presence of meaning in life showed, on average, a trend toward increasing across adulthood and old age; older adults (65 and older) reported the highest levels, followed by middle-aged adults (45–64), young adults (25–44), and emerging adults (18–24). Focusing on search for meaning, there was a reverse trend with emerging and young adults reporting the highest levels, followed by middle-aged and older adults.

One limitation the authors point out is the cross-sectional design of the study: it cannot be determined whether the observed pattern of age differences reflects actual age-related changes and whether the age differences are due to cohort effects. That is, by the time the youngest group (18–24 years) turns 65, they may have entirely different notions about what makes their lives meaningful than those who are currently 65. Steger and colleagues also note that "Future research should attempt to use longitudinal designs and sampling reflective of the demographics of the population" (p. 50).

Measurement invariance is often assumed yet rarely tested. The examination of measurement invariance in PTG research in populations from the adult life span is important because if the constructs (i.e., character strengths) are experienced and interpreted differently by younger versus older adults, it is imperative that the measuring device (scale) is adjusted accordingly. If a primary research goal is to assess the potential buffering effects of character strengths in the face of adversity, it would behoove the researcher to ensure that they are actually measuring the character strength of interest.

CONCLUSION

In this chapter, we outlined the most common approaches to the empirical study of character strengths. There is great hope in the study of character strengths, and the aim of this chapter is to both encourage researchers and pave the way to guide future avenues of inquiry into the field. Here, we raise significant conceptual and methodological considerations for future directions.

Conceptual Considerations

While research on character strengths has flourished in the past few years, there are limitations to current and past approaches to the study of these strengths. Here, we raise several points for future consideration. As should be clear from this chapter review, the evaluation of character strengths in adulthood and old age is scarce and inconsistent. Character strengths have been commonly examined across the life span, but many of the scales developed to measure character strengths are validated primarily on undergraduate college samples. Thus, given that character strengths may still be relevant well into adulthood and old age, we encourage researchers to further assess and validate findings in much older samples from diverse socioeconomic and cultural backgrounds and across a wide range of strengths.

Second, given that character strengths are relevant across the whole life span, it is also becoming increasingly critical to consider the extent to which these strengths remain static or are malleable. Many vital questions surround the idea that one's own ability to overcome obstacles through fortitude is something that can be inherently changed behaviorally. Therefore, more theoretical work needs to be done to evaluate whether and how specific character strengths are amenable to change based on specific situations and social roles across time. Initial work by Roberts and Jackson (2008; see also Roberts, 2018) discussed the idea that meaningful long-term gains in traits like conscientiousness are often seldom lost and instead are often triggered via enduring change due to situational contexts (i.e., traumatic event or environment and/or other changes). Recent work evaluating the stability and change in personality traits and goals in a sample from college to midlife found that social goals were higher than other goal like aesthetics, economic, etc. among individuals in midlife. However, this study only focused on evaluating developmental changes in goal importance but not the effort and goal commitment aspect. Therefore, more work needs to evaluate how effort toward achieving goals and character strengths associate with each other. Considering this, further evaluations of character strengths need to be undertaken by researchers across adulthood and across a range of several years to distill stability versus change.

We aim to address such limitations raised in this chapter in our research design that involves assessing individuals in midlife (aged 50–65) once a month for a period of 2 years, an portion of the life span that is especially ripe for the examination of PTG in the context of adversity. (Midlife broadly encompasses the age range of 40–60, plus or minus 5–10 years; Lachman, 2004.) Historically, midlife has been an understudied and underappreciated portion of the life course, with researchers and the lay public believing that not much is going on other than the possible "midlife crisis" or "empty nest syndrome" (Lachman et al., 2015). More recently, Infurna, Gerstorf, and Lachman (2020) have discussed midlife as being comprised of four distinct features that come to the forefront at this time, including simultaneous involvement in roles across family, friends, community, and work, life transitions, opportunities, and challenges. Midlife is also a critical point in the life span because of middle-aged adults' role in bridging younger and older generations and that they comprise a large segment of the workforce. There are various potential types of adversities that these individuals will confront, including singular, albeit major stressors (e.g., unemployment, bereavement) and chronic challenges (e.g., caregiving for an aging relative). Adversities can come about through intergenerational dynamics (caregiving for an aging parent, adult children not launching into adulthood, pressures of parenthood) and financial vulnerabilities (labor market instability, strained household budgets due to rising healthcare costs and stagnant wages, underemployment, rising housing costs).

Methodological Considerations

The importance of examining measurement invariance cannot be overstated. Often in psychological research, the investigator will use an existing scale that was developed on a convenience sample (e.g., undergraduate students) to study the same construct in a different sample. In doing so, the researcher assumes that the instrument is capturing the same construct, in the same scale, across groups. Failing to examine and establish measurement invariance calls into question the validity of inferences one can makes from the scores. When the measurement instrument is not actually measuring the same construct across groups, the investigator cannot make valid inferences from the data obtained. Furthermore, if the investigator wishes to compare factor scores and observed group differences, the need for strong measurement invariance is imperative. Otherwise, the comparisons may not be reasonable and observed group differences may (or may not) reflect actual differences in the common factor. The degree to which measurement bias is present must be considered.

Future Directions

We discussed various conceptual and methodological considerations when studying PTG, particularly in adult samples (e.g., middle-aged adults). A limitation that has been discussed extensively (Infurna & Jayawickreme, 2019) is how previous research has almost exclusively examined PTG through the PTGI, an inventory that retrospectively assesses whether individuals showed growth across five domains. To examine the degree to which growth occurs following adversity, prospective longitudinal data are essential. Another key point of contention lies in the measurement of key character strengths. The lack of proper scale development for measures of character strengths across the life span (i.e., young adulthood vs. midlife vs. old age) has led to broad inconsistencies in determining whether and to what extent they are malleable and/or remain static. Not only is it important to measure change in character strengths, but it also is important to consider whether, how, and for whom character growth happens. This reinforces the notion that character growth is a complex process and therefore, this section addresses the importance of continuing to study character strengths—especially in midlife—as well as research designs that are well-suited to examine character growth.

Research Designs

A limitation of most PTG research is that it utilizes a cross-sectional approach, limiting the ability to examine within-person changes both prior to and following adversity and the mechanisms that lead to character growth. Research from Peterson and colleagues (2008) found that individuals who reported experiencing more lifetime adversities showed a slight trend toward higher levels of certain types of character virtues, including kindness, honesty, perseverance, creativity, and religiousness. Furthermore, Peterson and Seligman (2004) found that individuals reported higher levels of seven character strengths—gratitude, hope, kindness, leadership, love, spirituality, and teamwork—following the September 11 terrorist attacks, which were sustained for up to 10 months following. This retrospective approach, while not uncommon, is lacking in untangling the complex nature surrounding character strengths. In response, some research designs have aimed at studying character strengths prospectively. Frazier and colleagues (2009) used prospective data over a 2-month period to examine growth following adversity and observed that perceived change does not translate to actual change. Although their prospective approach permitted the study of how individuals change both before and after adversity, the authors acknowledge that their sample was composed primarily of female undergraduate students and that they may have assessed (measured) perceived and actual growth too soon. What is needed are prospective longitudinal designs that span a sufficient amount of time to be able to detect actual change. The Pathways to Character empirical project attempted to address these limitations by assessing a group of adults (50–65 years) on a monthly basis for a period of 24 months. Frequent assessment over a long period of time in a sample of middle-aged adults allowed the researchers to explore the extent to which traumatic events impact character strengths for adults in this age group.

Another aspect of research design that may help in our understanding of the complex nature of character strengths is the use of informant reports in addition to self-reports. Utilizing informant reports has been shown to be a low-cost yet effective strategy that can help improve validity by providing a degree of consensus between self- and other reports, and they can shed light on new research questions that may otherwise be difficult to examine with self-reports alone (Vazire, 2006). The idea is that informant reports serve as an additional measure to gauge convergence between self and other reports. In addition to assessing 361 participants once a month for 24 months in the empirical Pathways to Character project, researchers also examined the concordance between self- and informant reports for several character strengths. To establish the informant as a reliable and valid source of information, participants were instructed to select an informant with whom they had regular contact and who knew them well. Once every 3 months, the informants completed an online questionnaire and were instructed to respond based on their perceptions of the participant. Due to the extensive design of this study, data involving informant reports are still being processed and analyzed.

Mixed-method approaches are increasingly called for in research designs. The term "mixed methods" has been defined as "research in which the investigator collects and analyzes data, integrates findings, and draws inferences from both quantitative and qualitative approaches in a single study" (Tashakkori & Creswell, 2007, p. 4). While mixed-method approaches are not new to the developmental psychology literature, they are garnering much more interest among the scientific community (Tashakkori & Teddlie, 2003; Tashakkori & Teddlie, 2010). Standardized questionnaires and assessments are important when comparing across samples and generalizing to a population. However, these standardized assessments only show one side of the story and may by their very nature limit phenomena under study (Castro, Kellison, Boyd, & Kopak, 2010). On the other hand, less structured, in-depth interviews allow for individuals to retell their experiences rather than fit their experiences into forced-choice responses. Therefore, relying on either approach in isolation can limit the breadth of the data and even the people being studied. A mixed-methods approach to studies can add significantly to the field of character strengths by investigating development at the individual, general, and theoretical levels. As a follow-up to the main 2-year project, the Pathways to Character study incorporated a qualitative component that involved hour-long interviews of 57 randomly chosen participants from the main study. These semi-structured interviews dealing with questions on adversity and the experience of being in midlife allowed an examination of character strengths on a more nuanced level that the quantitative data cannot reveal. Similar to this work, future research should aim to incorporate mixed-methods approaches at different stages of the life span to evaluate the complex nature of character growth.

REFERENCES

Allport, G. W. (1921). Personality and character. *Psychological Bulletin, 18*(9), 441–455. https://doi.org/10.1037/h0066265

Anusic, I., Lucas, R. E., & Donnellan, M. B. (2012). Dependability of personality, life satisfaction, and affect in short-term longitudinal data. *Journal of Personality, 80*(1), 33–58. https://doi.org/10.1111/j.1467-6494.2011.00714.x

Anusic, I., & Schimmack, U. (2016). Stability and change of personality traits, self-esteem, and well-being: Introducing the meta-analytic stability and change model of retest correlations. *Journal of Personality and Social Psychology, 110*(5), 766–781. https://doi.org/10.1037/pspp0000066

Azañedo, C. M., Fernández-Abascal, E. G., & Barraca, J. (2014). Character strengths in Spain: Validation of the Values in Action Inventory of Strengths (VIA-IS) in a Spanish sample. *Clínica y Salud, 25*(2), 123–130. https://doi.org/10.1016/j.clysa.2014.06.002

Blackie, L. E. R., Jayawickreme, E., Tsukayama, E., Forgeard, M. J. C., Roepke, A. M., & Fleeson, W. (2017). Post-traumatic growth as positive personality change: Developing a measure to assess within-person variability. *Journal of Research in Personality, 69*, 22–32. https://doi.org/10.1016/j.jrp.2016.04.001

Brown, S. L., Chopra, P. K., & Schiraldi, G. R. (2013). Validation of the Humility Inventory (HI), a five-factor, self-report measure of humility. *International Journal of Educational and Psychological Assessment*, 57–78.

Cabrera-Vélez, M., Lima-Castro, S., Peña-Contreras, E., Aguilar-Sizer, M., Bueno-Pacheco, A., & Arias-Medina, P. (2019). Adaptation and validation of the Gratitude Questionnaire GQ-6 for the Ecuadorian context. *Revista Avaliação Psicológica, 18*(02), 129–137. doi:10.15689/ap.2019.1802.15689.03

Castro, F. G., Kellison, J. G., Boyd, S. J., & Kopak, A. (2010). A methodology for conducting integrative mixed methods research and data analyses. *Journal of Mixed Methods Research, 4*(4), 342–360.

Chen, L. H., & Kee, Y. H. (2008). Gratitude and adolescent athletes' well-being. *Social Indicators Research, 89*(2), 361–373.

Christensen, L., & Mendoza, J. L. (1986). A method of assessing change in a single subject: An alteration of the RC index. *Behavior Therapy, 17*(3), 305–308. https://doi.org/10.1016/S0005-7894(86)80060-0

Cicchetti, D., & Toth, S. L. (2009). The past achievements and future promises of developmental psychopathology: The coming of age of a discipline. *Journal of Child Psychology and Psychiatry, 50*(1–2), 16–25.

Cole, D. A., & Martin, N. C. (2005). The longitudinal structure of the children's depression inventory: Testing a latent trait-state model. *Psychological Assessment, 17*(2), 144–155. https://doi.org/10.1037/1040-3590.17.2.144

Diener, E., Emmons, R. A., Larsen, R. J., & Griffin, S. (1985). The satisfaction with life scale. *Journal of Personality Assessment, 49*(1), 71–75.

Erikson, E. H. (1959). Identity and the life cycle. *Psychological Issues*, 1, 1–71.

Fleeson, W., Furr, R. M., Jayawickreme, E., Meindl, P., & Helzer, E. G. (2014). Character: The prospects for a personality-based perspective on morality. *Social and Personality Psychology Compass, 8*(4), 178–191. https://doi.org/10.1111/spc3.12094

Ford, J. D., Tennen, H., & Albert, D. (2008). A contrarian view of growth following adversity. In S. Joseph & P. A. Linley (Eds.), *Trauma, recovery, and growth: Positive psychological perspectives on posttraumatic stress* (pp. 297–324). Hoboken New Jersey: John Wiley & Sons, Inc.

Frazier, P., Anders, S., Perera, S., Tomich, P., Tennen, H., Park, C., & Tashiro, T. (2009). Traumatic events among undergraduate students: Prevalence and associated symptoms. *Journal of Counseling Psychology, 56*(3), 450–460. https://doi.org/10.1037/a0016412

Froh, J. J., Fan, J., Emmons, R. A., Bono, G., Huebner, E. S., & Watkins, P. (2011). Measuring gratitude in youth: assessing the psychometric properties of adult gratitude scales in children and adolescents. *Psychological Assessment, 23*(2), 311–324. doi:10.1037/a0021590.

Gillham, J., Adams-Deutsch, Z., Werner, J., Reivich, K., Coulter-Heindl, V., Linkins, M., . . . Seligman, M. E. P. (2011). Character strengths predict subjective well-being during adolescence. *Journal of Positive Psychology, 6*(1), 31–44. https://doi.org/10.1080/17439760.2010.536773

Gouveia, V. V., Ribeiro, M. G. C., de Aquino, T. A. A., Loureto, G. D. L., Nascimento, B. S., & Rezende, A. T. (2019). Gratitude Questionnaire (GQ-6): Evidence of construct validity in Brazil. *Current Psychology.* doi:10.1007/s12144-019-00197-x.

Gregorich, S. E. (2006). Do self-report instruments allow meaningful comparisons across diverse population groups? Testing measurement invariance using the confirmatory factor analysis framework. *Medical Care, 44*(11 Suppl 3), S78–S94.

Grühn, D., Rebucal, K., Diehl, M., Lumley, M., & Labouvie-Vief, G. (2008). Empathy across the adult life span: Longitudinal and experience-sampling findings. *Emotion, 8*(6), 753–765. https://doi.org/10.1037/a0014123

Güsewell, A., & Ruch, W. (2012). Are only emotional strengths emotional? Character strengths and disposition to positive emotions. *Applied Psychology. Health and Well-Being, 4*(2), 218–239. https://doi.org/10.1111/j.1758-0854.2012.01070.x

Hartshorne, H., May, M. A., Character Education Inquiry, Teachers College, Columbia University, & The Institute of Social and Religious Research. (1928). *Studies in the nature of character, [part] 1: Studies in deceit: book 1, General methods and results; book 2, Statistical methods and results.* MacMillan Co. https://doi.org/10.1037/13386-000

Hausler, M., Strecker, C., Huber, A., Brenner, M., Höge, T., & Höfer, S. (2017). Associations between the application of signature character strengths, health and well-being of health professionals. *Frontiers in Psychology, 8*, Article 1307. https://doi.org/10.3389/fpsyg.2017.01307

Horn, J. L., & McArdle, J. J. (1980). Perspectives on Mathematical/Statistical Model Building (MASMOB) in research on aging. In L. W. Poon (Ed.), *Aging in the 1980s: Psychological issues* (pp. 503–541). American Psychological Association. https://doi.org/10.1037/10050-037

Horn, J. L., & McArdle, J. J. (1992). A practical and theoretical guide to measurement invariance in aging research. *Experimental Aging Research, 18*(3), 117–144.

Herbst, J. H., McCrae, R. R., Costa, P. T. J., Feaganes, J. R., & Siegler, I. C. (2000). Self-perceptions of stability and change in personality at midlife: The UNC Alumni Heart Study. *Assessment, 7*(4), 379–388. doi:10.1177/107319110000700406

Infurna, F. J., Gerstorf, D., & Lachman, M. E. (2020). Midlife in the 2020s: Opportunities and challenges. *American Psychologist, 75*, 470–485.

Infurna, F. J., & Jayawickreme, E. (2019). Fixing the growth illusion: New directions for research in resilience and posttraumatic growth. *Current Directions in Psychological Science, 28*(2), 152–158. https://doi.org/10.1177/0963721419827017

Jayawickreme, E., & Blackie, L. E. (2014). Post–traumatic growth as positive personality change: Evidence, controversies and future directions. *European Journal of Personality, 28*(4), 312–331.

Jayawickreme, E., & Blackie, L. E. (2016). *Exploring the psychological benefits of hardship: A critical reassessment of posttraumatic growth.* Cham: Springer.

Jayawickreme, E., & Zachry, C. E. (2018). Positive personality change following adversity. In V. Zeigler-Hill & T. K. Shackelford (Eds.), *The SAGE Handbook of Personality and Individual Differences: Origins of Personality and Individual Differences* (pp. 450–464). Thousand Oaks, CA: Sage. https://doi.org/10.4135/9781526451200.n24

Linley, P. A., & Joseph, S. (2004). Positive change following trauma and adversity: A review. *Journal of Traumatic Stress, 17*(1), 11–21.

Joseph, S., & Linley, P. A. (2006). Growth following adversity: Theoretical perspectives and implications for clinical practice. *Clinical Psychology Review*, *26*(8), 1041–1053. https://doi.org/10.1016/j.cpr.2005.12.006

Kenny, D. A., & Zautra, A. (1995). The trait-state-error model for multiwave data. *Journal of Consulting and Clinical Psychology, 63*(1), 52–59. https://doi.org/10.1037/0022-006X.63.1.52

Kenny, D. A., & Zautra, A. (2001). Trait–state models for longitudinal data. In L. M. Collins & A. G. Sayer (Eds.), *Decade of behavior. New methods for the analysis of change* (pp. 243–263). American Psychological Association. https://doi.org/10.1037/10409-008

Kong, F., You, X., & Zhao, J. (2017). Evaluation of the Gratitude Questionnaire in a Chinese sample of adults: Factorial validity, criterion-related validity, and measurement invariance across sex. *Frontiers in Psychology, 8,* 1498, 1–6. doi:10.3389/fpsyg.2017.01498

Lachman, M. E. (2004). Development in midlife. *Annual Review of Psychology, 55,* 305–331.

Langer, A. I., Ulloa, V. G., Aguilar-Parra, J. M., Araya-Veliz, C., & Brito, G. (2016). Validation of a Spanish translation of the Gratitude Questionnaire (GQ-6) with a Chilean sample of adults and high schoolers. *Health and Quality of Life Outcomes, 14*(53) 1–9. doi:10.1186/s12955-016-0450-6.

Levinson, D. J. (1986). A conception of adult development. *American Psychologist, 41*(1), 3–13. https://doi.org/10.1037/0003-066X.41.1.3

Levinson D. J., & Levinson J. D. (1996). *The Seasons of a Woman's Life*. New York: Ballantine.

Lietz, C. A., Gerdes, K. E., Sun, F., Geiger, J. M., Wagaman, M. A., & Segal, E. A. (2011). The empathy assessment index (EAI): A confirmatory factor analysis of a multidimensional model of empathy. *Journal of the Society for Social Work and Research, 2*(2), 104–124. doi:10.5243/jsswr.2011.6.

Littman-Ovadia, H., & Lavy, S. (2012). Differential ratings and associations with well-being of character strengths in two communities. *Health Sociology Review, 21*(3), 299–312. https://doi.org/10.5172/hesr.2012.21.3.299

Lucas, R. E., & Donnellan, M. B. (2007). How stable is happiness? Using the STARTS model to estimate the stability of life satisfaction. *Journal of Research in Personality, 41*(5), 1091–1098. https://doi.org/10.1016/j.jrp.2006.11.005

Magallares, A., Recio, P., & Sanjuan, P. (2018). Factor structure of the Gratitude Questionnaire in a Spanish sample. *Spanish Journal of Psychology, 21*(E53), 1–7. doi:10.1017/sjp.2018.55.

Mangelsdorf, J., Eid, M., & Luhmann, M. (2019). Does growth require suffering? A systematic review and meta-analysis on genuine posttraumatic and postecstatic growth. *Psychological Bulletin, 145*(3), 302–338. https://doi.org/10.1037/bul0000173

Martínez-Martí, M. L., & Ruch, W. (2014). Character strengths and well-being across the life span: Data from a representative sample of German-speaking adults living in Switzerland. *Frontiers in Psychology*, *5*. https://doi.org/10.3389/fpsyg.2014.01253

Masten, A. S. (2004). Regulatory processes, risk, and resilience in adolescent development. In R. E. Dahl & L. P. Spear (Eds.), *Annals of the New York Academy of Sciences: Vol. 1021. Adolescent brain development: Vulnerabilities and opportunities* (pp. 310–319). New York Academy of Sciences.

McCullough, M. E., Emmons, R. A., & Tsang, J. A. (2002). The grateful disposition: A conceptual and empirical topography. *Journal of Personality and Social Psychology, 82*(1), 112–127. doi:10.1037//0022-3514.82.1.112

McCullough, M. E., & Snyder, C. R. (2000). Classical source of human strength: Revisiting an old home and building a new one. *Journal of Social and Clinical Psychology, 19*(1), 1–10. https://doi.org/10.1521/jscp.2000.19.1.1

McFarland, C., & Alvaro, C. (2000). The impact of motivation on temporal comparisons: Coping with traumatic events by perceiving personal growth. *Journal of Personality and Social Psychology, 79*(3), 327–343. doi:10.1037/0022-3514.79.3.327

McGrath, R. E. (2019). *Technical Report: The VIA Assessment Suite for Adults: Development and Initial Evaluation*, revised ed. Cincinnati, OH: VIA Institute on Character.

McGrath, R. E. (2014). Scale-and item-level factor analyses of the VIA Inventory of Strengths. *Assessment, 21*(1), 4–14. doi:10.1177/1073191112450612.

McGrath, R. E. (2015a). Integrating psychological and cultural perspectives on virtue: The hierarchical structure of character strengths. *Journal of Positive Psychology, 10*(5), 407–424.

McGrath, R. E. (2015b). Measurement invariance in translations of the VIA inventory of strengths. *European Journal of Psychological Assessment, 32*(3), 187–194.

McGrath, R. E. (2019). *Technical Report: The VIA Assessment Suite for Adults: Development and Initial Evaluation*, revised ed. Cincinnati, OH: VIA Institute on Character.

McGrath, R. E., & Wallace, N. (2021). Cross-validation of the VIA inventory of strengths-revised and its short forms. *Journal of Personality Assessment, 103*(1), 120–131.

Meredith, W. (1993). Measurement invariance, factor analysis and factorial invariance. *Psychometrika, 58*(4), 525–543.

Mischel, W. (1968). *Personality and Assessment*. New York: Wiley.

Mischel, W., Coates, B., & Raskoff, A. (1968). Effects of success and failure on self-gratification. *Journal of Personality and Social Psychology, 10*(4), 381–390. https://doi.org/10.1037/h0026800

Neff, K. D. (2003). The development and validation of a scale to measure self-compassion. *Self and Identity, 2*(3), 223–250.

Oh, J., Chopik, W. J., Konrath, S., & Grimm, K. J. (2019). Longitudinal changes in empathy across the life span in six samples of human development. *Social Psychological and Personality Science*. https://doi.org/10.1177/1948550619849429

Park, C. L., Cohen, L. H., & Murch, R. L. (1996). Assessment and prediction of stress-related growth. *Journal of Personality, 64*(1), 71–105. https://doi.org/10.1111/j.1467-6494.1996.tb00815.x

Park, C. L., & Helgeson, V. S. (2006). Introduction to the special section: Growth following highly stressful life events--Current status and future directions. *Journal of Consulting and Clinical Psychology, 74*(5), 791–796. https://doi.org/10.1037/0022-006X.74.5.791

Peterson, C. (1992). *Personality*, 2nd ed. Fort Worth, TX: Harcourt Brace Jovanovich.

Peterson, C., Park, N., & Seligman, M. E. (2005). Orientations to happiness and life satisfaction: The full life versus the empty life. *Journal of Happiness Studies, 6*(1), 25–41.

Peterson, C., Park, N., Pole, N., D'Andrea, W., & Seligman, M. E. (2008). Strengths of character and posttraumatic growth. *Journal of Traumatic Stress, 21*(2), 214–217.

Peterson, C., & Seligman, M. E. (2004). *Character Strengths and Virtues: A Handbook and Classification*, Vol. *1*. New York: Oxford University Press.

Proyer, R. T., Ruch, W., & Buschor, C. (2013). Testing strengths-based interventions: A preliminary study on the effectiveness of a program targeting curiosity, gratitude, hope, humor, and zest for enhancing life satisfaction. *Journal of Happiness Studies, 14*(1), 275–292. https://doi.org/10.1007/s10902-012-9331-9

Roberts, B. W., & Jackson, J. J. (2008). Sociogenomic personality psychology. *Journal of Personality, 76*(6), 1523–1544.

Roberts, B. W. (2018). A revised sociogenomic model of personality traits. *Journal of Personality, 86*(1), 23–35.

Robins, R. W., Noftle, E. E., Trzesniewski, K. H., & Roberts, B. W. (2005). Do people know how their personality has changed? Correlates of perceived and actual personality change in young adulthood. *Journal of Personality, 73*(2), 489–521. doi:10.1111/j.1467-6494.2005.00317.x

Ruch, W., Proyer, R. T., Harzer, C., Park, N., Peterson, C., & Seligman, M. E. P. (2010). Values in Action Inventory of Strengths (VIA-IS): Adaptation and validation of the German version and the development of a peer-rating form. *Journal of Individual Differences, 31*(3), 138–149. https://doi.org/10.1027/1614-0001/a000022

Ruch, W., Weber, M., Park, N., & Peterson, C. (2014). Character strengths in children and adolescents: Reliability and initial validity of the German Values in Action Inventory of Strengths for Youth (German VIA-Youth). *European Journal of Psychological Assessment, 30*(1), 57–64. https://doi.org/10.1027/1015-5759/a000169

Scheier, M. F., Carver, C. S., & Bridges, M. W. (1994). Distinguishing optimism from neuroticism (and trait anxiety, self-mastery, and self-esteem): A reevaluation of the Life Orientation Test. *Journal of Personality and Social Psychology, 67*(6), 1063.

Specht, J., Egloff, B., & Schmukle, S. C. (2011). Stability and change of personality across the life course: The impact of age and major life events on mean-level and rank-order stability of the Big Five. *Journal of Personality and Social Psychology, 101*(4), 862–882. doi:10.1037/a0024950

Sprecher, S., & Fehr, B. (2016). Compassionate love for close others and humanity. *Journal of Social and Personal Relationships, 22*(5), 629–651. doi:10.1177/0265407505056439.

Steger, M. F., Frazier, P., Oishi, S., & Kaler, M. (2006). The Meaning in Life Questionnaire: Assessing the presence of and search for meaning in life. *Journal of Counseling Psychology, 53*(1), 80–93. doi:10.1037/0022-0167.53.1.80.

Steger, M. F., Oishi, S., & Kashdan, T. B. (2009). Meaning in life across the life span: Levels and correlates of meaning in life from emerging adulthood to older adulthood. *Journal of Positive Psychology, 4*(1), 43–52. doi:10.1080/17439760802303127.

Tashakkori, A., & Creswell, J. W. (2007). The new era of mixed methods. *Journal of Mixed-Methods Research, 1*(1), 3–7.

Tashakkori, A., & Teddlie, C. (2003). Issues and dilemmas in teaching research methods courses in social and behavioural sciences: US perspective. *International Journal of Social Research Methodology, 6*(1), 61–77.

Tashakkori, A., & Teddlie, C. (2010). Putting the human back in "human research methodology": The researcher in mixed methods research [Editorial]. *Journal of Mixed Methods Research, 4*(4), 271–277. https://doi.org/10.1177/1558689810382532

Tedeschi, R. G., & Calhoun, L. G. (1996). The posttraumatic growth inventory: Measuring the positive legacy of trauma. *Journal of Traumatic Stress, 9*(3), 455–471.

Tedeschi, R. G., & Calhoun, L. G. (2004). Posttraumatic growth: Conceptual foundations and empirical evidence. *Psychological Inquiry, 15*(1), 1–18.

Tennen, H., & Affleck, G. (2009). Assessing positive life change: In search of meticulous methods. In C. L. Park, S. C. Lechner, M. H. Antoni, & A. L. Stanton (Eds.), *Medical illness and positive life change: Can crisis lead to personal transformation?* (pp. 31–49). Washington, DC US: American Psychological Association.

Valdez, J. P. M., Yang, W., & Datu, J. A. D. (2017). Validation of the Gratitude Questionnaire in Filipino secondary school students. *Spanish Journal Psychology, 20*, E45, 1–7. doi:10.1017/sjp.2017.51

Vazire, S. (2006). Informant reports: A cheap, fast, and easy method for personality assessment. *Journal of Research in Personality, 40*(5), 472–481.

12

Considering Characteristics of Events in Research on Post-Traumatic Growth

MAIKE LUHMANN AND INA FASSBENDER ■

Post-traumatic growth (PTG) occurs when people experience positive changes in personality traits after a traumatic experience (Jayawickreme & Blackie, 2014; Tedeschi & Calhoun, 2004). In close adherence to this definition, empirical research on PTG has traditionally focused on extreme adverse events as possible triggers of growth (Jayawickreme & Blackie, 2014). In recent years, however, there was an increasing tendency to include other types of events as well, for example, events that are adverse but not traumatic in the clinical sense (Seery & Kondrak, 2014), chronic stressors (Ruini, Offidani, & Vescovelli, 2015), and even positive events (Mangelsdorf, Eid, & Luhmann, 2019; Roepke, 2013). The assumption driving this broadening focus is that the mechanisms which are presumed to lead to growth (e.g., restructuring one's core belief systems or benefit finding; Affleck & Tennen, 1996; Park, 2010; Tedeschi & Calhoun, 2004)can also be triggered by events that are not highly adverse and traumatic (Blackie & Jayawickreme, 2014). At the same time, several studies indicated that growth after adversity might be less common than previously assumed, suggesting that even adverse events do not necessarily result in growth (Infurna & Jayawickreme, 2019). Hence, one important open question in this field is whether different events differ in their impact on personality change, and why (Blackie & Jayawickreme, 2014; Luhmann, 2014; Seery & Kondrak, 2014).

Traditionally, this question was addressed by studying a broad range of different types of events and comparing their effects on personality traits. We refer to this approach as the *typological approach* because events are assigned to distinct types, categories, or classes. If, for example, empirical studies showed repeatedly and reliably that growth (i.e., positive personality change) occurs after clinical trauma but not after nonclinical events, this finding would allow the conclusion that character growth is inextricably linked to clinical trauma. The typological approach is popular not only in research on PTG, but also in life events research more generally. For example, differential effects of major life events on subjective well-being are often explained by distinguishing positive and negative events, and this categorization is typically made by the researchers (e.g., Headey & Wearing, 1989).

Although widely used, the typological approach is associated with theoretical and practical limitations. In this chapter, we summarize these limitations and argue that differences among adverse events, and major life events more generally, should be studied using a dimensional approach that distinguishes events based on continuous characteristics instead of assigning them into distinct and mutually exclusive categories. We introduce the Event Characteristics Questionnaire (ECQ), a novel scale developed to measure nine empirically derived event characteristics. Finally, we lay out a research program for future theoretical and empirical research on event characteristics.

CLASSIFYING MAJOR LIFE EVENTS

The term *event* is not clearly defined in the psychological literature and can be used to refer to anything from a specific activity to a life-changing experience. To minimize ambiguity, we use the term *major life events*, which we define as events that are clearly timed, disrupt one's everyday routine, and are perceived as personally significant and memorable by those who experienced them (Filipp & Aymanns, 2010; Luhmann, Fassbender, Alcock, & Haehner, 2020). Given recent research showing that growth can also occur after positive events (Mangelsdorf et al., 2019), we consider it important that approaches to classifying major life events are not restricted to adverse events but include events of any valence, as it is the case for this definition.

Typological Approaches

In the typological approach, major life events are assigned to distinct categories. For example, many studies distinguish between positive/desirable and negative/undesirable major life events (Frederick & Loewenstein, 1999; Headey & Wearing, 1989; Jeronimus, Ormel, Aleman, Penninx, & Riese, 2013). Similarly common is the approach to distinguish major life events based on the life domain (e.g., work-related events, family-related events, or health-related events) (Bleidorn, Hopwood, & Lucas, 2018; Luhmann, Hofmann, Eid, & Lucas, 2012). However, these classification approaches are insufficient to explain differences in the effects of major life events on growth and other psychological outcomes. As an illustrative example, consider the finding that certain character strengths grew after the terrorist attacks of September 11, 2001 (Peterson & Seligman, 2003), but not after shooting tragedies (Schueller, Jayawickreme, Blackie, Forgeard, &

Roepke, 2015). Why do the findings diverge? Within the typological approach, one would conclude that terrorist attacks and mass shootings are different types of adverse events. However, it remains unclear why one type of event is associated with character growth and the other one is not. Is it because the two events differ on a multitude of characteristics such as level of exposure, surprise, or uncertainty (Bonanno, Romero, & Klein, 2015; Luhmann, 2014)? To develop a more comprehensive typology of adverse events, it would be necessary to study the effects of multiple different events on character growth and to then use the results of these studies to develop categories of events that each share similar characteristics and have similar effects on character growth. This approach is not only impractical because it would require hundreds of independent studies on character growth after adverse events, but it also has more general theoretical limitations.

These theoretical limitations of typological approaches are well known in related research domains such as personality psychology. Typological approaches such as the Myers-Briggs Type Indicator (Myers, 1962) remain popular in applied fields, but they are rarely used in contemporary personality research. A common limitation of personality typologies is that they are based on a very small number of personality traits and thereby cannot account for individual differences on other personality traits. Moreover, typologies are usually set up such that individuals are assigned to one specific category, and any differences among individuals belonging to the same type are deemed irrelevant or nonexistent. Describing individual differences more comprehensively would only be possible if the number of categories were increased dramatically.

The same limitation applies if one attempts to assign major life events to different categories. These categories would be based on a few event characteristics (e.g., traumatic vs. non-traumatic), and other event characteristics would be ignored. Furthermore, it would be assumed that all events belonging to one event category are more or less identical. Any differences among events belonging to the same category (so-called intracategorical variability; B. P. Dohrenwend, 2006) would be ignored. For example, terrorist attacks might be considered the same "type" of major life event but may nevertheless have very different effects on psychological outcomes depending, for example, on how surprising, how brutal, and how severe these particular events were. As a case in point, most research on the effects of terrorist attacks has been conducted in the context of the attacks of September 11, 2001 (Neria, DiGrande, & Adams, 2011). It is unclear to what extent these findings can be generalized to individuals experiencing terrorist attacks in time periods and countries where terrorist attacks are more common but also typically associated with fewer casualties than those of September 11, 2001.

Within the typological approach, the problem of intracategorical variability could only be resolved by dramatically increasing the number of categories. Hence, trying to understand when and why major life events differ in their effects on psychological outcomes by comparing different types of major life events is theoretically and practically challenging.

Dimensional Approaches

Dimensional approaches use different continues dimensions to describe differences among objects. For example, personality psychology relies on dimensional approaches such as the five-factor model (John, Naumann, & Soto, 2008) and the HEXACO model (Ashton & Lee, 2007) to describe differences among persons. Similarly, situation researchers have recently adopted the dimensional approach to describe differences among situations on multiple continuous dimensions, resulting in models such as the DIAMONDS (Rauthmann et al., 2014) and the CAPTION (Parrigon, Woo, Tay, & Wang, 2017).

We argue that the dimensional approach should also be preferred over the typological approach to describe differences among major life events. The dimensional approach has several advantages. First, by describing differences among events on multiple continuous characteristics, it is more likely that those characteristics that are psychologically meaningful and relevant for PTG and other psychological outcomes are included. Second, conclusions about the relevance of particular event characteristics can be generalized across different types of major life events. Third, this approach accounts for individual differences in how people perceive an event. For instance, divorce can be an extremely adverse experience for one person but a bittersweet relief for another. By assessing how individuals perceived the event, rather than just recording whether a specific type of major life event has occurred, we can take this source of interindividual variability into account. Finally, prospective longitudinal studies on major life events are easier to conduct because not all participants have to experience the exact same major life event as long as data on the perceived event characteristics can be collected.

EXISTING DIMENSIONAL APPROACHES

The idea that major life events can be described by different characteristics is as old as systematic research on major life events itself. One of the oldest scales to measure major life events, the Social Readjustment Scale (Holmes & Rahe, 1967), was designed to assess not only whether a specific event occurred, but also how much it required people to readjust after the event. One particular strength of this scale was that it was not restricted to adverse events, but also included major life events that most people would consider desirable (e.g., getting married). Hence, in this scale, it was recognized that even positive events can require people to readjust and, possibly, grow. However, the Social Readjustment Scale only assessed one event characteristic, and the average social readjustment score of each event was determined by asking people to rate hypothetical events rather than directly assessing the required amount of readjustment among those who actually had experienced the event.

The publication of the Social Readjustment Scale led to a surge in research on life events. In the 1970s and 1980s, dozens of approaches to measure major life events and their characteristics were published. In a systematic review of this literature (Luhmann et al., 2020), we identified seven continuous event characteristics that appeared recurrently in these early approaches: valence, attribution of causes and controllability, anticipation, familiarity, intensity and frequency, required adjustment and change, and emotional significance. However, no single empirical study measured all of these event characteristics. Instead, most approaches focused on a smaller number of characteristics, typically between one and four. This was particularly true for theory-driven approaches, in which the relevant characteristics were selected a priori based on theoretical frameworks such as appraisal theory (Folkman & Lazarus, 1985), causal attribution theory (Harvey & Weary, 1984), or life-stress approaches (Dohrenwend & Dohrenwend, 1974). Data-driven approaches, in contrast, used statistical techniques such as exploratory factor analysis, principal components analysis, or multidimensional scaling to derive event characteristics empirically. These approaches tended to yield a somewhat higher number of event characteristics, but none covered all of the main characteristics just listed. Furthermore, only three data-driven approaches included positive events (Buccheri, Musaad, Bost, & Fiese, 2018; Gall & Evans, 1987; Smith & Ellsworth, 1987), and these approaches were limited in other ways (for details, see Luhmann et al., 2020). In sum, despite decades of research and dozens of publications on characteristics of major life events, this research field has not yet delivered a broad and empirically validated taxonomy of continuous characteristics of major life events. To fill this gap, we developed the Event Characteristics Questionnaire.

THE EVENT CHARACTERISTICS QUESTIONNAIRE

The Event Characteristics Questionnaire (ECQ; Luhmann et al., 2020) was developed as a tool that could be applied to measure the characteristics of a wide range of different major life events without restrictions regarding valence, life domain, or severity. We focused on people's perceptions of event characteristics rather than on objective features of the events. Our goal was to develop a scale that was at the same time broad (i.e., included those characteristics that were frequently discussed in the literature) and parsimonious (i.e., excluded characteristics that were irrelevant to distinguish major life events). To find the right balance between breadth and parsimony, we adopted a data-driven approach where a long list of characteristics was reduced to empirically distinguishable and interpretable factors. This approach is similar to those used to derive taxonomies of characteristics of persons (Ashton & Lee, 2007; John et al., 2008) and characteristics of situations (Parrigon et al., 2017; Rauthmann et al., 2014).

The ECQ was developed in a multistep procedure (for details, see Luhmann et al., 2020). First, we conducted a systematic literature search to identify event characteristics frequently discussed in the life events literature (see earlier discussion). Second, we asked study participants to provide brief written descriptions of major life events they had recently experienced and analyzed these descriptions to identify additional event characteristics. Combining the results, we derived a broad list of event characteristics that was used to develop items. In three independent studies, we examined the psychometric properties and the factorial structure of these items and selected the final items.

The ECQ measures nine distinct event characteristics with four items per characteristic (Table 12.1). Five of these characteristics refer to the event itself (valence, challenge, predictability, external control, extraordinariness). Four characteristics refer to the perceived consequences of the event (impact, emotional significance, change in world views, change in social status). For a full list of the items, see Luhmann et al. (2020).

To provide initial evidence on the criterion validity of the ECQ, we conducted three studies in which we examined whether event characteristics were associated with interindividual differences in subjective well-being after major life events (for details, see Luhmann et al., 2020). Two studies used retrospective data of subjective well-being, the third study used a prospective longitudinal design. In all three studies, valence was the most important predictor of both remembered changes and actual changes in subjective well-being. For negative events, subjective well-being tended to decrease directly after the event and increase over the following months, reflecting an immediate negative reaction and subsequent adaptation. For negative events, the pattern was opposite (for remembered changes) or less pronounced (for actual changes). Furthermore, higher levels on social status changes, impact, and predictability were robustly associated with slower changes in remembered subjective well-being. Finally, higher levels on challenge, extraordinariness, impact, and social status changes were associated with more pronounced increases in subjective well-being after the event (for detailed discussions of these findings, see Luhmann et al., 2020). In sum, these findings indicate that event characteristics may indeed explain individual differences in how people change in the context of major life events.

Table 12.1 Event Characteristics Measured in the Event Characteristics Questionnaire (ECQ)

Dimension	**Description**
Valence	Positive and negative aspects of the event
Impact	Extent to which one's life has changed due to the event
Predictability	Extent to how suddenly or predictably the event had occurred
Challenge	Amount of stress and anxiety associated with the event
Emotional significance	Extent to which the event elicited strong feelings
Change in worldviews	Extent to which one's views have changed due to the event
Social status change	Extent of negative changes in one's social status
External control	Extent to which the event was controlled or caused by others
Extraordinariness	Extent of how ordinary or extraordinary the event was

DIRECTIONS FOR FUTURE RESEARCH ON EVENT CHARACTERISTICS

Measuring people's perceptions of characteristics of major life events provides the opportunity to investigate major life events from a novel perspective, but it also raises complex conceptual questions about the nature of event characteristics. In this section, we lay out what we perceive as the most pressing and most interesting questions for future research on event characteristics. We divide these questions into (a) conceptual groundwork that focuses on fostering a better theoretical and empirical understanding of event characteristics per se and (b) application, that is, theoretical and empirical work that integrates event characteristics into broader theoretical frameworks and research questions.

Conceptual Groundwork

Before event characteristics are integrated into broader research questions, it is necessary to understand how judgments of event characteristics are formed in the first place. To address this question systematically, we lean on the current literature on characteristics of situations (Rauthmann & Sherman, 2019; Rauthmann, Sherman, & Funder, 2015). Many of the conceptual issues discussed in the context of characteristics of situations also apply to characteristics of major life events.

As laid out by Rauthmann et al. (2015), judgments of situational characteristics are influenced by three general sources: objective features of the situation (called *cues* or *components* in the situation literature), characteristics of the persons who make the judgments, and the interaction between situation and person. Similarly, judgments of event characteristics are influenced by (a) relatively objective features of the major life event, (b) person characteristics, and (c) event × person interactions. The relatively objective features of the major life event refer to aspects of the event such as when, where, and to whom the event occurred; what exactly happened; and who was present. Notably, most attempts to classify major life events rely exclusively on these kinds of relatively objective features. However, as noted earlier, similar or even identical major life events are not perceived the same way by everyone involved (Dohrenwend, 2006). Individual differences in the perceptions of major life events can result from individual differences on stable traits that affect how people generally perceive major life events (e.g., higher levels of trait neuroticism might generally be associated with a more negative perception of the valence of major life events), from individual differences on variable states that may momentarily shape one's perceptions (e.g., negative momentary mood may be associated with less positive evaluations of a past event), and from the interaction between traits and specific features of an event (e.g., extraversion might be associated with individual differences in the perception of events in which other people were involved, but not in the perception of events in which no other people were involved). In sum, judgments of event characteristics can vary between different major life events (inter-event differences), between different persons (inter-individual differences), and even within persons (intra-individual differences).

Disentangling these different sources of variance is important to avoid the problem of circularity (Rauthmann et al., 2015). It is unclear to what extent the reported characteristics of a particular event are shaped by the actual event or by characteristics of the person. For example, people high in neuroticism may experience similar major life events as people low in neuroticism, but they consistently report having experienced more negative major life events because their level of neuroticism predisposes them to experience major life events as more negative (Headey & Wearing, 1989). In the most extreme case, all individual differences in reported event characteristics could be explained by individual differences in personality traits rather than by differences in the characteristics of the experienced major life events. If this were the case, measuring event characteristics would be obsolete. Hence, it is necessary to systematically investigate the relative importance of each of the sources of variance just listed.

The key to disentangling these different sources in judgments of event characteristics lies in assessing event characteristics with multiple methods. In parallel with situational characteristics (Rauthmann et al., 2015; Rauthmann & Sherman, 2019), methods to assess event characteristics can vary in terms of who makes the rating, what kind of event is rated, and when the event is rated. The raters can be *in situ* (i.e., having personally experienced the event and being personally affected by it), *juxta situm* (i.e., observing the event without being personally affected by it), and *ex situ* (i.e., not present at the event). One interesting question in this context is whether event characteristics are more predictive of outcomes if they are rated by the person who experienced them or by observers (e.g., a close friend or an interviewer). Furthermore, the event can be real (i.e., actually occurring in real life), artificial (i.e., constructed in the lab or in a virtual setting), or hypothetical (i.e., imagined). Finally, real and artificial events can be rated at the time when they occur (concurrent ratings) or afterward (retrospective ratings).

By gathering data from multiple rater perspectives, multiple events, and at multiple occasions, and by using statistical techniques such as structural equation models for multimethod data (Eid, 2006), it is possible to disentangle and quantify the relative importance of each of the sources of judgments just listed. This methodological approach can further be used to identify which traits and states in particular account for individual differences in judgments of event characteristics.

Application to Different Fields

Once we understand how judgments of event characteristics are formed, event characteristics can be integrated into theories and research questions in different fields. For example, PTG researchers might be particularly interested in identifying those event characteristics that are most predictive of changes in psychological outcomes such as gratitude, prosociality, or empathy. A further interesting question in this context is whether the effects found for these variables also apply to other psychological outcomes, such as subjective well-being or the Big Five personality traits. For example, it is possible that some event characteristics predict changes in most psychological outcomes, whereas others predict changes in a few specific psychological outcomes.

Research questions on the link between event characteristics and changes in psychological outcomes probably need to be addressed with a combination of theory-driven and exploratory empirical work. Due to the data-driven development of the ECQ, there is currently no comprehensive theoretical framework that allows specific hypotheses about the impact of every event characteristic included in the ECQ. However, some of the event characteristics that are measured in the ECQ have been examined in previous work, and it is therefore possible to come up with specific hypotheses for at least some of them. For example, valence or predictability are featured in several publications on major life events and PTG (Armeli, Gunthert, & Cohen, 2001; Mangelsdorf et al., 2019; Tedeschi & Calhoun, 2004). Furthermore, some of the ECQ dimensions tap into mechanisms that are assumed to underlie PTG. For example, changes in worldviews refer to the extent to which one's perspectives have changed, which is assumed to be one of the driving mechanisms of PTG (Affleck & Tennen, 1996; Park, 2010; Tedeschi & Calhoun, 2004). Measuring this and other consequence-related event characteristics repeatedly after the event would allow researchers to investigate this mechanism on a more fine-grained temporal scale than has typically been done in this field of research. In sum, even though a comprehensive theoretical framework is not yet available, it is possible to conduct theory-driven confirmative research for at least some event characteristics. However, we also see a clear need for exploratory work, where associations between event characteristics and changes in psychological outcomes are explored and replicated in multiple independent studies. Those exploratory findings that are replicable can then in turn be used to inform theory development.

Measuring event characteristics may also benefit research on specific major life events. There are many examples of studies that examine changes in one particular psychological outcome in the context of one particular major life event. One common finding in most of these studies is that there are significant individual differences in the trajectories of the psychological outcome (Bleidorn et al., 2018; Doré & Bolger, 2017; Lucas, 2007). Most attempts to explain these individual differences have focused on person characteristics (e.g., demographic characteristics such as age or gender (Kendler, Thornton, & Prescott, 2001; Luhmann et al., 2012) or personality traits such as the Big Five (Anusic, Yap, & Lucas, 2014; Boyce, Wood, & Ferguson, 2016) or perceived control) (Infurna & Luthar, 2016). We propose that individual differences in the characteristics of the major life event may also account for individual differences in changes after the event.

Finally, we note that the ECQ has been developed in one specific cultural and linguistic context (Germany) and was validated for major life events as defined earlier. An important direction for future research is to apply the concept of event characteristics in different contexts, cultures, and for a broader range of events, including daily events.

CONCLUSION

An important open question in the PTG literature and in research on major life events more generally is why people experience changes in psychological outcomes after some major life events but not after others. We propose that this question can best be addressed by adopting a dimensional approach to classifying major life events. Such a dimensional approach permits describing similarities and differences among a broad range of different major life events on dimensions that are psychologically meaningful and relevant. In this chapter, we described a newly developed scale to measure event characteristics, the ECQ, and laid out a plan for future research on event characteristics. Future research needs to resolve a number of complex conceptual question and requires collection of data on characteristics of major life events using multiple raters, events, time points, and contexts (Rauthmann et al., 2015; Rauthmann & Sherman, 2019). We are optimistic that a better understanding of the empirical and conceptual properties of event characteristics will enable us to better explain and predict when or for whom PTG can occur.

ACKNOWLEDGMENTS

Preparation of this chapter was supported by a generous award from the Pathways to Characters Project (John T. Templeton Foundation and Arizona State University) to Maike Luhmann.

REFERENCES

Affleck, G., & Tennen, H. (1996). Construing benefits from adversity: Adaptational significance and dispositional underpinnings. *Journal of Personality, 64*(4), 899–922. https://doi.org/10.1111/j.1467-6494.1996.tb00948.x

Anusic, I., Yap, S. C. Y., & Lucas, R. E. (2014). Does personality moderate reaction and adaptation to major life events? Analysis of life satisfaction and affect in an Australian national sample. *Journal of Research in Personality, 5*, 69–77. https://doi.org/10.1016/j.jrp.2014.04.009

Armeli, S., Gunthert, K. C., & Cohen, L. H. (2001). Stressor appraisals, coping, and post-event outcomes: The dimensionality and antecedents of stress-related growth. *Journal of Social and Clinical Psychology, 20*(3), 366–395. https://doi.org/10.1521/jscp.20.3.366.22304

Ashton, M. C., & Lee, K. (2007). Empirical, theoretical, and practical advantages of the HEXACO model of personality structure. *Personality and Social Psychology Review, 11*(2), 150–166. https://doi.org/10.1177/1088868306294907

Blackie, L. E. R., & Jayawickreme, E. (2014). Promoting change in post-traumatic growth research: Response to commentaries. *European Journal of Personality, 28*, 351–361. https://doi.org/10.1002/per.1970

Bleidorn, W., Hopwood, C. J., & Lucas, R. E. (2018). Life events and personality trait change. *Journal of Personality, 86*(1), 83–96. https://doi.org/10.1111/jopy.12286

Bonanno, G. A., Romero, S. A., & Klein, S. I. (2015). The temporal elements of psychological resilience: An integrative framework for the study of individuals, families, and communities. *Psychological Inquiry, 26*(2), 139–169. https://doi.org/10.1080/1047840X.2015.992677

Boyce, C. J., Wood, A. M., & Ferguson, E. (2016). For better or for worse: The moderating effects of personality on the marriage-life satisfaction link. *Personality and Individual Differences, 97*, 61–66. https://doi.org/10.1016/j.paid.2016.03.005

Buccheri, T., Musaad, S., Bost, K. K., & Fiese, B. H. (2018). Development and assessment of stressful life events subscales: A preliminary analysis. *Journal of Affective Disorders, 226*, 178–187. https://doi.org/10.1016/j.jad.2017.09.046

Dohrenwend, B. P. (2006). Inventorying stressful life events as risk factors for psychopathology: Toward resolution of the problem of intracategory variability. *Psychological Bulletin, 132*(3), 477–495. https://doi.org/10.1037/0033-2909.132.3.477

Dohrenwend, B. S., & Dohrenwend, B. P. (Eds.) (1974). *Stressful Life Events: Their Nature and Effects*. New York: Wiley.

Doré, B., & Bolger, N. (2017). Population- and individual-level changes in life satisfaction surrounding major life stressors. *Social Psychological and Personality Science, 9*(7), 875–884. https://doi.org/10.1177/1948550617727589

Eid, M. (2006). Methodological approaches for analyzing multimethod data. In M. Eid & E. Diener (Eds.), *Handbook of Multimethod Measurement in Psychology* (1st ed., pp. 223–230). Washington, DC: American Psychological Association.

Filipp, S.-H., & Aymanns, P. (2010). *Kritische Lebensereignisse und Lebenskrisen: Vom Umgang mit den Schattenseiten des Lebens*. Stuttgart: Verlag W. Kohlhammer.

Folkman, S., & Lazarus, R. S. (1985). If it changes it must be a process: Study of emotion and coping during three stages of a college examination. *Journal of Personality and Social Psychology, 48*(1), 150–170. https://doi.org/10.1037/0022-3514.48.1.150

Frederick, S., & Loewenstein, G. (1999). Hedonic adaptation. In D. Kahneman, E. Diener, & N. Schwarz (Eds.), *Well-Being: The Foundations of Hedonic Psychology* (pp. 302–329). New York: Russell Sage Foundation.

Gall, T. L., & Evans, D. R. (1987). The dimensionality of cognitive appraisal and its relationship to physical and psychological well-being. *Journal of Psychology: Interdisciplinary and Applied, 121*(6), 539–546. https://doi.org/10.1080/00223980.1987.9712682

Harvey, J. H., & Weary, G. (1984). Current issues in attribution theory and research. *Annual Review of Psychology, 35*, 427–459. https://doi.org/10.1146/annurev.ps.35.020184.002235

Headey, B., & Wearing, A. J. (1989). Personality, life events and subjective well-being: Toward a dynamic equilibrium model. *Journal of Personality and Social Psychology, 57*, 731–739. https://doi.org/10.1037/0022-3514.57.4.731

Holmes, T. H., & Rahe, R. H. (1967). The social readjustment rating scale. *Journal of Psychosomatic Research, 11*(2), 213–218. https://doi.org/10.1016/0022-3999(67)90010-4

Infurna, F. J., & Jayawickreme, E. (2019). Fixing the growth illusion: New directions for research in resilience and posttraumatic growth. *Current Directions in Psychological Science, 28*(2), 152–158. https://doi.org/10.1177/0963721419827017

Infurna, F. J., & Luthar, S. S. (2016). Resilience to major life stressors is not as common as thought. *Perspectives on Psychological Science, 11*(2), 175–194. https://doi.org/10.1177/1745691615621271

Jayawickreme, E., & Blackie, L. E. R. (2014). Post-traumatic growth as positive personality change: Evidence, controversies and future directions. *European Journal of Personality, 28*(4), 312–331. https://doi.org/10.1002/per.1963

Jeronimus, B. F., Ormel, J., Aleman, A., Penninx, B. W. J. H., & Riese, H. (2013). Negative and positive life events are associated with small but lasting change in neuroticism. *Psychological Medicine, 43*(11), 2403–2415. https://doi.org/10.1017/S0033291713000159

John, O. P., Naumann, L. P., & Soto, C. J. (2008). Paradigm shift to the integrative Big Five trait taxonomy: History, measurement, and conceptual issues. In O. P. John, R. W. Robins, & L. A. Pervin (Eds.), *Handbook of Personality: Theory and Research* (3rd ed., pp. 114–158). New York: Guilford.

Kendler, K. S., Thornton, L. M., & Prescott, C. A. (2001). Gender differences in the rates of exposure to stressful life events and sensitivity to their depressogenic effects. *American Journal of Psychiatry, 158*(4), 587–593. https://doi.org/10.1176/appi.ajp.158.4.587

Lucas, R. E. (2007). Adaptation and the set-point model of subjective well-being: Does happiness change after major life events? *Current Directions in Psychological Science, 16*(2), 75–79. https://doi.org/10.1111/j.1467-8721.2007.00479.x

Luhmann, M. (2014). Is studying traumatic events worth the effort? *European Journal of Personality, 28*(4), 343–344. https://doi.org/10.1002/per.1970

Luhmann, M., Fassbender, I., Alcock, M., & Haehner, P. (2020). A dimensional taxonomy of perceived characteristics of major life events. *Journal of Personality and Social Psychology.* Advance online publication. https://doi.org/10.1037/pspp0000291

Luhmann, M., Hofmann, W., Eid, M., & Lucas, R. E. (2012). Subjective well-being and adaptation to life events: A meta-analysis. *Journal of Personality and Social Psychology, 102*(3), 592–615. https://doi.org/10.1037/a0025948

Mangelsdorf, J., Eid, M., & Luhmann, M. (2019). Does growth require suffering? A systematic review and meta-analysis on genuine posttraumatic and postecstatic growth. *Psychological Bulletin, 145*(3), 302–338. https://doi.org/10.1037/bul0000173

Myers, I. B. (1962). *The Myers-Briggs Type Indicator: Manual (1962).* Palo Alto, CA: Consulting Psychologists Press. https://doi.org/10.1037/14404-000

Neria, Y., DiGrande, L., & Adams, B. G. (2011). Posttraumatic stress disorder following the September 11, 2001, terrorist attacks: A review of the literature among highly exposed populations. *American Psychologist, 66*(6), 429–446. https://doi.org/10.1037/a0024791

Park, C. L. (2010). Making sense of the meaning literature: An integrative review of meaning making and its effects on adjustment to stressful life events. *Psychological Bulletin, 136*(2), 257–301. https://doi.org/10.1037/a0018301

Parrigon, S., Woo, S. E., Tay, L., & Wang, T. (2017). Captioning the situation: A lexically-derived taxonomy of psychological situation characteristics. *Journal of Personality and Social Psychology, 112*(4), 642–681. https://doi.org/10.1037/pspp0000111

Peterson, C., & Seligman, M. E. P. (2003). Character strengths before and after September 11. *Psychological Science, 14*(4), 381–384. https://doi.org/10.1111/1467-9280.24482

Rauthmann, J. F., Gallardo-Pujol, D., Guillaume, E. M., Todd, E., Nave, C. S., Sherman, R. A., . . . Funder, D. C. (2014). The Situational Eight DIAMONDS: A taxonomy of major dimensions of situation characteristics. *Journal of Personality and Social Psychology, 107*(4), 677–718. https://doi.org/10.1037/a0037250

Rauthmann, J. F., & Sherman, R. (2019). Toward a research agenda for the study of situation perceptions: A variance componential framework. *Personality and Social Psychology Review, 23*(3), 238–266. https://doi.org/10.1177/1088868318765600

Rauthmann, J. F., Sherman, R. A., & Funder, D. C. (2015). Principles of situation research: Towards a better understanding of psychological situations. *European Journal of Personality, 29*(3), 363–381. https://doi.org/10.1002/per.1994

Roepke, A. M. (2013). Gains without pains? Growth after positive events. *Journal of Positive Psychology, 8*(4), 280–291. https://doi.org/10.1080/17439760.2013.791715

Ruini, C., Offidani, E., & Vescovelli, F. (2015). Life stressors, allostatic overload, and their impact on posttraumatic growth. *Journal of Loss and Trauma, 20*(2), 109–122. https://doi.org/10.1080/15325024.2013.830530

Schueller, S. M., Jayawickreme, E., Blackie, L. E. R., Forgeard, M. J. C., & Roepke, A. M. (2015). Finding character strengths through loss: An extension of Peterson and Seligman (2003). *Journal of Positive Psychology, 10*(1), 53–63. https://doi.org/10.1080/17439760.2014.920405

Seery, M. D., & Kondrak, C. L. (2014). Does trauma lead to "special" growth? *European Journal of Personality, 28*, 348–350. https://doi.org/10.1002/per.1970

Smith, C. A., & Ellsworth, P. C. (1987). Patterns of appraisal and emotion related to taking an exam. *Journal of Personality and Social Psychology, 52*(3), 475–488. https://doi.org/10.1037/0022-3514.52.3.475

Tedeschi, R. G., & Calhoun, L. G. (2004). Target Article: "Posttraumatic growth: Conceptual foundations and empirical evidence." *Psychological Inquiry, 15*(1), 1–18. https://doi.org/10.1207/s15327965pli1501_01

13

Openness to Experience and Post-Traumatic Growth

MARIE FORGEARD, ELANA BAYER-PACHT, PAUL J. SILVIA, ANN MARIE ROEPKE, AND THRÖSTUR BJÖRGVINSSON ■

Many people retrospectively report becoming more open to new ideas and possibilities following highly stressful events. Under these circumstances, individuals describe being compelled to question their most deeply held beliefs and becoming open to considering previously ignored ideas, perspectives, and opportunities (Tedeschi & Calhoun, 1996). Specific examples of this phenomenon vary widely and may, among other instantiations, take the form of adopting new hobbies or interests, starting projects or initiatives, beginning to volunteer for a cause, wanting to travel the world to discover unfamiliar places and cultures, or more generally developing curiosity and appreciation for new information or other viewpoints.

More broadly then, such anecdotal reports suggest that people may experience meaningful changes in the personality trait of openness to experience following major adversity. Individuals high in this trait are typically described as imaginative, curious, and creative, among other adjectives (Goldberg, 1992). At a more fundamental level, openness to experience can best be defined as the propensity to engage in cognitive exploration by seeking and engaging with unfamiliar and complex patterns of sensory and abstract information (DeYoung, 2015). It is therefore possible that adversity might increase people's "breadth, depth, and permeability of consciousness," as reflected in a "recurrent need to enlarge and examine experience" (McCrae & Costa, 1997, p. 826; McCrae & Sutin, 2009). Following adverse events, people may be more sensitive and receptive to inputs from their environment and more interested in understanding complex phenomena, including their inner/outer experiences (DeYoung, 2015).

This chapter reviews the body of literature investigating changes in openness to experience (from here on referred to as *openness*) following adversity. Given the relative paucity of research on this topic, we focus on openness broadly (as just defined) rather than examining its subcomponents. In doing so, we will therefore address the relevance of openness for understanding the phenomenon of post-traumatic growth (PTG), defined as positive changes reported following the experience of highly stressful events (Tedeschi & Calhoun, 2004). We first summarize findings supporting the notion that adversity could lead to positive changes in openness. Second, we discuss the hypotheses that openness may facilitate more general psychological growth by either moderating or mediating its occurrence. Third, we review contradictory findings suggesting that adversity is either negatively or not associated with changes in openness. Finally, we summarize key limitations of existing scholarship and propose a methodological agenda for future research on this topic.

CHANGES IN OPENNESS AS A MANIFESTATION OF GROWTH THROUGH ADVERSITY

Research on PTG has shown that people commonly report having identified new possibilities for their lives as a result of adversity, alongside four other domains of growth (i.e., enhanced relationships, personal strengths, appreciation for life, and spirituality) measured by the Post-Traumatic Growth Inventory (PTGI; Tedeschi & Calhoun, 1996). According to PTG theory, highly adverse events may by their very nature have the power to shatter people's basic assumptions about themselves and the world, forcing them to reconsider previously ingrained beliefs and allowing them to perceive and engage with new information and opportunities they might have otherwise ignored (Janoff-Bulman, 1992, 2006; Tedeschi & Calhoun, 2004).

While most studies suggesting growth in this domain do so by examining retrospective self-reports on the "New Possibilities" subscale of the PTGI, additional personality research has also produced some supporting evidence (but see later discussion for contradictory findings). For example, having experienced stress or trauma in childhood has been associated with higher levels of openness to experience later in life (Allen & Lauterbach, 2007; Williams, Rau, Cribbet, & Gunn, 2009). In addition, two longitudinal studies have found that adversity is associated with increases in openness, but only under certain circumstances. In a large sample drawn from the German Socio-Economic Panel, only men (but not women) experienced increases in openness following negative events (Specht, Egloff, & Schmukle, 2011). In a sample of undergraduate students, experiencing an adverse event was associated with small increases in openness over a 3-month period only if the experience was also construed as "highly central" (i.e., as a "turning point" in one's life) (Boals, Southard-Dobbs, & Blumenthal, 2015).

Scholarship relevant to closely related constructs can also help support the hypothesis that adversity enhances openness. For example, identifying new possibilities for one's life could take the form of creative pursuits or ideas, one of the behavioral hallmarks of openness to experience (Karwowski & Lebuda, 2016;

McCrae, 1987; Silvia, Nusbaum, Berg, Martin, & O'Connor, 2009). In keeping with this, self-reported creative growth following adversity has been associated with the perception of new possibilities for one's life, as well as with improvements in relationships (Forgeard, 2013). These findings are in line with historiometric and biographical findings showing that accomplished individuals are more likely than average to have lost a parent early in life (Csikszentmihalyi, 1996; Simonton, 1994) or to have experienced other forms of early adversity (Aldwin & Sutton, 1998; Bloom, 1998). Additional qualitative work has documented how the experience of chronic and/or severe illness can serve as a catalyst for creative and artistic work by offering new insights and possibilities (Reynolds, 2004; Zausner, 1998, 2007). Findings from the creativity literature therefore complement PTG research by suggesting that adversity may be associated with increases in one aspect of openness to experience (creativity).

Nonetheless, most of the evidence just reviewed only supports the claim that people's perceptions of their own openness changes following adverse events. As discussed later, little research has documented more extensive changes in people's thoughts, feelings, and behaviors over time. Nonetheless, if adversity is indeed meaningfully related to openness, one question that arises is whether this trait could help facilitate more general psychological growth either by acting as a moderator (are individuals high in openness to begin with more likely to grow from adversity in general?) or mediator (are individuals who grow in openness following adversity also then more likely to grow in general?).

CAN OPENNESS TO EXPERIENCE FACILITATE POSTTRAUMATIC GROWTH?

Preexisting Openness as a Moderator of Growth

Openness, along with extraversion, belongs to a broader meta-trait reflecting plasticity and potential for growth based on interactions with the environment (DeYoung, 2006; DeYoung, Peterson, & Higgins, 2002; Digman, 1997). Individuals high in openness are more attuned to and willing to take into consideration information they are exposed to and potentially to let this information change them. This framework suggests that people who are higher in openness to begin with may be more likely to grow from adverse experiences, though previous research suggests that plasticity may facilitate both positive and negative changes. For example, in a study of young German adults transitioning from high school to college, openness was associated with experiencing both positive and negative changes in self-care, relationships, and interests (Lüdtke, Roberts, Trautwein, & Nagy, 2011). In another study of the effects of moving on middle-aged women, openness was simultaneously associated with increases in both depressive symptoms and self-esteem (Kling, Ryff, Love, & Essex, 2003). If openness enhances people's sensitivity to new situations and information, it may therefore predispose them to be more vulnerable to the potential negative effects of stress, but also better able to make use of experiences to cope and grow (DeYoung, Grazioplene, & Peterson, 2012).

Some evidence has linked openness to experience to enhanced coping processes. Early PTG research found that the personality trait of openness to experience (especially openness to feelings) was modestly associated with retrospectively rated PTG (Tedeschi & Calhoun, 1996; Zoellner, Rabe, Karl, & Maercker, 2008). Openness has been associated with the ability to effectively deal with intercultural stress (Van Der Zee, Van Oudenhoven, De Grijs, 2004). In an experimental study during which participants were asked to describe and discuss a recent stressful event, high openness to experience was associated with increases in positive affect, suggesting that individuals effectively managed and regulated emotions associated with this recollection (Williams et al., 2009). Thus, openness may help regulate stress by promoting adaptive coping styles such as curiosity, humor, and acceptance of life's challenges and preventing maladaptive avoidance (McCrae & Costa, 1986; McCrae & Sutin, 2009; Schneider, Rench, Lyons, & Riffle, 2012; Weinstein & Ryan, 2011). Indeed, experiential avoidance (i.e., unwillingness to be in contact with distressing thoughts and feelings) combined with post-traumatic distress appears to make PTG less likely (Kashdan & Kane, 2011). More generally, a few studies have shown that increases in openness experienced during personality or clinical interventions are accompanied by decreases in neuroticism (e.g., Stieger et al., 2020) or depression symptoms (e.g., Forgeard et al., 2019), though more research is needed to understand this link.

Changes in Openness as a Mediator of Growth

Researchers interested in the phenomenon of PTG are understandably curious to understand what processes might facilitate the occurrence of positive changes. Increases in openness could constitute such a mechanism: as adversity compels individuals to consider new ideas, information, and possibilities, broader changes in a wider variety of domains may occur. For example, newfound openness may promote new relationships, a better ability to appreciate life's moments, or a spiritual awakening. Thus, it might be precisely because people become more open to new ideas, experiences, and opportunities (perhaps because the challenges they face require that they do so to process the experience) that they are able to experience additional positive transformations. In keeping with this, Roepke and Seligman (2015) found that engagement with new possibilities (i.e., perceiving "new doors opening") partially explained the cross-sectional relationship between disruption of core beliefs and psychological growth in a sample of adults. Relatedly, Roepke, Benson, Tsukayama, and Yaden (2018) tested an intervention that invited participants (who had recently experienced adversity) to think and write about new possibilities that might be emerging in their lives. Participants who were randomly assigned to this intervention, rather than to a factual writing or no writing control group, showed greater levels of PTG over time. Despite these findings, little research using other methods has followed up on this hypothesis to determine whether increases in openness might explain broader positive changes in personality.

CONTRADICTORY FINDINGS: DETERIORATION IN OPENNESS FOLLOWING ADVERSITY

Despite the intuitive appeal of the notion that adversity might enhance openness and the research reviewed supporting this claim, a broader look at the relevant literature quickly shows that evidence bearing on this topic is mixed. We now turn to reviewing contradictory findings in order to highlight key questions in this area deserving of further investigation.

Posttraumatic Growth Research

Several findings from the PTG literature suggest that the link between adversity and openness could actually be the reverse of what has been hypothesized earlier: under some circumstances, adversity might make people *less* open to new information and ideas. In a series of studies conducted in New York City and in Israel following terrorism/violence, high levels of PTG were associated with more rigid and less tolerant political attitudes and increased support for retaliatory violence (consequences suggesting lower openness), as well as heightened psychological distress (Hobfoll et al., 2007).

These findings lend credence to the idea that growth following adversity may have both a constructive/adaptive side and an illusory/self-deceptive side reflecting people's attempts to cope with extremely challenging circumstances (Maercker & Zoellner, 2004; Taylor, Kemeny, Reed, & Bower, 2000). Some people may accurately perceive increases in openness (and in many cases may demonstrate this through changes in cognitions and behaviors), while others may perceive similar increases that are either not accompanied by such meaningful changes in cognitions and/or behaviors or even accompanied by contradictory changes (Roepke, Forgeard, & Elstein, 2014). Discrepancies between people's subjective self-reports and what happens to them over time pose one of the greatest challenges to the study of PTG (Jayawickreme & Blackie, 2014), as further detailed in upcoming sections.

Longitudinal Personality and Developmental Research

Perhaps the most robust tests of changes in openness following adversity come from longitudinal studies in the areas of personality and developmental psychology, in which participants were followed over time to document changes in traits rather than relying on retrospective reports. However, the hypothesis that openness might increase following negative events is at odds with the more general observation that this trait is typically relatively stable over the life span, increasing somewhat in adolescence and young adulthood and then slowly declining afterward (Roberts, Walton, & Viechtbauer, 2006) despite the fact that most people experience highly adverse events during their lifetimes (Breslau et al., 1998).

To date, only a handful of studies have examined changes in openness specifically (and usually as part of a broader set of traits), yielding an inconsistent set of findings. In contrast with the replicated finding that neuroticism increases following adversity, openness and other traits have not yielded a consistent picture (Bleidorn, Hopwood, & Lucas, 2018; Costa, McCrae, & Löckenhoff, 2019). As already noted, two studies in this area found that adverse events were associated with openness only for some people (e.g., men but not women in Specht et al., 2011; those who rated adverse events as highly central in Boals et al., 2015). Most studies in this area have found no changes in openness following adverse events. Researchers examining resilience following the 2010–2011 Christchurch earthquake in New Zealand found no changes in openness (Milojev, Osborne, & Sibley, 2014). Similarly, another study following socioeconomically diverse families from Minneapolis for more than two decades found that adversity experienced in adolescence was not associated with changes in openness (in fact, openness was the most stable trait in this sample) (Shiner, Allen, & Masten, 2017). One study has also documented negative changes in openness following high stress. In an urban sample recruited from the East Baltimore Epidemiologic Catchment Study characterized by high levels of adversity, major stressors predicted decreases in openness to values and an increased tendency to embrace authority, dogma, and tradition over a period of 8 years (Löckenhoff, Terracciano, Patriciu, Eaton, & Costa, 2009).

Studies using sequential sample designs in which different (though large) sets of participants complete the same measures before and after an event (typically using the Values in Action Inventory of Strengths; Peterson & Seligman, 2004) have also yielded an inconsistent picture. In a study examining changes in character strengths before and after the September 11, 2001, terrorist attack on the United States, strengths related to openness were not among those showing increases during this time period (Peterson & Seligman, 2003; see also Schueller, Jayawickreme, Blackie, Forgeard, & Roepke, 2015). A more recent study examining changes in character strengths across three different countries (including France before and after the 2015 terror attacks, as well as the United States and Australia as controls) did not yield a pattern of findings consistent with previous research on this topic, leading the authors to question the reliability of within-nation findings using such designs (Lamade, Jayawickreme, Blackie, & McGrath, 2020).

Experimental Research

Last, evidence from experimental research also challenges the notion that stressful experiences could increase people's openness. However, it should be acknowledged that by testing the effects of more minor stressors on people's immediate thoughts, feelings, and behaviors, these studies do not provide insights into longer term ways in which significant adversity shapes personality. This is particularly relevant in light of research suggesting that increases in openness might be more likely after those adverse events that are highly central to an individual's life or identity (Boals et al., 2015). While a comprehensive review of this literature is beyond the scope of this chapter, this literature has for the most part shown that minor stressors lead to decreases in openness (though, as noted earlier, people who are already high in openness to begin with may fare better coping with stressors). Such stressors typically lead to "cognitive narrowing" by enhancing selective attention for threatening stimuli and impairing decision-making: for example, in multiple studies, acute stress led to increased attentional resources being directed toward threat-related stimuli regardless of whether participants were low or high in anxiety to begin with (Mogg, Mathews, Bird, & Macgregor-Morris, 1990). To cope with threat, individuals resort to increased black-and-white thinking to increase certainty and control (Dechesne & Kruglanski, 2004). Such motivated closed-mindedness in the face of threat has also been demonstrated with political attitudes, leading individuals to stop searching for information and endorse more conservative positions to satisfy a need for closure (Thórisdóttir & Jost, 2011). These experimental findings also echo insights from terror management theory research, which has demonstrated that exposure to reminders of one's mortality typically leads people to adhere more strongly to their ingroup's worldviews and beliefs and prevents them from considering other viewpoints (Greenberg et al., 1990).

ADDRESSING METHODOLOGICAL SHORTCOMINGS TO RECONCILE CONTRADICTORY FINDINGS

Our review of the literature suggests that while people subjectively report that they have become more open to new ideas and experiences following adversity, they do not show corroborating changes in personality when assessed over time. Perhaps the most obvious limitation of previous research is that very few studies have focused on openness as their main primary outcome. Instead, most studies have looked at this construct alongside other outcomes, precluding more nuanced approaches. The contradictory nature of these findings suggest that a much more careful look is needed to understand not just whether adversity leads to changes in openness (a question that so far has only yielded mixed findings, perhaps due to the heterogeneity of the research designs used), but more importantly to understand the circumstances under which any changes in openness might occur and under which conditions changes might be positive or negative in nature.

Many of the challenges involved in advancing our understanding of changes in openness following adversity are shared by research on PTG as a whole. As noted earlier, any positive changes reported following adversity may represent both actual constructive changes as well as positive illusions created and maintained in order to cope with the consequences of negative events (Jayawickreme & Blackie,

2014; Taylor & Armor, 1996). Such illusory growth can be adaptive (especially soon after the event), though it may also lead to difficulties if associated with avoidance or denial. Over time, more meaningful and constructive changes may occur, reflecting genuine growth (Maercker & Zoellner, 2004; Zoellner & Maercker, 2006). From a research perspective, disentangling growth from illusions has been challenging due to practical considerations in setting up research designs to adequately address this question. We highlight here several ways in which scholarship on this question can be enhanced by examining openness using multiple methods, complementing cross-sectional designs with longitudinal studies (including intensive longitudinal approaches), concurrently investigating the effect of major and more minor stressors, and advancing our understanding of potential moderators and mediators of growth in openness following adversity.

Examining Openness Using Multiple Methods

Although the studies just reviewed have included openness (or related constructs, such as the perception of new possibilities) as an outcome, none of these studies primarily focused on this variable specifically. Studies in the field of PTG have tended to take a general approach by looking at overall growth and/or assessing changes in several domains at the same time (e.g., the five domains represented in the PTGI, character strengths in general, etc.). Though this general approach allows researchers to compare how people fare in different domains, there might be great value in more focused studies carefully examining changes in one strength or trait at a time. This would allow for the use of multimethod strategies to corroborate any changes found and provide additional nuance about the different ways in which positive changes may (or may not) occur. Assessing openness using a combination of methods would allow researchers to, for example, document changes in self-perceptions over time and assess whether these are accompanied by changes in behaviors, beliefs, or explicit/implicit attitudes.

Going Beyond Retrospective Self-Reports

Documenting the existence of growth beyond subjective perceptions (adaptive or maladaptive) requires the use of longitudinal designs that can document trajectories of constructs of interest over time rather than rely on people's potentially flawed retrospective calculations of what has happened to them (Frazier et al., 2009; Jayawickreme & Blackie, 2014, 2016). As noted earlier, future research should attempt to use longitudinal methods whenever possible to better understand the time frame over which changes in openness do (or do not) occur (Infurna & Jayawickreme, 2019).

Researchers should also consider complementing waves of longitudinal assessments with intensive longitudinal approaches (e.g., experience-sampling; Blackie et al., 2017). Collecting in-the-moment assessments of openness would enable us to better understand how openness is manifested at the state level and how shifts in the frequency and intensity of state-level openness may, over a longer period of time, produce changes at the trait level (Fleeson, Furr, Jayawickreme, Meindl, & Helzer, 2014; Fleeson & Jayawickreme, 2015). A closer examination of openness states might also help generate a richer understanding of how openness manifests itself in daily life by answering the following questions, among others: What are people more open to? What does this look like in terms of behaviors or activities? Are people aware of this in the moment? Do people's assessments of their own openness (whether retrospective or at a particular timepoint) match up with more immediate reports of thoughts, feelings, and behaviors collected within the preceding time period using experience sampling?

Concurrently Examining the Effects of Major and Minor Stressors

Intensive longitudinal designs also provide an opportunity to examine not just how people's day-to-day functioning is affected by major adversity, but also how they fare in response to more minor stressors. This is especially noteworthy given previous research showing that significant stressors impact people's lives specifically by influencing responses to minor daily stressors (Miller & Rasmussen, 2010). It might therefore be that changes in people's personality are most obvious when they are dealing with ongoing life challenges. Integrative approaches that concurrently examine the influence of major and minor stressors on openness will help reconcile previous discrepancies in findings from both longitudinal and experimental research and advance our understanding of whether and when stressful experiences lead to changes in openness.

Moderators of Changes in Openness

As noted earlier, the most pressing question surrounding growth in openness following adversity is not whether changes in openness occur following major stressors, but rather when and how these occur (vs. do not occur). Thus, more research is needed to carefully investigate potential moderators facilitating versus impeding growth in openness. Many such variables may exist; we propose here a few that may be worthy of additional consideration.

First, the role of initial value effects—how someone's pre-adversity level of openness affects subsequent change—deserves more attention. One intuitive possibility is that some minimum level of openness is needed to further grow in this dimension. People who are at least average in openness, for example, have the hallmark motives and mindsets of open people—curiosity, creativity, and receptivity to novelty and change—that can serve as resources for growth. Alternately, people with notable levels of openness have less room to grow, representing a classic ceiling effect. In a recent study examining the effectiveness of a 2-week smartphone-based intervention designed to enhance openness to action specifically, individuals who were low on this facet of openness to begin with were more likely to want to increase on this trait than other participants and in turn experienced significant increases in openness to action during the intervention (Stieger et al., 2020). One could thus could reasonably predict the opposite initial value effect: people low in openness, because they have the most room to move, might show the greatest growth in openness following adversity. The limited longitudinal evidence base to date does not offer a way to settle these contrasting possibilities.

Second, other psychological resources may be needed to be able to grow in general and in openness specifically. For example, it might be useful to more closely study whether individual differences in vulnerability to stress relate to change. Earlier research has suggested that psychological distress is associated with retrospective reports of growth (Shakespeare-Finch & Lurie-Beck, 2014). This finding supports the notion that individuals need to be profoundly impacted and shaken by an event in order to experience positive changes (Tedeschi & Calhoun, 2004). However, recent studies using methods designed to reduce biases in participants' growth reports by either using neutrally worded items (Boals & Schuler, 2018) or longitudinal measurement strategies (Frazier et al., 2009) have shown psychological growth to instead predict lower levels of distress. Examining how vulnerability to stress relates to growth in openness (and how these relationships may vary over time) may offer additional insights into how openness following adversity can be facilitated (or conversely, whether openness might facilitate resilience).

Finally, other factors discussed in greater detail elsewhere in this volume may also be crucial for understanding when adversity increases openness. For example, it is unclear whether event characteristics shape such changes: perhaps only certain events (as described by type, severity, or personal meaning) may instill change. As with other potential domains of growth, the role of social and cultural norms has also been largely understudied. It would therefore be valuable to further investigate the role of culture in the context of understanding changes in openness (Calhoun, Cann, & Tedeschi, 2010; Kashyap & Hussain, 2018; Shakespeare-Finch & Copping, 2006; Splevins, Cohen, Bowley, & Joseph, 2010).

Explanations for Potential Changes in Openness

If openness does indeed change following experiences of adversity, more research is needed to understand exactly how this might be the case. Early PTG theory posited that growth occurs through cognitive changes, through a shift from intrusive and ineffective repetitive thinking toward more deliberate cognitive processing that enables growth (Tedeschi & Calhoun, 2004), a model supported by subsequent research (e.g., Chan, Ho, Tedeschi, & Leung, 2011; Garcia, Cova, Rincón, & Vázquez, 2015). Positive changes in openness may, of course, result from similar processes (a question that has yet to be examined), though processes specific to changes in this trait in particular may be worth investigating.

For example, previous research on the role of diversifying experiences for creativity (which, as noted earlier, is a known aspect of openness) may provide some direction. According to this perspective, adverse events may foster creative achievement by acting as diversifying experiences, defined as "highly unusual and unexpected events or situations that push individuals outside of the realm of 'normality,' enabling them to conceive ideas that are less bounded by conventional constraints" (Damian & Simonton, 2015, p. 623). Thus, negative events might foster greater flexibility in ideation and consideration for unusual ideas. However, and as noted by these authors, other types of events or circumstances may be just as likely to act as diversifying experiences and enhance receptiveness and generation of ideas (i.e., events do not need to be negative, and other experiences such as multicultural experiences, nontraditional backgrounds, or unusual positive events might be just as conducive) (Damian & Simonton, 2014). Relatedly, research on life events suggests that individuals report similar types of personal growth after positive experiences as after adverse or traumatic ones and that reports of growth are particularly likely if the individual saw the experience as one that involved perception of new opportunities for their life (Roepke, 2013). This hypothesis on diversifying experiences is in line with experimental research showing that such experiences (e.g., being presented with novel and incongruous stimuli) enhances creative thinking in the laboratory (e.g., Ritter, van Baaren, & Dijksterhuis, 2012). Thus, the mechanisms underlying increases in openness following adversity may partially consist of greater exposure to new and unexpected information and potentially greater receptiveness and ability to use this information effectively. Studies are needed to examine this theory using mediation models.

Extending research to understand exactly what is happening cognitively when individuals perceive, receive, and utilize novel information is an important challenge for this area of research. In this regard, related research on wisdom following adversity (a closely related construct, since wisdom is usually defined as a broader construct that includes open-mindedness to other perspectives; Grossmann, 2017) is a great model of how to study the ways in which people process information and how these might change following adversity. Scholarship in this area has shown that adverse experiences may promote growth in wisdom and well-being by enabling a more distanced (rather than immersed) perspective from the self, which is more conducive to growth (Dorfman, Oakes, Santos, & Grossmann, 2021; see also Kross & Grossmann, 2012). This type of research is uniquely useful because it can help explain when adversity fosters openness (vs. does not) and can also eventually help guide thoughtful interventions designed to help individuals cope and potentially grow from adversity.

Such efforts may therefore also benefit from insights drawn from relevant intervention research. For example, in their 2-week smartphone-based intervention study designed to increase openness to action, Stieger et al. (2020) designed their intervention to increase openness to action around four known change factors (Allemand & Flückiger, 2017): (a) accentuating participants' awareness of the discrepancy between their actual and desired personality (e.g., by generating and reviewing implementation intentions), (b) activating strengths and resources to change (e.g., by highlighting benefits of change), (c) targeting thoughts and feelings to realize insight (e.g., by encouraging participants to reflect on and address obstacles to change), and (d) practicing targeted behaviors (e.g., by creating "if-then" plans to facilitate implementation of desired changes). These factors deserve further investigation in the context of facilitating growth following adversity.

CONCLUSION

Many people report that going through significant hardship changed their outlook on life by opening their minds to new possibilities. Yet, as reviewed in this chapter, scientific evidence regarding this anecdotal claim remains limited and has produced contradictory findings. Such research is hampered by the fact that few studies have specifically centered on this trait to better understand the conditions under which it may grow or deteriorate following major stressors. More focused work looking at this trait might be especially important if changes in openness could help explain more general psychological growth, including growth in other domains. Given the alternative explanation that people may perceive themselves as more open without any actual changes in thoughts, feelings, and behaviors occurring over time, tackling this question with greater methodological rigor might help provide greater clarity. Such research will help accurately inform the scientific and public understanding of the consequences of adversity on personality and behavior. In doing so, it can then help add nuance to cultural narratives suggesting that most people experience growth, which may be experienced as invalidating or challenging for individuals coping with difficult events. In this light, future scholarship may also help inform strategies to help people effectively cope in the aftermath of adversity using sensitive expectations and appropriate resources and/or interventions.

ACKNOWLEDGMENTS

This work was made possible through the support of Grant 60699 Subaward 18-390 from the Pathways to Character Project (Arizona State University & Wake Forest University), funded by the John Templeton Foundation. The opinions expressed in this chapter are those of the authors and do not necessarily reflect the views of the funders.

REFERENCES

Aldwin, C. M., & Sutton, K. J. (1998). A developmental perspective on posttraumatic growth. In R. G. Tedeschi, C. L. Park & L. G. Calhoun (Eds.), *Posttraumatic growth: Positive changes in the aftermath of crisis* (pp. 43–64). Mahwah, NJ: Erlbaum.

Allemand, M., & Flückiger, C. (2017). Changing personality traits: Some considerations from psychotherapy process-outcome research for intervention efforts on intentional personality change. *Journal of Psychotherapy Integration, 27*, 476–494.

Allen, B., & Lauterbach, D. (2007). Personality characteristics of adult survivors of childhood trauma. *Journal of Traumatic Stress, 20*, 587–595.

Blackie, L. E. R., Jayawickreme, E., Tsukayama, E., Forgeard, M. J. C., Roepke, A. M., & Fleeson, W. (2017). Post-traumatic growth as positive personality change: Developing a measure to assess within-person variability. *Journal of Research in Personality, 69*, 22–32.

Bleidorn, W., Hopwood, C. J., & Lucas, R. E. (2018). Life events and personality trait change. *Journal of Personality, 86*, 83–96.

Bloom, S. L. (1998). By the crowd they have been broken, by the crowd they shall be healed: The social transformation of trauma. In R. G. Tedeschi, C. L. Park, & L. G. Calhoun (Eds.), *Posttraumatic Growth: Positive Changes in the Aftermath of Crisis* (pp. 173–208). Mahwah, NJ: Erlbaum.

Boals, A., & Schuler, K. L. (2018). Reducing reports of illusory posttraumatic growth: A revised version of the Stress-Related Growth Scale (SRGS-R). *Psychological Trauma: Theory, Research, Practice, and Policy, 10*, 190–198.

Boals, A., Southard-Dobbs, S., & Blumenthal, H. (2015). Adverse events in emerging adulthood are associated with increases in neuroticism. *Journal of Personality, 83*, 203–211.

Breslau, N., Kessler, R. C., Chilcoat, H. D., Schultz, L. R., Davis, G. C., & Andreski, P. (1998). Trauma and posttraumatic stress disorder in the community the 1996 Detroit area survey of trauma. *Archives of General Psychiatry, 55*, 626–632.

Calhoun, L. G., Cann, A., & Tedeschi, R. G. (2010). The posttraumatic growth model: Sociocultural considerations. In T. Weiss & R. Berger (Eds.), *Posttraumatic Growth and Culturally Competent Practice: Lessons Learned from Around the Globe* (pp. 1–14). Hoboken, NJ: Wiley.

Chan, M. W. C., Ho, S. M. Y., Tedeschi, R. G., & Leung, C. W. L. (2011). The valence of attentional bias and cancer-related rumination in posttraumatic stress and posttraumatic growth among women with breast cancer. *Psycho-Oncology, 20*, 544–552.

Costa, P. T., McCrae, R. R., & Löckenhoff, C. E. (2019). Personality across the lifespan. *Annual Review of Psychology, 70*, 423–448.

Csikszentmihalyi, M. (1996). *Creativity: Flow and the Psychology of Discovery and Invention*. New York: HarperCollins.

Damian, R. I., & Simonton, D. K. (2015). Psychopathology, adversity, and creativity: Diversifying experiences in the development of eminent African Americans. *Journal of Personality and Social Psychology, 108*, 623–636.

Dechesne, M., & Kruglanski, A. W. (2004). Terror's epistemic consequences: Existential threats and the quest for certainty and closure. In J. Greenberg, S. L. Koole, & T. Pyszczynski (Eds.), *Handbook of Experimental Existential Psychology* (pp. 247–262). New York: Guilford.

DeYoung, C. G. (2006). Higher-order factors of the Big Five in a multi-informant sample. *Journal of Personality and Social Psychology, 91*, 1138–1151.

DeYoung, C. G. (2015). Openness/Intellect: A dimension of personality reflecting cognitive exploration. In M. L. Cooper & R. J. Larsen (Eds.), *APA Handbook of Personality and Social Psychology: Personality Processes and Individual Differences.* Washington, DC: American Psychological Association.

DeYoung, C. G., Grazioplene, R. G., & Peterson, J. B (2012). From madness to genius: The Openness/Intellect trait domain as a paradoxical simplex. *Journal of Research in Personality, 46*, 63–78.

DeYoung, C. G., Peterson, J. B., & Higgins, D. M. (2002). Higher-order factors of the Big Five predict conformity: Are there neuroses of health? *Personality and Individual Differences, 33*, 533–552.

Digman, J. M. (1997). Higher-order factors of the Big Five. *Journal of Personality and Social Psychology, 73*, 1246–1256.

Dorfman, A., Oakes, H., Santos, H. C., & Grossmann, I. (2021). Self-distancing promotes positive emotional change after adversity: Evidence from a micro-longitudinal field experiment. *Journal of Personality, 89*(1), 132–144.

Fleeson, W., & Jayawickreme, E. (2015). Whole trait theory. *Journal of Research in Personality, 56*, 82–92.

Fleeson, W., Furr, M. R., Jayawickreme, E., Meindl, P., & Helzer, E. G. (2014). Character: The prospect for a personality-based perspective on morality. *Social and Personality Psychology Compass, 8*, 178–191.

Forgeard, M. J. C. (2013). Perceiving benefits after adversity: The relationship between self-reported posttraumatic growth and creativity. *Psychology of Aesthetics, Creativity, and the Arts, 7*, 245–264.

Forgeard, M., Herzhoff, K., Jayawickreme, E., Tsukayama, E., Beard, C., & Björgvinsson, T. (2019). Changes in daily manifestations of openness to experience during intensive cognitive-behavioral treatment. *Journal of Personality, 87*, 856–870.

Frazier, P., Tennen, H., Gavian, M., Park, C., Tomich, P., & Tashiro, T. (2009). Does self-reported posttraumatic growth reflect genuine positive change? *Psychological Science, 20*, 912–919.

García, F. E., Cova, F., Rincón, P., & Vázquez, C. (2015). Trauma or growth after a natural disaster? The mediating role of rumination processes. *European Journal of Psychotraumatology, 6*, 26557.

Goldberg, L. R. (1992). The development of markers for the big-five factor structure. *Psychological Assessment, 4*, 26–42.

Greenberg, J., Pyszczynski, T., Solomon, S., Rosenblatt, A., Veeder, M., Kirkland, S., & Lyon, D. (1990). Evidence for terror management theory II: The effects of mortality salience on reactions to those who threaten or bolster the cultural worldview. *Journal of Personality and Social Psychology, 58*, 308–318.

Grossmann, I. (2017). Wisdom in context. *Perspectives on Psychological Science, 12*, 233–257.

Hobfoll, S. E., Hall, B. J., Canetti-Nisim, D., Galea, S., Johnson, R. J., & Palmieri, P. A. (2007). Refining our understanding of traumatic growth in the face of terrorism: Moving from meaning cognitions to doing what is meaningful. *Applied Psychology, 56*, 345–366.

Infurna, F. J., & Jayawickreme, E. (2019). Fixing the growth illusion: New directions for research in resilience and posttraumatic growth. *Current Directions in Psychological Science, 28*, 152–158.

Janoff-Bulman, R. (1992). *Shattered Assumptions*. New York: Free Press.

Janoff-Bulman, R. (2006). Schema-change perspectives on posttraumatic growth. In L. G. Calhoun & R. G. Tedeschi (Eds.), *Handbook of Posttraumatic Growth* (pp. 81–99). Mahwah, NJ: Erlbaum.

Jayawickreme, E., & Blackie, L. E. R. (2014). Posttraumatic growth as positive personality change: Evidence, controversies and future directions. *European Journal of Personality, 28*, 312–331.

Jayawickreme, E., & Blackie, L. E. R. (2016). *Exploring the Psychological Benefits of Hardship: A Critical Reassessment of Posttraumatic Growth.* Cham: Springer.

Karwowski, M., & Lebuda, I. (2016). The big five, the huge two, and creative self-beliefs: A meta-analysis. *Psychology of Aesthetics, Creativity, and the Arts, 10*, 214–232.

Kashdan, T. B., & Kane, J. Q. (2011). Post-traumatic distress and the presence of post-traumatic growth and meaning in life: Experiential avoidance as a moderator. *Personality and Individual Differences, 50*, 84–89.

Kashyap, S., & Hussain, D. (2018). Cross-cultural challenges to the construct "posttraumatic growth." *Journal of Loss and Trauma, 23*, 51–69.

Kling, K. C., Ryff, C. D., Love, G., & Essex, M. (2003). Exploring the influence of personality on depressive symptoms and self-esteem across a significant life transition. *Journal of Personality and Social Psychology, 85*, 922–932.

Kross, E., & Grossmann, I. (2012). Boosting wisdom: Distance from the self enhances wise reasoning, attitudes, and behavior. *Journal of Experimental Psychology: General, 141*(1), 43–48.

Lamade, R. V., Jayawickreme, E., Blackie, L. E., & McGrath, R. E. (2020). Are sequential sample designs useful for examining post-traumatic changes in character strengths? *Journal of Positive Psychology, 15*, 292–299.

Löckenhoff, C. E., Terracciano, A., Patriciu, N. S., Eaton, W. W., & Costa, P. T. (2009). Self-reported extremely adverse life events and longitudinal changes in five-factor model personality traits in an urban sample. *Journal of Traumatic Stress, 22*, 53–59.

Lüdtke, O., Roberts, B. W., Trautwein, U., & Nagy, G. (2011). A random walk down university avenue: Life paths, life events, and personality trait change at the transition to university life. *Journal of Personality and Social Psychology, 101*, 620–637.

Maercker, A., & Zoellner, T. (2004). The Janus face of self-perceived growth: Toward a two-component model of posttraumatic growth. *Psychological Inquiry, 15*, 41–48.

McCrae, R. R. (1987). Creativity, divergent thinking, and openness to experience. *Journal of Personality and Social Psychology, 52*, 1258–1265.

McCrae, R. R., & Costa, P. T. (1986). Personality, coping, and coping effectiveness in an adult sample. *Journal of Personality, 54*, 385–405.

McCrae, R. R., & Costa, P. T. (1997). Conceptions and correlates of openness to experience. In R. Hogan, J. Johnson, & S. Briggs (Eds.), *Handbook of Personality Psychology* (pp. 825–847). San Diego, CA: Academic Press.

McCrae, R. R., & Sutin, A. R. (2009). Openness to experience. In M. R. Leary & R. H. Hoyle (Eds.), *Handbook of Individual Differences in Social Behavior* (pp. 257–273). New York: Guilford.

Miller, K. E., & Rasmussen, A. (2010). War exposure, daily stressors, and mental health in conflict and post-conflict settings: Bridging the divide between trauma-focused and psychological frameworks. *Social Science & Medicine, 70*, 7–16.

Milojev, P., Osborne, D., & Sibley, C. G. (2014). Personality resilience following a natural disaster. *Social Psychological and Personality Science, 5*, 760–768.

Mogg, K., Mathews, A., Bird, C., & Macgregor-Morris, R. (1990). Effects of stress and anxiety on the processing of threat stimuli. *Journal of Personality and Social Psychology, 59*, 1230–1237.

Peterson, C., & Seligman, M. E. P. (2003). Character strengths before and after September 11. *Psychological Science, 14*, 381–384.

Peterson, C., & Seligman, M. E. P. (2004). *Character Strengths and Virtues: A Handbook and Classification*. New York: Oxford University Press.

Reynolds, F. (2004). Conversations about creativity and chronic illness II: Textile artists coping with long-term health problems reflect on the creative process. *Creativity Research Journal, 16*, 79–89.

Ritter, S. M., van Baaren, R. B., & Dijksterhuis, A. (2012). Creativity: The role of unconscious processes in idea generation and idea selection. *Thinking Skills and Creativity, 7*, 21–27.

Roberts, B. W., Walton, K. E., & Viechtbauer, W. (2006). Patterns of mean-level change in personality traits across the life course: A meta-analysis of longitudinal studies. *Psychological Bulletin, 132*, 1–25.

Roepke, A. M. (2013). Gains without pains? Growth after positive events. *The Journal of Positive Psychology, 8*, 280–291.

Roepke, A. M., & Seligman, M. E. P. (2015). Doors opening: A mechanism for growth after adversity. *Journal of Positive Psychology, 10*, 107–115.

Roepke, A. M., Benson, L., Tsukayama, E., & Yaden, D. B. (2018). Prospective writing: Randomized controlled trial of an intervention for facilitating growth after adversity. *Journal of Positive Psychology, 13*, 627–642.

Roepke, A. M., Forgeard, M. J. C., & Elstein, J. G. (2014). Providing context for behavior: Cognitive change matters for posttraumatic growth. *European Journal of Personality, 28*, 347–348.

Schneider, T. R., Rench, T. A., Lyons, J. B., & Riffle. R. R. (2012). The influence of neuroticism, extraversion, and openness on stress responses. *Stress and Health, 28*, 102–110.

Schueller, S. M., Jayawickreme, E., Blackie, L. E. R., Forgeard, M. J. C., & Roepke, A. M. (2015). Finding character strengths through loss: An extension of Peterson and Seligman (2003). *Journal of Positive Psychology, 10*, 53–63.

Shakespeare-Finch, J., & Copping, A. (2006). A grounded theory approach to understanding cultural differences in posttraumatic growth. *Journal of Loss and Trauma, 11*, 355–371.

Shakespeare-Finch, J., & Lurie-Beck, J. (2014). A meta-analytic clarification of the relationship between posttraumatic growth and symptoms of posttraumatic distress disorder. *Journal of Anxiety Disorders, 28*, 223–229.

Shiner, R. L., Allen, T. A., & Masten, A. S. (2017). Adversity in adolescence predicts personality trait change from childhood to adulthood. *Journal of Research in Personality, 67*, 171–182.

Silvia, P. J., Nusbaum, E. C., Berg, C., Martin, C., & O'Connor, A. (2009). Openness to experience, plasticity, and creativity: Exploring lower-order, high-order, and interactive effects. *Journal of Research in Personality, 43*, 1087–1090.

Simonton, D. K. (1994). *Greatness: Who Makes History and Why*. New York: Guilford Press.

Specht, J., Egloff, B., Schmukle, S. C. (2011). Stability and change of personality across the life course: The impact of age and major life events on mean-level and rank-order stability of the Big Five. *Journal of Personality and Social Psychology, 101*, 862–882

Splevins, K., Cohen, K., Bowley, J., & Joseph, S. (2010). Theories of posttraumatic growth: Cross-cultural perspectives. *Journal of Loss and Trauma, 15*, 259–277.

Stieger, M., Wepfer, S., Rüegger, D., Kowatsch, T., Roberts, B. W., & Allemand, M. (2020). Becoming more conscientious or more open to experience? Effects of a two-week smartphone-based intervention for personality change. *European Journal of Personality, 34*, 345–366.

Taylor, S. E., & Armor, D. A. (1996). Positive illusions and coping with adversity. *Journal of Personality, 64*, 873–898.

Taylor, S. E., Kemeny, M. E., Reed, G., & Bower, J. (2000). Psychological resources, positive illusions, and health. *American Psychologist, 55*, 99–109.

Tedeschi, R. G., & Calhoun, L. G. (1996). The Posttraumatic Growth Inventory: Measuring the positive legacy of trauma. *Journal of Traumatic Stress, 9*, 455–472.

Tedeschi, R. G., & Calhoun, L. G. (2004). Posttraumatic growth: Conceptual foundations and empirical evidence. *Psychological Inquiry, 15*, 1–18.

Thórisdóttir, H., & Jost, J. T. (2011). Motivated closed-mindedness mediates the effect of threat on political conservatism. *Political Psychology, 32*, 785–811.

Van Der Zee, K., Van Oudenhoven, J. P., & De Grijs, E. (2004). Personality, threat, and cognitive and emotional reactions to stressful intercultural situations. *Journal of Personality, 72*, 1069–1096.

Weinstein, N., & Ryan, R. M. (2011). A self-determination theory approach to understanding stress incursion and responses. *Stress and Health, 27*, 4–17.

Williams, P. G., Rau, H. K., Cribbet, M. R., & Gunn, H. E. (2009). Openness to experience and stress regulation. *Journal of Research in Personality, 43*, 777–784.

Zausner, T. (1998). When walls become doorways: Creativity, chaos theory, and physical illness. *Creativity Research Journal, 11*, 21–28.

Zausner, T. (2007). *When Walls Become Doorways: Creativity and the Transforming Illness*. New York: Crown Archetype.

Zoellner, T., & Maercker, A. (2006). Posttraumatic growth in clinical psychology: A critical review and introduction of a two component model. *Clinical Psychology Review, 26*, 626–653.

Zoellner, T., Rabe, S., Anke, K., & Maercker, A. (2008). Posttraumatic growth in accident survivors: Openness and optimism as predictors of its constructive or illusory sides. *Journal of Clinical Psychology, 64*, 245–263.

14

The Relationship Between Narration and Character Growth After Interpersonal Failures and Transgressions

LAURA E. R. BLACKIE AND KATE C. MCLEAN ■

Can the experience of adversity act as a catalyst for self-development and personal growth? If so, under which conditions and for whom is self-development most likely to occur? These questions are at the center of research into post-traumatic growth (PTG; Tedeschi & Calhoun, 2004), which is the study of the positive changes that individuals report to their identity, relationships, and worldviews when coming to terms with the impact of highly challenging and difficult life experiences. Yet, despite over two decades of research into PTG, these questions still remain unanswered, largely due to methodological limitations with the study designs and self-report questionnaires used to measure this construct (Ford, Tennen, & Albert, 2008; Tennen & Affleck, 2002). In this chapter we capitalize on the promise of a narrative approach to understanding whether and how personality might change in response to adverse experiences, and we address how a prospective study of the narration of such experiences ameliorates some of the methodological concerns raised here. Specifically, we propose that individual differences in the written narration of adverse life experiences influences the likelihood of whether PTG is experienced. We focus on this within the context of romantic relationships, examining whether the act of narration of interpersonal transgressions is the mechanism for personality change in the interpersonal traits of empathy and humility.

CONTROVERSIES AND UNADDRESSED QUESTIONS IN POST-TRAUMATIC GROWTH RESEARCH

The most notable methodological limitations with PTG research are the prevailing use of cross-sectional study designs and retrospective questionnaires to test a theory that predicts change over time (Jayawickreme & Blackie, 2014). Currently research into PTG has most conclusively demonstrated that people frequently *self-report* PTG after a diverse range of adversities (Linley & Joseph, 2004). Thus, people *believe* they have changed in the aftermath of adversity, but the question of whether they *change in some objective way beyond those beliefs* over time is an intriguing hypothesis still awaiting conclusive empirical investigation with prospective longitudinal designs.

These methodological limitations are not the only issue with PTG; researchers have also disagreed that only traumatic experiences will result in some special form of personal growth that would not be observed in response to other adverse life experiences (Seery & Kondrak, 2014). Tedeschi and Calhoun (2004) developed PTG based on Janoff-Bulman's (1992) notion of "shattered assumptions," in which post-traumatic stress disorder (PTSD) and other clinical symptoms of distress are caused when the experience of a trauma severely challenges an individual's implicit assumptions about the benevolence and predictability of the world and their belief about how much control they have over the events in their own lives. Thus, in Tedeschi and Calhoun's model, clinical distress is the default response to the traumatic event and PTG is only experienced if individuals can disengage from the intrusive rumination characteristic of PTSD and try to make sense of their traumatic experience.

However, the notion of shattered assumptions has not been consistently supported empirically in PTG research. First, the conceptual notion of *shattered* assumptions is difficult to quantify and therefore measure accurately. As Seery and Kondrak (2014) have argued, without a minimum threshold to quantify schema-shattering trauma—and there currently is no recommended cutoff score in questionnaires used to measure disruption to core beliefs (Cann et al., 2010)—it is impossible to assess whether it is an independent mechanism for PTG. Second, although research into the time scale of PTG is rare, some longitudinal studies have observed remarkable stability in individuals' PTG over time shortly after diagnosis with cancer and throughout treatment (Danhauer et al., 2013, 2015). This is not consistent with Tedeschi and Calhoun's (2004) model of PTG, which proposes linear increases in PTG that slowly unfold over time as individuals rebuild their worldviews.

Although this evidence calls into question whether the experience of clinical trauma is necessary for PTG, it does not imply that all adverse experiences will result in PTG. The event still has to be psychologically significant to the individual, even if it does not shatter their worldviews. Indeed, research has found that the subjective impact of the adverse event (as rated by the individual) is an important predictor of whether PTG is associated with expected outcomes or not.

This research found that the subjective significance of the event was more predictive of outcomes compared to when the event was categorized into trauma using criteria of the *Diagnostic and Statistical Manual of Mental Disorders* (DSM) (Boals, Steward, & Schuettler, 2010). This is consistent with the narrative approach to processing life events, in which it is the subjective impact and interpretation of the event that is critical to understanding the role of the event in identity (e.g., McAdams, 2001). Thus, our study—the Dating Diaries Project—as outlined in the next section is designed on this premise and will test whether psychologically salient adverse events that happen within one's romantic relationships can lead to personality change in the associated interpersonal traits of empathy and humility.

AN INTRODUCTION TO THE DATING DIARIES PROJECT

In this section, we introduce our empirical research project that was funded under the Pathways to Character Project, which we called "Dating Diaries" and explain how it was designed to test some of the unresolved questions in the PTG literature. The aim of Dating Diaries is to examine whether narration is a mechanism through which PTG occurs when individuals have committed transgressions in their romantic relationships. We outline the theoretical contribution of testing whether narrative is a mechanism to promote PTG in due course, but we first outline how we operationalized PTG and how we designed our project to overcome some of the methodological flaws that have limited existing research.

In this project, we adopted Jayawickreme and Blackie's (2014) conceptualization of PTG as positive personality change. This definition of PTG posits that if trauma does cause positive and enduring shifts in peoples' self-views, relationships, and worldviews, then such changes should be observable as changes to relevant personality traits. Thus, PTG should manifest as positive changes to dispositional character. We further agree with Jayawickreme and Blackie (2016) that the conceptualization of PTG would benefit from drawing on the existing research on character development by defining positive change more specifically in terms of character virtues most likely to change over time in response to adversity. This is because the study of character is considered to be a more fine-grained analysis of a subset of personality characteristics that have evaluative significance insofar as they differentiate individuals on positive traits (or strengths) that promote moral excellence and human flourishing (Fleeson, Furr, Jayawickreme, Meindl, & Helzer, 2014). We focused on two relational character virtues—empathy and humility—because, similar to other researchers, we reasoned that the PTG experienced will vary depending on the nature of the event under study (Blalock, Calton, & Kashdan, 2014), and these two virtues are critical to successful conflict resolution and the maintenance of healthy romantic and/or family relationships (Worthington, 1998).

Research on forgiveness in married couples after interpersonal failures has shown that empathy is critical for predicting forgiveness and marital quality over time (Paleari, Regalia, & Fincham, 2005), and it acts as a mediator between therapeutic intervention and forgiveness (Sandage & Worthington, 2010; Burnette, Davis, Green, Worthington, & Bradfield, 2009). Worthington's (1998) model of forgiveness in family contexts recognizes the importance of empathy and humility, and more recent work has shown that intellectual humility—the ability to recognize the limits of one's knowledge of and perspective on a given situation—is critical for wise reasoning when applied to the resolution of interpersonal conflicts (Grossmann, 2017; Grossman & Kross, 2014; Kross & Grossmann, 2012). However, similar to PTG, this research has focused almost exclusively on how victims respond, but reconciliation is a dyadic process that requires an understanding of when, how, and why the individuals who commit such acts of interpersonal failure may show character growth. Our project therefore broadens the scope of research into PTG, which has thus far been narrowly focused on the victim-to-survivor transformation after clinical trauma (Blackie, Roepke, Hitchcott, & Joseph, 2016).

To overcome the methodological limitations of prior research into PTG, our project employed a prospective longitudinal design to investigate whether the way in which people revise their narrative of an interpersonal failure affects the development of empathy and humility over the course of a year. Specifically, we recruited 400 participants involved in committed romantic relationships into the baseline survey, where, among other measures, they completed questionnaires that assessed their trait standing on empathy and humility. Three months after the baseline, we asked participants to write a narrative about a significant incident in the past 3 months in which they had done something to upset and hurt their partners' feelings (or had done something that, while their partner was unaware, they felt violated the type of partner they ought to be). We asked participants to repeatedly narrate (in written form) this significant incident in three subsequent surveys and take the trait empathy and humility questionnaires again at 3-month intervals. (We note that when individuals could not remember what they had written about for the previous assessment, we asked them to narrate another, recent interpersonal failure. Our analyses will determine whether it matters if the same story is narrated or whether it is the activity of writing about such events that predicts changes in character growth over time.) Our focus was on acts of interpersonal failure, which we defined as the mistakes and wrongdoings individuals commit during the course of their relationships. Acts of interpersonal failure can range from minor disagreements to potentially more serious indiscretions, such as infidelity. Nascent research has shown that interpersonal failures are not necessarily committed with harm intended; hence, we reasoned that these acts could provide participants with an opportunity to reflect on the type of person they want to be and how they could change to achieve these self-aspirations (Lilgendahl, McLean, & Mansfield, 2013).

Our design affords three significant methodological improvements to PTG research. First, a prospective longitudinal design provides a baseline of participants' standings on trait empathy and humility and enables pre- to post-change to be observed over the course of a year after an individual has committed an act(s) of interpersonal failure. This overcomes issues associated with retrospective questionnaires of PTG, which require participants to engage in complicated arithmetic, where for each single question they must determine what their pre-trauma score was, what their post-trauma score is, the difference between these scores, and then how much of the difference was uniquely caused by the traumatic event (Ford et al., 2008).

Second, we explicitly measured character traits that are relevant to the context of interpersonal failure and thus avoided making implicit assumptions about the homogeneity of PTG outcomes without due consideration to how the type of event influences character growth (Blalock et al., 2014). In this respect, we avoid what Roberts (2011) has called "launching outcome fragmentation grenades," where researchers assess a wide diversity of psychological outcomes to determine what works empirically instead of focusing on the most theoretically meaningful outcomes.

Third, through the use of written narratives, we avoided the use of positively framed closed questionnaire assessments, such as the Post-Traumatic Growth Inventory (PTGI; Tedeschi & Calhoun, 1996), which may promote socially and culturally desirable responding and inflate reports of PTG. Indeed, Boals and Schuler (2018) found that simply revising the wording of the questions of the Stress-Related Growth Scale (SRGS; Park, Cohen, & Murch, 1996) to make them neutral and changing the response scale to give participants the chance to report positive and negative change reduced the likelihood of reports of illusory PTG. Specifically, while the standard PTGI was positively related to PTSD and avoidance coping and was unrelated to quality of life, the revised SRGS was found to be negatively associated with global distress and avoidance coping and positively related to reports of quality of life.

In addition to these methodological improvements, the Dating Diaries project offers the means to empirically test some of the psychological mechanisms that have theoretically been proposed to facilitate PTG. The extent to which an individual will experience PTG after interpersonal failure depends on individual differences in the subjective meaning that the individual attaches to the event. In Tedeschi and Calhoun's (2004) model of PTG, this notion is expressed through the construct of *deliberative rumination*, which, as outlined previously, is the extent to which individuals start to engage in an active search to make sense of the event and its impact on their life. Empirically this has been measured with the Event Related Rumination Inventory (Cann et al., 2011), but, similar to the PTGI or SRGS, this self-report questionnaire may inadvertently bias participants' responses. However, by analyzing participants' written narratives, we will be able to examine whether these self-reflective and ruminative processes are expressed organically in participants' own words and the impact of these narrative rumination styles on PTG.

However, deliberative rumination on its own is not sufficient for PTG. Tedeschi and Calhoun (2004) have theorized that revision to the life story (i.e., an individual's narrative identity) is also a key mechanism to PTG. For PTG to translate into enduring and meaningful character growth (rather than illusory growth), then the individual needs to incorporate the insights they have gained through self-reflection into their identity by revising their life story to connect how their experience has motivated them to change aspects of their personality moving forward. To our knowledge, this intriguing hypothesis is yet to be empirically tested within PTG research. We designed the Dating Diaries project to investigate whether the act of repeated narration serves as a mechanism for the development of empathy and humility after acts of interpersonal failure. In the following two sections, we provide an overview of the theory and research into narrative identity and discuss the types of narratives that are most likely to facilitate PTG after interpersonal failure.

NARRATIVE APPROACHES TO PERSONALITY DEVELOPMENT

We chose to examine narration as a mechanism of PTG in part because of Tedeschi and Calhoun's (2004) suggestions, which to our knowledge have yet to be empirically tested in a robust longitudinal design, and also because narration involves a reflective action of interpreting and understanding the psychological significance of past events—perhaps an optimal focus for understanding when revision to self-understanding and growth may occur. More specifically, the process of narrating important life events is both a sociocultural activity (Fivush & Haden, 2003) and representative of individual differences in personality (McAdams & McLean, 2013; McAdams & Pals, 2006). In terms of the latter, the concept of narrative is most often paired with McAdams's tripartite theory of personality structure (e.g., McAdams, 1995). The first level houses personality traits, reflecting the most stable and earliest appearing representation of individual differences. At the second level are characteristic adaptations—those aspects of personality more responsive to individual differences in approaches to developmental tasks and contextual shifts (e.g., attachment styles, coping styles, and goals). At the third level is narrative identity, which involves the work of constructing a coherent story that integrates one's past, present, and future to explain how one has come to be the person one currently is, which imbues one's life with a sense of coherence, meaning, and purpose (McAdams, 2001).

The sociocultural activity of narration is dynamic, subjective, and contextual. That is, narration occurs in particular situations with particular contextual constraints, affordances, and demands (e.g., Pasupathi, Fivush, & Hernandez-Martinez, 2016). For example, we tell different types of stories to different audiences (e.g., Pasupathi, McLean, Weeks, & Hynes, 2019), and those audiences can shape our later recall of the event (e.g., Pasupathi & Hoyt, 2010). This conceptualization of narrative highlights that they are not factual accounts of "what happened," but subjective accounts which bring the *interpretation* of past events to the fore.

Indeed, at the heart of theories about narrative identity development and personality functioning is the concept of *autobiographical reasoning* (Habermas & Bluck, 2000). That is, the construction of narrative identity is based on the ability to interpret past events in relation to current and future conceptions of self and linking those events together to create a sense of temporal continuity (Pasupathi, Mansour, & Brubaker, 2007). Through reasoning about the past, individuals are able to draw meaning from the past to make sense of who they were, are, and will be.

Like narration itself, this reasoning process is not static—the connections one makes between the past and present are up for revision and repetition as new opportunities for narration arise. In other words, as individuals engage in a process of recalling past events, considering them in relation to other important experiences, sharing them with others, and reflecting on their meaning, the opportunities arise for both solidifying self-views and revising ways of understanding oneself. Indeed, theorists have proposed that narrative is a *mechanism* for other aspects of self and personality development. For example, McLean, Pasupathi, and Pals (2007) proposed that aspects of self (e.g., traits) may impact how one perceives and narrates events and that the process of narration can serve to strengthen those aspects of self or shift them. From this perspective, it is more the *sociocultural activity* of narration that might be a mechanism for development in personality, and the change that results from this narrative process can take multiple forms. For example, it might cause a change in or cementing of one's full narrative identity, and it may also push for stability or change in other aspects of self at the level of traits or characteristic adaptations, the latter of which was the focus of the present investigation.

NARRATIVE AS A MECHANISM FOR TRAIT CHANGE AFTER INTERPERSONAL FAILURE

In the Dating Diaries project, we posited that reasoning about interpersonal failure in particular ways (as described in more detail in the next section) through repeated written narration might prompt positive change in the character traits of empathy and humility. To illustrate how the mechanism of repeated narration is theorized to operate, we provide two examples from the data of the Dating Diaries project. We first provide an example of how narration may function to cement or solidify self-views, resulting in stability and the very opposite of PTG. Thus, although a dynamic process of narration is occurring, it does not always prompt change—a possibility that is not well captured by the existing closed survey assessments typically used to assess PTG.

Madeline (a pseudonym) was a participant in our Dating Diaries project. At her baseline assessment she reported an intensely visceral low point narrative about having been in an abusive relationship, which involved being raped. She is clear about the pain, shame, and fear that this experience caused. She ended her narrative with the following:

> From that point forward, I had to accept what had happened, remove blame from myself, and move on. I am now stronger and I accept what happened to me as a part of my story. It still hurts me a lot, but I just take it in my stride.

Thus, here we see what appears to be a kind of redemption as she has apparently moved through this horrific experience with some resolution and potential growth. However, one might wonder what happens in Madeline's narratives over the course of the study. One unique aspect of our project is that we are able to determine whether narration of events remains consistent or if it changes over time. In her first two narratives of interpersonal failure, she writes about experiences in another abusive relationship with little elaboration or meaning—a simple recounting of events that occurred. In her third narrative of interpersonal failure, she writes a more elaborative accounting of an argument with a new partner and the meaning that she makes from it.

> I felt a lot of regret and like I had made a big mistake and that I shouldn't have spoken about the topic in such a way that made him feel that I was dominating it. I felt like it changed the dynamic of our relationship.

At the final assessment, she reports a narrative of a first date that goes awry, and at the end,

> It was my first date with somebody for a long while, and it really knocked my confidence. Now I am worried to go on any other dates because I feel self-conscious about the way I act. . . . I feel that this may have a lasting effect on me. I am completely unsure what he was/is feeling as there was no communication afterwards, but I must have gotten on his nerves or upset him somehow.

Thus, Madeline has had some extremely difficult, even traumatic, interpersonal experiences. If we had stopped at the low-point narrative, we might have assumed that the redemption and meaning made from the low-point narrative would have translated into narrative identity change and perhaps eventually changed her standing on personality traits or goals in some related way. Yet her subsequent narratives show either minimal elaboration or a narration of self-blame that may hinder positive change. This may be a narrative process that allows stability in self-views that center on continued feelings of blame in relational interactions. In terms of quantifying this narrative pattern, researchers could code Madeline's narratives to examine how she connects the events to her sense of self (Pasupathi et al., 2007). Madeline's later narratives evidence a pattern of stable and negative self-event connections where she feels responsible for upsetting her partners to the point where she is responsible for the relationships not lasting.

In contrast, Kelsie (a pseudonym) reported a series of narratives about fights she has had with her partner in which she had insulted him. In her initial narrative she describes this as "jokey," and it "shows the level of trust between us." In her next narrative, she describes an event in which she offends her partner in a moment of anger, and realizes,

> It is meaningful as I don't shout or get angry a lot but because I was stressed I was more emotional, it showed me how stress affects me and how it can then impact my relationship.

In her next two narratives she reiterates a theme of the importance of saying difficult things so that they can be "honest with each other and it not cause arguments." Thus, we see movement from seeing these interactions as jokey, to impactful, to changing their communication so that they do not have such arguments. This is the kind of narrative progression that may shift character traits like empathy and humility. As Kelsie has reflected on these interactions, she understands more about her role in the process, the importance of honesty, and how behavior patterns can change. Another way of thinking about this is that the opportunity to continue to narrate these interpersonal failures gives her space to reconsider their meaning and may provide the motivation for her to change her behavior. In terms of quantifying this narrative pattern, Kelsie's later narratives move toward a positive (change) self-event connection (Pasupathi et al., 2007), when she begins to understand when and why she argues with her partner and uses this knowledge to adopt an open and honest communication style.

These two examples, though different in their reasoning processes (and the types of events recalled), show that the act of narrating can work as an engine for development over time, whether that development is about solidifying or changing the self. Indeed, our theoretical position is that the revision of a narrative can serve as a mechanism that drives character growth.

Furthermore, this hypothesis fits nicely within theorizing regarding the cognitive-emotional processing that has been proposed to promote or hinder PTG. Specifically, Joseph and Linley (2005) proposed that there are three possible outcomes that may occur when an individual tries to make sense of a painful experience: assimilation, negative accommodation, and positive accommodation. It is the latter process that they claim results in PTG, which we saw evidenced in Kelsie's narratives as she was able to derive some meaning from the conflict with her partner and sought to adapt her communication style. Conversely, the process of assimilation was evidenced in Madeline's narratives, where she moved from one painful relationship to another and internalized blame for the failures she perceived within her dating life. Thus, the study of repeated narration in the Dating Diaries projects enables us to examine the cognitive-emotional processes that function to promote or hinder growth in empathy and humility while analyzing participants' own stories, told in their own words.

WHICH FACETS OF NARRATIVE ARE LIKELY TO FACILITATE PTG?

We are only aware of one study that demonstrated individuals who narrated a past trauma using positive self-event connections reported lower levels of distress and higher PTG (Merrill, Waters, & Fivush, 2016), but other, related work shows that there are likely to be reasonable connections between the two constructs. Most central to the present argument, the *redemption narrative* (McAdams, 2006) is viewed as a narrative expression of PTG, because a key component of the redemptive self is the construction of a narrative that turns emotionally negative experiences into positive outcomes. Though there are currently no extant studies of redemption and PTG, there is extensive cross-sectional and some longitudinal evidence to show that redemption is related to positive psychosocial outcomes. For example, redemptive narratives are associated with psychologically healthy and socially engaged adults who are invested in activities that promote the well-being of future generations (McAdams & Guo, 2015; Guo, Klevan, & McAdams, 2016). And, in one of the few longitudinal studies, Dunlop and Tracy (2013) found redemption narratives were associated with sobriety over a period of 4 months for newly sober alcoholics when compared to nonredemption narratives control group. Of greater relevance to our Dating Diaries project, in a 4-day diary study, Slotter and Ward (2015) found that people who used greater redemptive imagery in their journals on the previous day reported lower levels of emotional distress the next day when reflecting on the recent dissolution of their romantic relationships.

Furthermore, several other longitudinal studies have shown that individual differences in narrative processing that are conceptual neighbors to redemption are related to personal growth over time. Pals (2006), for instance, found that psychological maturity for women increased between the ages of 21 and 61 if they narrated a difficult experience at the age of 52 in a flexible, open, and reflective manner and with positive resolution (see also Lilgendahl, Helson, & John, 2013). Cox and McAdams (2014) found that positive meaning-making in high- and low-point narratives predicted emotion regulation 2 years later. Thus, the extant literature points to the role of the narration of difficult events in positive, growth-promoting ways is associated with psychological health.

The type of narrative that was the focus of our Dating Diaries project was unique. Indeed, interpersonal failures, or transgressions, are an intriguing place to examine narrative process of growth. These are the kinds of events that are reported to be least likely shared with others (Pasupathi, McLean, & Weeks, 2009) and which can pose a challenge to one's sense of self (e.g., Lilgendahl et al., 2013). Yet transgressions offer opportunities to think about the implications of one's actions, how those actions reflect one's identity, and whether and how one might want to shift behavior and perhaps one's conception of self to prevent such behavior in the future. Prior cross-sectional research has shown that people who reflect on interpersonal failures through narrative report higher levels of wisdom, self-compassion, and forgiveness (Mansfield, Pasupathi, & McLean, 2015; Mansfield, McLean, & Lilgendahl, 2010). Thus, these are events worthy of more rigorous longitudinal investigation to elucidate the role of narration in PTG.

We had three primary facets of narrative that we wanted to capture, which we thought would predict changes in empathy and humility over time. First, given the tight link between *redemption* and PTG, this was our first point of focus. We reasoned that those who are able to positively resolve a transgression might have the space to understand what they had done wrong and change for the better, as opposed to being mired in the negativity of the event.

However, positive resolution alone might not be enough, as redemption is primarily focused on the ending of the narrative and does not require reflection on how the event impacted one's identity. Thus, our second point of focus was on the construct of *self-event connections* (Pasupathi et al., 2007). These connections are a kind of autobiographical reasoning manifesting as explicit links between a past event and the self, and they can be positive (e.g., "when I comforted my partner I was able to express my compassionate side") or negative (e.g., "this shows what a hard time I have communicating my needs in relationships") in nature. Along with the PTG framework, and akin to our reasoning about redemption, we reasoned that connecting something about the event to the self in a positive manner would be more likely to promote growth than seeing only negative components of the self when reasoning about the past.

But this positive reasoning may still not be enough. Indeed, to truly learn from a transgression, the combination of redemption and positive self-event connections might be critical from a PTG perspective, but so might the degree to which one takes *responsibility* for one's actions. For example, taking responsibility for a past action is associated with understanding one's causal role in the act (Weiner, 2007), which sets one up for changing one's role in the future. If individuals mitigate their role in the transgression, the press for personal change may be lessened. Indeed, the experimental research on relational transgressions has found that people tend to minimize their role and justify their actions to greater degree when they are asked to consider a time when they were the cause of the transgression. Cameron, Ross, and Holmes (2002) recruited romantic couples into an experiment and asked them to work together to recall a transgression after one partner had been randomly assigned to the role of perpetrator of the action while the other was the victim of the action. Each partner independently wrote a narrative about the selected transgression. The narratives from the perpetrating partners minimized their blame and justified their actions to a greater degree than the narratives from the partners who were the victims.

Additionally, research has found that greater levels of guilt that signal a person has taken some responsibility for their actions are associated with conciliatory behaviors such as confession and apology in highly valued relationships (Baumeister, Stillwell, & Heatherton, 1995). Thus, although there are multiple levels of nuance in relation to how one might take responsibility for past actions (see Pasupathi & Wainryb, 2010), we viewed responsibility, broadly defined, to be an important part of the narration of transgressions. We reasoned that individuals who narrate their transgressions with greater levels of responsibility would be more likely to promote growth in empathy and humility over time.

IS THE NARRATION OF POST-TRAUMATIC GROWTH SIMPLY A CULTURAL EXPECTATION?

As we come to close this chapter, we raise one issue that involves a bigger picture of the issues we have been discussing, situating them within cultural context. One perspective on PTG is that it functions as a cultural expectation: when people experience trauma, we expect growth. And the "we" here may be particular to the United States, where the concept of redemption—growth from challenge—has been termed an "American master narrative" (Hammack, 2008; McAdams, 2006; McLean & Syed, 2015). A *master narrative* is a shared cultural story that shapes the beliefs, values, and behaviors of members of that culture and provides the social and historical context that influences the form that people's own personal narratives may take (McLean & Syed, 2015). According to this theory, a person's identity is deeply informed by the beliefs and values embedded in the master narrative, because the master narrative outlines what it means to be a good and valued member of society. Thus, in the United States, redemption is viewed as a culturally valued story and provides a blueprint for how individuals are expected to overcome and flourish in the wake of experiences of adversity, challenge, and failure (McAdams, 2006).

Recent data from one of our labs show the strength of the preference for trauma to be narrated as redemptive in the United States and also extends this idea to the novel findings that authors of redemptive narratives of trauma are perceived to be more likeable and to have more positive personality characteristics (McLean, Delker, Dunlop, Salton, & Syed, 2020). Thus, this cultural expectation may narrow the accepted responses to trauma and challenge, invalidating and silencing those whose experiences and stories do not fit this PTG framework. Such an invalidation can have implications for interpersonal misunderstanding or rejection, for the likelihood of seeking support or treatment, and even for the experience within a treatment setting (McLean & Syed, 2015; Delker, Salton, McLean, & Syed, 2020).

In short, cultural expectations may be intricately connected to the rise of PTG research and to the meaning of it. However, we know little about expectations around the narration of trauma in other cultures. Some recent preliminary data (Blackie, Colgan, McDonald, & McLean, 2020; Eriksson, McLean, & Frisen, 2020), suggest that different cultural contexts might have different narrative expectations. The Dating Diaries project is well placed to address this question as it collected data from both the United Kingdom and United States. In our analyses, we will determine whether the narrative themes that were outlined previously to predict growth in empathy and humility after interpersonal failure are dependent on sample location.

CONCLUSION

In summary, the Dating Diaries project was designed to test the function of repeated narration of challenging interpersonal transgressions in promoting the relational character traits of empathy and humility. This hypothesis was derived from personality research that claims narration might act as a mechanism for self-development (McLean et al., 2007), yet our theoretical rationale is also consistent with the psychosocial and emotional processes outlined in existing models of PTG (Joseph & Linley, 2005; Tedeschi & Calhoun, 2004) and thus provided an alternative paradigm with which to test these assumptions. Furthermore, we employed a methodologically rigorous prospective longitudinal design that avoided the social desirability concerns associated with closed survey assessments of PTG. Our approach to PTG offers an explanation about which types of narratives may promote stability and which may promote change—including negative change as opposed to PTG—in a person's identity.

In this project, we specifically conceptualize and measure PTG in terms of trait change in empathy and humility, consistent with definitions of PTG put forward previously (Jayawickreme & Blackie, 2014). However, in closing, we note that it if we find that narratives that focus on growth do *not* predict growth in trait-related characteristics, this opens an interesting line of questioning into how to conceptualize growth in personality more broadly. If we take seriously participants' narratives, an ethical imperative in narrative research (e.g., Adler, Lodi-Smith, Philippe, & Houle, 2016), can "real" growth occur at the narrative level of personality, even if it is unrelated to change in other aspects of personality? That is, the question of where growth is best captured within McAdams's tripartite theory of personality structure (e.g., McAdams & McLean, 2013) has yet to be addressed. We hope that our current dataset and the ideas that arise from the larger project continue to push the theoretical and empirical envelope regarding personality development and adverse life experiences.

ACKNOWLEDGMENTS

This publication was made possible through the support of Grant 60699 from the John Templeton Foundation. The opinions expressed in this publication are those of the authors and do not necessarily reflect the views of the John Templeton Foundation. Correspondence concerning this chapter should be addressed to Laura E. R. Blackie, School of Psychology, University of Nottingham, University Park Campus, Nottingham, Nottinghamshire, NG7 2RD, UK. Email: laura.blackie@nottingham.ac.uk

REFERENCES

Adler, J. M., Lodi-Smith, J., Philippe, F. L., & Houle, I. (2016). The incremental validity of narrative identity in predicting well-being: A review of the field and recommendations for the future. *Personality and Social Psychology Review, 20*(2), 142–175. https://doi.org/10.1177/1088868315585068

Baumeister, R. F., Stillwell, A. M., & Heatherton, T. F. (1995). Personal narratives about guilt: Role in action control and interpersonal relationships. *Basic and Applied Social Psychology, 17*(1–2), 173–198. https://doi.org/10.1080/01973533.1995.9646138

Blackie, E. R., Colgan, J., McDonald, S., & McLean, K. C. (2020, January, 27). A qualitative investigation into the cultural master narrative for overcoming trauma and adversity in the United Kingdom. *Qualitative Psychology.* Advance online publication. https://doi.org/10.1037/qup0000163

Blackie, L. E. R., Roepke, A. M., Hitchcott, N., & Joseph, S. (2016). Can people experience posttraumatic growth after committing violent acts? *Peace and Conflict: Journal of Peace Psychology, 22*(4), 409–412. https://doi.org/10.1037/pac0000218

Blalock, D. V., Carton, J. M., & Kashdan, T. B. (2014). Understanding post-traumatic growth by attending to contextual influences and developing wise interventions to measure it. *European Journal of Personality, 28*, 333–334. https://doi.org/10.1002/per.1970

Boals, A., & Schuler, K. L. (2018). Reducing reports of illusory posttraumatic growth: A revised version of the Stress-Related Growth Scale (SRGS-R). *Psychological Trauma: Theory, Research, Practice, and Policy, 10*(2), 190–198. https://doi.org/10.1037/tra0000267

Boals, A., Steward, J. M., & Schuettler, D. (2010). Advancing our understanding of posttraumatic growth by considering event centrality. *Journal of Loss and Trauma, 15*(6), 518–533. https://doi.org/10.1080/15325024.2010.519271

Burnette, J. L., Davis, D. E., Green, J. D., Worthington, E. L., & Bradfield, E. (2009). Insecure attachment and depressive symptoms: The mediating role of rumination, empathy, and forgiveness. *Personality and Individual Differences, 46*(3), 276–280. https://doi.org/10.1016/j.paid.2008.10.016

Cameron, J. J., Ross, M., & Holmes, J. G. (2002). Loving the one you hurt: Positive effects of recounting a transgression against an intimate partner. *Journal of Experimental Social Psychology, 38*(3), 307–314. https://doi.org/10.1006/jesp.2001.1506

Cann, A., Calhoun, L. G., Tedeschi, R. G., Kilmer, R. P., Gil-Rivas, V., Vishnevsky, T., & Danhauer, S. C. (2010). The Core Beliefs Inventory: A brief measure of disruption in the assumptive world. *Anxiety, Stress & Coping, 23*(1), 19–34. https://doi.org/10.1080/10615800802573013

Cann, A., Calhoun, L. G., Tedeschi, R. G., Triplett, K. N., Vishnevsky, T., & Lindstrom, C. M. (2011). Assessing posttraumatic cognitive processes: The Event Related Rumination Inventory. *Anxiety, Stress, & Coping, 24*(2), 137–156. https://doi.org/10.1080/10615806.2010.529901

Cox, K., & McAdams, D. P. (2014). Meaning making during high and low point life story episodes predicts emotion regulation two years later: How the past informs the future. *Journal of Research in Personality, 50*, 66–70. https://doi.org/10.1016/j.jrp.2014.03.004

Danhauer, S. C., Case, L. D., Tedeschi, R., Russell, G., Vishnevsky, T., Triplett, K., . . . Avis, N. E. (2013). Predictors of posttraumatic growth in women with breast cancer. *Psycho-oncology, 22*(12), 2676–2683. doi:10.1002/pon.3298

Danhauer, S. C., Russell, G., Case, L. D., Sohl, S. J., Tedeschi, R. G., Addington, E. L., . . . Avis, N. E. (2015). Trajectories of posttraumatic growth and associated characteristics in women with breast cancer. *Annals of Behavioral Medicine, 49*(5), 650–659. https://doi.org/10.1007/s12160-015-9696-1

Delker, B. C., Salton, R., McLean, K. C., & Syed, M. (2020). Who has to tell their trauma story and how hard will it be? Influence of cultural stigma and narrative redemption on the storying of sexual violence. *PloS one, 15*(6), e0234201.

Dunlop, W. L., & Tracy, J. L. (2013). Sobering stories: Narratives of self-redemption predict behavioral change and improved health among recovering alcoholics. *Journal of Personality and Social Psychology, 104*(3), 576–590. https://doi.org/10.1037/a0031185

Eriksson, P. L., McLean, K. C., & Frisén, A. (2020). Ta Det Onda Med Det Goda (Accepting the Bad that Comes with the Good)-A Cultural Framework for Identity Narratives of Difficult Experiences in Sweden. *Identity, 20*(3), 157–169.

Fivush, R., & Haden, C. A. (2003). *Autobiographical Memory and the Construction of a Narrative Self: Developmental and Cultural Perspectives.* New York: Psychology Press.

Fleeson, W., Furr, R. M., Jayawickreme, E., Meindl, P., & Helzer, E. G. (2014). Character: The prospects for a personality-based perspective on morality. *Social and Personality Psychology Compass, 8*(4), 178–191. https://doi.org/10.1111/spc3.12094

Ford, J. D., Tennen, H., & Albert, D. (2008). A contrarian view of growth following adversity. In S. Joseph & P. A. Linley (Eds.), *Trauma, Recovery, and Growth: Positive Psychological Perspectives on Posttraumatic Stress* (pp. 297–324). Hoboken, NJ: Wiley.

Grossmann, I. (2017). Wisdom in context. *Perspectives on Psychological Science, 12*(2), 233–257. https://doi.org/10.1177/1745691616672066

Grossman, I., & Kross, E. (2014). Exploring Solomon's paradox: Self-distancing eliminates the self-other asymmetry in wise reasoning about close relationships in younger and older adults. *Psychological Science, 25*(8), 1571–1580. https://doi.org/10.1177/0956797614535400

Guo, J., Klevan, M., & McAdams, D. P. (2016). Personality traits, ego development, and the redemptive self. *Personality and Social Psychology Bulletin, 42*(11), 1551–1563. https://doi.org/10.1177/0146167216665093

Habermas, T., & Bluck, S. (2000). Getting a life: The emergence of the life story in adolescence. *Psychological Bulletin, 126*(5), 748–769. DOI:10.1037/0033-2909.126.5.748

Hammack, P. L. (2008). Narrative and the cultural psychology of identity. *Personality and Social Psychology Review, 12*(3), 222–247. https://doi.org/10.1177/1088868308316892

Janoff-Bulman, R. (1992). *Shattered Assumptions: Towards a New Psychology of Trauma.* New York: Free Press.

Jayawickreme, E., & Blackie, L. E. R. (2014). Post-traumatic growth as positive personality change: Evidence, controversies and future directions. *European Journal of Personality, 28*(4), 312–331. https://doi.org/10.1002/per.1963

Jayawickreme, E., & Blackie, L. E. R. (2016). *Exploring the Psychological Benefits of Hardship: A Critical Reassessment of Posttraumatic Growth.* New York: Springer.

Joseph, S., & Linley, P. A. (2005). Positive adjustment to threatening events: An organismic valuing theory of growth through adversity. *Review of General Psychology, 9*(3), 262–280. https://doi.org/10.1037/1089-2680.9.3.262

Kross, E., & Grossmann, I. (2012). Boosting wisdom: Distance from the self enhances wise reasoning, attitudes, and behavior. *Journal of Experimental Psychology. General, 141*(1), 43–48. https://doi.org/10.1037/a0024158

Lilgendahl, J. P., Helson, R., & John, O. P. (2013). Does ego development increase during midlife? The effects of openness and accommodative processing of difficult events. *Journal of Personality, 81*(4), 403–416. https://doi.org/10.1111/jopy.12009

Lilgendahl, J. P., McLean, K. C., & Mansfield, C. D. (2013). When is meaning making unhealthy for the self? The roles of neuroticism, implicit theories, and memory telling in trauma and transgression memories. *Memory, 21*(1), 79–96. https://doi.org/10.1080/09658211.2012.706615

Linley, P. A., & Joseph, S. (2004). Positive change following trauma and adversity: A review. *Journal of Traumatic Stress, 17*(1), 11–21. https://doi.org/10.1023/B:JOTS.0000014671.27856.7e

Mansfield, C. D., McLean, K. C., & Lilgendahl, J. P. (2010). Narrating traumas and transgressions: Links between narrative processing, wisdom, and well-being. *Narrative Inquiry, 20*(2), 246–273. https://doi.org/10.1075/ni.20.2.02man

Mansfield, C. D., Pasupathi, M., & McLean, K. C. (2015). Is narrating growth in stories of personal transgressions associated with increased well-being, self-compassion, and forgiveness of others? *Journal of Research in Personality, 58*, 69–83. https://doi.org/10.1016/j.jrp.2015.05.008

McAdams, D. P. (1995). What do we know when we know a person? *Journal of Personality, 63*(3), 365–396. https://doi.org/10.1111/j.1467-6494.1995.tb00500.x

McAdams, D. P. (2001). The psychology of life stories. *Review of General Psychology, 5*(2), 100–122. https://doi.org/10.1037/1089-2680.5.2.100

McAdams, D. P. (2006). The redemptive self: Generativity and the stories Americans live by. *Research in Human Development, 3*(2–3), 81–100. https://doi.org/10.1080/15427609.2006.9683363

McAdams, D. P., & Guo, J. (2015). Narrating the generative life. *Psychological Science, 26*(4), 475–483. https://doi.org/10.1177/0956797614568318

McAdams, D. P., & McLean, K. C. (2013). Narrative identity. *Current Directions in Psychological Science, 22*(3), 233–238. https://doi.org/10.1177/0963721413475622

McAdams, D. P., & Pals, J. L. (2006). A new Big Five: Fundamental principles for an integrative science of personality. *American Psychologist, 61*(3), 204–217. https://doi.org/10.1037/0003-066X.61.3.204

McLean, K. C., Delker, B. C., Dunlop, W. L., Salton, R., & Syed, M. (2020). Redemptive stories and those who tell them are preferred in the U.S. *Collabra: Psychology, 6*(1), 39. doi:https://doi.org/10.1525/collabra.369

McLean, K. C., Pasupathi, M., & Pals, J. L. (2007). Selves creating stories creating selves: A process model of self-development. *Personality and Social Psychology Review, 11*(3), 262–278. https://doi.org/10.1177/1088868307301034

McLean, K. C., & Syed, M. (2015). Personal, master, and alternative narratives: An integrative framework for understanding identity development in context. *Human Development, 58*(6), 318–349. https://doi.org/10.1159/000445817

Merrill, N., Waters, T. E. A., & Fivush, R. (2016). Connecting the self to traumatic and positive events: Links to identity and well-being. *Memory, 24*(10), 1321–1328. https://doi.org/10.1080/09658211.2015.1104358

Paleari, F. G., Regalia, C., & Fincham, F. (2005). Marital quality, forgiveness, empathy, and rumination: A longitudinal analysis. *Personality and Social Psychology Bulletin, 31*(3), 368–378. https://doi.org/10.1177/0146167204271597

Pals, J. L. (2006). Narrative identity processing of difficult life experiences: Pathways of personality development and positive self-transformation in adulthood. *Journal of Personality, 74*(4), 1079–1110. https://doi.org/10.1111/j.1467-6494.2006.00403.x

Park, C. L., Cohen, L. H., & Murch, R. L. (1996). Assessment and prediction of stress-related growth. *Journal of Personality, 64*(1), 71–105. https://doi.org/10.1111/j.1467-6494.1996.tb00815.x

Pasupathi, M., Fivush, R., & Hernandez-Martinez, M. (2016). Talking about it: Stories as paths to healing after violence. *Psychology of Violence, 6*(1), 49–56. https://doi.org/10.1037/vio0000017

Pasupathi, M., & Hoyt, T. (2010). Silence and the shaping of memory: How distracted listeners affect speakers' subsequent recall of a computer game experience. *Memory, 18*(2), 159–169. https://doi.org/10.1080/09658210902992917

Pasupathi, M., Mansour, E., & Brubaker, J. R. (2007). Developing a life story: Constructing relations between self and experience in autobiographical narratives. *Human Development, 50*(2–3), 85–110. https://doi.org/10.1159/000100939

Pasupathi, M., McLean, K. C., & Weeks, T. (2009). To tell or not to tell: Disclosure and the narrative self. *Journal of Personality, 77*(1), 89–124. https://doi.org/10.1111/j.1467-6494.2008.00539.x

Pasupathi, M., McLean, K. C., Weeks, T. L., & Hynes, W. (2019). Tailoring narration for distinct audiences in emerging adulthood. *Emerging Adulthood.* Advance online publication. https://doi.org/10.1177/2167696819856753

Pasupathi, M., & Wainryb, C. (2010). Developing moral agency through narrative. *Human Development, 53*(2), 55–80. https://doi.org/10.1159/000288208

Roberts, B. W. (2011). Personality psychology has a serious problem (and so do many other areas of psychology). The Online Newsletter for Personality Science. http://www.personality-arp.org/html/newsletter06/problem.html

Sandage, S., & Worthington, E. (2010). Comparison of two group interventions to promote forgiveness: Empathy as a mediator of change. *Journal of Mental Health Counseling, 32*(1), 35–57. https://doi.org/10.17744/mehc.32.1.274536n518571683

Seery, M. D., & Kondrak, C. L. (2014). Does trauma lead to special growth? *European Journal of Personality, 28*, 348–350. https://doi.org/10.1002/per.1970

Slotter, E. B., & Ward, D. E. (2015). Finding the silver lining: The relative roles of redemptive narratives and cognitive reappraisal in individuals' emotional distress after the end of a romantic relationship. *Journal of Social and Personal Relationships, 32*(6), 737–756. https://doi.org/10.1177/0265407514546978

Tedeschi, R. G., & Calhoun, L. G. (1996). The Posttraumatic Growth Inventory: Measuring the positive legacy of trauma. *Journal of Traumatic Stress, 9*(3), 455–472. https://doi.org/10.1002/jts.2490090305

Tedeschi, R. G., & Calhoun, L. G. (2004). Posttraumatic growth: Conceptual foundations and empirical evidence. *Psychological Inquiry, 15*(1), 1–18. https://doi.org/10.1207/s15327965pli1501_01

Tennen, H., & Affleck, G. (2002). Benefit-finding and benefit-reminding. In C. R. Snyder & S. J. Lopez (Eds.), *Handbook of Positive Psychology* (pp. 584–597). New York: Oxford University Press.

Weiner, B. (2007). On responsibility inferences and the perceived moral person. *International Journal of Existential Positive Psychology, 1*(1), 1696–1708.

Worthington, Everett L. (1998). An empathy-humility-commitment model of forgiveness applied within family dyads. *Journal of Family Therapy, 20*(1), 59–76. https://doi.org/10.1111/1467-6427.00068

15

Pathways from Adversity to Wisdom

ANNA DORFMAN, DAVID A. MOSCOVITCH, AND IGOR GROSSMANN ■

Philosophers and lay people have long thought that mastering adversity contributes to growth in wisdom—adaptability to the situation, perspectivism, dialectical thinking, and epistemic humility. But existing research on outcomes of adversity appears inconclusive, suggesting a puzzle: on the one hand, cross-sectional studies have found that adversity leads to post-traumatic growth (PTG) in character strengths such as wisdom. On the other hand, adverse experiences have been shown to exacerbate negative emotions and thoughts and undermine health and well-being over time. Our chapter highlights the idea that outcomes of adversity may depend on the way one approaches and reflects on adverse experiences: whereas self-distancing can foster growth in wisdom in the face of adversity, self-immersing can put one on a path toward maladaptive rumination, depression, and further distress. We review evidence-based advances in the study of daily adversity and wisdom, specifically focusing on evidence from longitudinal and randomized control trial studies. We conclude by outlining several questions for future research as well as clinical implications of self-distancing for growth in wisdom.

DEFINING WISDOM

Wisdom has long been considered a cardinal virtue in Eastern and Western philosophy (Baltes & Kunzmann, 2004; Dahlsgaard, Peterson, & Seligman, 2005; Grossmann, Kung, & Santos, 2019; Grossmann et al., 2012) and has recently become a topic of interest in behavioral and social sciences (Grossmann, Westrate et al., 2020; Jayawickreme & Blackie, 2016; Peterson & Seligman, 2004; Swartwood

& Tiberius, 2019). According to the recently emerged consensus among behavioral and cognitive sciences, the Common Wisdom Model across empirical sciences chiefly aims to assess "morally-grounded excellence in social-cognitive processing" (Grossmann, Weststrate et al., 2020). In this consensus definition, wisdom involves moral aspirations such as pursuit of truth, orientation toward shared humanity, and balance of self- and other-oriented interests. Moreover, wisdom involves certain meta-cognitive characteristics:

- Context-adaptability (e.g., pragmatic reasoning, adjusting to the situation).
- Perspectivism (e.g., considering diverse perspectives, foresight and long-term thinking).
- Dialectical thinking (e.g., balancing and integration of viewpoints, entertaining opposites).
- Epistemic humility (e.g., unbiased/accurate thinking, understanding one's limitations).

In this chapter, we focus on these characteristics to address the question of change after encountering adversity. Notably, existing research on outcomes of adversity suggests a puzzle. On the one hand, akin to Nietzsche's famous phrase "that which does not kill us makes us stronger," some research indicates that wise characteristics can develop as a result of facing and mastering adverse life experiences (Ferrari, Grossmann, Grimm & Staffel, 2019; Grossmann, 2017; Staudinger & Glück, 2011). On the other hand, people's attempts to work through adversity can lead to a decline in mental health and well-being (e.g., Hankin, Stone, & Wright, 2010; Lyubomirsky & Nolen-Hoeksema, 1995; Nolen-Hoeksema & Morrow, 1991). To start unpacking the puzzle of adversity and wisdom, we will first consider how different ways of reflecting on adversity may impact changes in wisdom.

DOES ADVERSITY MAKE US STRONGER?

The idea that mastering adversity can promote character strengths, and specifically wisdom, is very compelling. It suggests a silver-lining of living through difficult, sometimes devastating, life events. Folk notions of wisdom hold that struggles make people wiser—more open-minded, intellectually humble, empathetic to others' opinions and willing to compromise. Emerging empirical findings on wisdom provide some indirect support to this intuition, showing, for example, that economic hardships can be associated with greater wisdom. For instance, a recent study examining wisdom among different socioeconomic strata of the US population found a higher propensity of reasoning wisely about challenging interpersonal situations among participants from lower social classes (Brienza & Grossmann, 2017). As individuals from lower social classes are likely to experience more adversity, such as economic setbacks, discrimination, and decreases in health in general and mental health in particular (e.g., Karlsen & Nazroo, 2002), such difficult life circumstances could be related to their gain of wise characteristics observed in the study. Also, older adults, who are more likely than younger adults to have experienced adversity, tend to show more wisdom in reasoning about social conflicts (Grossmann, Varnum, Park, Kitayama, & Nisbet, 2010).

The idea of enhanced wisdom following adversity is closely related to the concept of PTG. PTG is broadly defined as self-reported positive change following traumatic events (Tedeschi & Calhoun, 2004). Such positive change can be reflected in personal characteristics such as open-mindedness, perception of personal strength, spirituality, sense of meaning, appreciation of life, and wisdom (Affleck, Tennen, & Gershman, 1985; Jayawickreme & Blackie, 2014; Park, 2010; Roepke, Jayawickreme, & Riffle, 2014; Tedeschi & Callhoun, 2004). In an early study on PTG (Calhoun, Cann, Tedeschi, & McMillan, 2000), students who experienced severe adversity retrospectively reported their experience of PTG, to what extent they engaged in "rumination" 2 weeks after the adverse event occurred, and their religious orientation (i.e., expectation that religiosity will change and grow). PTG was assessed with the Post-Traumatic Growth Inventory (PTGI; Tedeschi & Calhoun, 1996) in five domains: personal strength (e.g., "I discovered that I'm stronger than I thought I was"), interpersonal relationships (e.g., "I learned a great deal about how wonderful people are"), spirituality (e.g., "I have a stronger religious faith"), new possibilities for one's life (e.g., "New opportunities are available which wouldn't have been otherwise"), and appreciation of life (e.g., "An appreciation for the value of my own life"). This well-cited study found positive relationships between reports of ruminations, religious orientation, and PTG. The more participants reported ruminating about the adverse event after it had occurred, the more they reported PTG. Several subsequent cross-sectional studies also found PTG following adverse events in student samples as well as among breast cancer patients and refugees (e.g., Cordova, Cunningham, Carlson, & Andrykowski, 2001; Powell, Rosner, Butollo, Tedeschi, & Calhoun, 2003; Shakespeare-Finch & Enders, 2008; Widows, Jacobsen, Booth-Jones, & Fields, 2005). Conceptual models of PTG have proposed that a traumatic event invokes a cognitive process that leads to change in "life-narrative," namely the way people make meaning of their lives (Pals & McAdams, 2004; Park, 2010; Pennebaker, 1997; Tedeschi & Calhoun, 2004). The change in life narratives, in turn, leads to PTG.

DOES ADVERSITY MAKE US WEAKER?

Though the idea that one can gain wisdom by overcoming struggles and adversities appears straightforward, another sizable body of research indicates that attempts to work through adverse experiences often backfire. According to this line of work, when people try to focus on adverse experiences, negative thoughts become more accessible, which leads to a vicious cycle of rumination, maintaining and exacerbating distress in the short term and undermining health and well-being over time (e.g., Lyubomirsky & Nolen-Hoeksema; 1995; Nolen-Hoeksema & Morrow, 1991). Focus on adverse experiences can increase anxiety, dysphoria, social and interpersonal stagnation, and avoidance of similar situations in the present and future, leading to life interference and distress (e.g., Chiupka, Moscovitch, & Bielak, 2012; Gavric, Moscovitch, Rowa, & McCabe, 2017). In addition, some studies that examined PTG failed to find growth in spirituality and empathy, suggesting that adverse events do not necessarily promote PTG. Specifically, the few studies that have tackled the question of the long-term stability of PTG found that perceived growth remained stable from several weeks to several years after the event and, in some cases, even declined over time (Affleck, Tennen, Croog, & Levine, 1987; Dekel, Ein-Dor, & Solomon, 2012; Davis et al., 2021; Frazier, Conlon, & Glaser, 2001).

Another body of literature on positive psychology also suggests an inverse relationship between adversity and wisdom. The *broaden-and-build hypothesis* (Fredrickson, 2001) posits that positive emotional experiences are essential for broadening people's cognitive horizon. The above-mentioned central wise characteristics—reflective open-minded thinking, consideration of diverse perspectives, balancing of viewpoints, and epistemic humility—are linked to cognitive broadening (Santos & Grossmann, 2021). Adversity, through increased negative emotions could inhibit cognitive broadening, which in turn could inhibit wise characteristics.

Taken together, the inconsistent findings present a complex picture of adversity's outcomes. Adverse experiences may lead to growth in valued personal characteristics. But it can also lead to maladaptive cognitions (e.g., rumination, brooding) and behaviors (e.g., withdrawal, avoidance) which may result in life interference. These contradicting outcomes of adversity suggest a puzzle: Do adverse events encourage growth in wisdom, or do they lead to stagnation and decline?

While character growth is not the only possible trajectory of experiencing adverse life events (Infurna & Luthar, 2016), the mechanisms through which adverse experiences may facilitate wisdom are currently underspecified. A closer look at clinical treatments for negative outcomes following adverse life experiences and recent empirical research on regulation of negative emotions suggests that examining one's mindset concerning the adverse experience may hold the key to solving the puzzle of adversity and wisdom. Specifically, the mindset with which one approaches and processes an adverse event can differently impact the subsequent outcomes of adversity (e.g., Bernstein et al., 2015; Gross, 1998; Lazarus & Alfert, 1964).

HOW TO MASTER ADVERSITY: MINDSETS MATTER

When spontaneously reflecting on adverse past experiences, people, especially in North America, habitually adopt a self-immersed mindset. They tend to visualize the event through their own eyes, focusing on the specific details and emotions they experienced as the event was unfolding (e.g., Grossmann & Kross, 2010;

McIsaac & Eich, 2004; Nigro & Neisser, 1983; Wu & Keysar, 2007). However, research suggests that this type of self-immersed reflection is associated with narrow thinking (e.g., Grossmann & Jowhari, 2018), negative emotionality, distress, and depressive symptomatology (Tackman et al., 2019). At the same time, one can also approach adverse experience via a self-distanced mindset, which involves "taking a step back" from the current experience (Kross & Ayduk, 2017). Though it is not habitual, people vary in the extent to which they adopt either mindset spontaneously (e.g., Grossmann & Kross, 2010) and can also be instructed to use either mindset via training (e.g., Dorfman, Oakes, Santos, & Grossmann, 2021).

When facing an adverse experience, which mindsets can enhance wisdom, and which would lead to decline? Approaching or reflecting on adversity with different mindsets may have different effects on wisdom, with some mindsets more likely to encourage wise reasoning. Most of the evidence for the role of mindsets in coping with adversity comes from affective sciences. Two decades of research on cognitive reappraisal have shown that when reflecting on adverse experiences, people's mindsets impact their emotional reactions to adversity. Numerous studies have found that when reflecting on an adverse experience, reconstruction or reappraisal of the experience reduces negative emotions and distress compared to immersing in the adverse experience, suppressing the negative emotions, or distracting oneself from the emotion (e.g., McLean & Foa, 2017; Gross, 2008; Gross & John, 2003; Gross & Thompson, 2007; Lazarus, 2006). Cognitive reappraisal of the adverse experience changes the emotional experience, expression, and physiological response to negative emotions (Buhle et al., 2014; Morawetz, Bode, Derntl, & Heekeren, 2017; Webb, Miles, & Sheeran, 2012). Daily use of reappraisal has been associated with higher well-being (Bruehlman-Senecal, Ayduk, & John, 2016) and fewer mental health difficulties (Aldao, Nolen-Hoeksema, & Schweizer, 2010; Garnefski, Kraaij, & Spinhoven, 2001; McRae, Jacobs, Ray, John, & Gross, 2012; Troy, Wilhelm, Shallcross, & Mauss, 2010).

Central to cognitive reappraisal is the notion of psychological distance from the self (Beck, 2002; Kross & Ayduk, 2017). An example of such a self-distanced mindset would be to imagine oneself asking for a friend's advice on an emotionally charged event one is currently experiencing (Kross, Ayduk, & Mischel, 2005; Kross & Ayduk, 2017). Because the friend is not directly involved in the event, they can think about it in a more analytical and reflective manner (Grossmann & Kross, 2014). Studies on emotion regulation have used different methods for cuing the self-distanced mindset, such as imagining the situation as happening to someone else, thinking about the situation as an uninvolved observer would, imagining looking at the situation from a distant vantage point (like "a fly on the wall" would), and reflecting on the situation using third-person pronouns (i.e., as one would when describing someone else's experience) (Grossmann & Kross, 2014; Kross et al., 2014; Nook, Schleider, & Somerville, 2017). The self-distanced mindset is instrumental in reducing stress and improving well-being (Blascovich & Mendes, 2000; Finkel, Slotter, Luchies, Walton, & Gross, 2013; Grossmann & Kross, 2010; Kross et al., 2005, 2014; Moscovitch et al., 2012; Reimer & Moscovitch, 2015). The self-distanced mindset is more likely than the self-immersed mindset to promote shifts in focus from recounting adverse experience to the "big picture" reconstruing of the experience, ultimately resulting in less distress following the reflection (Grossmann & Kross, 2010).

A meta-analysis comparing different types of emotion regulation strategies found that cognitive reappraisal reduces the experience of negative emotions, with the strongest effects observed for *distancing* (and mixed strategies that involve distancing) (Webb et al., 2012). More recently, a longitudinal study compared the effects of distancing, reinterpretation, and a no-instructions control on negative affect and perceived stress in four laboratory sessions (Denny & Ochsner, 2014). Participants were randomly assigned to practice distancing or reinterpretation. The control group received no instructions. In each session, participants were instructed to use their assigned strategy during an experimentally induced negative experience (i.e., viewing unpleasant images). After each image, participants rated the strength of their negative affect. Participants who used distancing reported the lowest negative affect. Moreover, the distancing group participants showed a decrease in general perceived stress from the first session, while participants in the other two groups showed no such decrease. Taken together, these findings suggest that facing an adverse experience with a self-distanced mindset is likely to enhance wise characteristics and possibly even allow for subsequent growth in wisdom.

ROLE OF MINDSETS FOR CHANGE IN WISDOM AFTER ADVERSITY

The mindset with which one approaches the adverse experience extends beyond emotion regulation to change in wisdom-related characteristics. A self-distanced mindset promotes a "big picture" view and reconstructive reasoning (Huynh, Yang, & Grossmann, 2016; McIsaac & Eich, 2004; Pronin & Ross, 2006; Robinson & Swanson, 1993; Vasquez & Buehler, 2007). Based on this notion, several studies examined the idea that reflecting on adversity with a self-distanced rather than a self-focused mindset can enhance wise characteristics such as dialectical thinking and perspectivism (Kross & Grossmann, 2012; Grossmann & Kross, 2014; Huynh, Oakes, Shay, & McGregor, 2017; Staudinger & Baltes, 1996 see Grossmann, 2017, for a review).

In one of the earliest experimental studies on wisdom, participants reflected on an interpersonal dilemma (Staudinger & Baltes, 1996). One group of participants reflected on the dilemma as they would typically think about social problems. Another group of participants was instructed to adopt a different mindset: they considered what other individuals whose opinions they value might say about this dilemma. Content-analyses of participants' reflections for wisdom-related aspects indicated that participants who adopted a mindset different from their habitual mindset were more likely to show wise characteristics (epistemic humility and recognition of uncertainty and change) as compared to participants who reflected on the dilemma as they normally would.

In another study (Kross & Grossmann, 2012), cuing participants to reason about personally meaningful issues (e.g., how an economic crisis would affect them) with a self-distanced versus self-immersed mindset enhanced wise characteristics of epistemic humility, dialectical thinking, and perspectivism. More recently, Grossmann and Kross (2014) examined the effects of framing a hypothetical situation as distant from the self (happening to another person) versus proximal (happening to the self) on wisdom-related characteristics. Participants were assigned to read and reason about a serious relationship in which one of the partners admitted to cheating. Participants in the self condition read that their partner cheated. Participants in the friend condition read that their friend's partner cheated. Participants reflected on this situation, described their thoughts about the future development of the relationship, and answered directed questions about various aspects related to wise characteristics. Participants in the friend condition showed wise characteristics (epistemic humility, perspectivism, dialectic reasoning, and compromise seeking) in their reasoning to a greater extent as compared to participants in the self condition. In another set of studies, Grossmann and Kross (2014; Studies 2–3) showed that the differences between self and friend conditions were driven by mindsets that participants in these conditions were asked to adapt: when instructed to reflect on the friend and self scenarios in a self-distanced, third-person language, the difference between friend and self conditions dissipated. This set of findings suggests that people tend to display more wisdom-related characteristics when they adopt a self-distanced mindset, a result that has since been independently replicated by another research group (Huynh et al., 2017).

GROWING FROM ADVERSITY: LONGITUDINAL STUDIES

Experimental studies (Kross & Grossmann, 2012; Grossmann & Kross, 2014) have shown that inducing a self-distanced (vs. self-immersed) mindset can boost wise characteristics. Other studies have provided cross-sectional support for the idea that self-distanced reflection on adverse events can boost wisdom (Sternberg, & Jordan, 2005). Yet, because these studies used only experimental and cross-sectional designs, they could not explore the idea that self-distanced mindsets can *prospectively* facilitate changes in wise characteristics over time. To fill this gap, we recently conducted several longitudinal investigations examining the prospective effects of adopting different mindsets on wisdom-related characteristics in the aftermath of adverse experiences.

In a micro-longitudinal diary study, Dorfman et al. (2021) examined changes in positive and negative emotionality following reflections on experiences with self-distanced and self-immersed mindsets. Participants were randomly assigned to two groups, instructed either to reflect on daily events with a self-distanced mindset (using third-person pronouns in their reflection) or with the habitual self-immersed mindset (using first-person pronouns in their reflection). For 4 weeks, each weekday, they were instructed to adopt their randomly assigned mindset, recall the daily event, and reflect on this event using either a self-distanced or a self-immersed mindset (on day 7 of each week, participants reflected on an event from the past week without receiving their assigned mindset instructions). To induce a self-distanced mindset, the instructions directed participants to recall and reflect on the daily event using their name and third-person pronouns. In the self-immersed mindset group, participants were instructed to write about a daily event using first-person pronouns. After the reflection, participants reported on their emotional reactions (the importance of different positive and negative emotions) to the daily negative event. Participants who adopted the self-distanced mindset, but not participants who adopted the habitual self-immersed mindset, reported greater emotional dialecticism (Grossmann, Huynh, & Ellsworth, 2016)—that is, an increasing importance of positive as well as negative emotions in adverse experiences over time (Figure 15.1). Self-distanced reflections may have broadened participants' emotional repertoire, allowing them to experience a more balanced emotional reaction overall, one that includes both negative and positive emotions.

Another set of micro-longitudinal randomized control trial studies with a pre-post experimental design (Grossmann, Dorfman, Oakes, Santos, Vohs, & Scholer, 2021) directly examined the effects of repeatedly adopting a self-distanced (vs. self-immersed) mindset on wise characteristics. First, participants were invited to a laboratory session. They reflected on a social adverse event they recently experienced (e.g., a social conflict, an argument with a close other) and described in detail their stream of thoughts about this event.

Figure 15.1 Effects of self-distanced versus self-immersed mindsets on importance of positive and negative emotions (from Dorfman et al., 2019). Estimated marginal means and 95% confidence bands from the generalized mixed effects model with mindset, day, and emotion valence as predictors of emotion importance.

Next, participants completed diaries for 4 weeks, during which time they repeatedly adopted either a self-distanced or a self-immersed mindset when reflecting on a daily event. For the proposes of this investigation, the diary portion of the study was considered as training in adopting a self-distanced mindset. After the conclusion of the diary study, participants were invited back to the laboratory. As in the pre-diary sessions, during the post-diary training session participants reflected on a new social adverse event and described their stream of thoughts. Importantly, reflection in the pre- and post-sessions did not include instructions to adopt a self-distanced or self-immersed mindset.

This study assessed the actual display of wise characteristics in participants' reflections. Two blind coders coded the detailed stream-of-thoughts descriptions from the pre- and post-sessions for instances of epistemic humility, dialectical thinking, and perspectivism, as well as the willingness to seek compromise/integration of different perspectives. Results showed that adopting the self-distanced mindset enhanced wise characteristics from the pre-diary to the post-diary measure (Figure 15.2). The increase in wise characteristics was robust when controlling for time of day event occurred, duration of adverse events, the length of participants' written reflections, and number of adverse experiences reported during the diary-based training.

A second 1-week micro-longitudinal study replicated these findings, adding a no-instruction control group (Grossmann et al., 2021). This study largely replicated the results of the original study. The results from this replication showed that

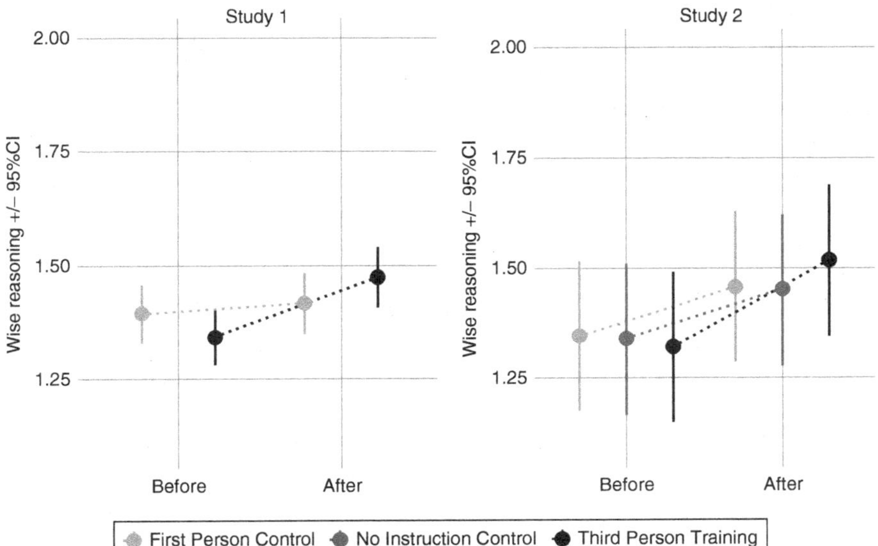

Figure 15.2 Effects of self-distanced reflection training on wisdom in Studies 1 and 2 (Grossmann et al., 2020). "Third Person" refers to the self-distanced mindset; "First-Person Control" refers to the self-immersed mindset. Mean estimates across all subdimensions with 95% confidence intervals.

participants who trained in adopting a self-distanced mindset showed the largest increase in wise characteristics from before to after the training. This suggests that individuals' wise characteristics can be enhanced by repeatedly adopting a self-distanced mindset. In other words, wisdom can be trained depending on the mindset one adopts when reflecting on experiences.

Finally, to track changes in wise characteristics following adverse experiences over time Dorfman, Moscovitch, Chopik, and Grossmann (2021) conducted a year-long four-wave longitudinal study. The research examined associations between adopting a self-distanced mindset and the propensity to display wise characteristics when reflecting on adverse experiences. Study waves were set approximately 2.5 months apart, with each wave including 10 daily surveys. On the first day of each wave, participants reported the main measures of the study. They first recalled the most significant recent adverse event they experienced. (On the subsequent days of each study wave (days 2-10), participants reported on a daily event, wise reasoning about the event, the tendency to self-distance from the event, and emotional experiences following the event. These data were analyzed separately and are not reported here.) Adverse events were defined as "a state or instance of difficulty or misfortune. Such adversity can include economic setbacks (e.g., loss of a job), health-related challenges (e.g., illness, pregnancy), marital conflict (e.g., separation), a loss of a loved one (e.g., ending a relationship or death), a serious scare (e.g., being a victim of a crime/accident, distress over future events, loved one's health), a serious conflict with another person or any other serious difficulty or challenge you may have encountered in your life." Participants reflected on the adverse experience and described their stream of thoughts. Next, wise characteristics were assessed with Situated Wise Reasoning Scale (SWiS; Brienza, Kung, Santos, Bobocel, & Grossmann, 2018). Using the SWiS, participants rated the extent to which they engaged in 21 thoughts and actions as the adverse experience unfolded. A wisdom score was computed based on these ratings.

Next, on a separate scale, participants reported the extent to which they adopted a self-distant mindset by responding to four items: "Wondered what I would think if I was somebody else watching the situation," "Tried to see the conflict from the point of view of an uninvolved person," "Asked myself what other people might think or feel if they were watching the conflict," and "Thought about whether an outside person might have a different opinion from mine about the situation." Trait (overall, across 4 waves) and state (for each wave) self-distancing scores were computed.

The data revealed a positive association between the tendency to adopt a self-distanced mindset and wisdom-related characteristics in each of the four study waves (Figure 15.3). The more participants reported that they engaged in self-distanced reflection, the more they reported wisdom-related characteristics. This pattern was observed for the overall wisdom score and for each of the wise characteristics included in the scale, including epistemic humility (i.e., ability to recognize the limitations of their knowledge), dialectical thinking (i.e., ability to recognize different ways in which the situation can unfold), perspectivism (i.e.,

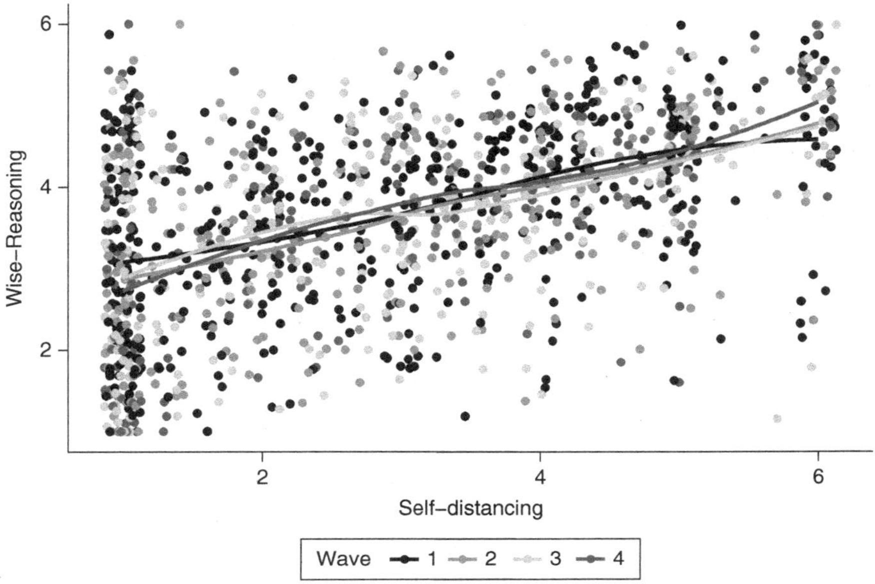

Figure 15.3 The positive relationship between self-distanced reflection and wisdom in four waves of the longitudinal study (from Dorfman et al., 2020).

ability to consider the perspectives of others involved in the situation), and prosocial aspirations (seeking compromise and conflict resolution).

The longitudinal data collected in this study also allowed us to examine changes in wise characteristics over time. Participants who reported engaging in less self-distancing when reflecting on the adverse event exhibited a decline in wise characteristics over time, whereas those who reported engaging in more self-distancing did not show this decline. Unpacking this general finding, we looked at specific types of reported adverse events, such as social conflicts (e.g., break-up, marital problems, conflicts with close family members and friends), economic hardships, career setbacks, trauma, and health-related adversity. We found that the relationship between self-distancing and wisdom over time was most pronounced for adverse social events such as social conflicts and arguments. For reflections on social conflicts, participants who reported less self-distancing when reflecting showed a decline over time in wise characteristics, whereas participants who reported more self-distancing maintained their wise characteristics. These findings suggest that while there may be no actual increase in wisdom over time following adverse events, self-distancing when reflecting on adversity can help to prevent decline in wise characteristics such as epistemic humility, perspectivism, and dialectical reasoning. Our longitudinal findings suggest the possibility that what appears as PTG in cross-sectional studies is actually resilience, or lack of decline, in the aforementioned personal characteristics, a decline that can result from the hyperfocus on the self, intrusive thoughts, ruminations, and distress that often follow adverse experiences (Nolen-Hoeksema, Wisco, & Lyubomirsky, 2008). Because adopting a self-distanced mindset decreases distress and rumination (e.g., Webb et al., 2012), increases positive emotional experiences (Dorfman et al., 2021), and leads to less (vs. more) self-focus, this mindset is likely to prevent such decline.

Whether or not preventing decline can be considered as growth is another important question. The answer would depend on the definition of growth, a fuzzy construct that is usually defined as positive change in personality characteristics (Jayawickreme & Blackie, 2014). One way to address this question is to define the expected trajectory of wise characteristics following adverse life events. If we expect an overall decline in wise characteristics following adverse life events (e.g., break-up with a partner, conflicts with close others) due to enhanced self-focus, rumination, and negative emotionality, then preventing such naturally occurring decline through the adoption of a self-distanced mindset can be viewed as *relative* growth. At the same time, attenuated decline may also fit the notion of resilience—the ability to maintain relatively stable levels of psychological and physical functioning following adversity (e.g., Bonanno, 2004)—rather than actual growth (i.e., positive change) in personality characteristics.

It is noteworthy that, while there was within-person stability in the tendency to adopt a self-distanced perspective (i.e., suggesting this tendency is trait-like), we found considerable within-person variability in displays of wise characteristics across the four waves of the study, suggesting that wise characteristics are not fixed personality traits. This finding is consistent with previous findings regarding the intrapersonal variability in wisdom (Grossmann, 2017; Grossmann, Kung, & Santos, 2019), indicating that wisdom may be contingent not only on the type of mindset adopted but also on features of the adverse situation. This finding is also in line with the idea that the same individual may, in different types of situations, be more or less likely to show wise characteristics. For example, for the same individual, a social conflict might encourage wise reasoning whereas an economic hardship may not. This also suggests that one's capacity for wisdom can fluctuate over time rather than show a linear trajectory of growth or decline. Measuring actual personality change often requires a longer time span than 1 year (e.g., McAdams & Olson, 2010). Therefore, micro-longitudinal studies (e.g., Dorfman et al., 2020, 2021; Grossmann et al., 2020) may not provide a full picture about how personality changes over one's life span. On the other hand, examining the manifestation of wise characteristics across life events in micro-longitudinal data is in line with a dynamic view to virtue development (e.g., Jayawickreme & Fleeson, 2017). According to this view, changes in the frequency with which wisdom is observable in a person over time can speak to possible underlying changes toward an "unwise" character in this person. The question of whether adversity would lead to an overall permanent change in wise characteristics remains open, awaiting future exploration.

IMPLICATIONS AND FUTURE DIRECTIONS

We started this chapter with a question about the role of adversity for character growth, with a particular focus on growth in wisdom. From the outset, research on this topic presents a puzzle: on the one hand, theorizing and cross-sectional studies suggested that adversity leads to PTG. On the other hand, a sizable literature shows that adversity leads to increased distress, more negative ruminations, and decrease in mental health and well-being. To tackle this puzzle, in this chapter we suggest that the outcomes of adversity depend on one's mindset. Specifically, though one may be habitually inclined to reflect and work through adverse experiences by adapting a self-immersed mindset, this mindset may not necessarily put one on the path to growth when encountering adversity. In contrast, a self-distanced mindset may have the potential to promote wisdom-related growth and resilience in the face of major stressors and daily challenges.

Adopting a self-immersed mindset tends to narrow people's attentional focus onto the specific negative experience, leading to more rumination and feelings of distress. Such a mindset appears to inhibit wise characteristics and reasoning, preventing growth. Habitually adopting a self-immersed mindset may account for the lack of PTG evidence in several longitudinal studies (e.g., Davis et al., 2021). Conversely, "taking a step back" from the current experience and psychologically distancing the self from the situation can help to downregulate negative emotions, reduce distress, and enhance wise reasoning about personally relevant challenges (e.g., Kross & Grossmann, 2012; Grossmann & Kross, 2014; Kross & Ayduk, 2017). Reflecting on negative events with a self-distanced mindset can also enhance positive emotional reactions to adversity over time, potentially enhancing well-being over time (Dorfman et al., 2021). Furthermore, adopting a self-distanced mindset repeatedly over the course of 1 month or even 1 week can lead to growth in wisdom when reasoning about adverse events (Grossmann et al., 2020). Finally, spontaneously adopting a self-distanced mindset when reflecting on major life stressors sustains one's ability to reason wisely about adversity over the course of a year, whereas spontaneously adopting a self-immersed mindset results in a decline in wise reasoning over the same time period (Dorfman et al., 2020).

These observations raise intriguing questions about how long-lasting the effects of self-distancing on wisdom might be. Existing studies have not examined effects extending beyond 1 year. Additional longitudinal investigations are necessary to explore the relationship between adversity, self-distancing, and wisdom over longer periods of time. Related research on the longitudinal relationship of well-being and wisdom may suggest a likely direction. Analyzing large-scale longitudinal data, Santos and Grossmann (2021) recently found that wisdom predicts higher well-being over 20 years, but not vice versa, indicating that well-being (as a proxy for low level of adversity) does not promote growth in wisdom. However, establishing the role of a self-distanced mindset for promoting growth in wisdom over longer periods of time awaits future research.

Our research has also revealed that the impact of a self-distanced mindset on growth in wisdom may also be contingent on the domain of the adverse events. For example, Dorfman et al.'s (2021) findings suggest that self-distancing is linked to growth in wisdom for social conflicts but not for other types of adversity such as economic hardship or health problems. The interpersonal nature of wisdom may be more transferable from adverse events that concern interpersonal matters. According to this view, wisdom is a social feature of human cognition, and these wise characteristics would develop from experiences involving other people (Grossmann, Dorfman, & Oakes, 2020). Future research is needed to further explore whether growth in wisdom is more likely for social (vs. self-focused) adverse experiences.

Another important question is whether adverse events with broader impact on one's life (i.e., events that affect several life domains at once) encourage greater growth in wisdom than adverse events that are more specific in their impact on particular life domains. On the one hand, it is possible that wisdom can be gained from the adversity that affects many life domains because it can be viewed as more generalizable to different situations. On the other hand, adversity that has widespread effects on one's life can be experienced as too threatening and intense, thus inhibiting growth or leading to stagnation (see Ferrari et al., 2019, for similar arguments). Current research in our labs on the impact of COVID-19 will begin to address these questions, as will future research utilizing longitudinal designs that specifically target different types of adverse situations.

CAN COGNITIVE THERAPY CONTRIBUTE TO GROWTH IN WISDOM?

Although cognitive behavioral therapy (CBT) and related contemporary evidence-based psychological interventions for mental health difficulties do not directly focus on the development of wisdom, they are designed to target clients' negative appraisals of past adverse experiences (Antony, 2019; Moscovitch et al., 2012). Training clients to adopt an adaptive mindset with reappraisal strategies may facilitate the development of wise characteristics by promoting changes in one's viewpoint when reflecting on past adversity and when facing new adverse situations. For example, cognitive interventions can reduce negative self-focus. Indeed, cognitive interventions focused on reappraisal have been shown to reduce the negative self-focused cognitions that are associated with elevated symptoms of social anxiety (Hofmann, Moscovitch, Kim, & Taylor, 2004). Moreover, inducing clients to adopt a self-compassionate mindset when rescripting socially traumatic experiences promotes significant decreases in symptoms of anxiety and negative self-focused beliefs (Reimer & Moscovitch, 2015; Romano, Moscovitch, Huppert, Reimer, & Moscovitch, 2020). A self-compassionate mindset also promotes adaptive coping in response to distressing adverse events (Dupasquier, Kelly, Moscovitch, & Vidovic, 2020; Dupasquier, Kelly, Waring, & Moscovitch, 2020). Outside the therapy room, experimental evidence suggests that reducing self-focus can boost wisdom, at least temporarily (for reviews, see Grossmann, 2017; Santos, Huynh, & Grossman, 2017).

The process of engaging in cognitive reappraisal typically involves challenging one's initial negative beliefs and assumptions about an adverse situation by adopting a rational approach and weighing evidence for and against one's original interpretation or construal about the meaning of the situation (Antony, 2019). Reappraisal helps to promote the recognition that one's initial viewpoint is not the only possible way to view a situation. Engaging in this process could, therefore, encourage the development of wisdom, including (1) intellectual humility (understanding that one's knowledge is limited), (2) open-mindedness to future changes and uncertainly, (3) empathy toward viewpoints of other people involved in the situation, and (4) willingness to compromise by integrating different viewpoints. The formal process of reappraisal may not be essential for such changes to occur. Indeed, many types of empirically supported therapies, including both cognitive therapies and "third-wave" acceptance-based approaches, encourage clients to engage in mindful, self-distanced reflection on their thoughts, feelings, and associated internal experiences. Any intervention that utilizes or promotes a self-distanced mindset is likely to lead to growth in wise characteristics such as increased epistemic humility, reflective thinking, and perspectivism.

Future research should address the process through which a self-distanced mindset can promote development in wisdom. Like the process-oriented accounts of emotion regulation (Sheppes, Scheibe, Suri, & Gross, 2011; Smith & Kirby, 2009), it is important to identify the steps in the relationship between adversity, self-distanced mindset, and wisdom. For example, adopting a self-distanced mindset at the time of an ongoing adverse experience, or in anticipation of a future adverse event could have a different effect on wise characteristics than adopting a self-distanced mindset during a reflection on past adverse experience.

AUTHOR'S NOTE

Correspondence should be addressed to Anna Dorfman, Department of Psychology, University of Waterloo. E-mail: anna.dorfman@uwaterloo.ca or Igor Grossmann, Department of Psychology, University of Waterloo. E-mail: igrossma@uwaterloo.ca

REFERENCES

Affleck, G., Tennen, H., Croog, S., & Levine, S. (1987). Causal attribution, perceived benefits, and morbidity after a heart attack: An 8-year study. *Journal of Consulting and Clinical Psychology, 55*, 29–35.

Affleck, G., Tennen, H., & Gershman, K. (1985). Cognitive adaptations to high-risk infants: The search for mastery, meaning, and protection from future harm. *American Journal of Mental Deficiency, 89*, 653–656.

Aldao, A., Nolen-Hoeksema, S., & Schweizer, S. (2010). Emotion-regulation strategies across psychopathology: A meta-analytic review. *Clinical Psychology Review, 30*, 217–237.

Antony, M. M. (2019). Behavior therapy. In D., Wedding & R. J., Corsini (Eds.), *Current Psychotherapies* (11th ed., pp. 199–236). Boston, MA: Cengage Learning.

Baltes, P. B., & Kunzmann, U. (2004). The two faces of wisdom: Wisdom as a general theory of knowledge and judgment about excellence in mind and virtue vs. wisdom as everyday realization in people and products. *Human Development, 47*, 290–299.

Beck, A. T. (2002). Cognitive models of depression. *Clinical Advances in Cognitive Psychotherapy: Theory and Application, 14*, 29–61.

Bernstein, A., Hadash, Y., Lichtash, Y., Tanay, G., Shepherd, K., & Fresco, D. M, (2015). Decentering and related constructs: A critical review and metacognitive processes model. *Perspectives on Psychological Science, 10*, 599–617.

Blascovich, J., & Mendes, W. B. (2000). Challenge and threat appraisals. In J. Forgas (Ed.,) *Feeling and Thinking: The Role of Affect in Social Cognition* (pp. 59–82). New York: Cambridge University Press.

Bonanno, G. A. (2004). Loss, trauma, and human resilience: Have we underestimated the human capacity to thrive after extremely aversive events. *American Psychologist, 59*, 20–28

Brienza, J. P., & Grossmann, I. (2017). Social class and wise reasoning about interpersonal conflicts across regions, persons and situations. *Proceedings of the Royal Society B: Biological Sciences, 284*(1869), 20171870.

Brienza, J. P., Kung, F., Santos, H. C., Bobocel, D. R., & Grossmann, I. (2018). Wisdom, bias, and balance: Toward a process-sensitive measurement of wisdom-related cognition. *Journal of Personality and Social Psychology, 115*, 1093–1126. doi:10.1037/pspp0000171

Bruehlman-Senecal, E., Ayduk, Ö., & John, O. P. (2016). Taking the long view: Implications of individual differences in temporal distancing for affect, stress reactivity, and well-being. *Journal of Personality and Social Psychology, 111*, 610–635. https://doi.org/10.1037/pspp0000103

Buhle, J. T., Silvers, J. A., Wager, T. D., Lopez, R., Onyemekwu, C., Kober, H., . . . Ochsner, K. N. (2014). Cognitive reappraisal of emotion: A meta-analysis of human neuroimaging studies. *Cerebral Cortex, 24*, 2981–2990.

Calhoun, L. G., Cann, A., Tedeschi, R. G., & McMillan, J. (2000). A correlational test of the relationship between posttraumatic growth, religion, and cognitive processing. *Journal of Traumatic Stress, 13*, 521–527.

Chiupka, C. A., Moscovitch, D. A., & Bielak, T. (2012). In vivo activation of anticipatory vs. post-event autobiographical images and memories in social anxiety. *Journal of Social and Clinical Psychology, 31*, 783–809.

Cordova, M. J., Cunningham, L. L., Carlson, C. R., & Andrykowski, M. A. (2001). Posttraumatic growth following breast cancer: A controlled comparison study. *Health Psychology, 20*, 176–185.

Davis, E. B., Van Tongeren, D. R., McElroy-Heltzel, S. E., Davis, D. E., Rice, K. G., Hook, J. N., . . . Lemke, A. W. (2021). Perceived and actual posttraumatic growth in religiousness and spirituality following disasters. *Journal of Personality, 89*(1), 68–83.

Dahlsgaard, K., Peterson, C., & Seligman, M. E. P. (2005). Shared virtue: The convergence of valued human strengths across culture and history. *Review of General Psychology. 9*, 203–213.

Dekel, S., Ein-Dor, T., & Solomon, Z. (2012). Posttraumatic grown and posttraumatic distress: A longitudinal study. *Psychological Trauma: Theory, Research, Practice, and Policy, 4*, 94–101.

Denny, B. T., & Ochsner, K. N. (2014). Behavioral effects of longitudinal training in cognitive reappraisal. *Emotion, 14*, 425–433.

Dorfman, A., Moscovitch, D. A., Chopik, W. J., & Grossmann, I. (2020). *Does Self-Distancing Cultivate Wisdom? Evidence from a Four-Wave Longitudinal Diary Study.* Manuscript in preparation. Department of Psychology, University of Waterloo.

Dorfman, A., Oakes, H., Santos, H. C., & Grossmann, I. (2021). Self-distancing promotes positive emotional change after adversity: Evidence from a micro-longitudinal field experiment. *Journal of Personality, 89*(1), 132–144.

Dupasquier, J. R., Kelly, A. C., Moscovitch, D. A., & Vidovic, V. (2020). Cultivating self-compassion promotes disclosure of experiences that threaten self-esteem. *Cognitive Therapy and Research, 44*, 108–119. https://doi.org/10.1007/s10608-019-10050-x

Dupasquier, J. R., Kelly, A. C., Waring, S. V., & Moscovitch, D. A. (2020). Self-compassionate college women report receiving more social support in the face of distress: Evidence from a daily diary study. *Personality and Individual Differences, 154*, 109680.

Ferrari, M., Grossmann, I., Grimm, S., & Staffel, J. (2019). A process model of wisdom from adversity. *Journal of Value Inquiry, 53*, 471–473.

Finkel, E. J., Slotter, E. B., Luchies, L. B., Walton, G. M., & Gross, J. J. (2013). A brief intervention to promote conflict reappraisal preserves marital quality over time. *Psychological Science, 24*, 1595–1601.

Frazier, P., Conlon, A., & Glaser, T. (2001). Positive and negative life changes following sexual assault. *Journal of Consulting and Clinical Psychology, 69*, 1048–1055.

Fredrickson, B. L. (2001). The role of positive emotions in positive psychology: The broaden-and-build theory of positive emotions. *American Psychologist, 56*, 218–226.

Garnefski, N., Kraaij, V., & Spinhoven, P. (2001). Negative life events, cognitive emotion regulation and emotional problems. *Personality and Individual Differences, 30*, 1311–1327.

Gavric, D., Moscovitch, D. A., Rowa, K., & McCabe, R. E. (2017). Post-event processing in social anxiety disorder: Examining the mediating roles of positive metacognitive beliefs and perceptions of performance. *Behaviour Research and Therapy, 91*, 1–12.

Gross, J. J. (1998). The emerging field of emotion regulation: An integrative review. *Review of General Psychology, 2*, 271–299.

Gross, J. J. (2008). Emotion regulation. In M. Lewis, J. M. Haviland-Jones, & L. F. Barrett (Eds.), *Handbook of Emotions* (pp. 497–512). New York: Guilford.

Gross, J. J., & John, O. P. (2003). Individual differences in two emotion regulation processes: Implications for affect, relationships, and well-being. *Journal of Personality and Social Psychology, 85*, 348–362.

Gross, J. J., & Thompson, R. A. (2007). Emotion regulation: Conceptual foundations. In J. J. Gross (Ed.), *Handbook of Emotion Regulation* (pp. 3–24). New York: Guilford.

Grossmann, I. (2017). Wisdom in context. *Perspectives on Psychological Science, 12*, 233–257.

Grossmann, I., Dorfman, A., & Oakes, H. (2020). Wisdom is a social-ecological rather than person-centric phenomenon. *Current Opinion in Psychology, 32*, 66–71.

Grossmann, I., Dorfman, A., Oakes, H., Santos, H. C., Vohs, K. D., & Scholer, A. A. (2021). Training for wisdom: The distanced-self-reflection diary method. *Psychological Science, 32*(3), 381–394.

Grossmann, I., Huynh, A. C., & Ellsworth, P. C. (2016). Emotional complexity: Clarifying definitions and cultural correlates. *Journal of Personality and Social Psychology, 111*(6), 895–916. https://doi.org/10.1037/pspp0000084

Grossmann, I., & Jowhari, N. (2018). Cognition and the self: Attempt of an independent close replication of the effects of self-construal priming on spatial memory recall. *Journal of Experimental Social Psychology, 74*, 65–73. doi:10.1016/j.jesp.2017.08.005

Grossmann, I., Karasawa, M., Izumi, S., Na, J., Varnum, M. E. W., Kitayama, S., & Nisbett, R. E. (2012). Aging and wisdom: Culture matters. *Psychological Science, 23*, 1059–1066. doi:10.1177/0956797612446025

Grossmann, I., & Kross, E. (2010). The impact of culture on adaptive vs. maladaptive self-reflection. *Psychological Science, 21*, 1150–1157. doi:10.1177/0956797610376655

Grossmann, I., & Kross, E. (2014). Exploring Solomon's Paradox: Self-distancing eliminates the self-other asymmetry in wise reasoning about close relationships in younger and older adults. *Psychological Science, 25*, 1571–1580. https://doi.org/10.1177/0956797614535400

Grossmann, I., Kung, F. Y. H., & Santos, H. C. (2019). Wisdom as state versus trait. In R. J. Sternberg & J. Glück (Eds.), *The Cambridge Handbook of Wisdom* (pp. 249–273). New York: Cambridge University Press. https://doi.org/10.1017/9781108568272.013

Grossmann, I., Na, J., Varnum, M. E. W., Park, D. C., Kitayama, S., & Nisbett, R. E. (2010). Reasoning about social conflicts improves into old age. *Proceedings of the National Academy of Sciences of the United States of America, 107*, 7246–7250. doi:10.1073/pnas.1001715107

Grossmann, I., Weststrate, N. M., Ardelt, M., . . .Vervaeke, J. (2020). The science of wisdom in a polarized world: Knowns and unknowns. *Psychological Inquiry, 31*, 1–31. doi:10.1080/1047840X.2020.1750917

Hankin, B. L., Stone, L., & Wright, P. A. (2010). Corumination, interpersonal stress generation, and internalizing symptoms: Accumulating effects and transactional influences in a multiwave study of adolescents. *Development and Psychopathology, 22*, 217–235.

Hofmann, S. G., Moscovitch, D. A., Kim, H. J., & Taylor, A. N. (2004). Changes in self-perception during treatment of social phobia. *Journal of Consulting and Clinical Psychology, 72*, 588–596.

Huynh, A. C., Oakes, H., Shay, G. R., & McGregor, I. (2017). The wisdom in virtue: Pursuit of virtue predicts wise reasoning about personal conflicts. *Psychological Science, 28*, 1848–1856.

Huynh, A. C., Yang, D. Y. J., & Grossmann, I. (2016). The value of prospective reasoning for close relationships. *Social Psychological and Personality Science, 7*, 893–902. https://doi.org/10.1177/19485 50616660591

Infurna, F. J., & Luthar, S. S. (2016). Resilience to major life stressors is not as common as thought. *Perspectives on Psychological Science, 11*, 175–194

Jayawickreme, E., & Blackie, L. E. (2014). Post-traumatic growth as positive personality change: Evidence, controversies and future directions. *European Journal of Personality, 28*, 312–331.

Jayawickreme, E., & Blackie, L. E. R. (2016). *Exploring the Psychological Benefits of Hardship*. New York: Springer. doi:10.1007/978-3-319-47989-7_5

Jayawickreme, E., & Fleeson, W. (2017). Does whole trait theory work for the virtues? In W. Sinnott-Armstrong & C.B. Miller (Eds.), *Moral Psychology, Volume V: Virtue and Happiness* (pp. 75–103). Cambridge, MA: MIT Press.

Karlsen, S., & Nazroo, J. Y. (2002). Relation between racial discrimination, social class, and health among ethnic minority groups. *American Journal of Public Health, 92*, 624–631, https://doi.org/10.2105/AJPH.92.4.624

Kross, E., & Ayduk, O. (2017). Self-distancing: Theory, research and current directions. In J. Olson & M. Zanna (Eds.), *Advances in Experimental Social Psychology* (Vol. 55, pp. 81–136). Cambridge, MA: Academic Press.

Kross, E., Ayduk, O., & Mischel, W. (2005). When asking "why" does not hurt distinguishing rumination from reflective processing of negative emotions. *Psychological Science, 16*, 709–715.

Kross, E., Bruehlman-Senecal, E., Park, J., Burson, A., Dougherty, A., Shablack, H., . . . Ayduk, O. (2014). Self-talk as a regulatory mechanism: How you do it matters. *Journal of Personality and Social Psychology, 106*, 304–324.

Kross, E., & Grossmann, I. (2012). Boosting wisdom: Distance from the self enhances wise reasoning, attitudes, and behavior. *Journal of Experimental Psychology: General, 141*, 43–48.

Lazarus, R. S. (2006). Emotions and interpersonal relationships: Toward a person-centered conceptualization of emotions and coping. *Journal of Personality, 74*, 9–46.

Lazarus, R. S., & Alfert, E. (1964). Short-circuiting of threat by experimentally altering cognitive appraisal. *Journal of Abnormal and Social Psychology, 69*, 195–205.

Lyubomirsky, S., & Nolen-Hoeksema, S. (1995). Effects of self-focused rumination on negative thinking and interpersonal problem solving. *Journal of Personality and Social Psychology, 69*, 176–190. https:// doi.org/10.1037/0022-3514.69.1

McAdams, D. P., & Olson, B. D. (2010). Personality development: Continuity and change over the life course. *Annual Review of Psychology, 61*, 517–542.

McIsaac, H. K., & Eich, E. (2004). Vantage point in traumatic memory. *Psychological Science, 15*, 248–253. https://doi.org/10.1111/j.0956-7976.2004.00660.x

McLean, C. P., & Foa, E. B. (2017). Emotions and emotion regulation in posttraumatic stress disorder. *Current Opinion in Psychology, 14*, 72–77.

McRae, K., Jacobs, S. E., Ray, R. D., John, O. P., & Gross, J. J. (2012). Individual differences in reappraisal ability: Links to reappraisal frequency, well-being, and cognitive control. *Journal of Research in Personality, 46*, 2–7.

Morawetz, C., Bode, S., Derntl, B., & Heekeren, H. R. (2017). The effect of strategies, goals and stimulus material on the neural mechanisms of emotion regulation: A meta-analysis of fMRI studies. *Neuroscience & Biobehavioral Reviews, 72*, 111–128.

Moscovitch, D. A., Gavric, D. L., Senn, J., Santesso, D. L., Miskovic, V., Schmidt, L. A., . . . Antony, M. M. (2012). Changes in judgment biases and use of emotion regulation strategies during cognitive-behavioral therapy for social anxiety disorder: Distinguishing treatment responders from nonresponders. *Cognitive Therapy and Research, 36*, 261–271.

Nigro, G., & Neisser, U. (1983). Point of view in personal memories. *Cognitive Psychology, 15*, 467–482. https://doi. org/10.1016/0010-0285(83)90016-6

Nolen-Hoeksema, S., & Morrow, J. (1991). A prospective study of depression and posttraumatic stress symptoms after a natural disaster: The 1989 Loma Prieta Earthquake. *Journal of Personality and Social Psychology, 61*, 115–121.

Nolen-Hoeksema, S., Wisco, B. E., & Lyubomirsky, S. (2008). Rethinking rumination. *Perspectives on Psychological Science, 3*, 400–424. https://doi.org/10.1111/j.1745-6924.2008.00088.x

Nook, E. C., Schleider, J. L., & Somerville, L. H. (2017). A linguistic signature of psychological distancing in emotion regulation. *Journal of Experimental Psychology: General, 146*, 337–346. https://doi. org/10.1037/xge0000263

Pals, J. L., & McAdams, D. P. (2004). The transformed self: A narrative understanding of posttraumatic growth. *Psychological Inquiry, 15*, 65–69.

Park, C. L. (2010). Making sense of the meaning literature: An integrative review of meaning making and its effects on adjustment to stressful life events. *Psychological Bulletin, 136*, 257–301. https:// doi.org/10.1037/a0018301

Pennebaker, J. W. (1997). Writing about emotional experiences as a therapeutic process. *Psychological Science, 8*, 162–166.

Peterson, C., & Seligman, M. E. P. (2004). *Character Strengths and Virtues: A Handbook and Classification*. Washington, DC: American Psychological Association.

Powell, S., Rosner, R., Butollo, W., Tedeschi, R. G., & Calhoun, L. G. (2003). Posttraumatic growth after war: A study with former refugees and displaced people in Sarajevo. *Journal of Clinical Psychology, 59*, 71–83.

Pronin, E., & Ross, L. (2006). Temporal differences in trait self-ascription: When the self is seen as another. *Journal of Personality and Social Psychology, 90*, 197–209. doi:10.1037/0022-3514.90.2.197

Reimer, S. G., & Moscovitch, D. A. (2015). The impact of imagery rescripting on memory appraisals and core beliefs in social anxiety disorder. *Behaviour Research and Therapy, 75*, 48–59.

Robinson, J. A., & Swanson, K. L. (1993). Field and observer modes of remembering. *Memory, 1*, 169–184.

Roepke, A. M., Jayawickreme, E., & Riffle, O. M. (2014). Meaning and health: A systematic review. *Applied Research in Quality of Life, 9*, 1055–1079. https://doi.org/10.1007/s11482-013-9288-9

Romano, M., Moscovitch, D. A., Huppert, J. D., Reimer, S. G., & Moscovitch, M. (2020). The effects of imagery rescripting on memory outcomes in social anxiety disorder. *Journal of Anxiety Disorders, 69*, 102169.

Santos, H. C., & Grossmann, I. (2021). Cross-temporal exploration of the relationship between wisdom-related cognitive broadening and subjective well-being: Evidence from a cross-validated national longitudinal study. *Social Psychological and Personality Science, 12*(4), 506–516.

Santos, H. C., Huynh, A. C., & Grossmann, I. (2017). Wisdom in a complex world: A situated account of wise reasoning and its development. *Social and Personality Psychology Compass*. doi:10.1111/spc3.12341

Shakespeare-Finch, J., & Enders, T. (2008). Corroborating evidence of posttraumatic growth. *Journal of Traumatic Stress, 21*, 421–424.

Sheppes, G., Scheibe, S., Suri, G., & Gross, J. J. (2011). Emotion-regulation choice. *Psychological Science, 22*, 1391–1396.

Smith, C. A., & Kirby, L. D. (2009). Putting appraisal in context: Toward a relational model of appraisal and emotion. *Cognition and Emotion, 23*, 1352–1372.

Staudinger, U. M., & Baltes, P. B. (1996). Interactive minds: A facilitative setting for wisdom-related performance?. *Journal of Personality and Social Psychology, 71*, 746–762.

Staudinger, U. M., & Glück, J. (2011). Psychological wisdom research: Commonalities and differences in a growing field. *Annual Review of Psychology, 62*, 215–241.

Sternberg, R., & Jordan, J. (Eds.). (2005). *A Handbook of Wisdom: Psychological Perspectives*. New York: Cambridge University Press.

Swartwood, J., & Tiberius, V. (2019). Philosophical foundations of wisdom. In R. Sternberg & J. Gluek (Eds.), *The Cambridge Handbook of Wisdom* (pp. 10–39). Cambridge: Cambridge University Press.

Tackman, A. M., Sbarra, D. A., Carey, A. L., Donnellan, M. B., Horn, A. B., Holtzman, N. S., . . . Mehl, M. R. (2019). Depression, negative emotionality, and self-referential language: A multi-lab, multi-measure, and multi-language-task research synthesis. *Journal of Personality and Social Psychology, 116*, 817–834. https://doi. org/10.1037/pspp0000187

Tedeschi, R. G., & Calhoun, L. G. (1996). The Posttraumatic Growth Inventory: Measuring the positive legacy of trauma. *Journal of Traumatic Stress, 9*, 455–471.

Tedeschi, R. G., & Calhoun, L. G. (2004). Posttraumatic growth: Conceptual foundations and empirical evidence. *Psychological Inquiry, 15*, 1–18.

Troy, A. S., Wilhelm, F. H., Shallcross, A. J., & Mauss, I. B. (2010). Seeing the silver lining: Cognitive reappraisal ability moderates the relationship between stress and depressive symptoms. *Emotion, 10*, 783–795.

Vasquez, N. A., & Buehler, R. (2007). Seeing future success: Does imagery perspective influence achievement motivation?. *Personality and Social Psychology Bulletin, 33*, 1392–1405.

Webb, T. L., Miles, E., & Sheeran, P. (2012). Dealing with feeling: A meta-analysis of the effectiveness of strategies derived from the process model of emotion regulation. *Psychological Bulletin, 138*, 775–808.

Widows, M. R., Jacobsen, P. B., Booth-Jones, M., & Fields, K. K. (2005). Predictors of posttraumatic growth following bone marrow transplantation for cancer. *Health Psychology, 24*, 266–273.

Wu, S., & Keysar, B. (2007). The effect of culture on perspective taking. *Psychological Science, 18*, 600–606. https://doi. org/10.1111/j.1467-9280.2007.01946.x

16

Redesigning Research on Post-Traumatic Growth

Current Knowledge and New Directions

FRANK J. INFURNA AND ERANDA JAYAWICKREME ■

A cultural narrative has emerged that suggests exposure to adversity could—and in certain cases *should*—lead to personal growth. From Paul Tough's popular *New York Times* magazine article, "What If the Secret to Success Is Failure?" (Tough, 2011) to Jessica Lahey's book *The Gift of Failure* (Lahey, 2015), people are encouraged to embrace failure and the potential for positive downstream effects. This belief is best expressed by Friedrich Nietzsche's famous quote, "From life's school of war: What does not kill me makes me stronger." Embedded within these cultural narratives and statements is the notion that adversity can potentially lead to the strengthening of character and virtue development. These narratives have found some support in research on post-traumatic growth (PTG; e.g., Tedeschi & Calhoun, 2004). Yet, despite the promise of adversity potentially leading to meaningful character growth, a significant limitation with PTG research is that it lacks robust empirical evidence of support (Infurna & Jayawickreme, 2019; Jayawickreme & Blackie, 2014; Jayawickreme et al., 2021). An overwhelming number of the studies examining PTG have been cross-sectional or used research designs with retrospective self-perceived assessment. Additionally, while research on the structure and development of character as well as specific character strengths and virtues has grown significantly in the past 15 years (Fleeson et al., 2015; Jayawickreme & Fleeson, 2017a,b), relatively little is still known about which specific characteristics may respond to and potentially grow in response to specific features of adversity, challenge, or failure.

This edited volume has the ambitious goal of outlining the next generation of research on the possibilities for growth following adversity. The origins of this volume lie in the Pathways to Character Project, a major initiative based at

Arizona State University and Wake Forest University that we co-led between 2016 and 2019, with the goal of improving the quality of PTG research. While the idea that growth is possible following adversity, especially during the COVID-19 pandemic of 2020–2021 (the context in which this volume came together), provides a hopeful and optimistic view of how individuals are able to cope, grow, and move past adversity, it currently lacks robust empirical evidence of support. Despite the predominance of cultural narratives promoting such beliefs as well as several decades of research on PTG and resilience, a number of important empirical questions remain unanswered and were the target of the funding competition we ran as part of this Project, which included,

1. Is it possible for our character to grow following adversity, challenge, or failure possible?
2. Can we accurately conceptualize and prospectively assess character growth following adversity, challenge, or failure, and, if so, how?

These two big questions were the focus of the Request for Proposals (RFP) that aimed to stimulate research on the significance of character growth and adversity and ultimately provide greater clarity in the literature. This edited volume features contributions from each of the research projects involved in the RFP, in addition to chapters from leading scholars in the field of PTG. We hope this volume fills an important gap in the literature by examining key conceptual and methodological considerations centered on PTG. Specifically, this volume will provide a comprehensive overview of current limitations in research on PTG, highlight research that addresses these limitations, and provide a clear roadmap for how methodologically rigorous basic and applied research on this topic should be conducted. In accomplishing this task, we are hopeful that this volume will have a transformative impact on the field by setting new standards for high-quality research on this topic.

In this final chapter, we provide an overview of key topics that were covered in the RFP and reflected in each of the chapters. We first discuss the importance of studying adversity and why character strengths could have the potential to change and, for that matter, potentially grow following adversity. We then provide a brief overview of each of the four major questions that are the focus of this volume: (1) current challenges in examining PTG, (2) methodological advancements (with a focus on innovative assessment strategies), (3) research in specific populations, and (4) new directions for research.

WHY IS IT IMPORTANT TO STUDY THE POTENTIAL POSITIVE IMPACT OF ADVERSITY, CHALLENGES, AND FAILURES?

Over the course of the life span, individuals encounter adversities, life challenges, or traumas that may qualitatively change their life circumstances (Hultsch &

Plemons, 1979). Different types of life challenges that have been defined in the literature include daily stressors (e.g., challenges at home or work), adverse life events (e.g., bereavement, unemployment), chronic stressors (e.g., living with significant illness, caregiving for a family member), and clinical trauma (e.g., being involved in a major accident). These life challenges are uniquely characterized by discrete and, in principle, observable environmental and social changes (Dohrenwend, 2006). These changes are potentially threatening because they precipitate the need for adjustment in identity or life routines (Gray, Litz, Hsu, & Lombardo, 2004; Turner & Wheaton, 1995). More specific examples include challenges at the workplace that accumulate over time, loss of one's spouse or child, marital separation/divorce, or health adversities like cancer recovery and disability. Epidemiological studies have shown that the lifetime prevalence of such adversities or traumas is 75%, and each year, one in five persons is likely to experience an adversity or trauma (Kessler, Sonnega, Bromet, Hughes, & Nelson, 1995).

Consistent across these adversities is their potential to have long-lasting impacts, both good and bad. Various trajectories or courses of changes that have been identified following such adversities include the extent to which individuals are able to overcome and bounce back (recovery), maintain previous levels of functioning (resilient), or show improvements in functioning (growth). The resilience (Infurna & Luthar, 2018; Luthar, Cicchetti, & Becker, 2000; Masten & Narayan, 2012) and PTG (Jayawickreme & Blackie, 2014; Jayawickreme et al., 2021) literatures go hand in hand in this regard, providing conceptual and methodological frameworks to study change as a function of adversity and factors that promote positive outcomes such as PTG and resilience.

As a result of the great amount of interest in research on PTG and resilience, cultural narratives have emerged that focus on the typical response that individuals *should* display following an adversity or trauma. For example, the resilience literature in adulthood and old age has proposed that resilience, defined as exhibiting stable, healthy levels of psychological functioning before and after adversity, is the most common response to adversity. However, this dialogue is problematic because if individuals struggle for a period of time following the adversity, this can invoke discussions of blaming the victim; recent research has countered such claims by documenting that this research is a function of methodological assumptions and that, instead, a recovery trajectory characteristic of declines as a result of the adversity followed by a return back to previous levels over time is the most common response to adversity (Infurna & Luthar, 2016, 2018). A similar narrative has emerged in the PTG literature, with research proclaiming that some good should come out of tragedy as evinced by most individuals reporting that they had experienced growth to some degree following adversity/trauma (Joseph, 2011). For example, PTG research suggests that as many as 70% of survivors of various forms of trauma report experiencing positive changes in at least one domain of life (Linley & Joseph, 2004). However, a notable limitation of this research is the extensive use of the Post-Traumatic Growth Inventory (PTGI), a retrospective assessment that is frequently used in cross-sectional studies. The primary limitation of the PTGI is that it is a mentally taxing procedure: it requires people to make causal attributions of personality change to specific adversity, which is a problematic procedure (Nisbett & Wilson, 1977), and the measure may reflect the ability to find perceived silver linings as opposed to representing lasting and genuine transformation, which prevents its effectiveness in determining whether growth actually occurred (for discussion, see Jayawickreme & Blackie, 2014).

The research literature on PTG and resilience has been instrumental in documenting the human capacity to overcome adversity by illuminating that there are different pathways following adversity, including (but not limited to) resilience, recovery, and growth. There is continued and increased interest in these literatures, as shown by recent debates and controversies coming to light (see Infurna & Luthar, 2016; Jayawickreme & Blackie, 2014). The recent debates highlight numerous important avenues to pursue in the PTG and resilience literatures. For example, these literatures need greater clarity, specifically in the examination of claims that growth should come out of tragedy (e.g., Does growth occur when studied prospectively?) and the domains through which growth is likely to manifest as a function of adversity. One of the overarching goals of this edited volume is to provide clarity to such claims that growth is possible and should occur in character strengths and virtues for individuals following adversity.

The second Big Question focuses on the possibilities for assessing character growth following adversity. The PTG literature has unfortunately focused almost exclusively on retrospective reports in the examination of whether growth is actually evident following adversity (for discussion, see Jayawickreme & Blackie, 2014). PTG has been theorized as a process (Tedeschi & Calhoun, 2004) and, given this, requires a methodological design to match the theory/concept. PTG is broadly considered positive *enduring* change or improvements in psychological functioning following adversity (Jayawickreme & Blackie, 2014; Tedeschi & Calhoun, 2004). Our views align with PTG having to be the study of actual change versus retrospective self-perceived change as assessed through the PTGI, which assesses five domains of growth: appreciation of life, new possibilities, personal strength, spiritual change, and relatedness with others. In this regard, to examine the degree to which growth occurs following adversity, prospective longitudinal data is *essential* (Tennen & Affleck, 2009). In one of the few prospective examinations, Frazier and colleagues (2009) found that perceived change does not translate to actual change; their methodological approach permitted the study of how individuals change from before and after the adversity experienced. The Frazier and colleagues (2009) study was instrumental because it had closely spaced prospective data, putting it in the position to study short-term changes over a 2-month period of time. Similarly, Blackie, Jayawickreme, and colleagues (2017) comprehensively examined the structure of the PTGI domains at one point in time (i.e., between-person level) and its concordance to fluctuations in these domains in daily life (i.e., within-person level; Jayawickreme et al., 2017) through the use of experience sampling methodology. The authors found that the PTGI domains assessed retrospectively following an experienced adversity (as has been overwhelmingly assessed in the literature) were not associated with the experience of PTGI domains from day to day (with the single exception of spirituality); these findings reinforce notions that self-perceived retrospective growth does not translate to its manifestation in daily life (for further discussion, see Fleeson, 2014). This line of thinking is along the lines suggested by Clement and Bollinger (2016), who discussed the importance of longitudinal data for disentangling whether character strengths and virtues are distinct from one another and whether they co-develop. Another important idea discussed by Clement and Bollinger (2016) was the notion of what individual differences or experiences contribute to the emergence of one specific character strength and not the other. With prospective longitudinal data, these types of research questions can begin to be answered. Our hope is that the collective projects from the RFP will be able to shed light on the potential of PTG when studied using prospective longitudinal data.

THE ROLE OF ADVERSITY IN CHARACTER DEVELOPMENT

The research literature examining change following adversity has thus far been dominated by well-being and mental health outcomes (i.e., anxiety, depressive symptoms, life satisfaction, posttraumatic stress; for discussions, see Helzer & Jayawickreme, 2015; Infurna & Luthar, 2018). Much less is known regarding whether growth in character strengths and virtues is possible following adversity, challenge, or failure, as well as whether the nature of growth is tied to specific domains of functioning and the adversity experienced. This notion of multidimensionality is drawn from life span (Baltes, 1987), resilience (Luthar, Doemberger, & Zigler, 1993), relational developmental systems meta-theory (Lerner & Callina, 2014), and PTG (Miller, 2014) literatures. Miller (2014) addresses the notion of "across the board" PTG, or, put differently, where we should draw the line in terms of domains to assess PTG. In a recent examination, Infurna and Luthar (2017) examined resilience to spousal loss across five relevant domains—life satisfaction (66%), positive affect (26%), negative affect (19%), general health (37%), and physical functioning (28%)—and found stark differences in the proportion deemed resilient across domains (in parentheses). When considered together, only 8% of individuals showed "across the board" resilience, whereas 20% did not show resilience across all five outcomes considered. One can apply this multidimensional approach and reasoning to examine which domains are more or less likely to exhibit growth following specific adversities and the extent to which growth coexists with resilience and recovery. It may be that certain character virtues are more likely to show growth following specific adversities and that growth in certain character virtues is more likely to coexist with resilience, recovery, and positive mental health.

For the purposes of the RFP, we hypothesize that altruism, humility, gratitude, relatedness/empathy, spirituality, and open-mindedness (a key component of wisdom) may be key character strengths and virtues that are likely to show growth through adversity, challenge, or failure. Part of our interest in these specific character strengths and virtues is that while the past few years have seen an increased interest in the scientific assessment and exploration of character virtues (Campbell,

Jayawickreme, & Hanson, 2015; Fleeson et al., 2014; Peterson & Seligman, 2004; McGrath, 2015), *little is known about both the developmental trajectory of such traits and the possible role that adversity may have in acting as a catalyst for change.* Conceptual work points to these virtues being most likely to be sensitive to the experience of adversity, challenge, and failure (Jayawickreme & Blackie, 2016; Tiberius, 2008). Furthermore, limited empirical evidence suggests that these character strengths and virtues could potentially grow as a function of adversity. For example, Peterson and Seligman (2003) observed that, following the terrorist attacks of September 11, 2001, the virtues of gratitude, hope, kindness, leadership, love, spirituality, and teamwork showed growth up to 10 months following the attacks. Similarly, Frazier and colleagues (2009) observed that a subset of individuals exhibited growth over a 2-month period, following a clinical trauma, in positive relations with others, meaning in life, life satisfaction, gratitude, and religious commitment. Furthermore, theoretical notions also detail how altruism could be born of suffering (Vollhardt, 2009). Therefore, while character strengths and virtues have shown the potential to change, more research is needed.

As described earlier, character strengths and virtues broadly encompass what is right about people and specifically about what makes the good life possible. These are core characteristics and psychological ingredients that are ubiquitously recognized and valued across individuals, communities, and societies (Peterson & Seligman, 2004). People who possess a deep understanding of these character strengths can potentially enter into heightened spiritual states of consciousness and imbue their daily activities with a sense of the divine (Emmons, 1999). One important question that has yet to be answered satisfactorily is whether and how these character virtues can be fostered and developed through the experience of adversity, challenge or failure. We therefore view character strengths and virtues as important outcomes to study because they pertain directly to whether and how individuals relate (1) directly with one another, (2) to their immediate and distal context, and (3) more broadly, with their community and society.

This volume therefore fills an important gap in the literature by examining key conceptual and methodological considerations pertaining to PTG. Specifically, this volume will provide a comprehensive overview of current limitations in research on PTG, highlight research that addresses these limitations, and provide a clear roadmap for how methodologically rigorous basic and applied research on this topic should be conducted. In accomplishing this task, we are hopeful that this volume will have a transformative impact on the field by setting new standards for high-quality research on this topic.

We next briefly summarize the main take-home points from each chapter across the four sections of the edited volume.

CURRENT CHALLENGES IN EXAMINING PTG

Tiberius tackles the question of PTG through a philosophical lens. In Chapter 1, her focus is on evaluating the concepts that are linked to PTG, intertwining discussion of various well-being outcomes that are pertinent to study, and ending with a discussion of measurement issues for research on PTG. She discusses how philosophers use the term "thick concepts" for concepts that are used both to report the facts *and* convey an evaluation of those facts. Concepts that merely describe the facts (e.g., "square") or concepts that mere convey evaluations (e.g., "good") are "thin concepts." The word "growth" is considered a thick concept and defined in terms of "increasing, developing, or maturing," which is naturally interpreted teleologically: something that is growing is making progress toward its natural telos. The word has a positive evaluative spin. "Change" is not like this. Something may change for the better or the worse, and no particular direction is implied when the word is used.

In thinking about PTG, the concept of change infers that there needs to be something that is studied that could change. Here, Tiberius discusses various theories and orientations toward studying well-being, including psychological concepts pertaining to life satisfaction and the philosophical theories of hedonism, objective list theories, and desire satisfaction theories. When it comes to indicators/ingredients of well-being, there are numerous to choose from, and it largely depends on one's orientation and judgment, which could include happiness, health, friendship and family relationships, meaningful work, personal liberty, pleasure, and virtues of various kinds. Tiberius ends by discussing solutions to examining the different components of well-being, such as the use of multiple methods ranging from self- and informant-report to qualitative interviews.

In Chapter 2, Park and Boals cover various important components, ranging from the various measures of perceived and actual PTG to limitations of these measures, mixed results when trying to validate self-reports of PTG, and efforts to modify measures to reduce bias, and they end with suggestions for future research. The core components of their chapter focus on the topics of the most widely used measures of self-report for PTG, their limitations, and ways to reduce their bias toward reporting growth. Their focus then moves to discussing what the measures of PTG actually tap into and assess that concept. For us, the biggest take-home message from Park and Boals is their discussion of measurement validation. They write that current assessments of PTG "omitted a key step in standard psychological science: Validation of the self-report instruments used to assess the construct." This is an absolutely critical component when conducting research, one that is often overlooked and taken for granted. The methodology behind what we are studying is of utmost importance. The PTG research in the late 1980s and early 1990s took off after initial research showing the potential for growth following adversity using retrospective assessment; however, when researchers began raising issues with the approach, it unfortunately fell on deaf ears. We hope this edited volume helps change the narrative and methodology toward studying PTG.

In Chapter 3, Roepke and colleagues tackle the issue of whether PTG can be initiated via intervention. They discuss challenges and criticism of PTG intervention research, intervention approaches ranging from cognitive-behavioral therapy (CBT) or narrative writing, and psychosocial and educational programs, and they end the chapter by focusing on methodological considerations for PTG, such as more nuanced measurement; examining growth, distress, and their relationships; minding multiple comparisons; careful selection of control groups; mediation and moderation; and quality standards for reporting RCTs.

Given the challenging circumstances of COVID-19, discussion centering on measurement issues pertaining to PTG and the potential negative consequences from intentionally targeting PTG in interventions is especially pertinent. People may not be ready just now, if ever, to PTG following adversity. Various interventions tested in randomized controlled trial (RCT) designs have been found to raise scores on the PTGI or similar retrospective self-report measures. However, several important questions remain unanswered, including the difference between self-perceived PTG versus other indicators of PTG: Do our interventions only influence self-perceptions? Or do they also help people to grow and change in ways that might be reflected in behavior and observable to those around them? Do they impact personality traits and the expression of those traits in daily life (e.g., becoming more agreeable or more open to experience)? Do they change an individual's level of functioning in well-being domains and PTG-relevant domains (e.g., meaning in life, gratitude, or intimacy)?

METHODOLOGICAL ADVANCEMENTS

In Chapter 4, Baez and colleagues take the approach of examining PTG and character strengths in the context of dynamic theories of personality. These theories broadly focus on the distribution of states, which represent one's personality, and accumulation of state, which explains one's state distribution. To examine these processes, researchers can harness the utility of cognitive and behavioral neuroscience to consider the factors that contribute to PTG.

An additional focus is the myriad of ways for collecting data beyond that of self-report. Their discussion in this regard focuses on using mHealth (or ambulatory assessment) methods, which refer to a set of methods for collecting data "in the field" as individuals traverse everyday life. Typical methods include (1) ecological momentary assessment (EMA), which can involve sending an SMS message containing a URL which leads to a self-report survey several times throughout the day for a period of days or weeks; (2) geolocation, which passively tracks an individual's movements; and (3) other movement (pedometer/accelerometer) data. Timing of measurements is critical in relation to PTG in the context of adversity—too frequently or not frequently enough may lead to missing out on potential changes. Another point of consideration that they elaborate is privacy: with the treasure trove of data that can be collected, it needs to be safely stored. Analyzing this data can take the form of multilevel modeling and network modeling, among numerous other methods.

In Chapter 5, Jayawickreme and Mendonça provide an overview of how methodological and theoretical innovations in personality psychology can be utilized in the service of developing a more robust science of PTG. Methods such as informant assessments and experience sampling methodology (ESM) can help corroborate people's narratives of perceived growth and allow for the in-depth examination of how changes following adversity can be detected in daily life. Moreover, recent advances in personality dynamics (which examine how and why people systematically change their thoughts, feelings, and behavior over time) point the way toward more plausible theoretical accounts for how adversity can lead to enduring positive personality change.

In Chapter 6, Laceulle and colleagues approach to and research design for PTG is innovative for several reasons. Methodologically, they incorporate multiple methods for addressing their research questions, such as EMA, qualitative interviews, naturalistic audio recordings, and focus groups, and they use active community participation to ensure the findings are relevant for their population of interest: Syrian refugees. Exposure to adversity may trigger a range of emotional experiences such as sorrow, guilt, trepidation, nostalgia, compassion, gratitude, and love. These emotional experiences, in turn, may drive personality change. The research project by Laceulle and colleagues, named Karakter, is a 13-month longitudinal study examining how emotional experiences in everyday life may contribute to the link between adversity and personality change in Syrian-origin young adults who have recently resettled in the Netherlands. An important point to highlight is the need for cultural sensitivity when initiating such a project. The goals of this project are advanced through creating a partnership with young adults of Syrian origin. The research team organized a cultural advisory board that included people of Syrian heritage or who held expertise in interacting with Syrian youth in the Netherlands, which helped build trust in the community and further advance their active community participation approach.

In Chapter 7, Luong and colleagues focus their attention on the examination of PTG in older adults who are making the transition to an assisted living facility. It is no secret that the population is graying, and their study targets a transition that is not intensively studied but is important because of the multiple components involved and the disruptions it may cause. To study the extent to which PTG is possible during this transition, they utilize a multiple time scale research design. This involves repeated "bursts" of assessment, where participants complete questionnaires at four different time points: one before the transition and three in the months thereafter. Within each "burst," participants complete a 7-day EMA that involves assessments of well-being and character strengths. The benefits of this research design involve its ability to examine both more global aspects of PTG and, more importantly, aspects of character strengths at the daily level of assessments. Furthermore, the rich data source that will be compiled through this design will afford the researchers the ability to utilize cutting-edge methods for statistical analyses in the family of differential equation modeling and vector autoregressive contexts, such as GIMME frameworks and regime-switching models. Each of these statistical methods of analysis are known for its ability to examine how individuals are changing continuously over time. The study is also embedded in the community that it serves and employs a community-based participatory research design. This approach blends the movement toward evidence-based practice with the expertise and experience of practitioners in service settings. This will provide mutual benefit by integrating academic and service settings for the betterment of the community.

RESEARCH IN SPECIFIC POPULATIONS

In Chapter 8, Cheung and colleagues focus on how individuals and couples are impacted by and able to effectively manage a cancer diagnosis. Their discussion begins by discussing how findings in the literature examining PTG in the context of cancer diagnosis are mixed and have relied heavily on the use of the retrospective PTGI. They also elaborate on theoretical debates and methodological considerations within this research arena. Some of the theoretical models posit that positive changes in relation to cancer are illusory, whereas others argue that PTG is real due to an individual's struggle with trauma or adversity leading to the reconstruction of basic beliefs and world assumptions. The rest of their chapter focuses on how their research project aims to overcome previous limitations in the literature by developing a dyadic model of character growth in the context of cancer diagnosis. As they discuss, previous studies have primarily examined positive changes in the cancer patient and caregiver as separate, parallel processes and have not considered a shared interpersonal context or whether a cancer diagnosis can lead to positive changes in a relationship. Their prospective longitudinal research design involves repeated assessments of both the patient and caregiver across many character strengths and relationship strengths, with the goal of identifying whether there are discrete profiles of character and couple growth in cancer patients and caregivers following a cancer diagnosis.

In Chapter 9, White and colleagues focus on how PTG may constitute something different across cultures/minority groups. They argue how incorporating culturally and contextually informed theorizing into PTG is essential. Such an approach can advance the literature by providing an overview of how culturally informed theorizing can support sophisticated psychological research designs. They discuss how contextually informed theorizing is the process of developing ideas about the ways in which variables that describe within- and between-setting diversity might intersect with existing psychological knowledge and/or theory related to PTG.

Culturally and contextually informed theorizing should be the basis for selecting a study's design via its impact on the development of research questions and hypotheses. White and colleagues are applying this rationale to their work with Mexicans in the United States to identify, for example, (a) the relevant mechanisms for growth, (b) the types of adversities we should assess, and (c) the possible domains of growth to consider. Furthermore, culturally and contextually informed theorizing can be used to delineate appropriate sampling frames and samples derived from a target bounded group-community. There may be within-group heterogeneity in the characteristics and outcomes of interest in the group-community even if the sample is homogenous based on minority status. These types of research designs additionally require the potential need to have multiple-language versions of available measures and must address measurement equivalence, which is a question of the similarity of reliability and construct validity of a measure across two or more groups. The chapter provides a guidepost for researchers who are interested in examining research questions pertaining to PTG in the context of persons from various cultures or minority groups.

In Chapter 10, Chopik focuses his discussion in on modeling PTG and resilience among military personnel using large-scale longitudinal panel surveys. He additionally devotes time and attention to how using different statistical models can yield different results, thereby greatly influencing one's findings. He starts out by discussing the advantages of using longitudinal panel surveys over cross-sectional designs, which include being able to prospectively examine change over a period of time, have access to large sample sizes that preclude the use of many longitudinal research methods, and the ability to model the mechanisms that give rise to character development.

To illustrate his arguments pertaining to statistical modeling he provides an example of how analytic flexibility can influence findings. Analytic flexibility focuses on traditional, longer term change among individuals assessed over multiple years and does so by examining whether and how disability impacts well-being on veterans' depressive symptoms. The two analytic approaches include the use of multilevel modeling and growth mixture modeling. Multilevel modeling has the advantage of examining within-person changes in depressive symptoms before and after disability onset and assessing the extent to which between-person changes occur in levels and rates of change in depressive symptoms. Advantages include the modeling of within-person change at the population-level and, if between-person differences exist, the inclusion of predictors of levels and rates of change. Growth mixture modeling allows researchers to examine whether there are distinct subgroups within the data that show specific trajectories of change before and after adversity onset. Recent considerations have shown that, depending on the methodological assumptions, this greatly influences the findings. Chopik uses data from the Health and Retirement Study to illustrate how the use of each of these methods can impact the interpretation and take-home message arising from the findings.

In Chapter 11, Staben and colleagues focus on important conceptual and methodological considerations when conducting PTG research in samples consisting of adults in midlife and old age. Conceptually, the authors focus their attention on discussing theoretical and empirical age-related trends of character strengths that are most relevant to midlife and older adults, and they highlight key areas of research, namely, longitudinal examination of character strengths and the stability of these strengths. Methodologically, the focus is on the measurement equivalence of the measures of character strengths that are commonly used to determine PTG. Many measures of character strengths, such as meaning-making and gratitude, were developed on samples of undergraduates who are typically between the ages of 18 and 25. When using these constructs in samples consisting of persons in adulthood and old age, researchers are assuming that they are measuring the same construct. Some scales, like meaning-making, do, whereas others do not. This importantly demonstrates that although a measure has been established, it is an open question as to whether the scale is measuring the same construct across population groups. For example, gratitude may connote something different across young adulthood, midlife, and old age, which could lead to different conclusions being drawn.

NEW DIRECTIONS FOR RESEARCH

In Chapter 12, Luhmann and Fassbender focus on comparing and contrasting the typological approach to studying PTG using a dimensional approach that distinguishes events based on continuous characteristics instead of assigning them into distinct and mutually exclusive categories. In doing so, they discuss the Event Characteristics Questionnaire (ECQ), a novel scale developed to measure nine empirically derived event characteristics. They argue how, in the typological approach, major life events are assigned to distinct categories. For example, many studies distinguish between positive/desirable and negative/undesirable major life events. Similarly common is the approach to distinguish major life events based on the life domain (e.g., work-related events, family related events, or health-related events). They argue that the dimensional approach should be preferred over the typological approach to describe differences among major life events. The dimensional approach has several advantages. First, it permits empirical conclusions about which event characteristics are psychologically meaningful and which are not. Second, these conclusions can be generalized across different types of major life events. Third, this approach considers that major life events that may look similar to observers can be perceived very differently by those who experienced them. For instance, divorce can be an extremely adverse experience for one person but a bittersweet relief for another. By assessing how individuals perceived the event, rather than just recording whether a specific type of major life event has occurred, we can take this source of interindividual variability into account. Finally, prospective longitudinal studies on major life events are easier to conduct because not all participants have to experience exactly the same major life event as long as data on the perceived event characteristics can be collected.

Based on this motivation and study, they developed the ECQ. The ECQ was developed as a tool that could be applied to measure the characteristics of a wide range of different major life events without restrictions regarding valence, life domain, or severity. The authors focused on people's perceptions of event characteristics rather than on objective features of the events. Their goal was to develop a scale that was at the same time comprehensive (i.e., including all characteristics that were frequently discussed in the literature) and parsimonious (i.e., excluding characteristics that were irrelevant to distinguish major life events).

Chapter 13, by Forgeard and colleagues, focuses on openness to experience in the context of research on PTG. To stimulate future theoretical and empirical work in this area, their chapter reviews and discusses existing scientific research pertaining to changes in the personality trait of openness to experience following experiences of adversity. Studies using retrospective self-reports have shown that people judge themselves as more open following highly stressful events. Such research also suggests that changes in openness could even help foster more general psychological growth. Most longitudinal studies examining changes in personality over time have found no changes in openness following negative events. To help reconcile previous contradictory findings, they propose a methodological agenda including using multiple methods to assess openness, complementing correlational with longitudinal methods to examine changes over time, studying everyday manifestations of openness (including how people deal with everyday stressors), and investigating potential moderators and mediators of growth in this trait. Such research will help increase clarity about the circumstances under which people may (or may not) become more open as a result of adversity. Future research would benefit from using multiple methods when studying openness to experience in the context of PTG. This would involve going beyond retrospective self-reports by using longitudinal research designs that prospectively assess openness to experience and other outcomes of interest. Collecting in-the-moment assessments would enable researchers to better understand how openness is manifested at the state level and how shifts in the frequency and intensity of state-level openness may, over a longer period of time, produce changes at the trait level. Intensive longitudinal designs would permit for conjointly examining both major life stressors and minor stressors to allow an examination of not just how people's daily lives are affected by major adversity, but how it impacts minor stressors. This daily impact potentially could lead to long-term change.

In Chapter 14, Blackie and McLean discuss how written narratives could be a mechanism driving interpersonal failures and transgressions that ultimately lead to PTG. They begin their chapter by outlining how the PTG literature has suffered from several methodological limitations, with the most notable of these being the prevailing use of cross-sectional and retrospective study designs to test a theory that predicts change over time (Jayawickreme & Blackie, 2014). Current research into PTG has most conclusively demonstrated that people frequently self-report PTG after a diverse range of adversities (Linley & Joseph, 2004). Thus, people *believe* they have changed in the aftermath of adversity, but the question of whether they *change in some objective way beyond those beliefs* over time is an intriguing hypothesis still awaiting conclusive empirical investigation.

When discussing relevant outcomes, these authors explicitly focused on measured character traits that are relevant to the context of interpersonal failure, and thus they avoided making implicit assumptions about the homogeneity of PTG outcomes without due consideration to how the type of event influences character growth (Blalock et al., 2014); what Roberts (2011) has called the "launching outcome fragmentation grenades," where researchers assess a wide diversity of psychological outcomes to determine what works empirically instead of focusing on the most theoretically meaningful outcomes.

To address their research questions, they utilize a longitudinal research design that involves repeated assessments of individuals using global questionnaires, but also presents participants with the opportunity to write narratives pertaining to interpersonal failures and transgressions. By analyzing participants' written narratives, researchers are positioned to examine whether these self-reflective and ruminative processes are expressed organically in participants' own words and the impact of these narrative rumination styles on PTG (Blackie et al., 2017).

In Chapter 15, Dorfman and colleagues focus their attention on the importance of mindsets in the context of adversity. They start by discussing how, depending on one's cultural background, one's mindset may differ. For example, when spontaneously reflecting on past experiences, people, especially in North America, habitually adopt a self-immersed mindset. They tend to visualize the event through their own eyes, focusing on the specific details and emotions they experienced as the event was unfolding. However, research suggests that this type of self-immersed reflection is associated with narrow thinking, negative emotionality, distress, and depressive symptomatology. At the same time, one can also approach adverse experience via a self-distanced mindset, which involves "taking a step back" from the current experience. Although not habitual, people vary in the extent to which they adopt either mindset spontaneously, and they can also be trained to use either mindset. The mindset with which one approaches the adverse experience extends beyond emotion regulation to change in wisdom-related characteristics. A self-distanced mindset promotes a "big picture" view and reconstructive reasoning.

The authors conclude by providing an overview of how longitudinal studies that utilize a prospective longitudinal design are best positioned to examine whether adversity facilitates changes in wisdom characteristics. To this end, this research group has recently conducted several longitudinal investigations examining the prospective effects of adopting different mindsets on wisdom-related characteristics in the aftermath of adverse experiences. Participants who adopted the self-distanced mindset, but not participants who adopted the habitual self-immersed mindset, reported greater emotional dialecticism—an increasing importance of positive as well as negative emotions in adverse experiences over time. The ability of participants in the self-distanced group to experience both negative *and* positive emotions following an adverse event suggests that these participants regulated their emotional experiences by boosting the importance of positive emotions (although they still reported experiencing negative emotions). Self-distanced reflections may have broadened participants' emotional repertoire, allowing them to experience a more balanced emotional reaction overall, one that includes both negative and positive emotions.

CONCLUSION

We believe that the chapters in this volume together outline a fruitful path for future research on PTG. Given the ongoing debate within psychology about the credibility of the research produced in the field, we hope that both junior and senior researchers will use the insights provided here as a jumping-off point for theoretically grounded and methodologically rigorous research programs that help answer the perennial question of whether adversity can, in fact, build our characters.

AUTHOR'S NOTE

Both authors contributed equally to this chapter. Address questions and comments to Frank J. Infurna, Arizona State University, Department of Psychology, 950 S. McAllister Ave., Tempe, AZ 85287, frank.infurna@asu.edu or Eranda Jayawickreme, Wake Forest University, Department of Psychology, P.O. Box 7778, Winston-Salem, NC 27109, jayawide@wfu.edu

REFERENCES

Baltes, P. B. (1987). Theoretical propositions of life-span developmental psychology: On the dynamics between growth and decline. *Developmental Psychology, 23*, 611–626.

Blackie, L. E. R., Jayawickreme, E., Tsukayama, E., Forgeard, M. J., Roepke, A. M., & Fleeson, W. (2017). Post-traumatic growth as positive personality change: Developing a measure to assess within-person variability. *Journal of Research in Personality, 69*, 22–32.

Blackie, L. E. R., Jayawickreme, E., Hitchcott, N., & Joseph, S. (2017). Distinguishing post-traumatic growth from psychological adjustment among Rwandan genocide survivors. In D. Carr (Ed.), *Varieties of Virtue Ethics* (pp. 299–317). Palgrave Macmillan UK.

Blalock, D. V., Calton, J. M., & Kashdan, T. B. (2014). Understanding post-traumatic growth by attending to contextual influences and developing wise interventions to promote it. *European Journal of Personality, 28*, 333–334. doi:10.1002/per.1970

Campbell, J. B., Jayawickreme, E., & Hanson, E. (2014). Measures of values and moral personality. In G. Boyle (Ed.), Handbook of Personality and Social Psychological Constructs (pp. 505–529). New York: Elsevier.

Clement, S., & Bollinger, R. (2016). Commentary: Perspectives on character development. *Research in Human Development, 13*, 174–181.

Dohrenwend, B. P. (2006). Inventorying stressful life events as risk factors for psychopathology: Toward resolution of the problem of intracategory variability. *Psychological Bulletin, 132*, 477–495.

Emmons, R. A. (1999). *The Psychology of Ultimate Concerns: Motivation and Spirituality in Personality*. New York: Guilford Press.

Fleeson, W. (2014). Four ways of (not) being real and whether they are essential for post-traumatic growth. *European Journal of Personality, 28*, 336–337.

Fleeson, W., Furr, R. M., Jayawickreme, E., Helzer, E. G., Hartley, A. G., & Meindl, P. (2015). Personality science and the foundations of character. In C. B. Miller, R. M. Furr, A. Knobel, & W. Fleeson (Eds.), *Character: New Directions from Philosophy, Psychology, and Theology* (pp. 41–71). Oxford University Press.

Frazier, P., Tennen, H., Gavian, M., Park, C., Tomich, P., & Tashiro, T. (2009). Does self-reported posttraumatic growth reflect genuine positive change? *Psychological Science, 20*, 912–919.

Gray, M. J., Litz, B. T., Hsu, J. L., & Lombardo, T. W. (2004). Psychometric properties of the life events checklist. *Assessment, 11*(4), 330–341.

Helzer, E. G., & Jayawickreme, E. (2015). Control and the "good life" primary and secondary control as distinct indicators of well-being. *Social Psychological and Personality Science, 6*(6), 653–660.

Hultsch, D. F., & Plemons, J. K. (1979). Life events and life-span development. In P. B. Baltes & O. G. Brim, Jr. (Eds.), *Life-span Development and Behavior* (Vol. 2, pp. 1–36). New York: Academic Press.

Infurna, F. J., & Jayawickreme, E. (2019). Fixing the growth illusion: New directions for research in resilience and post-traumatic growth. *Current Directions in Psychological Science, 28*, 152–158.

Infurna, F. J., & Luthar, S. S. (2016). Resilience to major life stressors is not as common as thought. *Perspectives on Psychological Science, 11*, 175–194.

Infurna, F. J., & Luthar, S. S. (2017). The multidimensional nature of resilience to spousal loss. *Journal of Personality and Social Psychology, 112*, 926–947.

Infurna, F. J., & Luthar, S. S. (2018). Re-evaluating the notion that resilience is commonplace: A review and distillation of directions for future research, practice, and policy. *Clinical Psychology Review, 65*, 43–56.

Jayawickreme, E., & Blackie, L. E. R. (2014). Post-traumatic growth as positive personality change: Evidence, controversies and future directions. *European Journal of Personality, 28*, 312–331.

Jayawickreme, E., & Blackie, L. E. (2016). *Exploring the psychological benefits of hardship: A critical reassessment of posttraumatic growth*. Cham: Springer.

Jayawickreme, E., & Fleeson, W. (2017a). Whole trait theory can explain virtues. In *Moral Psychology, Volume V: Virtue and Happiness*. Ed. Walter Sinnott-Armstrong and Christian B. Miller (pp. 121–129). Cambridge: MIT Press.

Jayawickreme, E., & Fleeson, W. (2017b). Does whole trait theory work for the virtues? In *Moral Psychology, Volume V: Virtue and Happiness*. Ed. Walter Sinnott-Armstrong and Christian B. Miller (pp. 75–103). Cambridge: MIT Press.

Jayawickreme, E., Infurna, F. J., Alajak, K., Blackie, L. E., Chopik, W. J., Chung, J. M., . . . Zonneveld, R. (2021). Post-traumatic growth as positive personality change: Challenges, opportunities, and recommendations. *Journal of Personality, 89*(1), 145–165.

Jayawickreme, E., Tsukayama, E., & Kashdan, T. B. (2017). Examining the effect of affect on life satisfaction judgments: A within-person perspective. *Journal of Research in Personality, 68*, 32–37.

Joseph, S. (2011). *What doesn't kill us: The new psychology of posttraumatic growth*. Basic Books.

Kessler, R. C., Sonnega, A., Bromet, E., Hughes, M., & Nelson, C. B. (1995). Posttraumatic stress disorder in the National Comorbidity Survey. *Archives of General Psychiatry, 52*(12), 1048–1060.

Lahey, J. (2015). *The Gift of Failure*. London: Short Books.

Lerner, R. M., & Callina, K. S. (2014). The study of character development: Towards tests of a relational developmental systems model. *Human Development, 57*(6), 322–346.

Linley, P. A., & Joseph, S. (2004). Positive change following trauma and adversity: A review. *Journal of Traumatic Stress, 17*(1), 11–21.

Luthar, S. S., Cicchetti, D., & Becker, B. (2000). The construct of resilience: A critical evaluation and guidelines for future work. *Child Development, 71*, 543–562.

Luthar, S. S., Doernberger, C. H., & Zigler, E. (1993). Resilience is not a unidimensional construct: Insights from a prospective study of inner-city adolescents. *Development and Psychopathology, 5*, 703–717.

Masten, A. S., & Narayan, A. J. (2012). Child development in the context of disaster, war, and terrorism: Pathways of risk and resilience. *Annual Review of Psychology, 63*, 227–257.

McGrath, R. E. (2015). Character strengths in 75 nations: An update. *Journal of Positive Psychology, 10*(1), 41–52.

Miller, C. B. (2014). A satisfactory definition of "post-traumatic growth" still remains elusive. *European Journal of Personality, 28*, 344–346.

Nisbett, R. E., & Wilson, T. D. (1977). Telling more than we can know: Verbal reports on mental processes. *Psychological Review, 84*(3), 231–259. https://doi.org/10.1037/0033-295X.84.3.231

Peterson, C., & Seligman, M. E. (2003). Character strengths before and after September 11. *Psychological Science, 14*(4), 381–384.

Peterson, C., & Seligman, M. E. (2004). *Character Strengths and Virtues: A Handbook and Classification*. New York: Oxford University Press.

Roberts, B.W. (2011). Personality Psychology Has a Serious Problem (And so Do Many Other Areas of Psychology). *P: The Online Newsletter for Personality Science*, Issue 6, November 2011.

Tedeschi, R. G., & Calhoun, L. G. (2004). Posttraumatic growth: Conceptual foundations and empirical evidence. *Psychological Inquiry, 15*, 1–18.

Tennen, H., & Affleck, G. (2009). Assessing positive life change: In search of meticulous methods. In C. L. Park, S. C. Lechner, M. H. Antoni, & A. L. Stanton (Eds.), *Medical illness and positive life change: Can crisis lead to personal transformation?* (pp. 31–49). Washington, DC US: American Psychological Association.

Tiberius, V. (2008). *The reflective life: Living wisely with our limits*. New York: Oxford University Press.

Tough, P. (2011). What if the secret to success is failure? *New York Times*, September 14, 2011.

Turner, R. J., & Wheaton, B. (1995). Checklist measurement of stressful life events. In S. Cohen, R. C. Kessler, & L. U. Gordon (Eds.), *Measuring stress: A guide for health and social scientists* (pp. 29–58). Oxford University Press.

Vollhardt, J. R. (2009). Altruism born of suffering and prosocial behavior following adverse life events: A review and conceptualization. *Social Justice Research, 22*(1), 53–97.

INDEX

For the benefit of digital users, indexed terms that span two pages (e.g., 52–53) may, on occasion, appear on only one of those pages.

Tables, figures, and boxes are indicated by *t*, *f*, and *b* following the page number

Triggering situations, Expectancies, State/State expressions, and ReActions (TESSERA) theory, 81–82